Get the eBook FREE!

(PDF, ePub, Kindle, and liveBook all included)

We believe that once you buy a book from us, you should be able to read it in any format we have available. To get electronic versions of this book at no additional cost to you, purchase and then register this book at the Manning website.

Go to https://www.manning.com/freebook and follow the instructions to complete your pBook registration.

That's it!
Thanks from Manning!

Mastering Large Datasets with Python

Mastering Large Datasets with Python

Parallelize and Distribute Your Python Code

J.T. Wolohan

MANNING
Shelter Island

For online information and ordering of this and other Manning books, please visit www.manning.com. The publisher offers discounts on this book when ordered in quantity. For more information, please contact

Special Sales Department
Manning Publications Co.
20 Baldwin Road
PO Box 761
Shelter Island, NY 11964
Email: orders@manning.com

Manning Publications Co.
20 Baldwin Road
PO Box 761
Shelter Island, NY 11964

Development editor: Marina Michaels
Technical development editor: Michael Smolyak
Review editor: Aleksandar Dragosavljević
Production editor: Deirdre Hiam
Copy editor: Carl Quesnel
Proofreader: Keri Hales
Technical proofreader: Al Krinker
Typesetter: Dennis Dalinnik
Cover designer: Marija Tudor

ISBN: 9781617296239
Printed in the United States of America

brief contents

contents

preface

The idea for this book came to me in the summer of 2018 after working with some especially talented developers who had managed to go a significant portion of their careers without learning how to write scalable code. I realized then that a lot of the techniques for "big data" work, or what we'll refer to in this book as "large dataset" problems, are reserved for those who want to tackle these problems exclusively. Because a lot of these problems occur in enterprise environments, where the mechanisms to produce data at this scale are ripe, books about this topic tend to be written in the same enterprise languages as the tools, such as Java.

This book is a little different. I've noticed that large dataset problems are increasingly being tackled in a distributed manner. Not distributed in the terms of distributed computing—though certainly that as well—but distributed in terms of who's doing the work. Individual developers or small development teams, often working in rapid prototyping environments or with rapid development languages (such as Python), are now working with large datasets.

My hope is that this book can bring the techniques for scalable and distributed programming to a broader audience of developers. We're living in an era where big data is becoming increasingly prevalent. Skills in parallelization and distributed programming are increasingly vital to developers' day-to-day work. More and more programmers are facing problems resulting from datasets that are too large for the way they've been taught to think about them. Hopefully, with this book, developers will have the tools to solve those big data problems and focus on the ones that got them interested in programming in the first place.

acknowledgments

A special thanks to all the developers of and contributors to the excellent tools I've covered in this book, as well as all the wonderful folks at Manning who helped make this book possible: Stephen Soehnlen, Marina Michaels, Aleksandar Dragosavljevic, Deirdre Hiam, Carl Quesnel, Keri Hales, and Barbara Mirecki. Also thank you to my technical proofer, Al Krinker, and technical developmental editor, Michael Smolyak.

To all the reviewers: Aditya Kasuhik, Al Krinker, Ariel Gamino, Craig E. Pfeifer, David Jacobs, Diego Casella, Duncan McRae, Gary Bake, Hawley Waldman, Jason Rendel, Jibesh Patra, Joseph Wang, Justin Fister, Maxim Kupfer, Richard Meinsen, Richard Tobias, Sayak Paul, Simone Sguazza, Stuart Woodward, Taylor Dolezal, and Vitosh K. Doynov, your suggestions helped make this a better book.

about this book

Who should read this book

The goal of this book is to teach a scalable style of programming. To do that, we'll cover a wider range of material than you might be familiar with from other programming or technology books. Where other books might cover a single library, this book covers many libraries—both built-in modules, such as functools and itertools, as well as third-party libraries, such as toolz, pathos, and mrjob. Where other books cover just one technology, this book covers many, including Hadoop, Spark, and Amazon Web Services (AWS). The choice to cover a broad range of technologies is admitting the fact that to scale your code, you need to be able to adapt to new situations. Across all the technologies, however, I emphasize a "map and reduce" style of programming in Python.

You'll find that this style is a constant throughout the changing environment in which your code is running, which is why I adopted it in the first place. You can use it to rapidly adapt your code to new situations. Ultimately, the book aims to teach you how to scale your code by authoring it in a map and reduce style. Along the way, I also aim to teach you the tools of the trade for big data work, such as Spark, Hadoop, and AWS.

I wrote this book for a developer or data scientist who knows enough to have gotten themselves into a situation where they're facing a problem caused by having too much data. If you know how to solve your problem, but you can't solve it fast enough at the scale of data with which you're working, this book is for you. If you're curious about Hadoop and Spark, this book is for you. If you're looking for a few pointers on how to bring your large data work into the cloud, this book could be for you.

How this book is organized: A roadmap

In chapter 1, I introduce the map and reduce style of programming and what I'll cover in this book. I discuss the benefits of parallel programming, the basics of distributed computing, the tools we'll cover for parallel and distributed computing, and cloud computing. I also provide a conceptual model for the material that I cover in this book.

In chapter 2, I introduce the map part of the map and reduce style, and we look at how to parallelize a problem to solve it faster. I cover the process of pickling in Python—how Python shares data during parallelization—and we'll tackle an example using parallelization to speed up web scraping.

In chapter 3, we'll use the `map` function to perform complex data transformations. In this chapter, I teach how you can chain small functions together into function pipelines or function chains to great effect. I also show how you can parallelize these function chains for faster problem solving on large datasets.

In chapter 4, I introduce the idea of laziness and how you can incorporate laziness to speed up your large data workflows. I show how lazy functions allow you to tackle large dataset problems locally, how you can create your own lazy functions, and how to best combine lazy and hasty approaches to programming. We'll use these lazy methods to solve a simulation problem.

In chapter 5, I cover accumulation transformations with the `reduce` function. I also teach the use of anonymous or lambda functions. In this chapter, we'll use the `reduce` function to calculate summary statistics on a large dataset.

In chapter 6, I cover advanced parallelization techniques using both `map` and `reduce`. You'll learn advanced functions for parallelization in Python, as well as how and when to pursue a parallel solution to your problem. In this chapter, you'll also learn how to implement parallel reduce workflows.

In chapter 7, I introduce the basics of distributed computing as well as the technologies of Hadoop and Spark. You'll write introductory programs in Hadoop and Spark, and learn the benefits of each framework. We'll also cover the situations in which Hadoop is preferable over Spark, and when Spark is preferable over Hadoop.

In chapter 8, I cover how to use Hadoop streaming to run your map-and-reduce–style code on a distributed cluster. I also introduce the mrjob library for writing Hadoop jobs in Python. We'll cover how to move complex data types between Hadoop job steps. We'll cement these principles with hands-on examples analyzing web traffic data and tennis match logs.

In chapter 9, we dive into using Spark for distributing our Python code. I cover Spark's RDD data structure as well as convenience methods of the `RDD` that you can use to implement your code in a map and reduce style. We'll also implement the classic PageRank algorithm on the tennis match log data from chapter 8.

In chapter 10, we look at one of the most popular applications of Spark: parallel machine learning. In this chapter, we cover some of the basics of machine learning.

We'll practice these principles by implementing decision trees and forests to predict whether mushrooms are poisonous or not.

In chapter 11, I cover the basics of cloud computing and the nature of cloud storage. We'll put our learning into practice by loading data into Amazon S3 using both the web GUI and the boto3 AWS API wrapper library for Python.

In chapter 12, we use Amazon ElasticMapReduce to run distributed Hadoop and Spark jobs in the cloud. You'll learn how to set up an elastic Hadoop cluster from the console using mrjob and from the AWS browser-based GUI. Once you've mastered this chapter, you'll be ready to tackle datasets of any size.

About the code

On the journey to mastering large datasets with Python, you'll need a few tools, the first of which is a recent version of Python. Throughout this book, any version of Python 3.3+ will work. For the most part, you can install the remainder of the software you'll need with a single pip command:

```
pip install toolz pathos pyspark mrjob --user
```

If you'd like to set up a virtual environment to keep the packages installed with this book separate from Python packages you currently have installed on your path, you can do this with a few lines of code as well:

```
$ python3 -m venv mastering_large_datasets
$ pip install toolz pathos pyspark mrjob --user
$ source mastering_large_datasets/bin/active
```

If you set up a virtual environment, remember that you'll need to run the source command to activate it so you can access the libraries inside of it.

Beyond Python, the only software that you'll need for this book is Hadoop. The easiest way to install Hadoop is to go to the Hadoop website and follow the instructions for downloading Hadoop there: https://hadoop.apache.org/releases.html. Hadoop is written in Java, so you'll also need to have a Java Development Kit installed to run it. I recommend OpenJDK. You can download OpenJDK from the OpenJDK website: https://openjdk.java.net/.

Finally, to complete the last two chapters of the book, you'll need an AWS account. You can create a new AWS account by going to https://aws.amazon.com, selecting "Sign in to the Console," and then creating a new AWS account. To set up your account, you'll need to provide a payment method. Amazon will use this method to charge you for resources you use. For this book, you won't need more than $5 of resources from AWS. To ensure you don't spend more than you're comfortable with, you can get a prepaid Visa card and set that up as your payment method. You can find prepaid Visa cards at stores like CVS, Walgreens, Rite-Aid, Target, and Walmart, as well as many convenience stores and gas stations. You won't need an AWS account until chapter 11.

liveBook discussion forum

Purchase of *Mastering Large Datasets with Python* includes free access to a private web forum run by Manning Publications where you can make comments about the book, ask technical questions, and receive help from the author and from other users. To access the forum, go to https://livebook.manning.com/book/mastering-large-datasets/welcome/v-5/discussion. You can also learn more about Manning's forums and the rules of conduct at https://livebook.manning.com/#!/discussion.

Manning's commitment to our readers is to provide a venue where a meaningful dialogue between individual readers and between readers and the author can take place. It is not a commitment to any specific amount of participation on the part of the author, whose contribution to the forum remains voluntary (and unpaid). We suggest you try asking the author some challenging questions, lest his interest stray! The forum and the archives of previous discussions will be accessible from the publisher's website as long as the book is in print.

about the author

J.T. Wolohan is a senior artificial intelligence and natural language processing architect at Booz Allen Hamilton. He has taught programming to learners of all levels: from elementary and middle school students up to graduate students and professionals. In addition to his interests in distributed and parallel computing, J.T. enjoys running, cooking, and spending time with his family.

about the cover illustration

The figure on the cover of *Mastering Large Datasets with Python* is captioned "Costumes civils actuels de tous les peuples connus," or "Current Civilian Costumes of All Known Peoples." The illustration is taken from a collection of dress costumes from various countries by Jacques Grasset de Saint-Sauveur (1757–1810), titled *Costumes de Différents Pays*, published in France in 1797. Each illustration is finely drawn and colored by hand. The rich variety of Grasset de Saint-Sauveur's collection reminds us vividly of how culturally apart the world's towns and regions were just 200 years ago. Isolated from each other, people spoke different dialects and languages. In the streets or in the countryside, it was easy to identify where they lived and what their trade or station in life was just by their dress.

The way we dress has changed since then and the diversity by region, so rich at the time, has faded away. It is now hard to tell apart the inhabitants of different continents, let alone different towns, regions, or countries. Perhaps we have traded cultural diversity for a more varied personal life—certainly for a more varied and fast-paced technological life.

At a time when it is hard to tell one computer book from another, Manning celebrates the inventiveness and initiative of the computer business with book covers based on the rich diversity of regional life of two centuries ago, brought back to life by Grasset de Saint-Sauveur's pictures.

Part 1

Part 1 explores the map and reduce style of computing. We'll introduce map and reduce, as well as the helper and convenience functions that you'll need to get the most out of this style. In this section, we'll also cover the basics of parallel computing. The tools and techniques in this part are useful for large data in categories 1 and 2: tasks that are both storable and computable locally, and tasks that are not storable locally but are still computable locally.

1 Introduction

> ***This chapter covers***
>
> - Introducing the map and reduce style of programming
> - Understanding the benefits of parallel programming
> - Extending parallel programming to a distributed environment
> - Parallel programming in the cloud

This book teaches a set of programming techniques, tools, and frameworks for mastering large datasets. Throughout this book, I'll refer to the style of programming you're learning as a *map and reduce* style. The map and reduce style of programming is one in which we can easily write parallel programs—programs that can do multiple things at the same time—by organizing our code around two functions: `map` and `reduce`. To get a better sense of why we'll want to use a map and reduce style, consider this scenario:

SCENARIO Two young programmers have come up with an idea for how to rank pages on the internet. They want to rank pages based on the importance of the other sites on the internet that link to them. They think the internet should be just like high school: the more the cool kids talk about you, the more important you are. The two young programmers love the idea, but how can they possibly analyze the entire internet?

A reader well versed in Silicon Valley history will recognize this scenario as the Google.com origin story. In its early years, Google popularized a way of programming called *MapReduce* as a way to effectively process and rank the entire internet. This style was a natural fit for Google because

1. Both of Google's founders were math geeks, and MapReduce has its roots in math.
2. Map and reduce-centric programming results in simple parallelization when compared with a more traditional style of programming.

> **`map` and `reduce` vs. MapReduce**
>
> I'm going to refer to a map and reduce style of programming a lot in this book. Indeed, this style is the primary means through which I'll be teaching you how to scale up your programs beyond your laptop. Though this style is similar in name and functionality to MapReduce, it is distinct from and more general than MapReduce. MapReduce is a framework for parallel and distributed computing. The map and reduce style is a style of programming that allows programmers to run their work in parallel with minimal rewriting and extend this work to distributed workflows, possibly using MapReduce, or possibly using other means.

In this book, we'll tackle the same issues Google tackled in their early stages. We'll look at a style of programming that makes it easy to take a good idea and scale it up. We'll look at a way of programming that makes it easy to go from doing work as an individual to doing work on a team, or from doing work on your laptop to doing work in a distributed parallel environment. In other words, we'll look at how to master large datasets.

1.1 What you'll learn in this book

In this book, you'll learn a style of programming that makes parallelization easy. You'll learn how to write scalable, parallel code that will work just as well on one machine as it will on thousands. You'll learn how to

- chunk large problems into small pieces
- use the `map` and `reduce` functions
- run programs in parallel on your personal computer
- run programs in parallel in distributed cloud environments

and you'll learn two popular frameworks for working with large datasets: Apache Hadoop and Apache Spark.

This book is for the programmer who can write working data-transformation programs already and now needs to scale those programs up. They need to be able to work with more data and to do it faster.

1.2 Why large datasets?

You've probably heard conversations about an amorphous set of problems in modern computing that revolve around the notion of *big data*. Big data tends to mean different things to different people. I find that most people use that phrase to mean that the data "feels" big—it's uncomfortable to work with or unwieldy.

Because one of the goals of this book is to get you comfortable with any size dataset, we'll work with *large datasets*. As I think of it, large dataset problems come in three sizes:

1. The data can both fit on and be processed on a personal computer.
2. The solution for the problem can be executed from a personal computer, but the data can't be stored on a personal computer.
3. The solution for the problem can't be executed on a personal computer, and the data can't be stored on one either.

You likely already know how to solve problems that fall in the first category. Most problems—especially those that are used to teach programming—fall into this first category. The second group of problems is a bit harder. They require a technique called *parallel computing* that allows us to get the most out of our hardware. Lastly, we have the third group of problems. These problems are expensive, requiring either more money or more time to solve. To solve them, we'll want to use a technique called *distributed computing*.

Dask—A different type of distributed computing

The map and reduce style of programming puts data at the forefront and is excellent for working with data, from small data transformations up to large distributed data stores.

If you aren't interested in learning a style of programming that will make your Python code easier to read and easier to scale, but you still want to be able to manage large datasets, one tool out there for you is Dask. Dask is a Python framework for distributed data frames with a NumPy and pandas look-alike API. If that sounds like something you're interested in, I recommend *Data Science with Python and Dask*, by Jesse Daniel (Manning, 2019; http://mng.bz/ANxg).

Through this book, you'll learn a style of programming that allows you to write code in the same way for problems of all three sizes. You'll also learn about parallel computing and two distributed computing frameworks (Hadoop and Spark), and we'll explore how to use those frameworks in a distributed cloud environment.

1.3 What is parallel computing?

Parallel computing, which I'll also refer to as *parallel programming* and *parallelization*, is a way to get your computer to do multiple things at once. For example, referring to the scenario you saw earlier, our young programmers are going to need to process more than one web page at a time; otherwise, they might never finish—there are a lot of web pages. Even processing one page per half second wouldn't bring them to 200,000 pages a day. To scrape and analyze the entire internet, they're going to need to be able to scale up their processing. Parallel computing will allow them to do just that.

1.3.1 Understanding parallel computing

To understand parallel programming, let's first talk about what happens in standard procedural programming. The standard procedural programming workflow typically looks like this:

1. A program starts to run.
2. The program issues an instruction.
3. That instruction is executed.
4. Steps 2 and 3 are repeated.
5. The program finishes running.

This is a straightforward way of programming; however, it limits us to executing one instruction at a time (figure 1.1). Steps 2 and 3 need to resolve before we can move on to Step 4. And Step 4 routes us back to Steps 2 and 3, leaving us in the same pickle.

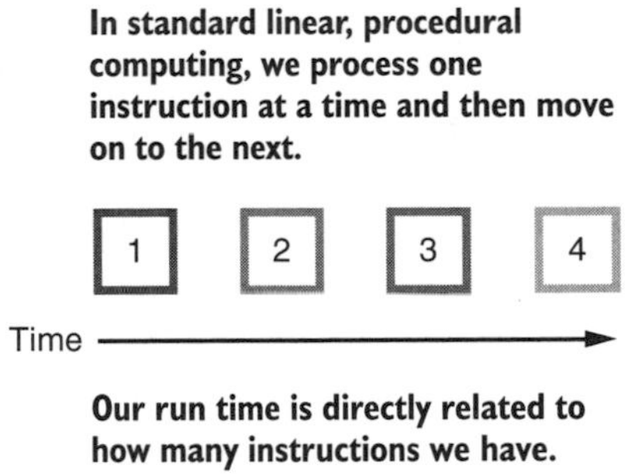
In standard linear, procedural computing, we process one instruction at a time and then move on to the next.
1
2
3
4
Time
Our run time is directly related to how many instructions we have.

Figure 1.1 The procedural computing process involves issuing instructions and resolving them in sequence.

In a standard linear program, if the instructions in Step 2 take a long time to execute, then we won't be able to move on to the next section of the problem. Imagine what this looks like for our young programmers trying to scrape the entire internet. How many of their instructions are going to be "scrape web page abc.com/xyz"? Probably a lot. What's more, we know that the scraping of one web page (like the Amazon homepage, for instance) is in no way going to alter the content of other web pages (such as the *New York Times* homepage).

Parallel programming allows us to execute all of these similar and independent steps simultaneously. In parallel programming, our workflow is going to look more like this:

1. A program starts to run.
2. The program divides up the work into chunks of instructions and data.
3. Each chunk of work is executed independently.
4. The chunks of work are reassembled.
5. The program finishes running.

By programming this way, we free ourselves from the instruction-execution loop we were trapped in before (figure 1.2). Now we can split our work up into as many chunks as we'd like, as long as we have a way of processing them.

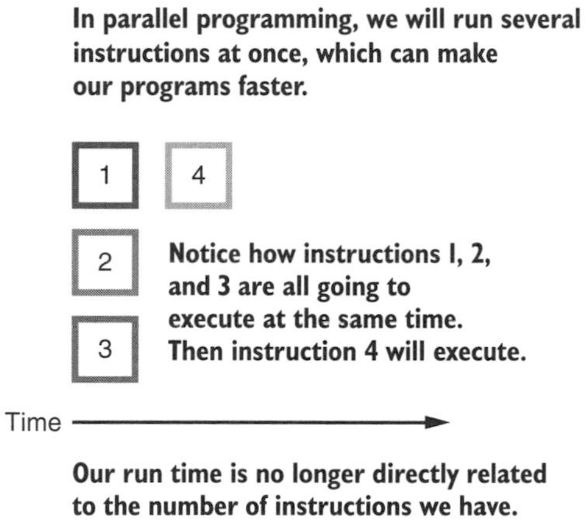
In parallel programming, we will run several instructions at once, which can make our programs faster.
1
4
2
3
Notice how instructions 1, 2, and 3 are all going to execute at the same time. Then instruction 4 will execute.
Time
Our run time is no longer directly related to the number of instructions we have.

Figure 1.2 The parallel computing process divides work into chunks that can be processed separately from one another and recombined when finished.

This process would be much better for the young programmers wishing to scrape the entire internet. They still need to find a way to get enough computing resources to process all of the chunks, but every time they acquire a new machine, they make their process that much faster. And indeed, even early-stage Google was running on a cluster of thousands of computers.

1.3.2 Scalable computing with the map and reduce style

When we think about the map and reduce style of computing, it's important to do so in the context of both the size of our data and the capacity of the compute resources available to us (figure 1.3). With normal-sized data—which allows us to use personal computer-scale resources to work on data we can store on a personal computer—we can rely on the fundamentals of the map and reduce style and standard Python code. In this area, we won't see much difference from other styles of programming.

Moving up in size of data, we arrive at a place where we can use our personal computer hardware to process the data, but we're having trouble storing the data on a

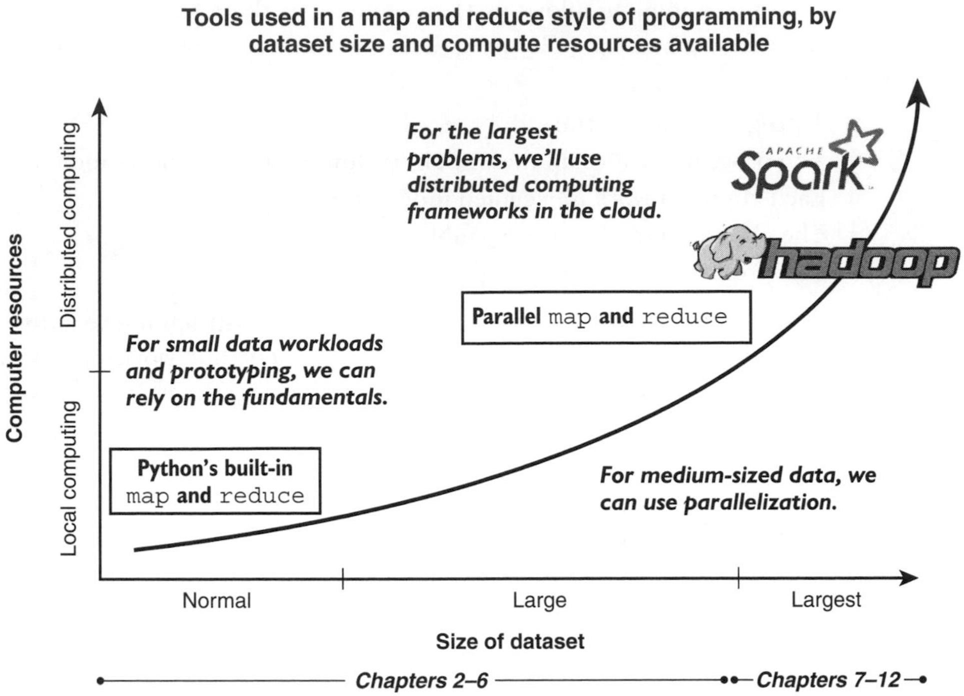
Tools used in a map and reduce style of programming, by dataset size and compute resources available
Computer resources
Distributed computing
Local computing
For the largest problems, we'll use distributed computing frameworks in the cloud.
APACHE Spark
hadoop
Parallel map and reduce
For small data workloads and prototyping, we can rely on the fundamentals.
Python's built-in map and reduce
For medium-sized data, we can use parallelization.
Normal
Large
Largest
Size of dataset
Chapters 2–6
Chapters 7–12

Figure 1.3 We can think of the map and reduce style of programming as a construction project: from blueprints, which help us organize our work; to the transformation of raw material; to the assembly of parts into a final product.

personal computer. At this point, we could, if we wanted to, work on our job in a cluster, but it's not a necessity. Here, the benefits of the map and reduce style start to become apparent. We can use a slightly modified version of our code from the smaller sized data to work on data in this size category.

And finally, we arrive at the final and largest category of data. This is data that we need to both process and store in a distributed environment. Here, we can use distributed computing frameworks such as Hadoop and Spark. And although we can't use the exact same code, we can use the principles and patterns from the smaller sizes. We'll often also need to use a cloud computing service, such as AWS.

Other large data technologies: Splunk, Elasticsearch, Pig, and Hive

Because this book focuses on scalable workflows, I intentionally omitted big data tools that only make sense to operate once you're already in a high-volume environment, including Splunk, Elasticsearch, Apache Pig, and Apache Hive. The latter two, built on the Hadoop stack, are natural bedfellows with Hadoop and Spark. If you're operating with a large volume of data, investigating these tools is well worth your while.

We can see this at play in figure 1.3. Figure 1.3 shows how the techniques taught in this book match up against the various sizes of data and the compute resources available. We begin by covering techniques that you can use on your laptop or personal computer: the built-in map and reduce and parallel computing abilities of Python. In the final two sections (from chapter 7 and on), we cover distributed computing frameworks such as Hadoop and Spark, as well as how to deploy these services on the cloud using Amazon Web Services EMR.

1.3.3 When to program in a map and reduce style

The map and reduce style of programming is applicable everywhere, but its specific strengths are in areas where you may need to scale. Scaling means starting with a small application, such as a little game you might build on your laptop in an evening as a pet project, and applying it to a much larger use case, such as a viral game that *everyone* is playing on their cell phones.

Consider one small step in our hypothetical game: improving the AI. Say we have an AI opponent against which all the players compete, and we want the AI to improve every 1,000 matches. At first, we'll be able to update our AI on a single machine. After all, we only have 1,000 matches, and it's trivial to process them. Even as the number of players picks up, we'll only have to run this improvement every few hours. Eventually, however, if our game gets popular enough, we'll have to dedicate several machines to this task—the amount of information they'll need to process will be larger (there will be more matches in the match history), and they'll need to process the information faster (because the rate of plays will be faster). This would be an excellent application for a map and reduce style because we could easily modify our code to be parallel, allowing us to scale our AI improvements up to any number of users.

1.4 The map and reduce style

The parallel programming workflow has three parts that distinguish it from the standard linear workflow:

1. Divide the work into chunks.
2. Work on those chunks separately.
3. Reassemble the work.

In this book, we'll let the functions `map` and `reduce` handle these three parts for us.

1.4.1 The map function for transforming data

`map` is a function we'll use to transform sequences of data from one type to another (figure 1.4). The function gets its name from mathematics, where some mathematicians think of functions as rules for taking an input and returning the single corresponding output. Considering again our young and ambitious programmers, they

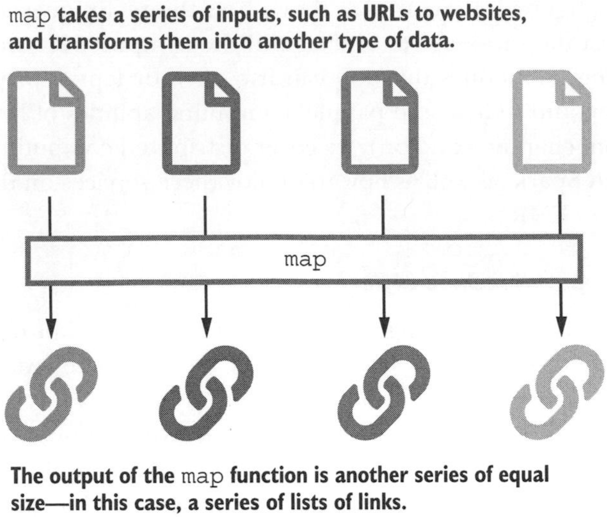
map takes a series of inputs, such as URLs to websites, and transforms them into another type of data.
map
The output of the map function is another series of equal size—in this case, a series of lists of links.

Figure 1.4 We can use the `map` function to transform a sequence of data from one type to another, such as transforming web page URLs into lists of links found on those pages.

may want to `map` a sequence of web pages (or the sequence of all web pages) into the URLs that those pages contain. They could then use those URLs to see which pages were linked to most often and by whom.

A key thing to remember about `map` is that it always retains the same number of objects in the output as were provided in the input. For example, if we wanted to get the outbound links on 100,000 websites with `map`, then the resulting data structure would be 100,000 lists of links.

> **NOTE** `map` and `reduce` have their roots in a style of programming called declarative programming. Declarative programming focuses on explaining the logic of our code and not on specifying low-level details. That's why scaling our code is natural in the map and reduce style: the logic stays the same, even if the size of the problem changes.

It's worth taking a look at a small example of `map` in action now because of how fundamental it is to what we'll be doing throughout this book. Let's imagine we want to add seven to a sequence of four numbers: –1, 0, 1, and 2. To do this, we write a small function called `add_seven` that takes a number `n` and returns `n+7`. To do this for our sequence of numbers, we'd simply call `map` on `add_seven` and our sequence (figure 1.5).

You'll note that, like we touched on previously, we have the same number of inputs (4) as outputs (4). Also, these inputs and outputs have a direct 1 to 1 relationship: a particular output corresponds to each and every input.

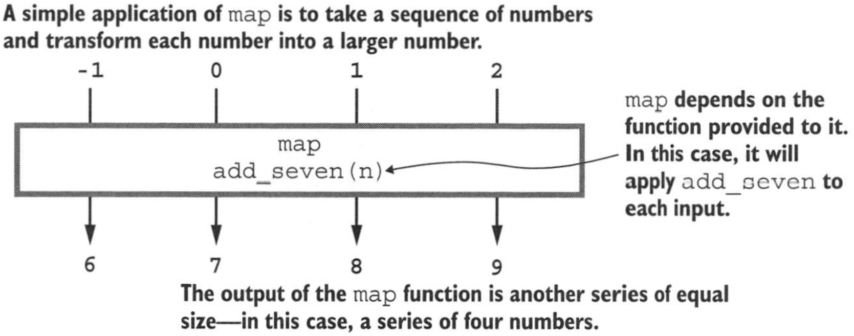
A simple application of map is to take a sequence of numbers and transform each number into a larger number.
-1
0
1
2
map
add_seven(n)
map depends on the function provided to it. In this case, it will apply add_seven to each input.
6
7
8
9
The output of the map function is another series of equal size—in this case, a series of four numbers.

Figure 1.5 A basic use of `map` would be to increment a sequence of numbers, such as changing –1, 0, 1, and 2 into 6, 7, 8, and 9.

1.4.2 The reduce function for advanced transformations

If we want to take that sequence and turn it into something of a different length, we'll need our other critical function: `reduce`. `reduce` allows us to take a sequence of data and transform it into a data structure of any shape or size (figure 1.6). For example, if our programmers wanted to take those links and turn them into frequency counts—finding which pages are linked to the most—they would need to use `reduce`, because it is possible that the number of pages linked to is different from the number of pages crawled. We can easily imagine that 100 web pages might link to anywhere between 0 and 1 million external pages, depending on what the web pages in question are.

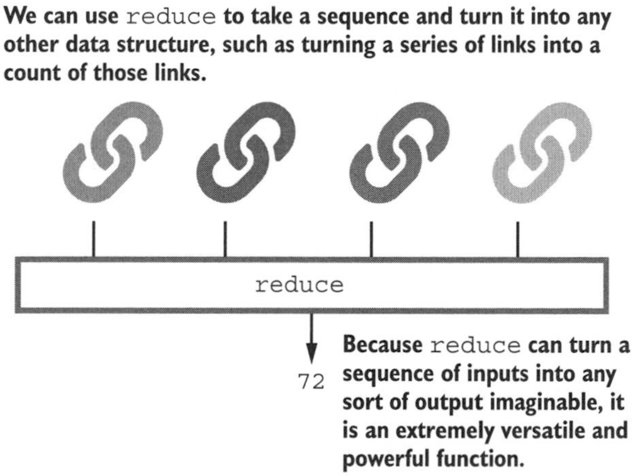
We can use reduce to take a sequence and turn it into any other data structure, such as turning a series of links into a count of those links.
reduce
72
Because reduce can turn a sequence of inputs into any sort of output imaginable, it is an extremely versatile and powerful function.

Figure 1.6 We can use the `reduce` function to turn a sequence of data of one type into something else: another sequence or even a primitive.

We can even use `reduce` to turn a sequence of data into a primitive data type if we'd like, such as an integer or a string. For example, we could use `reduce` to find the number of outbound links on 100 web pages (an integer) or we could use it to find the longest word in a long text document, such as a book (a string). In this way, `reduce` is a lot more flexible than `map`.

1.4.3 Map and reduce for data transformation pipelines

Often, we'll want to use `map` and `reduce` together, one right after another. This pattern gives rise to the *MapReduce* programming pattern. The MapReduce programming pattern relies on the `map` function to transform some data into another type of data and then uses the `reduce` function to combine that data. A mathematical example might be taking the sum of the greatest prime factor of a sequence of numbers. We can use `map` to transform each number into its greatest prime factor and then use `reduce` to take their sum. A more practical example may be finding the longest word on a sequence of web pages, when all we have is the URLs. We can use `map` to turn the URLs into text and `reduce` to find the longest word (figure 1.7).

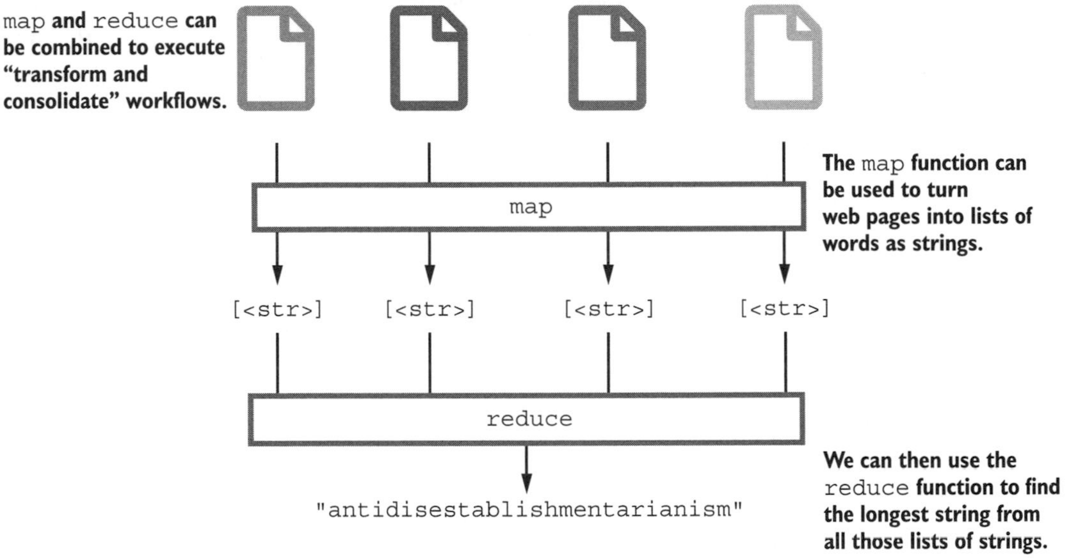
map and reduce can be combined to execute "transform and consolidate" workflows.
The map function can be used to turn web pages into lists of words as strings.
map
[<str>] [<str>] [<str>] [<str>]
reduce
"antidisestablishmentarianism"
We can then use the reduce function to find the longest string from all those lists of strings.

Figure 1.7 The functions `map` and `reduce` are often used together to perform complex transformations of large amounts of data quickly.

1.5 Distributed computing for speed and scale

To get the most out of parallel programming, we need to be working in a distributed environment, that is, an environment where it's possible to spread the workload out across several machines. Consider the following scenario.

SCENARIO A financial trading firm has come up with a way of forecasting the next day's market activity based on the overnight taxi and rideshare traffic in New York City, combined with the morning's fish prices. The firm's simulation is perfect, but it takes five hours to run. The traffic results are considered final at 3:00 a.m., and the markets don't open until 9:00 a.m. That would give it plenty of time, except the fish prices aren't available until 6:00 a.m. on some days. How can the trading firm get its model to run in time?

In the above scenario, our traders are out of luck if they are hoping to input the actual fish price data for that day. Lucky for them, it's possible to distribute this problem over a network of computers and have them each compute a separate scenario. That way, no matter what the fish price data says, they'll already have the results on hand.

Distributed computing is an extension of parallel computing in which the compute resource we are dedicating to work on each chunk of a given task is its own machine. This can get complex. All of these machines have to communicate with the machine that splits the tasks up and combines the results. The benefit is that many, many complex tasks—like financial simulations—can be performed simultaneously and have their results brought together (figure 1.8).

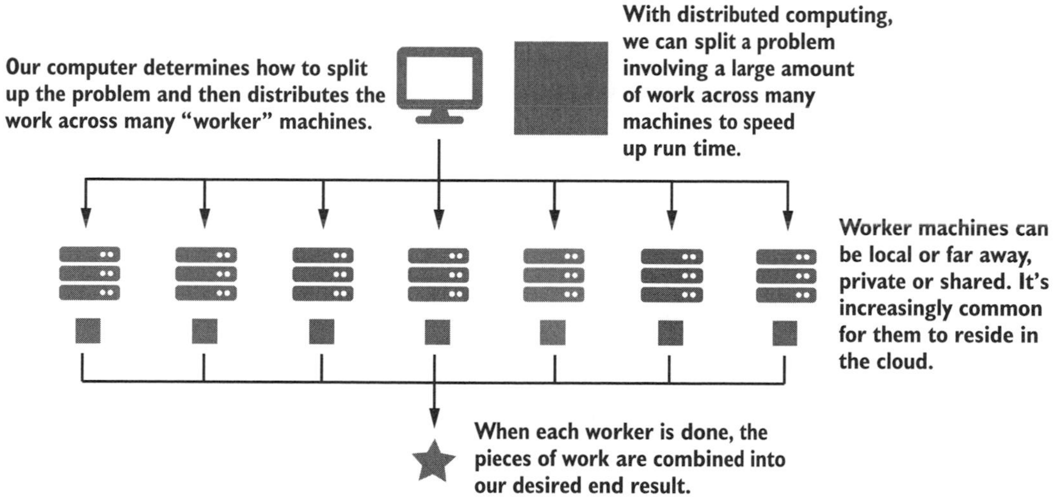
Our computer determines how to split up the problem and then distributes the work across many "worker" machines.
With distributed computing, we can split a problem involving a large amount of work across many machines to speed up run time.
Worker machines can be local or far away, private or shared. It's increasingly common for them to reside in the cloud.
When each worker is done, the pieces of work are combined into our desired end result.

Figure 1.8 We can use distributed computing to run sophisticated scenarios simultaneously and return the results to a single location.

Importantly, for problems that we can execute in a distributed manner, we can often speed them up simply by distributing the work over more and more machines or by improving the capability of the machines that the tasks are being distributed across. Which, if either, solution is going to result in faster code depends on the problem. The good news for our financial trading firm, though, is that they probably have the money for either one.

1.6 Hadoop: A distributed framework for map and reduce

To learn more about distributed computing, we'll first look at a specific form of distributed computing called *Apache Hadoop*, or simply *Hadoop*. Hadoop was designed as an open source implementation of Google's original MapReduce framework and has evolved into distributed computing software that is used widely by companies processing large amounts of data. Examples of such companies include Spotify, Yelp, and Netflix.

> **SCENARIO** Spotify is a cloud music provider that has two signature offerings: free music over the internet and customized, curated playlists that help you discover new music. These custom playlists work by comparing songs you like and listen to with what other users listen to, then suggesting songs that you may have missed. The challenge is that Spotify has hundreds of millions of users. How can Spotify compare the musical taste of all these users?

To create their music recommendations, Spotify uses Hadoop. Hadoop allows Spotify to store its listening logs (petabytes of information) on a distributed filesystem and then regularly analyze that information. The volume of data is the reason Hadoop is so valuable.

If Spotify had a smaller amount of information, it could use a relational database. With many petabytes of data, though, that becomes infeasible. For comparison, since we're talking about music, a 10 PB playlist of MP3s would take about 20,000 years to play. If someone started playing it before humans domesticated livestock, you could finish the playlist in your lifetime.

Using Hadoop means that the data storage and the processing both can be distributed, so Spotify doesn't have to pay attention, necessarily, to how much data it has. As long as it can pay for new machines to store the data on, it can pull them together with Hadoop (figure 1.9).

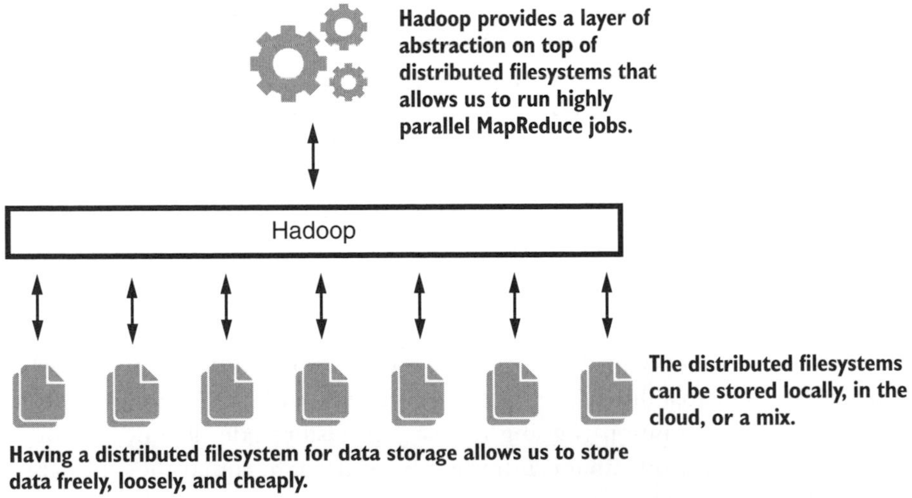
Hadoop provides a layer of abstraction on top of distributed filesystems that allows us to run highly parallel MapReduce jobs.
Hadoop
The distributed filesystems can be stored locally, in the cloud, or a mix.
Having a distributed filesystem for data storage allows us to store data freely, loosely, and cheaply.

Figure 1.9 Hadoop allows us to store data on a distributed file system of nodes and analyze the data with a highly parallel MapReduce process.

1.7 Spark for high-powered map, reduce, and more

We'll also touch on *Apache Spark* (or simply *Spark*) as a distributed computing framework. Spark is something of a successor to the Apache Hadoop framework that does more of its work in memory instead of by writing to files. The memory referenced in this case is not the memory of a single machine but, rather, the memories of a cluster of machines.

The result is that Apache Spark can be much faster than Apache Hadoop. By Apache's own estimations, Spark can run more than 100 times faster than Hadoop, though both will significantly increase your speed when compared to a linear process on a single machine. Spark also has some nice libraries for machine learning that we'll take a look at.

Ultimately, whether you decide you want to use Spark or Hadoop for your work will be up to you. Spark, like Hadoop, is being used by a lot of large organizations, such as Amazon, eBay, and even NASA. Both are excellent choices.

1.8 AWS Elastic MapReduce—Large datasets in the cloud

One of the most popular ways to implement Hadoop and Spark today is through Amazon's Elastic MapReduce. Elastic MapReduce (EMR) joins the MapReduce framework we've been talking about with Amazon's "elastic" series of cloud computing APIs, such as Elastic Cloud Compute (EC2). These tools have a very relevant purpose: allowing software developers to focus on writing code and not on the procurement and maintenance of hardware.

In traditional distributed computing, an individual—or more often a company—has to own all the machines. They then have to unite those machines into a cluster, ensure those machines stay up to date with all the latest software, and otherwise ensure that all of the machines stay running. With EMR, all we need to dabble in distributed computing is some spare change, and Amazon handles the rest.

Because EMR allows us to run distributed jobs on demand, without having to own our own cluster, we can expand the scope of problems we want to solve with parallel programming. EMR allows us to tackle small problems with parallel programming because it makes it cost effective. We don't have to make an up-front investment in servers to prototype new ideas. EMR also allows us to tackle large problems with parallel programming because we can procure as many resources as we need, whether that's tens or thousands of machines (figure 1.10).

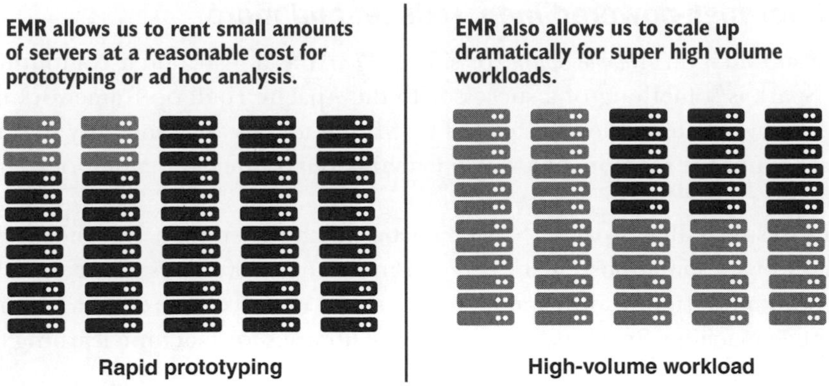
EMR allows us to rent small amounts of servers at a reasonable cost for prototyping or ad hoc analysis.
EMR also allows us to scale up dramatically for super high volume workloads.
Rapid prototyping
High-volume workload

Figure 1.10 EMR allows us to run small parallel jobs more cheaply, while also allowing us to expand when we need to run large jobs.

Summary

- We can use the map and reduce style of programming to solve problems on our local machine or in a distributed cloud environment.
- Parallel programming helps us speed up our programs by running many operations at the same time on different processors or on different machines.
- The `map` function performs one-to-one transformations and is a great way to transform data so it is more suitable for use.
- The `reduce` function performs one-to-any transformations and is a great way to assemble data into a final result.
- Distributed computing allows us to solve problems rapidly if we have enough computers.
- We can do distributed computing a number of ways, including using the Apache Hadoop and Apache Spark libraries.
- AWS is a cloud computing environment that makes it easy and cost-effective to do massive parallel work.

2 Accelerating large dataset work: Map and parallel computing

This chapter covers

- Using `map` to transform lots of data
- Using parallel programming to transform lots of data
- Scraping data from the web in parallel with `map`

In this chapter, we'll look at `map` and how to use it for parallel programming, and we'll apply those concepts to complete two web scraping exercises. With `map`, we'll focus on three primary capabilities:

1. We can use it to replace `for` loops.
2. We can use it to transform data.
3. Map evaluates only when necessary, not when called.

These core ideas about `map` are also why it's so useful for us in parallel programming. In parallel programming, we're using multiple processing units to do partial work on a task and combining that work later. Transforming lots of data from one type to another is an easy task to break into pieces, and the instructions for doing so are generally easy to transfer. Making code parallel with `map` can be as easy as adding four lines of code to a program.

2.1 An introduction to map

In chapter 1, we talked a little bit about `map`, which is a function for transforming sequences of data. Specifically, we looked at the example of applying the mathematical function `n+7` to a list of integers: [–1,0,1,2]. And we looked at the graphic in figure 2.1, which shows a series of numbers being mapped to their outputs.

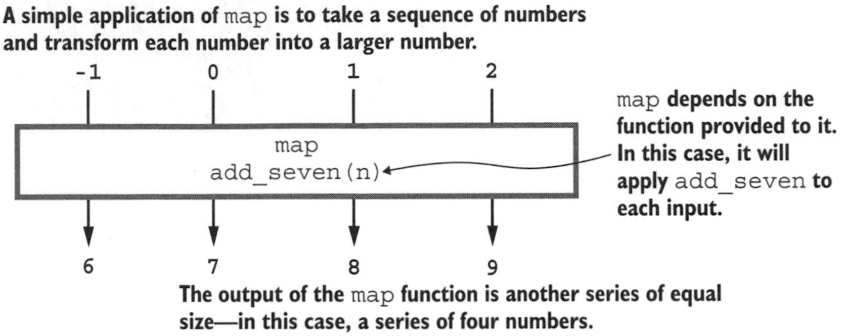
A simple application of map is to take a sequence of numbers and transform each number into a larger number.
-1
0
1
2
map
add_seven(n)
map depends on the function provided to it. In this case, it will apply add_seven to each input.
6
7
8
9
The output of the map function is another series of equal size—in this case, a series of four numbers.

Figure 2.1 The `map` function applies another function to all the values in a sequence and returns a sequence of their outputs: transforming [–1, 0, 1, 2] into [6, 7, 8, 9].

This figure shows the essence of `map`. We have an input of some length, in this case four, and an output of that same length. And each input gets transformed by the same function as all the other inputs. These transformed inputs are then returned as our output.

> **Some Python knowledge required**
>
> We will cover some advanced topics in this book as we work up to dealing with large datasets. That said, in the first section of this book (chapters 1 through 6), one of my goals is to provide all my readers with background knowledge that may be missing from their programming education. Depending on your experience, you may already be familiar with some of the concepts, such as regular expressions, classes and methods, higher order functions, and anonymous functions. If not, you will be by the end of chapter 6.
>
> By the end of this first section, my goal is to have you ready to learn about distributed computing frameworks and processing large datasets. If at any point you feel like you need more background knowledge on Python, I recommend Naomi Ceder's *The Quick Python Book* (Manning, 2018; http://mng.bz/vl11).

That's all fine and good, but most of us aren't concerned with middle-school math problems such as applying simple algebraic transformations. Let's take a look at a few ways that `map` can be used in practice so we can really begin to see its power.

> **SCENARIO** You want to generate a call list for your sales team, but the original developers for your customer sign-up form forgot to build data validation checks into the form. As a result, all the phone numbers are formatted differently. For example, some will be formatted nicely—(123) 456-7890; some are just numbers—1234567890; some use dots as separators—123.456.7890; and others, trying to be helpful, include a country code—+1 123 456-7890.

First, let's tackle this problem in a way that you're probably familiar with already: `for` looping. We'll do that in listing 2.1. Here, we first create a regular expression that matches all numbers and compile that. Then, we go through each phone number and get the digits out of that number with the regular expression's `.findall` method. From there, we count off the digits from the right. We assign the first four from the right as the last four, the next three as the first three, and the next three as an area code. We assume any other digits would just be a country code (+1 for the United States). We store all of these in variables, and then we use Python's string formatting to append them to a list to store our results: `new_numbers`.

Listing 2.1 Formatting phone numbers with a `for` loop

```
import re

phone_numbers = [
    "(123) 456-7890",
    "1234567890",
    "123.456.7890",
    "+1 123 456-7890"
]

new_numbers = []

R = re.compile(r"\d")                      # Compiles our regular expression

for number in phone_numbers:               # Loops through all the phone numbers
  digits = R.findall(number)


  area_code = "".join(digits[-10:-7])      # Gathers the numbers into variables
  first_3 = "".join(digits[-7:-4])
  last_4 = "".join(digits[-4:len(digits)])

  pretty_format = "({}) {}-{}".format(area_code,first_3,last_4)
  new_numbers.append(correct_format)       # Appends the numbers in the right format
```

How do we tackle this with `map`? Similarly, but with `map`, we have to separate this problem into two parts. Let's separate it like this:

1. Resolving the formatting of a phone number
2. Applying that solution to all the phone numbers we have

First up, we'll tackle formatting the phone numbers. To do that, let's create a small class with a method that finds the last 10 numbers of a string and returns them in our pretty format. That class will compile a regular expression to find all the numbers. We can then use the last seven numbers to print a phone number in the format we desire. If there are more than seven, we'll ignore the country code.

> **NOTE** We want to use a *class* (instead of a function) here because it will allow us to compile the regular expression once but use it many times. Over the long run, this will save our computer the effort of repeatedly compiling the regular expression.

We'll create a `.pretty_format` method that expects a misformatted phone number (a string) and uses the compiled regular expression to find all of the numbers. Then, just as we did in the previous example, we'll take matches at positions –10, –9, and –8, using e slice syntax, and assign them to a variable named `area code`. These numbers should be our area code. We'll take the matches at positions –7, –6, and –5 and assign them to be the first three numbers of the phone number. And we'll take the last four numbers to be the last four of the phone numbers. Again, any numbers that occur before –10 will be ignored. These will be country codes. Lastly, we'll use Python's string formatting to print the numbers in our desired format. The class would look something like the following listing.

Listing 2.2 A class for reformatting phone numbers with `map`

```
import re

class PhoneFormatter:                    # Creates a class to hold our compiled regular expression
  def __init__(self):                    # Creates an initialization method to compile the regular expression
    self.r = re.compile(r"\d")

  def pretty_format(self, phone_number):   # Creates a format method to do the formatting
    phone_numbers = self.r.findall(phone_number)   # Gathers the numbers from the phone number string
    area_code = "".join(phone_numbers[-10:-7])
    first_3 = "".join(phone_numbers[-7:-4])
    last_4 = "".join(phone_numbers[-4:len(phone_numbers)])
    return "({}) {}-{}".format(area_code,    # Returns the numbers in the desired "pretty" format
                              first_3,
                              last_4)
```

Now that we're able to turn phone numbers of any format into phone numbers in a pretty format, we can combine our class with `map` to apply it to a list of phone numbers of any length. To combine the two, we'll instantiate our class and pass the method as the function that `map` will apply to all the elements of a sequence. We can do that as shown in the following listing.

Listing 2.3 Applying the `.pretty_format` method to phone numbers

```
phone_numbers = [
  "(123) 456-7890",
  "1234567890",
  "123.456.7890",
  "+1 123 456-7890"
]

P = PhoneFormatter ()
print(list(map(P.pretty_format, phone_numbers)))
```

Initializes test data to validate our function

Initializes our class so we can use its method

Maps the .pretty_format method across the phone numbers and prints the results

You'll notice at the very bottom that we convert our `map` results to a `list` before we print them. If we were going to use them in our code, we would not need to do this; however, because `map`s are lazy if we print them without converting them to a `list`, we'll just see a generic `map` object as output. This isn't as satisfying as the nicely formatted phone numbers that we expected.

Another thing you'll notice about this example is that we were set up perfectly to take advantage of `map` because we were doing a 1-to-1 transformation. That is, we were transforming each element of a sequence. In essence, we've turned this problem into our middle-school algebra example: applying `n+7` to a list of numbers.

In figure 2.2, we can see the similarities between the two problems. For each problem, we're doing three things: taking a sequence of data, transforming it with some function, and getting the outputs. The only difference between the two is the data type (integers versus phone number strings) and the transformation (simple arithmetic versus regular expression pattern matching and pretty printing).

The key with `map` is recognizing situations where we can apply this three-step pattern. Once we start looking for it, we'll start to see it everywhere. Let's take a look at another, and more complex, version of this pattern: web scraping.

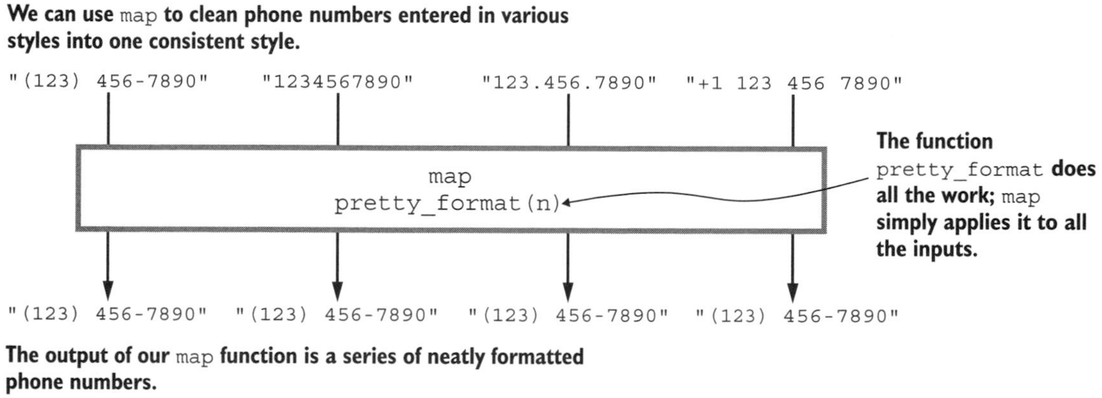
We can use map to clean phone numbers entered in various styles into one consistent style.
"(123) 456-7890"
"1234567890"
"123.456.7890"
"+1 123 456 7890"
map
pretty_format(n)
The function pretty_format does all the work; map simply applies it to all the inputs.
"(123) 456-7890"
"(123) 456-7890"
"(123) 456-7890"
"(123) 456-7890"
The output of our map function is a series of neatly formatted phone numbers.

Figure 2.2 We can use `map` to clean text strings into a common format by applying a cleaning function to all of them.

SCENARIO In the early 2000s, your company's archrival may have posted some information about their top-secret formula on their blog. You can access all their blog posts through a URL that includes the date the post was made (e.g., https://arch-rival-business.com/blog/01-01-2001). Design a script that can retrieve the content of every web page posted between January 1, 2001, and December 31, 2010.

Let's think about how we're going to get the data from our archrival's blog. We'll be retrieving data from URLs. These URLs, then, can be our input data. And the transformation will take these URLs and turn them into web page content. Thinking about the problem like this, we can see that it's similar to the others we've used `map` for in this chapter.

Figure 2.3 shows the problem posed in the same format as the previous problems we've solved with `map`. On the top, we can see the input data. Here, however, instead of phone numbers or integers, we'll have URLs. On the bottom, again, we have our output data. This is where we'll eventually have our HTML. In the middle, we have a function that will take each URL and return HTML.

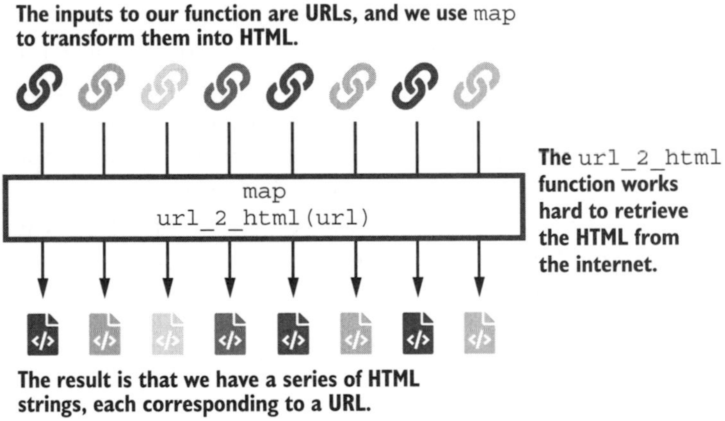
The inputs to our function are URLs, and we use map to transform them into HTML.
map
url_2_html(url)
The url_2_html function works hard to retrieve the HTML from the internet.
The result is that we have a series of HTML strings, each corresponding to a URL.

Figure 2.3 We also can use `map` to retrieve the HTML corresponding to a sequence of URLs, once we write a function that can do that for a single URL.

2.1.1 *Retrieving URLs with map*

With the problem posed like this, we know we can solve it with `map`. The question, then, becomes: How can we get a list of all these URLs? Python has a handy datetime library for solving problems like this. Here, we create a generator function that takes start and end date `tuples` in `(YYYY,MM,DD)` format and produces a list of dates between them. We use a generator instead of a normal loop because this prevents us from storing all the numbers in memory in advance. The keyword `yield` in the following listing distinguishes this as a generator, instead of a traditional function that uses `return`.

Listing 2.4 A date range generating function

```
from datetime import date

def days_between(start, stop):
  today = date(*start)
  stop = date(*stop)
  while today < stop:
   datestr = today.strftime("%m-%d-%Y")
   yield http://jtwolohan.com/arch-rival-blog/"+ datestr
    today = date.fromordinal(today.toordinal()+1)
```

- Imports the datetime library's date class
- Creates our generator function
- Unpacks the date start and stop tuples to store them as dates
- Loops through all the dates until we've reached our stop date
- Returns the date as a path
- Increments the date by one day

TAKING ADVANTAGE OF DATETIME

The majority of the work this function does comes from Python's datetime library's `date` class. The datetime `date` class represents a date and contains knowledge about the Gregorian calendar and some convenience methods for working with dates. You'll notice that we import the `date` class directly as `date`. In our function, we instantiate two of these classes: one for our start date and one for our stop date. Then, we let our function generate new dates until we hit our stop date.

The last line of our function uses the ordinal date representation, which is the date as the number of days since January 1, year 1. By incrementing this value and turning it into a `date` class, we can increase our date by one. Because our `date` class is calendar aware, it will automatically progress through the weeks, months, and years. It will even account for leap years.

Lastly, it's worth looking at the line our `yield` statement is on. This is where we output URLs. We take the base URL of the website—http://jtwolohan.com/arch-rival-blog/—and append the date formatted as a MM-DD-YYYY string to the end, just like our problem specified. The `.strftime` method from the `date` class allows us to use a date formatting language to turn dates into strings formatted however we want.

TURNING INPUT INTO OUTPUT

Once we've got our input data, the next step is coming up with a function to turn our input data into the output data. Our output data here is going to be the web content of the URL. Lucky for us again, Python provides some useful tools for that in its urllib.request library. Taking advantage of that, a function like the following may work for us:

```
from urllib import request

def get_url(path):
  return request.urlopen(path).read()
```

This function takes a URL and returns the HTML found at that URL. We rely on Python's request library's `urlopen` function to retrieve the data at the URL. This data is returned to us as an HTTPResponse object, but we can use its .read method to return the HTML as a string. It's worth trying this function out in your REPL environment on a URL for a website you visit often (like www.manning.com) to see the function in action.

Then, like in previous scenarios, we can apply this function to all the data in our sequence, using map like this:

```
blog_posts = map(get_url,days_between((2000,1,1),(2011,1,1)))
```

This single line of code takes our get_url function and applies it to each and every URL generated by our days_between function. Passing the start and end dates ((2000,1,1) and (2011,1,1)) to our days_between function results in a generator of days between January 1, 2000, and January 1, 2011: every day of the first decade of the 21st century. The values that this function returns are stored in the variable blog_posts.

If you run this on your local machine, the program should finish almost instantly. How is that possible? Certainly we can't scrape 10 years of web pages that quickly, can we? Well, no. But with our generator function and with map, we don't actually try to.

2.1.2 The power of lazy functions (like map) for large datasets

map is what we call a lazy function. That means it doesn't actually evaluate when we call it. Instead, when we call map, Python stores the instructions for evaluating the function and runs them at the exact moment we ask for the value. That's why when we've wanted to see the values of our map statements previously, we've explicitly converted the maps to lists; lists in Python require the actual objects, not the instructions for generating those objects.

If we think back to our first example of map—mapping n+7 across a list of numbers: [–1,0,1,2]—we used figure 2.4 to describe map.

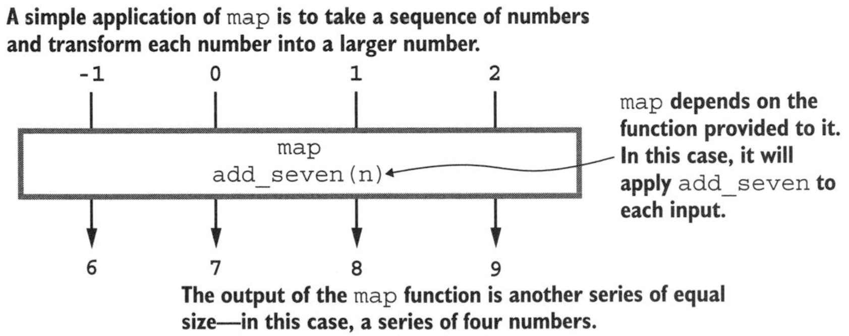
A simple application of map is to take a sequence of numbers and transform each number into a larger number.
-1
0
1
2
map
add_seven(n)
map depends on the function provided to it. In this case, it will apply add_seven to each input.
6
7
8
9
The output of the map function is another series of equal size—in this case, a series of four numbers.

Figure 2.4 We initially thought about map as something that transforms a sequence of inputs into a sequence of outputs.

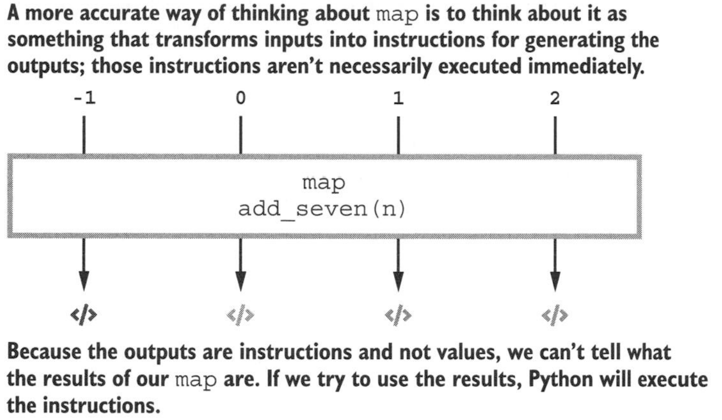
A more accurate way of thinking about map is to think about it as something that transforms inputs into instructions for generating the outputs; those instructions aren't necessarily executed immediately.
-1
0
1
2
map
add_seven(n)
</>
</>
</>
</>
Because the outputs are instructions and not values, we can't tell what the results of our map are. If we try to use the results, Python will execute the instructions.

Figure 2.5 In Python, the base `map` turns a sequence of inputs into instructions for computing a sequence of outputs—not the sequence itself.

It is, however, a little more accurate to think about `map` like in figure 2.5.

In figure 2.5, we have the same input values on the top and the same function we're applying to all of those values; however, our outputs have changed. Where before we had 6, 7, 8, and 9, now we have instructions. If we had the computer evaluate these instructions, the results would be 6, 7, 8, and 9. Often in our programs, we will act like these two outputs are equal. However, as programmers, we'll need to remember that there's a slight difference: the default `map` in Python doesn't evaluate when called, it creates instructions for later evaluation.

As a Python programmer, you've probably already seen lazy data floating around. A common place to find lazy objects in Python is the `range` function. When moving from Python2 to Python3, the Python folks decided to make `range` lazy so that Python programmers (you and me) can create huge ranges without doing two things:

1. Taking the time to generate a massive list of numbers
2. Storing all those values in memory when we may only need a few

These benefits are the same for `map`. We like a lazy `map` because it allows us to transform a lot of data without an unnecessarily large amount of memory or spending the time to generate it. That's exactly how we want it to work.

2.2 Parallel processing

Great, so now we have a way to get all of our data from the internet using `map`. But using `map` to get that data offline one page at a time is going to be very slow. If it takes us 1 second to scrape a single webpage, and we need to scrape 3,652 web pages, then it will take us a little more than an hour to download all the data (3,652 pages × 1 second per page/60 seconds per minute = 61 minutes). This is not an incredibly long time to wait, but it's long enough that we want to avoid it if we can. And we can.

How can we avoid this wait? Well, what if instead of downloading a single page at a time, we downloaded multiple pages at once? Using parallel programming, we can do just that.

Parallel programming means to program in such a way that we divide our problem into chunks that can then be processed separately and simultaneously. Typically, the work we'll want to do on each of these chunks is going to be the same. For example, in our case, we want to process each URL (a separate piece of data, unrelated to any other URL) and retrieve a website at that URL (a common process).

Figure 2.6 shows the difference between downloading URLs with standard linear processing and with parallel processing.

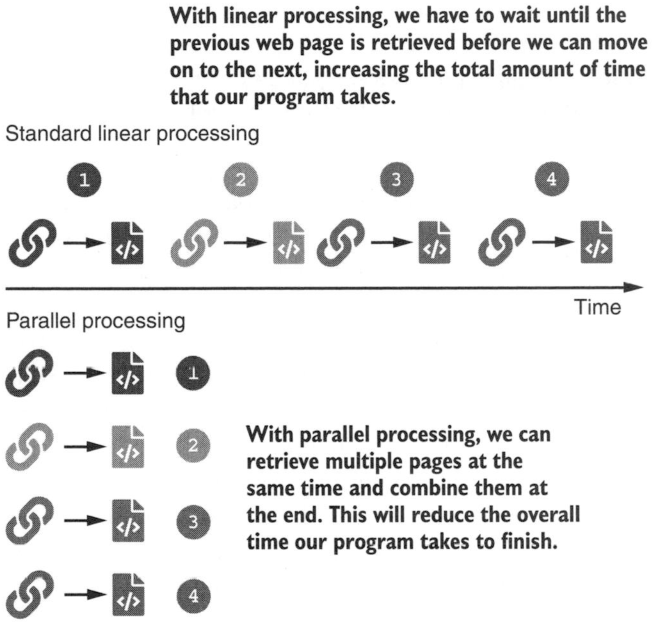
With linear processing, we have to wait until the previous web page is retrieved before we can move on to the next, increasing the total amount of time that our program takes.
Standard linear processing
1
2
3
4
Time
Parallel processing
1
2
3
4
With parallel processing, we can retrieve multiple pages at the same time and combine them at the end. This will reduce the overall time our program takes to finish.

Figure 2.6 Reading one web page at a time is slow; we can speed this up with parallel programming.

Using linear processing, we'd be processing URLs and turning them into web pages one at a time. We'd work on one URL, get the data, then work on the next URL. Parallel programming allows us to split this task up and process it faster. When we write parallel code, we assign a number of "workers" (typically CPUs) to the task. Each of these workers then takes a chunk of our data and processes it.

In figure 2.6, the data is the same and the data transformation is the same. The only change in our setup is the number of tasks we're performing at once. Where before we were doing one task at a time, now we're doing four. This will make our work go four times more quickly.

2.2.1 Processors and processing

If four is better, why not eight? Why not 10? Why not 1,000? Well, that's a really good question. Something most people don't think about when they're working on computers, something that most programmers don't even think about, is the effect computer hardware has on how the computer behaves. Most people will know, for example, whether they have a Mac or a PC; however, unless they have an Intel sticker on their computer somewhere, most people probably couldn't say what type of processor they have.

In parallel programming, though, these processors are our heroes. Processors are little circuit boards that are capable of executing instructions, that is, actually doing work. Often, we think of our computer's memory as the limiting factor to what we can do, and it certainly can be. But our CPU can be just as important. Having a lot of memory with a weak processor is like being in the buffet line with only one plate: sure, there's a lot of food, but most of it won't ever get eaten. If our CPU has multiple cores, it's like getting extra plates: every time we go to the buffet, we'll be able to bring that much more food back to the table.

With CPUs, like with plates, more is better. The more we have, the more we can assign to tasks, and the more work we can do. You can check how many CPUs you have on your machine by running the following Python command in your Python REPL:

```
import os
os.cpu_count()
```

Alternatively, you can run the following command from the terminal:

```
python3 -c "import os; print(os.cpu_count())"
```

Both of these commands do the same thing. The first bit imports the `os` module from the Python standard library, and the second bit checks how many CPUs you have. The `os` module, if you're not familiar with it, is stocked full of tools for interacting with your operating system. Depending on which operating system you're using, the exact details of some of these functions will change. It's worthwhile to familiarize yourself with the details before using too much of this module.

These commands are useful because they tell you how much of a speed increase you'll get from your standard parallel programming implementation. When we implement code in parallel in Python, by default Python will use all of our CPUs. If we don't want it to, we'll have to specify that we want it to use fewer.

But that's jumping a little ahead. What does it even look like to implement parallel code in Python? Let's return to our URL downloading example. We want to scrape web pages in parallel. How much do we have to modify our code? The following listing will give you an idea.

Listing 2.5 Web scraping in parallel

```
from datetime import date
from urllib import request

from multiprocessing import Pool          <-- Imports the multiprocessing library

def days_between(start,stop):
  today = date(*start)
  stop = date(*stop)
  while today < stop:
    datestr = today.strftime("%m-%d-%Y")
    yield "http://jtwolohan.com/arch-rival-blog/"+datestr
    today = date.fromordinal(today.toordinal()+1)

def get_url(path):
  return request.urlopen(path).read()

with Pool() as P:          <-- Gathers our processors with Pool()

  blog_posts = P.map(get_url,
                     days_between((2000,1,1),
                                  (2011,1,1)))     <-- Performs our map in parallel
```

As we can see in listing 2.5, the code doesn't have to change very much at all. Because we organized our code using `map` in the first place, making our code parallel for this problem required only two new lines of code and adding two characters to a third line. If you have four CPUs on your machine, this program should run about four times faster than the nonparallel version. That would cut our hypothetical one-hour run time down to about 15 minutes.

That was pretty easy, and it should be. This type of task falls under the umbrella of tasks that are dismissively referred to as *embarrassingly parallel*. In other words, the solution to speeding up these tasks is embarrassingly easy. That said, some problems can pop up when doing parallel programming.

Some of the problems we may encounter when working with parallelization in Python are

- The inability to pickle data or functions, causing our programs to not run
- Order-sensitive operations returning inconsistent results
- State-dependent operations returning inconsistent results

2.2.2 Parallelization and pickling

When we write code in parallel—for example, when we called our parallel `map` function previously—Python does a lot of work behind the scenes. When our parallelizations don't work, it's usually because we aren't fully thinking through the work that Python is hiding from us. One of the things that Python hides from us is *pickling*.

Pickling is Python's version of object serialization or marshalling, with object serialization being the storing of objects from our code in an efficient binary format on the disk that can be read back by our program at a later time. The term *pickling* comes from Python's `pickle` module, which provides functions for pickling data and reading pickled data.

The pickling and unpickling process looks something like figure 2.7.

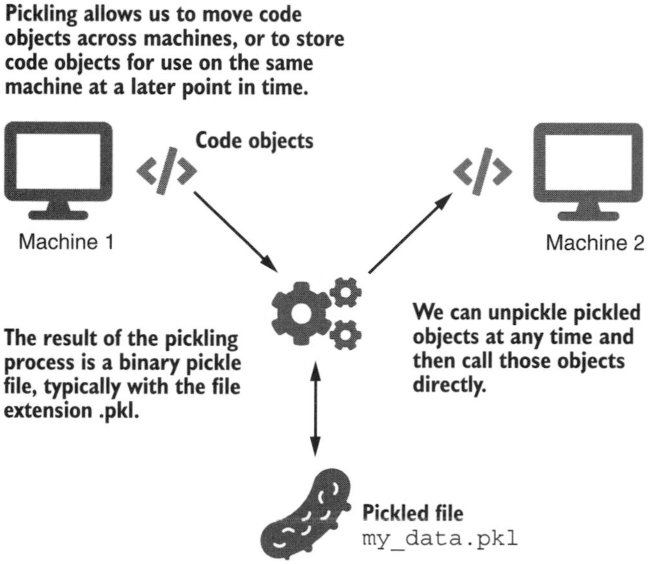
Pickling allows us to move code objects across machines, or to store code objects for use on the same machine at a later point in time.
Code objects
Machine 1
Machine 2
The result of the pickling process is a binary pickle file, typically with the file extension .pkl.
We can unpickle pickled objects at any time and then call those objects directly.
Pickled file
my_data.pkl

Figure 2.7 Pickling allows us to save data and instructions in a machine-readable state so Python can reuse it later.

On the left, we begin the process with our original programming environment and our original code objects. Nothing special is going on at this point; we're just programming in Python as usual. Next, we pickle our code objects. Now our code objects are saved in a binary file on a disk. Next, we read the pickled file from a new programming environment, and our original code objects become accessible to us in the new environment. Everything that we pickled in the first environment is now accessible to us in the new one just as it was previously.

> **NOTE** Our code can sit in the pickled format for as long as we'd like. In parallel programming, usually we read the file back into a Python environment quickly, but there's no reason we couldn't leave the pickled objects on the disk for a longer amount of time. However, pickling data for long-term storage is not a good idea, because if you upgrade your Python version, the data may become unreadable.

Why do we use pickling in parallel programming? Remember how we talked about parallel programming allowing our program to do multiple things at the same time? Python pickles objects—functions and data—to transfer the work to each of the processors that will be working on our problem. That process looks something like figure 2.8.

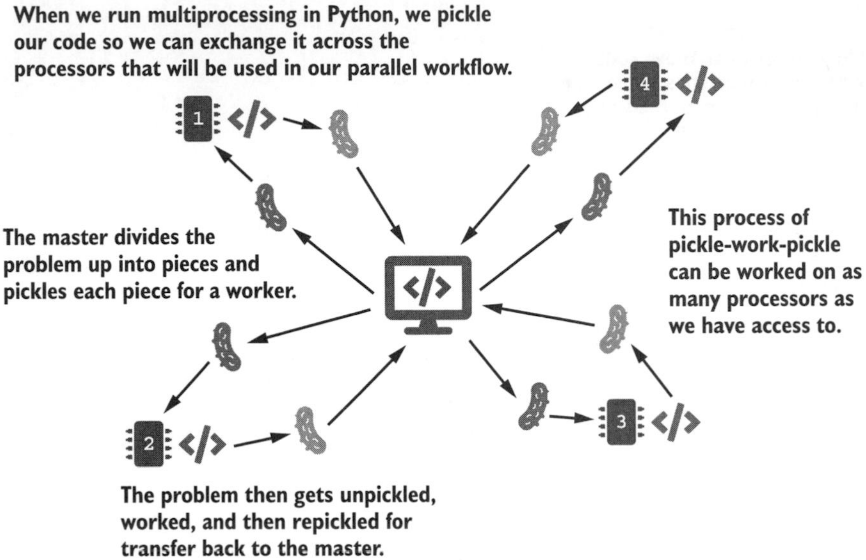
When we run multiprocessing in Python, we pickle our code so we can exchange it across the processors that will be used in our parallel workflow.
1
4
The master divides the problem up into pieces and pickles each piece for a worker.
This process of pickle-work-pickle can be worked on as many processors as we have access to.
2
3
The problem then gets unpickled, worked, and then repickled for transfer back to the master.

Figure 2.8 Pickling allows us to share data across processors or even across machines, saving the instructions and data and then executing them elsewhere.

We start with our code operating on only one processor; this is the standard way of coding. To work our code in parallel, Python then divides our problem into parts that can each be tackled by an individual processing unit. The master work stream then pickles these parts. This pickling ensures that the processor will know how to perform the work we need it to do. When the processing unit is ready to do the work, it reads the pickled file from the disk and does the work. Then, finally, the worker pickles the result and returns it to the master.

Most of the time, this approach works flawlessly; however, only some types of Python objects can be pickled. If we try to use parallel methods on objects that can't be pickled, Python will throw an error. Luckily for us, most standard Python objects are pickleable and, therefore, usable in parallel Python code. Python can naturally pickle the following types:

- None, True, and False
- Integers, floating-point numbers, complex numbers
- Strings, bytes, bytearrays

- Tuples, lists, sets, and dictionaries containing only pickleable objects
- Functions defined at the top level of a module
- Built-in functions defined at the top level of a module
- Classes that are defined at the top level of a module

We can't pickle the following types of objects:

- Lambda functions
- Nested functions
- Nested classes

The easiest way to avoid problems with the unpickleable types is to avoid using them when working with Python's built-in multiprocessing module. For situations where we absolutely must use them, a community library called *pathos* solves many of these problems with a module called `dill` (Get it? Dill pickles?). The `dill` module takes a different approach to pickling that allows us to pickle just about anything we'd like, including the three object types we weren't able to pickle before.

Using pathos and `dill` is not much different from using the multiprocessing module. The first thing we have to do is install the library. From the command line, run

```
pip3 install pathos
```

In addition to installing pathos, Python also will install some of the libraries pathos depends on, including `dill`. With pathos installed, we can now call on it, and it will use `dill` behind the scenes. If you remember back to our multiprocessing example, it looked something like this:

```
from multiprocessing import Pool

# ... other code here ...

with Pool() as P:
  blog_posts = P.map(get_url,days_between((2000,1,1),(2011,1,1)))
```

To convert this to pathos, we just have to make a few changes. Our new code will look like this:

```
from pathos.multiprocessing import ProcessPool

# ... other code here ...

with ProcessPool(nodes=4) as P:
  blog_posts = P.map(get_url,days_between((2000,1,1),(2011,1,1)))
```

Moving from multiprocessing to pathos requires only two real changes. First, we have to import from pathos instead of from multiprocessing. Also, in pathos the pool we want is called `ProcessPool` instead of just `Pool`. Just like `Pool`, `ProcessPool` is the function that will recruit worker processor units for us. We need to call `ProcessPool` in place of `Pool`. As with `Pool`, we only need to specify the number of nodes if we want to use fewer than the maximum number of nodes. We're specifying it here for demonstration purposes. With our `ProcessPool` now accessible as `P`, we can call it just like we called our `multiprocessing.Pool` object: `P.map`.

2.2.3 Order and parallelization

Another condition that can cause us problems when we're working in parallel is order sensitivity. When we work in parallel, we're not guaranteed that tasks will be finished in the same order they're input. This means that if we're doing work that needs to be processed in a linear order, we probably shouldn't do it in parallel.

To test this for yourself, try running this command in Python:

```
with Pool() as P:
  P.map(print,range(100))
```

If we do this with a `for` loop, we expect to get a nice ordered list of every number between 0 and 99 printed to our screen. With our `map` construction, though, we don't get this. With `map`, we get a somewhat ordered, somewhat mismatched sequence printed to our screen and a list of `None`s. What's going on?

When Python parallelizes our code, it chunks our problem up for our processing units to work on. Our processing units, for their part, grab the first available chunk every time they have capacity to work on the problem. They then work this problem until it's complete, then they grab the next available chunk to work. When chunks are available out of order, they will be completed out of order. We can visualize this process as shown in figure 2.9.

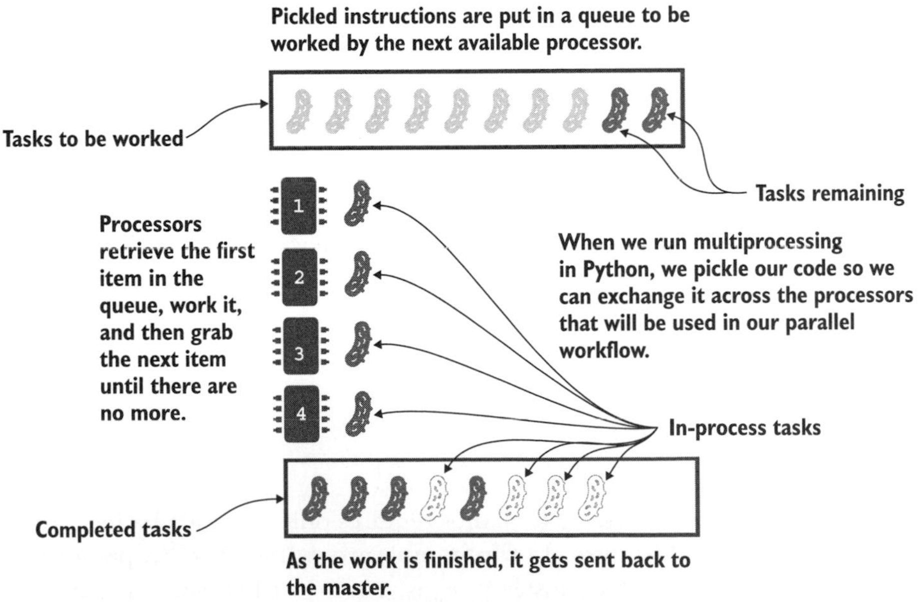
Pickled instructions are put in a queue to be worked by the next available processor.
Tasks to be worked
Tasks remaining
1
2
3
4
Processors retrieve the first item in the queue, work it, and then grab the next item until there are no more.
When we run multiprocessing in Python, we pickle our code so we can exchange it across the processors that will be used in our parallel workflow.
In-process tasks
Completed tasks
As the work is finished, it gets sent back to the master.

Figure 2.9 Parallel processing doesn't necessarily finish tasks in order, so we have to know if that is acceptable before we use parallel techniques.

In figure 2.9, our problem starts at the top. We've chunked the problem into 10 pieces and put them in a queue. As the processors become available, they'll pull a task from the queue, work it, and send the results to the completed tasks area at the bottom. The processors then grab the next available tasks and process them until all of the tasks are finished. But the time it takes for these operations to finish varies. For example, in the completed tasks area we can see that tasks 1, 2, 3, and 5 have been completed, and tasks 4, 6, 7, and 8 are currently being worked. Tasks 9 and 10 are still queued up, unassigned to a processor. A situation like this can easily occur if tasks 1 (or 2 or 3) and 5 are short, but task 4 is long, such that two tasks can be completed in the time it takes the single task 4 to finish.

All that said, even though Python may not complete the problems in order, it still remembers the order in which it was supposed to do them. Indeed, our `map` returns in the exact order we would expect, even if it doesn't process in that order. To demonstrate that, we can run the following code:

```
def print_and_return(x):
  print(x); return x

with Pool() as P:
  P.map(print_and_return, range(20))
```

The printed output won't be ordered, but the list that's returned will be. The printed output shows the order in which the chunks were worked; the list output shows the data structure that was returned. We can see that even though Python works the problem in the "wrong" order, it still orders the results properly. When is this going to cause problems for us? Well, if we rely on state for one.

2.2.4 State and parallelization

In object-oriented programming, we'll often write methods that rely on the state of the class. Consider the fizz/buzz problem. The fizz/buzz problem is a problem that's often used to introduce programming language syntax. It involves looping through numbers and returning *fizz* if a number is not evenly divisible by three (or five, or some other number), and returning *buzz* if it is. The expected output is a sequence of fizzes and buzzes at the appropriate intervals.

In Python, we could solve the fizz/buzz problem with a class, as shown in the following listing.

Listing 2.6 Classic fizz/buzz problem with a `for` loop

```
class FizzBuzzer:
  def __init__(self):
    self.n = 0                  # The counter starts at 0.
  def foo(self,_):              # foo function that decides on fizzes and buzzes
    self.n += 1                 # Increments the counter each time the function is run
    if (self.n % 3) == 0:       # If the counter is divisible by three, buzz.
      x = "buzz"
```

```
    else: x = "fizz"
    print(x)
    return x

FB = FizzBuzzer()
for i in range(21):
  FB.foo(i)
```

If it's not, fizz.

Both prints the statement and returns it

Tests that the class is working

The class pays attention to how many times we've called its .foo method, and every third time it will print and return buzz instead of fizz. We use it in a loop to demonstrate that it's working properly. If you run this on your local machine, you'll see that this works just like we expect: we print out fizzes, with a buzz interjected in every third spot. However, something strange happens when we try to do the same thing using a parallel map:

```
FB = fizz_buzzer()
With Pool() as P:
  P.map(FB.foo, range(21))
```

What's going on here? Why do we only get fizz and no buzz? Let's return to something we talked about earlier when we were discussing map. Remember how we said that map doesn't actually do the calculations, it simply stores the instructions for the calculations? That's why we call it lazy. Well, in this case, the instructions to do the calculations for FB.foo include the state of FB at the time we ask for it. So since FB.n is 0 at the time we ask for the instructions, map uses FB.n = 0 for all of the operations, even if FB.n changes by the time we use it. And since FB.n = 0 will always produce a fizz, all we get is fizz.

We can test this by changing FB.n to 2, which should always produce a buzz, and running the same command. That would look something like this:

```
FB = FizzBuzzer()
FB.n = 2
with Pool() as P:
  P.map(FB.foo, range(21))
```

Here, like we expect, we store the instructions for FB.foo when FB.n = 2, and the result is that we get all buzz and no fizz.

What can we do instead? Often, situations like this simply require us to rethink the problem. A common solution is to take internal state and make it an external variable. For example, we could use the numbers generated by range instead of the internal values stored by FB. We could then also replace the class with a simple function, like this:

```
def foo(n):
  if (n % 3) == 0:
    x = "buzz"
  else: x = "fizz"
  print(x)
  return x
```

This function does exactly what the `.foo` method does, but it relies on the value of an external variable `n` instead of an internal state `self.n`. We can then apply this to the numbers generated by range with a parallel `map` and get our results back, just like we expect.

```
with Pool() as P:
  print(P.map(foo, range(1,22)))
```

When you run this, note that the printed values don't return in the correct order. That's because, as we noted in the previous section, the processors are grabbing the first available job off the stack and completing it as fast as they can. Sometimes, a fizz job will go slower than a buzz, and two buzzes will be printed in a row. Other times, a buzz will take longer, and we'll see three or more fizzes in a row. The resulting data, though, will be in the proper order: fizz, fizz, buzz . . . fizz, fizz, buzz . . . fizz, fizz, buzz.

It's worth taking a second to look at how this would be depicted visually. We'll look first at what happens when we attempt to do parallelization with state, then at what happens without it. To start, let's recall figure 2.8 (as duplicated in figure 2.10).

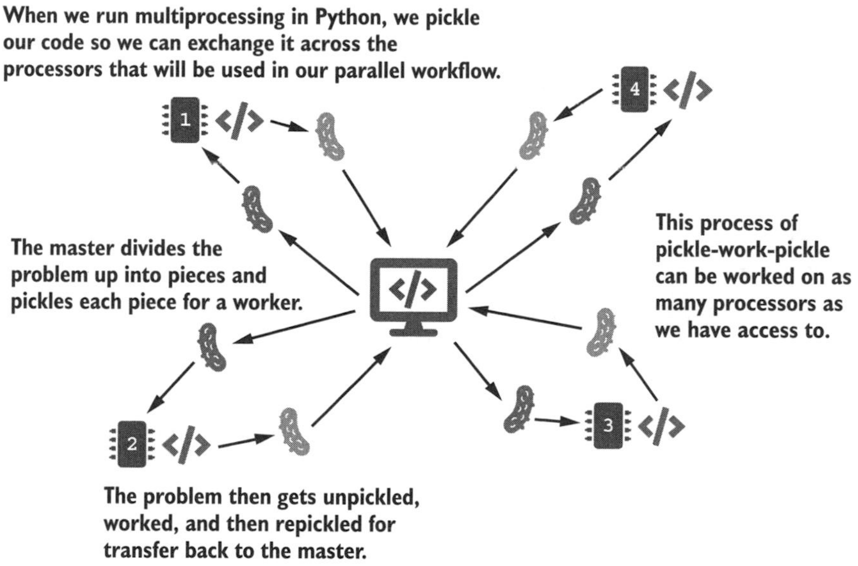
When we run multiprocessing in Python, we pickle our code so we can exchange it across the processors that will be used in our parallel workflow.
The master divides the problem up into pieces and pickles each piece for a worker.
This process of pickle-work-pickle can be worked on as many processors as we have access to.
The problem then gets unpickled, worked, and then repickled for transfer back to the master.

Figure 2.10 When we pickle work and distribute it with a parallel `map`, we're pickling state information as well. This allows us to execute the work in parallel but may produce unexpected results.

This graphic demonstrates what's happening when we're performing parallel calculations: first we chop our task up into chunks—in this case, four—then we save those chunks to the disk in a pickled format. Our processors then grab them and work them until they're all complete. With respect to state, it's this second step—pickling the data—that we need to be most aware of.

At the first step, `map` provides instructions for each part of the problem. This step is akin to our parallelization step, where we chunk the problem. Remember, `map` doesn't do the work of the problem immediately, it writes the instructions and does them later—it's lazy. Second, we save the instructions to a disk. `map` already captured these instructions, so it's easy to do. However, note that we're saving the instructions for the problem. That means that any state we needed is going to be stored as well, such as when we store `FB.n`. Then, the last step, our processors read the instructions and execute them.

2.3 Putting it all together: Scraping a Wikipedia network

We've covered a lot of powerful stuff in this chapter. To wrap it all up, let's consider one final scenario involving creating a network graph, such as the one in Figure 2.11.

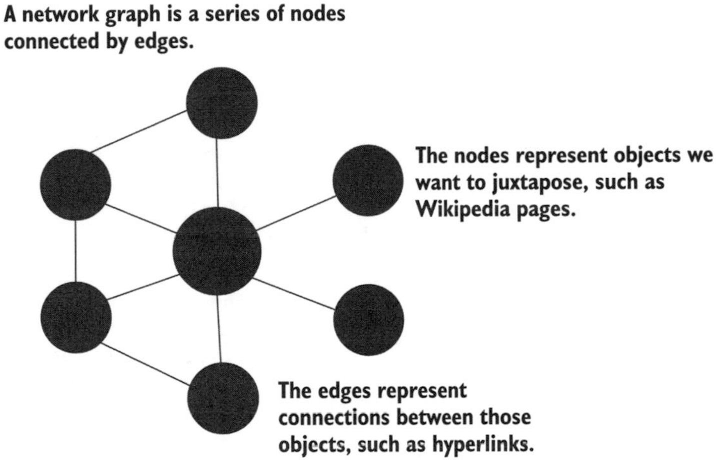
A network graph is a series of nodes connected by edges.
The nodes represent objects we want to juxtapose, such as Wikipedia pages.
The edges represent connections between those objects, such as hyperlinks.

Figure 2.11 A network graph is a series of nodes connected by edges that is often used to display relationships between objects, such as friendship between people, communication between systems, or roads between cities.

> **SCENARIO** We want to create a topic network graph from Wikipedia. That is, we want to be able to enter a term (for example: *parallel computing*) and find all the Wikipedia pages in that page's immediate *network*—pages that link to that page or that that page links to. The result will be a graph of all the pages in our network.

Let's begin by thinking about the problem at hand and sketching out a solution. Wikipedia has a nice API for getting data about Wikipedia pages, so we'll want to use that. And we know we're going to start from a single page, so we'll want to use that page as a starting point for our network. From that page, we'll want to get all the inbound and outbound links, which will be other nodes in our graph. Then, for each of the other nodes, we'll want to get the nodes to which those are related.

We can break that down further into a to-do list:

1 Write a function that gets the inbound and outbound links of a Wikipedia page.
2 Get the inbound and outbound links from our initial page.
3 Gather those pages in one long list.
4 Get the inbound and outbound links from all of those pages.
5 We'll do this in parallel, to speed things up.
6 Represent all our links as edges between pages.
7 Bonus: Use a graphing library (like networkx) to display the graph.

Let's first write a function to get the inbound and outbound links of a Wikipedia page based on its title. We'll start by importing the `JSON` module and the `requests` class from the `urllib` module. You'll remember `urllib` from before: this module helps us with getting data from the internet, which is exactly what we'll want to be doing with our Wikipedia pages. The `JSON` module is a module for parsing data in JSON format. It reads JSON into native Python types. We'll use this to convert the data Wikipedia provides us into an easily manageable format.

Next, we'll create a little function to help us turn Wikipedia page links into just the titles of those pages. Wikipedia naturally packages these links as JSON objects—we only want the title string.

Then, finally, we get to creating our actual function for getting information from Wikipedia. Our function, `get_wiki_links` expects a page title and turns that into a `dict` of inbound and outbound links. This `dict` will allow us easy access to those links later on.

The first thing we do in this function is create the URL for our query. If you're curious about where the URL comes from, Wikipedia has a well-documented API online; however, I'll explain the pertinent parts here. The `/w/api.php` tells Wikipedia that we want to use its API and not request a standard web page. The `action=query` tells Wikipedia that we'll be doing a query action. Query is one of the many actions Wikipedia makes available. It's tailored for getting metadata about pages, such as which pages link to and are linked from a given page.

The `prop=links|linkshere` tells the Wikipedia API that the properties we're interested in are the page's links and which pages link to the page. `pllimt` and `lhlimit` tell the API that we want to get at most 500 results. This is the maximum number of results we can get without registering ourselves as a bot. The `title` parameter is where we put the title of the page we want, and the `format` parameters define how the data returned to us should be formatted. We'll choose JSON for convenience's sake.

Next, with our URL set, we can pass it `request.urlopen`, which opens the URL with a `get` request. Wikipedia takes our request to its API and passes us back the information we requested. We can read this information into memory with the `.read` method, and we do. Since we asked Wikipedia to return this information as JSON, we can then read the JSON string with `json.reads`, which turns JSON strings into Python objects. The resulting object `j` is a `dict` that represents the JSON object that Wikipedia returns.

Now we can wade through those objects and pull out the links, which will be four levels deep at `page['query']['pages'][0]["links"]` and `page['query']['pages'][0]["linkshere"]`. The former object contains the pages to which our current page links, and the latter contains the pages that link to our current page. The Wikipedia API defines this structure, which is how we know where to find the data we need. These objects—the `links` and `linkshere`—as we noted before, are not the page titles but JSON objects, with the title as an element. To get just the title, we'll use our `link_to_title` function. Because we'll have more than one link and these links will be in a list, we'll use `map` to transform all of the objects to just their titles.

Finally, we'll return these objects as a `dict`. Altogether, that will look like the following listing.

Listing 2.7 A function for retrieving a Wikipedia page's network from its title

```
import json                                     # Imports the libraries we'll need
from urllib import request, parse

def link_to_title(link):                        # Creates a helper function for getting the title from a link result
  return link["title"]

def clean_if_key(page,key):                     # Creates a helper function that gets titles for the links found, if they exist
    if key in page.keys():
        return map(link_to_title,page[key])
    else: return []

def get_wiki_links(pageTitle):                  # Defines our get_wiki_links function
    safe_title = parse.quote(pageTitle)         # Quotes the title to ensure it's URL-safe
    url = "https://en.wikipedia.org/w/api.php?action=query&
prop=links|linkshere&pllimit=500&lhlimit=500&titles={}&
format=json&formatversion=2".format(safe_title)
    page = request.urlopen(url).read()          # Sends an HTTP request to the URL and reads the response
    j = json.loads(page)                        # Parses the response as JSON
    jpage = j["query"]["pages"][0]
    inbound = clean_if_key(jpage,"links")       # Cleans the inbound and outbound links if they exist
    outbound = clean_if_key(jpage,"linkshere")
    return {"title": pageTitle,                 # Returns the page's title and its inbound and outbound links
            "in-links":list(inbound),
            "out-links":list(outbound)}
```

At this point, we've tackled item 1 on our to-do list and put ourselves in a good position to tackle 2 and 3. We can do that now by writing a small function and creating an *only on execute* section of our script. Let's do that now.

Next, here's a simple function that will flatten the page's inbound and outbound links into one big list:

```
def flatten_network(page):
    return page["in-links"]+page["out-links"]
```

And here's the part of our code that will run if and only if we call this script with Python3:

```
if __name__ == "__main__":
  root = get_wiki_links ("Parallel_computing")
  initial_network = flatten_network(root)
```

The `if __name__ == "__main__"` tells Python only to use this code if it's called directly as a script. The line after that says to get all the links from the parallel computing page on Wikipedia using our function. And the last line stores the network in a variable.

Next, let's use this list, and the function we just wrote, to get all of the Wikipedia pages in the network of the parallel computing page. We'll do this in parallel to speed things up. To do that, we're going to want to extend the *run only when executed* section of our code from before. We'll add a few lines so it looks like this:

```
if __name__ == "__main__":
    root = get_wiki_links ("Parallel_computing")
    initial_network = flatten_network(root)
    with Pool() as P:
        all_pages = P.map(get_wiki_links, initial_network)
```

We've called `Pool` again to round up some processors to use in parallel programming. We then use those processors to get the Wikipedia page info for each page that either linked to or was linked to by our root page: parallel computing. Assuming we have four processors, we're completing this task in one-quarter the time it would take if we got the info for the pages one by one.

Now we want to represent each of these page objects as the edges between pages. What is this going to look like? A good representation of this will be a `tuple`, with the object in first position representing the page doing the linking and the object in second position representing the page being linked to. If `Parallel_computing` links to Python, we'll want a `tuple` like this: `("Parallel_computing", "Python")`.

To create these, we'll need another function. This function will turn each page `dict` into a list of these edge `tuples`.

```
def page_to_edges(page):
    a = [(page['title'],p) for p in page['out-links']]
    b = [(p,page['title']) for p in page['in-links']]
    return a+b
```

This function loops through each page in a page's network, creating a list of `tuples` for all the pages in the out-links, of the form `(page,out-link)`, and for all the pages in the in-links, of the form `(in-link,page)`. We'll then add these two lists together and return them.

We'll also need to update the script portion of our code. That section now looks like this:

```
from multiprocessing import Pool

if __name__ == "__main__":
    root = get_wiki_links ("Parallel_computing")
```

```
    initial_network = flatten_network(root)
    with Pool() as P:
        all_pages = P.map(get_wiki_links, initial_network)
        edges = P.map(page_to_edges, all_pages)
```

We've added a line that applies this `page_to_edges` function to all the pages we gathered with our previous function. Because we still have all those processors handy, let's just use them again to get this task done faster too.

The last thing we'll want to do is flatten this list of edges into one big list. The best way to do so is to use Python's itertools `chain` function. The `chain` function takes an iterable of iterables and chains them together so they can all be accessed one after another. For example, it allows us to treat [[1,2,3],[1,2],[1,2,3]] as if it was [1,2,3,1,2,1,2,3].

We'll use this chain function on our `edges` object. At this point, we're done needing our processors for parallelization, so we'll out-dent, moving out of this block of code, and let our processors go.

```
from itertools import chain

edges = chain.from_iterable(edges)
```

The `chain` function is lazy by default, so we'll need to wrap it in a `list` call, just like `map`, if we want to print it to the screen. If you do decide to print it to the screen, don't expect to see much. You'll be looking at 1,000,000 string-string `tuples` (1,000 `tuples` for each of the 1,000 pages in our network).

NOTE We just wrote about 50 lines of code, piece by piece. When we code like this, sometimes we can miss little things that cause our code to break. If you ever have trouble getting your code to run, remember that you can find the source code for this book online. Please refer to it if you ever spend more than a few minutes debugging: www.manning.com/downloads/1961.

2.3.1 Visualizing our graph

The best way to visualize our graph is to take it out of Python and import it into Gephi, a dedicated piece of graph visualization software. Gephi is well known in the social sciences for being an excellent network and graph visualization tool. It can work with data in many formats but prefers a custom format called .gefx. We'll use a Python library called *networkx* to export our graph to this format. That whole process will look something like this:

```
import networkx as nx

G = nx.DiGraph()
    for e in edges:
        G.add_edge(*e)
    nx.readwrite.gexf.write_gexf(G,"./MyGraph.gexf")
```

What we're doing here is creating a directed graph (`nx.DiGraph`) object and adding edges to it by iterating through our chained edges. The graph object has a method,

.add_edge, that allows us to construct a graph by declaring its edges one by one. Once this is done, all that's left to do is export the graph in the Gephi format, .gefx. The networkx library has a convenience function for that called `write_gefx`. We'll use that on our graph object and provide a path name. The graph is then saved in .gefx format at that path. On my machine, the output file is just under 36 MB.

> **NOTE** Gephi is excellent graph visualization software; however, this is not a book on visualizing graphs. If you don't think you'll find it satisfying to visualize your web scraping, or if you get frustrated using Gephi, feel free to skip ahead. We won't use Gephi again in this book.

From here, we can load up Gephi, import our .gefx file, and view our graph. If you don't have Gephi installed, you can find it at https://gephi.org. Gephi is free software, distributed under an open source license, and runs on Windows, MacOS, and Linux.

When you open Gephi, you may have to play around with the settings a bit with the graph to get it to show something pretty. I'll leave the graph visualization up to you and your creativity because I'm far from an expert in this area.

If you're short on patience for learning how to visualize a graph with more than 100,000 nodes, change the settings on our query to retrieve a smaller number of pages. I'll also leave it up to you to look back through the code and figure out how to do that. (Hint: It's in our request to the Wikipedia API.)

When I request only 50 neighbors from each page, I end up with a network of about 1,300 nodes that looks something like figure 2.12 by default in Gephi.

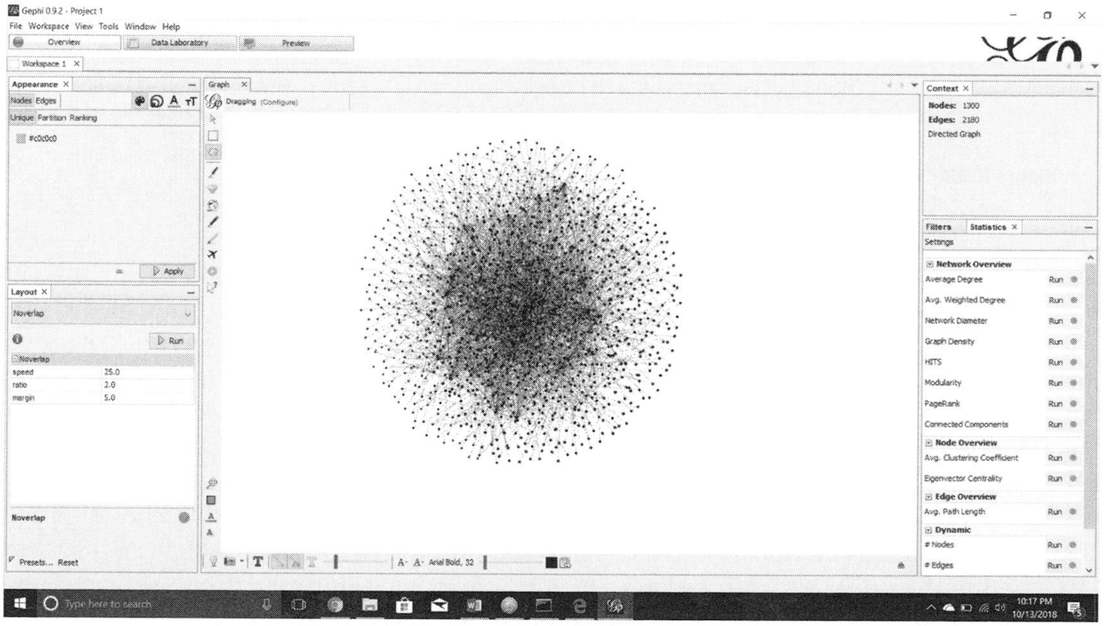
Gephi 0.9.2 - Project 1
File Workspace View Tools Window Help
Overview
Data Laboratory
Preview
Workspace 1
Appearance
Nodes Edges
Unique Partition Ranking
#c0c0c0
Apply
Layout
Noverlap
Run
speed 25.0
ratio 2.0
margin 5.0
Presets... Reset
Graph
Dragging (Configure)
Context
Nodes: 1300
Edges: 2180
Directed Graph
Filters
Statistics
Settings
Network Overview
Average Degree
Avg. Weighted Degree
Network Diameter
Graph Density
HITS
Modularity
PageRank
Connected Components
Node Overview
Avg. Clustering Coefficient
Eigenvector Centrality
Edge Overview
Avg. Path Length
Dynamic
Nodes
Edges
Run
Arial Bold, 32
Type here to search
10:17 PM
10/13/2018

Figure 2.12 Network of Wikipedia pages surrounding *parallel computing*

2.3.2 Returning to map

Before we wrap up the chapter, it's worth looking at how what we've done fits into the `map` diagrams we've been using. Coming back to the `map` data transformation diagrams is useful because it allows us to contextualize a complex task—web scraping and creating an entity network—in a simple way.

First, let's start with a diagram of the entire process (figure 2.13). On the left, we start with our seed document. We apply our `get_wiki_links` function to this document to get all the pages in our network: the inbound and outbound linking pages. From there, and secondly, we map the `get_wiki_links` function across all of these pages. This returns the extended network, that is, the pages that link to and are linked from the pages that link to and are linked from our seed page. Third, we convert all of these links into edges. This transforms the data from a more implicit data structure to a more explicit definition of a graph. And finally, we use each of these edges to construct the graph.

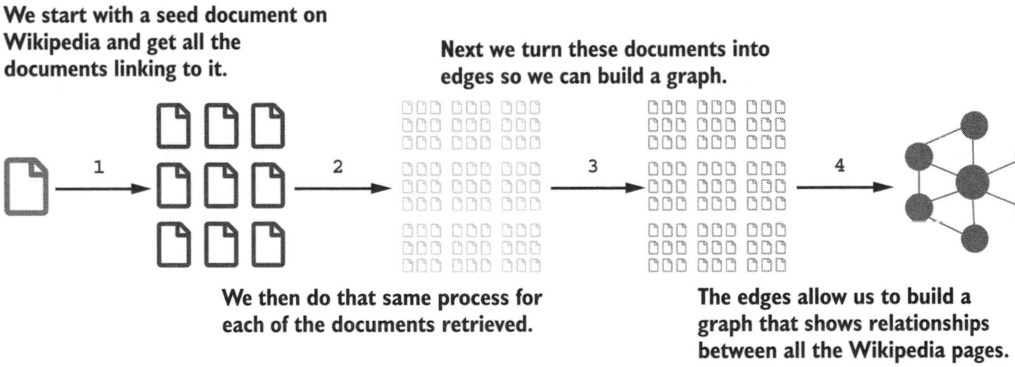
We start with a seed document on Wikipedia and get all the documents linking to it.
Next we turn these documents into edges so we can build a graph.
1
2
3
4
We then do that same process for each of the documents retrieved.
The edges allow us to build a graph that shows relationships between all the Wikipedia pages.

Figure 2.13 We'll turn a single seed page into a network of pages in four steps.

In this process, we used two map statements: one to turn our initial network into an extended network, and one to turn our extended network into edges. In the first instance, shown in figure 2.13, we take all of the links that we retrieved from our seed scrape, we scrape these, and we return the network of each link. The result is that where before we had a list of pages (or, if you remember what the data looked like, a `dict` with the page title, the inbound links, and the outbound links), we now have a list of lists of pages (or again: a list of these "page" `dict`s). Though there is a lot happening in between—we ping the Wikipedia API, the Wikipedia API fetches the page and returns the result, we parse that result into JSON, we sort through the JSON to find the values we want, we store them in a `dict` and return the `dict`—we can represent all of this as a data transformation from one object to the next.

Next, we complete the third step of taking the networks retrieved in our second step and turning them into a list of edges that we can use to define a directed graph. We wrote a `path_to_edges` function to use for this purpose. What we're doing is not that complicated: we're taking two lists of strings and turning them into a single list of `tuples`; however, abstracting that away with the `path_to_edges` function allows us to visualize the entire transformation at a higher level. This higher-level understanding corresponds directly with our overall process and highlights what's going on: our link networks are being transformed into edges.

Looking back at the Wikipedia scraping, network creation program we just wrote, we can see that using `map` is quite natural for a lot of tasks. Indeed, anytime we're converting a sequence of some type into a sequence of another type, what we're doing can be expressed as a map. I like to refer to these situations as N-to-N transformations because we're converting some number of data elements, N, into that same number of data elements but in a different format.

In just this last example, we encountered two of these N-to-N situations. We first turned N links into N networks of links. Then we turned N networks of links into N edges. In each of these situations, we used a map, as we just diagrammed.

We also used parallel programming in each of these situations to complete the task more quickly. They were excellent candidates for parallel programming because we had time-consuming, repetitive tasks that we could express neatly in self-contained instructions. We used a parallel `map` to accomplish this. The parallel `map` allows us to express our desire for parallelization and use syntax similar to what we'd use if we were doing a nonparallel `map`. All in all, the amount of effort it takes to make this problem parallel only adds up to four lines of code: one import; wrangling our processors with `Pool()`; and modifying our `map` statements to use `Pool`'s `.map` method.

2.4 Exercises

2.4.1 Problems of parallelization

Parallelization is an effective way to speed up our programs but may come with a few problems. Earlier in this chapter, I named three. How many can you remember, and what are they?

2.4.2 Map function

The `map` function is a key piece of how we'll approach large datasets in this book. Which sentence best describes the map function?

- `map` transforms a sequence of data into a different, same-sized sequence.
- `map` allows us to process data conditionally, replacing `if-else` statements.
- `map` replaces conditional `while` loops with optimized bytecode.

2.4.3 Parallelization and speed

Parallelization is useful because it allows us to process large datasets more quickly. Which of the following explains how parallelization works?

- Parallelization optimizes our code during compilation.
- Parallelization computes similar tasks on several compute resources.
- Parallelization removes duplication from our code and reduces the number of expensive operations.

2.4.4 Pickling storage

Which of the following is *not* a good use for pickling?

- Short-term, single-machine storage
- Sharing data between compute tasks on a cluster
- Long-term storage where data integrity is key

2.4.5 Web scraping data

In web scraping, one of the most common things we'll have to do is transform `dicts` into something else. Use `map` to transform a list of `dicts` into only the page text, with this as your input data:

```
[{"headers":(01/19/2018,Mozilla,300),
  "response":{"text":"Hello world!","encoding"0:"utf-8"}},
     {"headers":(01/19/2018,Chrome,404),
  "response":{"text":"No page found","encoding":"ascii"}},
     {"headers":(01/20/2018,Mozilla,300),
  "response":{"text":"Yet another web page.","encoding":"utf-8"}}]
```

Your resulting list should be `["Hello world!","No page found","Yet another web page."]`.

2.4.6 Heterogenous map transformations

So far, we've only looked at using `map` to transform homogenous lists, which contain data of all the same type. There's no reason, though, why we couldn't use `map` to transform a list of heterogenous data. Write a function that turns `[1, "A", False]` into `[2,"B",True]`.

Summary

- `map` statements are an excellent way to transform a sequence of data (such as data in a list or a tuple) into a sequence of data of some other type.
- Whenever we encounter a `for` loop, we should look for the opportunity to replace that loop with a `map`.

- Because `map` defines rules for transformations, instead of performing the actual transformations, it is readily paired with parallel techniques that can allow us to speed up our code.
- We can use `map` to scrape data from Wikipedia, or anywhere on the web, if we know a sequence of URLs that we want to scrape or APIs we want to call.
- Because `map` creates instructions and doesn't immediately evaluate them, it doesn't always play nicely with stateful objects, especially when applied in parallel.

Function pipelines for mapping complex transformations

This chapter covers

- Using `map` to do complex data transformations
- Chaining together small functions into pipelines
- Applying these pipelines in parallel on large datasets

In the last chapter, we saw how you can use `map` to replace `for` loops and how using `map` makes parallel computing straightforward: a small modification to `map`, and Python will take care of the rest. But so far with `map`, we've been working with simple functions. Even in the Wikipedia scraping example from chapter 2, our hardest working function only pulled text off the internet. If we want to make parallel programming *really* useful, we'll want to use `map` in more complex ways. This chapter introduces how to do complex things with `map`. Specifically, we're going to introduce two new concepts:

1. Helper functions
2. Function chains (also known as pipelines)

We'll tackle those topics by looking at two very different examples. In the first, we'll decode the secret messages of a malicious group of hackers. In the second, we'll help our company do demographic profiling on its social media followers. Ultimately, though, we'll solve both of these problems the same way: by creating function chains out of small helper functions.

3.1 Helper functions and function chains

Helper functions are small, simple functions that we rely on to do complex things. If you've heard the (rather gross) saying, "The best way to eat an elephant is one bite at a time," then you're already familiar with the idea of helper functions. With helper functions, we can break down large problems into small pieces that we can code quickly. In fact, let's put forth this as a possible adage for programmers:

> *The best way to solve a complex problem is one helper function at a time.*
>
> —J.T. Wolohan

Function chains or *pipelines* are the way we put helper functions to work. (The two terms mean the same thing, and different people favor one or the other; I'll use both terms interchangeably to keep from overusing either one.) For example, if we were baking a cake (a complex task for the baking challenged among us), we'd want to break that process up into lots of small steps:

1. Add flour.
2. Add sugar.
3. Add shortening.
4. Mix the ingredients.
5. Put the cake in the oven.
6. Take the cake from the oven.
7. Let the cake set.
8. Frost the cake.

Each of these steps is small and easily understood. These would be our helper functions. None of these helper functions by themselves can take us from having raw ingredients to having a cake. We need to chain these actions (functions) together to bake the cake. Another way of saying that would be that we need to pass the ingredients through our cake making pipeline, along which they will be transformed into a cake. To put this another way, let's take a look at our simple `map` statement again, this time in figure 3.1.

As we've seen several times, we have our input values on the top, a function that we're passing these values through in the middle, and on the bottom, we have our output values. In this case, `n+7` is our helper function. The `n+7` function does the work in this situation, not `map`. `map` applies the helper function to all of our input values and provides us with output values, but on its own, it doesn't do us too much good. We need a specific output, and for that we need `n+7`.

It's also worth taking a look at function chains, sequences of (relatively) small functions that we apply one after another. They also have their basis in math. We get them from a rule that mathematicians call *function composition.*

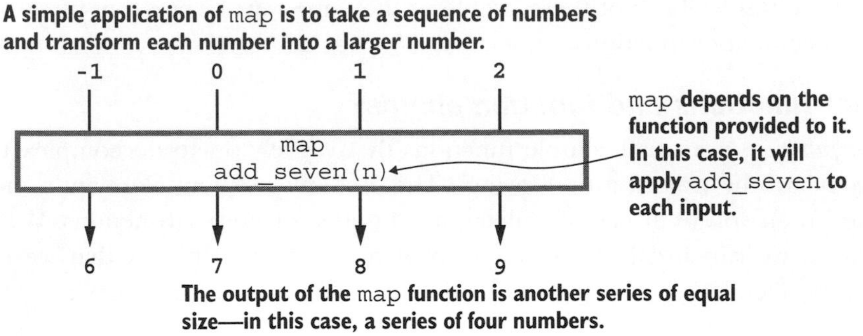
A simple application of map is to take a sequence of numbers and transform each number into a larger number.
-1
0
1
2
map
add_seven(n)
map depends on the function provided to it. In this case, it will apply add_seven to each input.
6
7
8
9
The output of the map function is another series of equal size—in this case, a series of four numbers.

Figure 3.1 The standard map statement shows how we can apply a single function to several values to return a sequence of values transformed by the function.

Function composition says that a complex function like j(x) = $((x+7)^2-2)*5$ is the same as smaller functions chained together that each do one piece of the complex function. For example, we might have these four functions:

1. $f(x) = x+7$
2. $g(x) = x^2$
3. $h(x) = x - 2$
4. $i(x) = x * 5$

We could chain them together as `i(h(g(f(x))))` and have that equal `j(x)`. We can see that play out in figure 3.2.

As we move through the pipeline in figure 3.2, we can see our four helper functions: f, g, h, and i. We can see what happens as we input 3 for x into this chain of

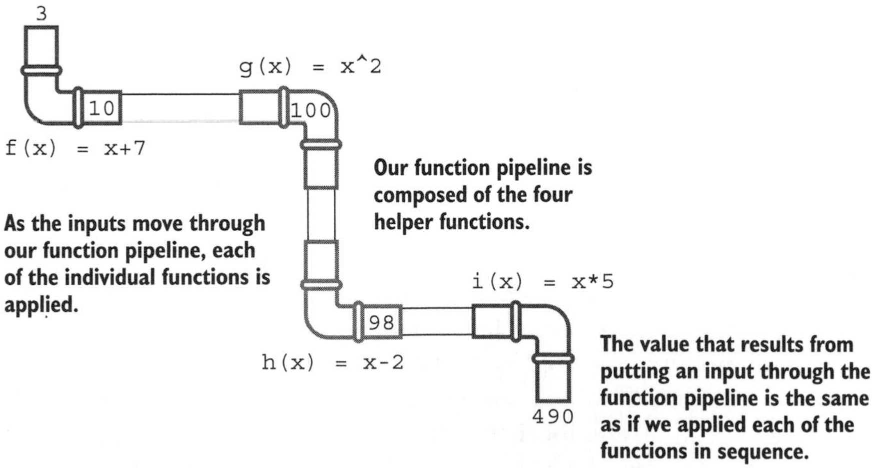
3
g(x) = x^2
10
100
f(x) = x+7
Our function pipeline is composed of the four helper functions.
As the inputs move through our function pipeline, each of the individual functions is applied.
i(x) = x*5
98
h(x) = x-2
490
The value that results from putting an input through the function pipeline is the same as if we applied each of the functions in sequence.

Figure 3.2 Function composition says that if we apply a series of functions in sequence, then it's the same as if we applied them all together as a single function.

functions. First, we apply f to x and get 10 (3+7). Then we apply g to 10 and get 100 (10^2). Then we apply h to 100 and get 98 (100–2). Then, lastly, we apply i to 98 and get 490 (98*5). The resulting value is the same as if we had input 3 into our original function j.

With these two simple ideas—helper functions and pipelines—we can achieve complex results. In this chapter, you'll learn how to implement these two ideas in Python. As I mentioned in the chapter introduction, we'll explore the power of these ideas in two scenarios:

1. Cracking a secret code
2. Predicting the demographics of social media followers

3.2 Unmasking hacker communications

Now that we're familiar with the concept of function pipelines, let's explore their power with a scenario. Here, we'll conquer a complex task by breaking it up into many smaller tasks.

> **SCENARIO** A malicious group of hackers has started using numbers in place of common characters and Chinese characters to separate words to foil automated attempts to spy on them. To read their communications—and find out what they're saying—we need to write some code that will undo their trickery. Let's write a script that turns their hacker speak into a list of English words.

We'll solve this problem like we've solved the previous problems in the book: by starting with `map`. Specifically, we'll use the idea of `map` to set up the big picture data transformation that we're doing. For that, we'll visualize the problem in figure 3.3.

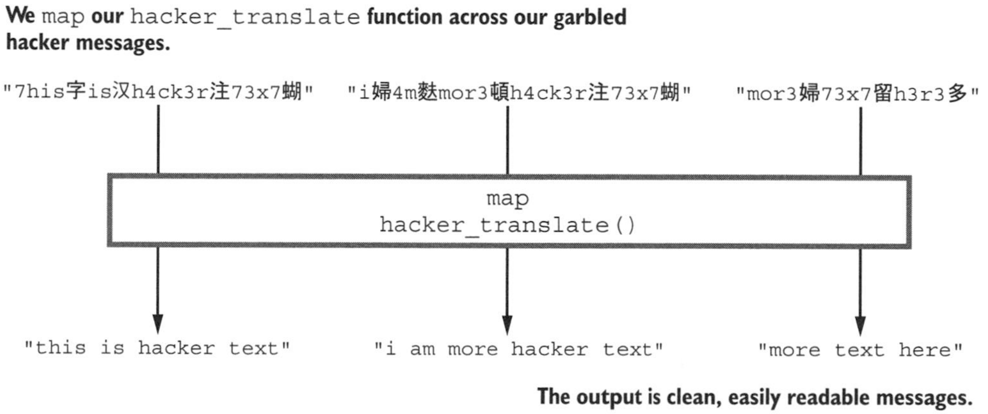
We map our hacker_translate function across our garbled hacker messages.
"7his字is汉h4ck3r注73x7蝴"
"i婦4m麩mor3頓h4ck3r注73x7蝴"
"mor3婦73x7留h3r3多"
map
hacker_translate()
"this is hacker text"
"i am more hacker text"
"more text here"
The output is clean, easily readable messages.

Figure 3.3 We can express our hacker problem as a `map` transformation in which we start with hard-to-read hacker messages as input. Then, after we clean them with our `hacker_translate` function, they become plain English text.

On the top, we have our input values. We can see that they're some pretty hard-to-read hacker communications, and at first glance they don't make a lot of sense. In the middle, we have our `map` statement and our `hacker_translate` function. This will be our heavy lifter function. It will do the work of cleaning the texts. And finally, on the bottom, we have our outputs: plain English.

Now this problem is not a simple problem; it's more like baking a cake. To accomplish it, let's split it up into several smaller problems that we can solve easily. For example, for any given hacker string, we'll want to do the following:

- Replace all the 7s with t's.
- Replace all the 3s with e's.
- Replace all the 4s with a's.
- Replace all the 6s with g's.
- Replace all the Chinese characters with spaces.

If we can do these five things for each string of hacker text, we'll have our desired result of plain English text. Before we write any code, let's take a look at how these functions will transform our text. First, we'll start with replacing the 7s with t's in figure 3.4.

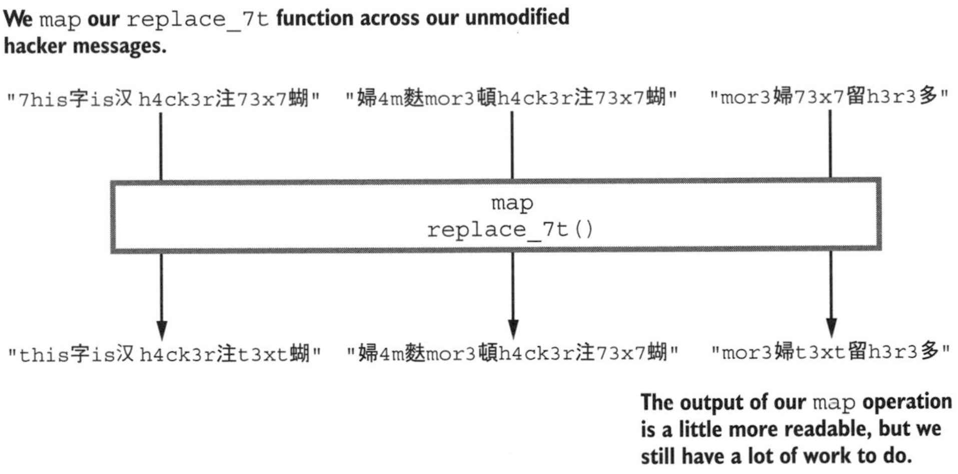
We map our replace_7t function across our unmodified hacker messages.
"7his字is汉 h4ck3r注73x7蝴"
"婦4m麩mor3頓h4ck3r注73x7蝴"
"mor3婦73x7留h3r3多"
map
replace_7t()
"this字is汉 h4ck3r注t3xt蝴"
"婦4m麩mor3頓h4ck3r注73x7蝴"
"mor3婦t3xt留h3r3多"
The output of our map operation is a little more readable, but we still have a lot of work to do.

Figure 3.4 Part of our hacker translate pipeline will involve replacing 7s with t's. We'll accomplish that by mapping a function that performs that replacement on all of our inputs.

At the top of figure 3.4, we see our unchanged input texts: garbled unreadable hacker communications. In the middle, we have our function `replace_7t`, which will replace all the 7s with t's. And on the bottom, we have no 7s in our text anywhere. This makes our texts a little more readable.

Moving on, we'll replace all the 3s in all the hacker communications with e's. We can see that happening in figure 3.5.

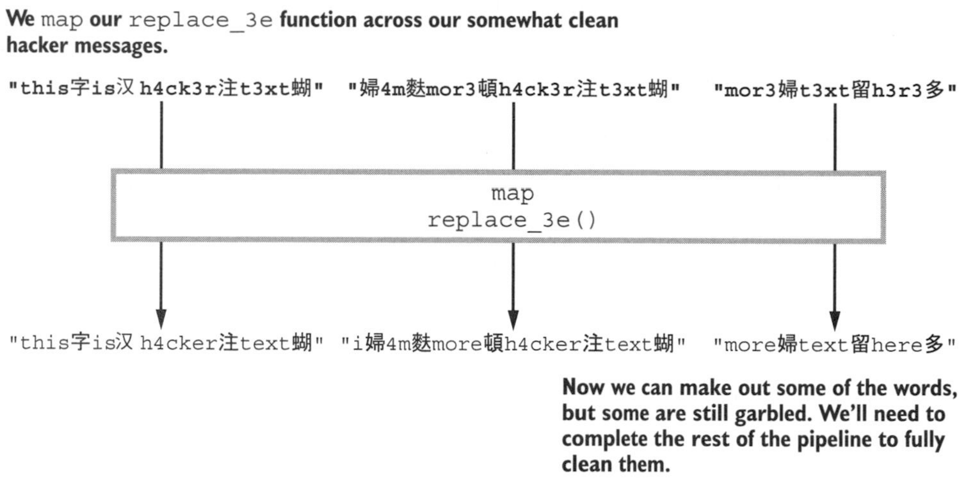
We map our replace_3e function across our somewhat clean hacker messages.
"this字is汉 h4ck3r注t3xt蝴"
"婦4m麩mor3頓h4ck3r注t3xt蝴"
"mor3婦t3xt留h3r3多"
map
replace_3e()
"this字is汉 h4cker注text蝴"
"i婦4m麩more頓h4cker注text蝴"
"more婦text留here多"
Now we can make out some of the words, but some are still garbled. We'll need to complete the rest of the pipeline to fully clean them.

Figure 3.5 The second step in our hacker translate pipeline will involve replacing 3s with e's. We'll accomplish that by mapping a function that performs that replacement on all of our inputs.

At the top of figure 3.5, we see our slightly cleaned hacker texts; we've already replaced the 7s with t's. In the middle, we have our `replace_3e` function, which works to replace the 3s with e's. And on the bottom, we have our now more readable text. All the 3s are gone, and we have some e's in there.

Continuing on, we'll do the same thing with 4s and a's and 6s and g's, until we've removed all our numbers. We'll skip discussing those functions for the sake of avoiding repetition. Once we've completed those steps, we're ready to tackle those Chinese characters. We can see that in figure 3.6.

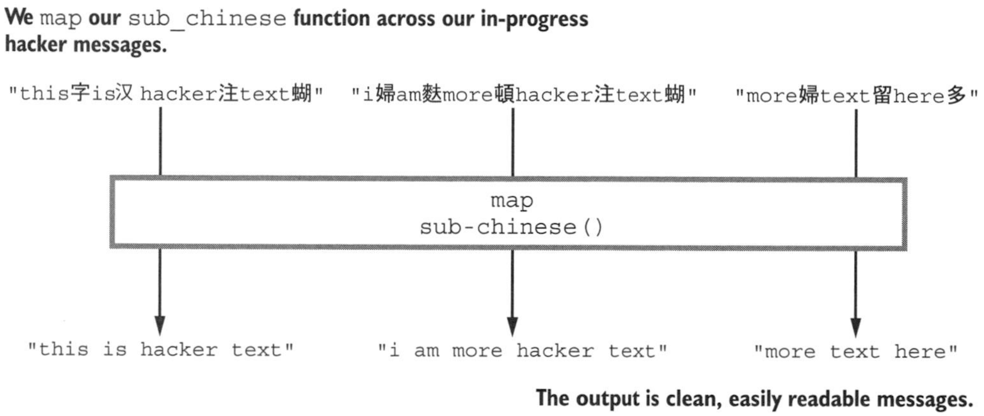
We map our sub_chinese function across our in-progress hacker messages.
"this字is汉 hacker注text蝴"
"i婦am麩more頓hacker注text蝴"
"more婦text留here多"
map
sub-chinese()
"this is hacker text"
"i am more hacker text"
"more text here"
The output is clean, easily readable messages.

Figure 3.6 Subbing on Chinese characters is going to be the last step in our `hacker_translate` function chain, and we can tackle it with a `map` statement.

In figure 3.6, we see at the top we have mostly English sentences with Chinese characters smooshing the words together. In the middle, we have our splitting function: `sub_chinese`. And on the bottom, finally, we have our fully cleaned sentences.

3.2.1 Creating helper functions

Now that we've got our solution sketched out, let's start writing some code. First, we'll write all our replacement helper functions.

We'll write all of these functions at once because they all follow a similar pattern: we take a string, find all of some character (a number) and replace it with some other character (a letter). For example, in `replace_7t`, we find all of the 7s and replace them with t's. We do this with the built-in Python string method `.replace`. The `.replace` method allows us to specify as parameters which characters we want to remove and the characters with which we want to replace them, as shown in the following listing.

Listing 3.1 Replacement helper functions

```
def replace_7t(s):                    <-- Replaces all the 7s with t's
    return s.replace('7','t')
def replace_3e(s):                    <-- Replaces all the 3s with e's
    return s.replace('3','e')
def replace_6g(s):                    <-- Replaces all the 6s with g's
    return s.replace('6','g')
def replace_4a(s):                    <-- Replaces all the 4s with a's
    return s.replace('4'.,'a')
```

That takes care of the first handful of steps. Now we want to split where the Chinese text occurs. This task is a little more involved. Because the hackers are using different Chinese characters to represent spaces, not just the same one again and again, we can't use `replace` here. We have to use a regular expression. Because we're using a regular expression, we're going to want to create a small class that can compile it for us ahead of time. In this case, our `sub_chinese` function is actually going to be a class method. We'll see that play out in the following listing.

Listing 3.2 Split on Chinese characters function

```
import re

class chinese_matcher:      <-- We compile our regular expression
                                on initialization of the class.
    def __init__(self):
        self.r = re.compile(r'[\u4e00-\u9fff]+')   <-- In this case, we want to match one
                                                       or more Chinese characters. Those
                                                       characters can be found in the
                                                       Unicode range from 4e00 to 9fff.
    def sub_chinese(self,s):
        return self.r.sub(s, " ")   <-- Now we can use this compiled regular
                                        expression in a method that uses the
                                        expression pattern's split method.
```

The first thing we do here is create a class called `chinese_matcher`. Upon initialization, that class is going to compile a regular expression that matches all the Chinese characters. That regular expression is going to be a range regular expression that looks up the Unicode characters between `\u4e00` (the first Chinese character in the Unicode standard) and `\u9fff` (the last Chinese character in the Unicode standard). If you've used regular expressions before, you should already be familiar with this concept for matching capital letters with regular expressions like `[A-Z]+`, which matches one or more uppercase English characters. We're using the same concept here, except instead of matching uppercase characters, we're matching Chinese characters. And instead of typing in the characters directly, we're typing in their Unicode numbers.

Having set up that regular expression, we can use it in a method. In this case, we'll use it in a method called `.sub_chinese`. This method will apply the regular expression method `.split` to an arbitrary string and return the results. Because we know our regular expression matches one or more Chinese characters, the result will be that every time a Chinese character appears in the string, we'll change that character to a space.

3.2.2 Creating a pipeline

Now we have all of our helper functions ready and we're ready to bake our hacker-foiling cake. The next thing to do is to chain these helper functions together. Let's take a look at three ways to do this:

1. Using a sequence of maps
2. Chaining functions together with `compose`
3. Creating a function pipeline with `pipe`

A SEQUENCE OF MAPS

For this method, we take all of our functions and map them across the results of one another.

- We map `replace_7t` across our sample messages.
- Then we map `replace_3e` across the results of that.
- Then we map `replace_6g` across the results of that.
- Then we map `replace_4a` across the results of that.
- Finally, we map `C.sub_chinese`.

The solution shown in listing 3.3 isn't pretty, but it works. If you print the results, you'll see all of our garbled sample sentences translated into easily readable English, with the words split apart from one another—exactly what we wanted. Remember, you need to evaluate `map` before you can print it!

Listing 3.3 Chaining functions by sequencing `maps`

```
C = chinese_matcher()

map(C.sub_chinese,
        map(replace_4a,
```

```
        map(replace_6g,
            map(replace_3e,
                map(replace_7t, sample_messages)))))
```

CONSTRUCTING A PIPELINE WITH COMPOSE

Although we certainly can chain our functions together this way, there are better ways. We'll take a look at two functions that can help us do this:

1. `compose`
2. `pipe`

Each of these functions is in the toolz package, which you can install with `pip` like you would most python packages: `pip install toolz`.

First, let's look at `compose`. The `compose` function takes our helper functions in the reverse order that we would like them applied and returns a function that applies them in the desired order. For example, `compose(foo, bar, bizz)` would apply `bizz`, then `bar`, then `foo`. In the specific context of our problem, that would look like listing 3.4.

In listing 3.4, you can see that we call the `compose` function and pass it all the functions we want to include in our pipeline. We pass them in reverse order because `compose` is going to apply them backwards. We store the output of our `compose` function, which is itself a function, to a variable. And then we can call that variable or pass it along to `map`, which applies it to all the sample messages.

Listing 3.4 Using `compose` to create a function pipeline

```
from toolz.functoolz import compose

hacker_translate = compose(C.sub_chinese, replace_4a, replace_6g,
                           replace_3e, replace_7t)

map(hacker_translate, sample_messages)
```

If you print this, you'll notice that the results are the same as when we chained our functions together with a sequence of `map` statements. The major difference is that we've cleaned up our code quite a bit, and here we only have one `map` statement.

PIPELINES WITH PIPE

Next, let's look at `pipe`. The `pipe` function will pass a value through a pipeline. It expects the value to pass and the functions to apply to it. Unlike `compose`, `pipe` expects the functions to be in the order we want to apply them. So `pipe(x, foo, bar, bizz)` applies `foo` to x, then `bar` to that value, and finally `bizz` to that value. Another important difference between `compose` and `pipe` is that `pipe` evaluates each of the functions and returns a result, so if we want to pass it to `map`, we actually have to wrap it in a function definition. Again, turning to our specific example, that will look something like the following listing.

Listing 3.5 Using `pipe` to create a function pipeline

```
from toolz.functoolz import pipe

def hacker_translate(s):
        return pipe(s, replace_7t, replace_3e, replace_6g,
                       replace_4a, C.sub_chinese)

    map(hacker_translate,sample_messages)
```

Here, we create a function that takes our input and returns that value after it has been piped through a sequence of functions that we pass to `pipe` as parameters. In this case, we're starting with `replace_7t`, then applying `replace_3e`, `replace_6g`, `replace_4a`, and lastly `C.sub_chinese`, in that order. The result, as with `compose`, is the same as when we chained the functions together using a sequence of `map`s—you're free to print out the results and prove this to yourself—but the way we get there is a lot cleaner.

Creating pipelines of helper functions provides two major advantages. The code becomes

- Very readable and clear
- Modular and easy to edit

The former advantage, increasing readability, is especially true when we have to do complex data transformations or when we want to perform a sequence of possibly related, or possibly unrelated, actions. For example, having just been introduced to the notion of `compose`, I'm pretty confident you could make a guess at what this pipeline does:

```
my_pipeline = compose(reverse, remove_vowels, make_uppercase)
```

The latter advantage, making code modular and easy to edit, is a major perk when we're dealing with dynamic situations. For example, let's say our hacker adversaries change their ruse so they're now replacing even more letters! We could simply add new functions into our pipeline to adjust. If we find that the hackers stop replacing a letter, we can remove that function from the pipeline.

A HACKER TRANSLATE PIPELINE

Lastly, let's return to our `map` example of this problem. At the beginning, we'd hoped to have one function, `hacker_translate`, that took us from garbled hacker secrets to plain English. We can see what we really did in figure 3.7.

Figure 3.7 shows our input values up top and our output values on the bottom, and through the middle we see how our five helper functions change our inputs. Breaking our complicated problem up into several small problems made coding the solution to this problem rather straightforward, and with `map`, we can easily apply the pipeline to any number of inputs that we need.

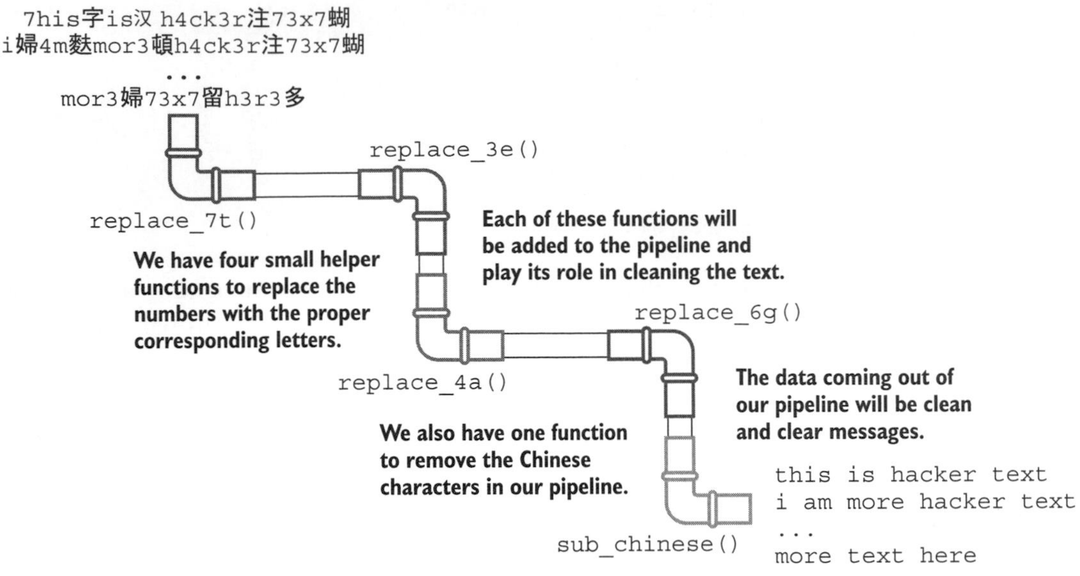
7his字is汉 h4ck3r注73x7蝴
i婦4m麩mor3頓h4ck3r注73x7蝴
...
mor3婦73x7留h3r3多
replace_3e()
replace_7t()
Each of these functions will be added to the pipeline and play its role in cleaning the text.
We have four small helper functions to replace the numbers with the proper corresponding letters.
replace_6g()
replace_4a()
The data coming out of our pipeline will be clean and clear messages.
We also have one function to remove the Chinese characters in our pipeline.
this is hacker text
i am more hacker text
...
more text here
sub_chinese()

Figure 3.7 We can solve the hacker translation problem by constructing a chain of functions that each solve one part of the problem.

3.3 Twitter demographic projections

In the previous section, we looked at how to foil a group of hackers by chaining small functions together and applying them across all the hackers' messages. In this section, we'll dive even deeper into what we can do using small, simple helper functions chained together.

> **SCENARIO** The head of marketing has a theory that male customers are more likely to engage with our product on social media than female customers and has asked us to write an algorithm to predict the gender of Twitter users mentioning our product based on the text of their posts. The marketing head has provided us with lists of Tweet IDs for each customer. We have to write a script that turns these lists of IDs into both a score representing how strongly we believe them to be of a given gender and a prediction about their gender.

To tackle this problem, again, we're going to start with a big picture `map` diagram. We can see that in figure 3.8.

The `map` diagram in figure 3.8 allows us to see our input data on the top and our output data on the bottom, which will help us think about how to solve the problem. On the top, we can see that we have a sequence of lists of numbers, each representing a Tweet ID. That will be our input format. And on the bottom, we see that we have a sequence of `dicts`, each with a key for `"score"` and `"gender"`. This gives us a sense of what we'll have to do with our function `gender_prediction_pipeline`.

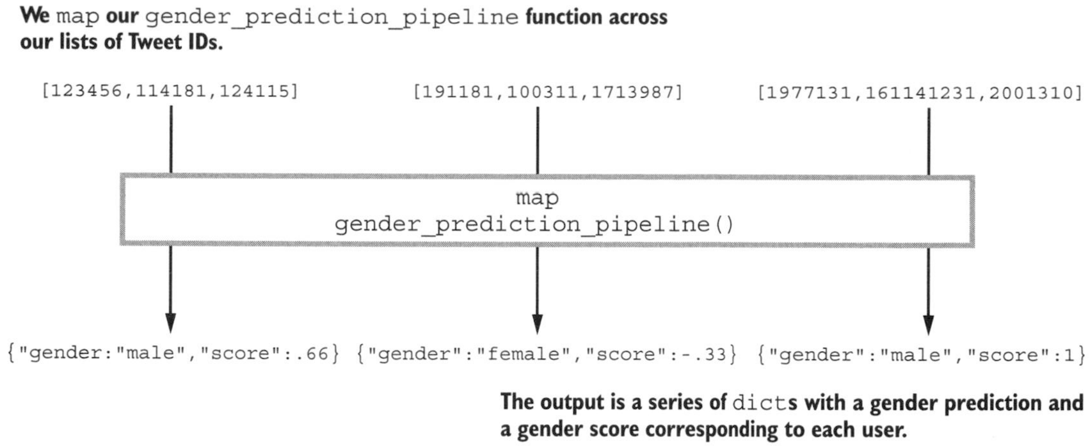
We map our gender_prediction_pipeline function across our lists of Tweet IDs.
[123456,114181,124115]
[191181,100311,1713987]
[1977131,161141231,2001310]
map
gender_prediction_pipeline()
{"gender:"male","score":.66}
{"gender":"female","score":-.33}
{"gender":"male","score":1}
The output is a series of dicts with a gender prediction and a gender score corresponding to each user.

Figure 3.8 The map diagram for our `gender_prediction_pipeline` demonstrates the beginning and end of the problem: we'll take a list of Tweet IDs and convert them into predictions about a user.

Now, predicting the gender of a Twitter user from several Tweet IDs is not one task; it's actually several tasks. To accomplish this, we're going to have to do the following:

- Retrieve the tweets represented by those IDs
- Extract the tweet text from those tweets
- Tokenize the extracted text
- Score the tokens
- Score users based on their tweet scores
- Categorize the users based on their score

Looking at the list of tasks, we can actually break down our process into two transformations: those that are happening at the user level and those that are happening at the tweet level. The user-level transformations include things like scoring the user and categorizing the user. The tweet-level transformations include things like retrieving the tweet, extracting the text, tokenizing the text, and scoring the text. If we were still working with `for` loops, this type of situation would mean that we would need a nested `for` loop. Since we're working with `map`, we'll have to have a `map` inside our `map`.

3.3.1 Tweet-level pipeline

Let's look at our tweet-level transformation first. At the tweet level, we'll convert a Tweet ID into a single score for that tweet, representing the gender score of that tweet. We'll score the tweets by giving them points based on the words they use. Some words will make the tweet more of a "man's tweet," and some will make the tweet more of a "woman's tweet." We can see this process playing out in figure 3.9.

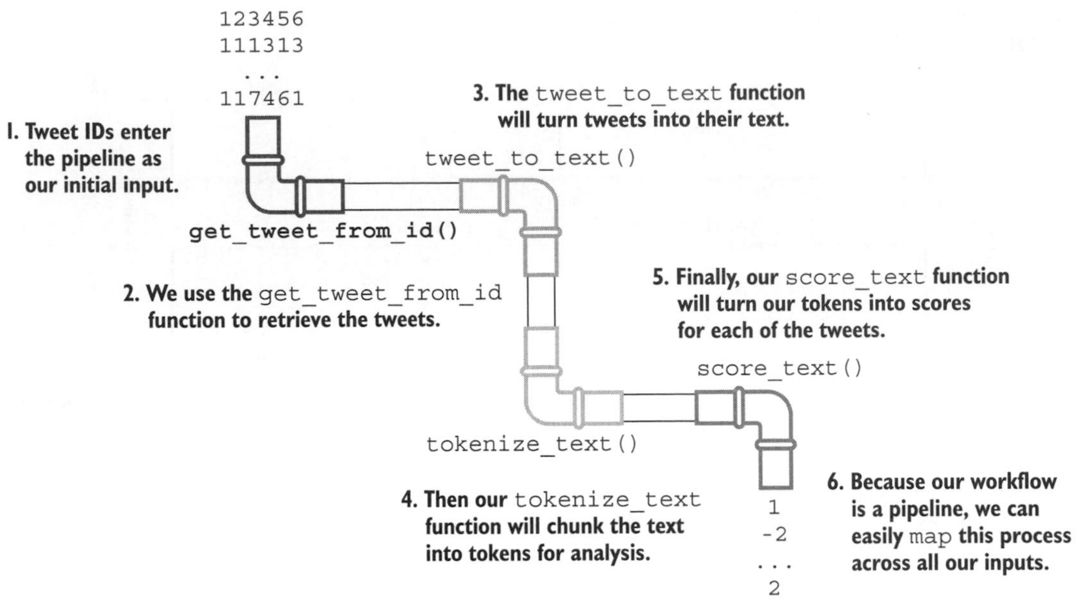
123456
111313
...
117461
1. Tweet IDs enter the pipeline as our initial input.
get_tweet_from_id()
2. We use the get_tweet_from_id function to retrieve the tweets.
3. The tweet_to_text function will turn tweets into their text.
tweet_to_text()
tokenize_text()
4. Then our tokenize_text function will chunk the text into tokens for analysis.
5. Finally, our score_text function will turn our tokens into scores for each of the tweets.
score_text()
1
-2
...
2
6. Because our workflow is a pipeline, we can easily map this process across all our inputs.

Figure 3.9 We can chain four functions together into a pipeline that will accomplish each of the subparts of our problem.

> **Text classification**
>
> Classifying a tweet by assigning scores to words it uses may seem simplistic, but it's actually not too far from how both academia and industry approach the situation. Lexicon-based methods of classification, which assign words points and then roll those points up into an overall score, achieve remarkable performance given their simplicity. And because they are transparent, they offer the benefit of interpretability to practitioners.
>
> In this chapter, we only approximate the real thing, but you can find a state-of-the art classifier on my GitHub page: https://github.com/jtwool/TwitterGenderPredictor.

Figure 3.9 shows the several transformations that our tweets will undertake as we transform them from ID to score. Starting at the top left, we see that we start with Tweet IDs as an input, then we pass them through a `get_tweet_from_id` function and get tweet objects back. Next, we pass those tweet objects through a `tweet_to_text` function, which turns the tweet objects into the text of those tweets. Then, we tokenize the tweets by applying our `tokenize_text` function. After that, we score the tweets with our `score_text` function.

Turning our attention to user-level transformations, the process here is a little simpler:

1. We apply the tweet-level process to each of the user's tweets.
2. We take the average of the resulting tweet scores to get our user-level score.
3. We categorize the user as either `"male"` or `"female"`.

Figure 3.10 shows the user-level process playing out.

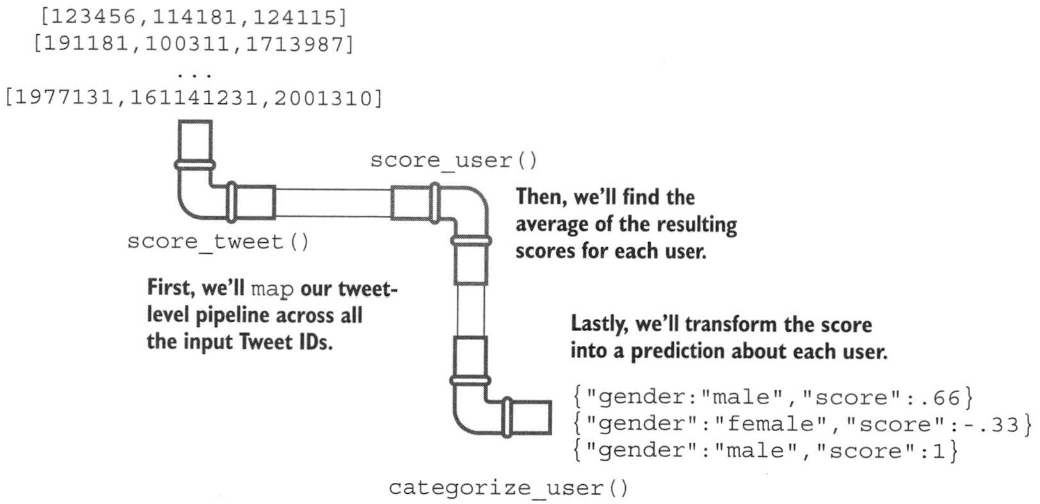
[123456,114181,124115]
[191181,100311,1713987]
...
[1977131,161141231,2001310]
score_user()
Then, we'll find the average of the resulting scores for each user.
score_tweet()
First, we'll map our tweet-level pipeline across all the input Tweet IDs.
Lastly, we'll transform the score into a prediction about each user.
{"gender:"male","score":.66}
{"gender":"female","score":-.33}
{"gender":"male","score":1}
categorize_user()

Figure 3.10 We can chain small functions together to turn lists of users' Tweet IDs into scores, then into averages, and, finally, into predictions about their demographics.

We can see that each user starts as a list of Tweet IDs. Applying our `score_user` function, across all of these lists of Tweet IDs, we get back a single score for each user. Then, we can use our `categorize_user` function to turn this score into a `dict` that includes both the score and the predicted gender of the user, just like we wanted at the outset.

These `map` diagrams give us a roadmap for writing our code. They help us see what data transformations need to take place and where we're able to construct pipelines. For example, we now know that we need two function chains: one for the tweets and one for the users. With that in mind, let's start tackling the tweet pipeline.

Our tweet pipeline will consist of four functions. Let's tackle them in this order:

1. `get_tweet_from_id`
2. `tweet_to_text`
3. `tokenize_text`
4. `score_text`

Our `get_tweet_from_id` function is responsible for taking a Tweet ID as input, looking up that Tweet ID on Twitter, and returning a tweet object that we can use. The easiest way to scrape Twitter data will be to use the `python-twitter` package. You can install `python-twitter` easily with `pip`:

```
pip install python-twitter
```

Once you have `python-twitter` set up, you'll need to set up a developer account with Twitter. (See the "Twitter developer accounts" sidebar.) You can do that at https://developer.twitter.com/. If you have a Twitter account already, there's no need to create another account; you can sign in with the account you already have. With your account set up, you're ready to apply for what Twitter calls an *app*. You'll need to fill out an application form, and if you tell Twitter that you're using this book to learn parallel programming, they'll be happy to give you an account. When you're prompted to describe your use case, I suggest entering the following:

> The core purpose of my app is to learn parallel programming techniques. I am following along with a scenario provided in chapter 3 of *Mastering Large Datasets with Python*, by JT Wolohan, published by Manning Publications.
>
> I intend to do a lexical analysis of fewer than 1,000 Tweets.
>
> I do not plan on using my app to Tweet, Retweet, or "like" content.
>
> I will not display any Tweets anywhere online.

Twitter developer accounts

Because this scenario involves Twitter scraping, the automated collection of Twitter data, I would like to offer you the opportunity to do real Twitter scraping. Doing so requires you to request a Twitter developer account. These developer accounts used to be much easier to get. Twitter is beginning to restrict who can develop on its platform because it wants to crack down on bots. If you don't want to sign up for Twitter, you don't want to sign up for a developer account, or you don't want to wait, you can proceed without signing up for a developer account.

In the repository for this book, I include text that can stand in for the tweets, and you can omit the first two functions (`get_tweet_from_id` and `tweet_to_text`) from your tweet-level pipeline.

Once you have your Twitter developer account set up and confirmed by Twitter (this may take an hour or two), you'll navigate to your app and find your consumer key, your consumer secret, your access token key, and your access token secret (figure 3.11). These are the credentials for your app. They tell Twitter to associate your requests with your app.

With your developer account set up and `python-twitter` installed, we're finally ready to start coding our tweet-level pipeline. The first thing we do is import the

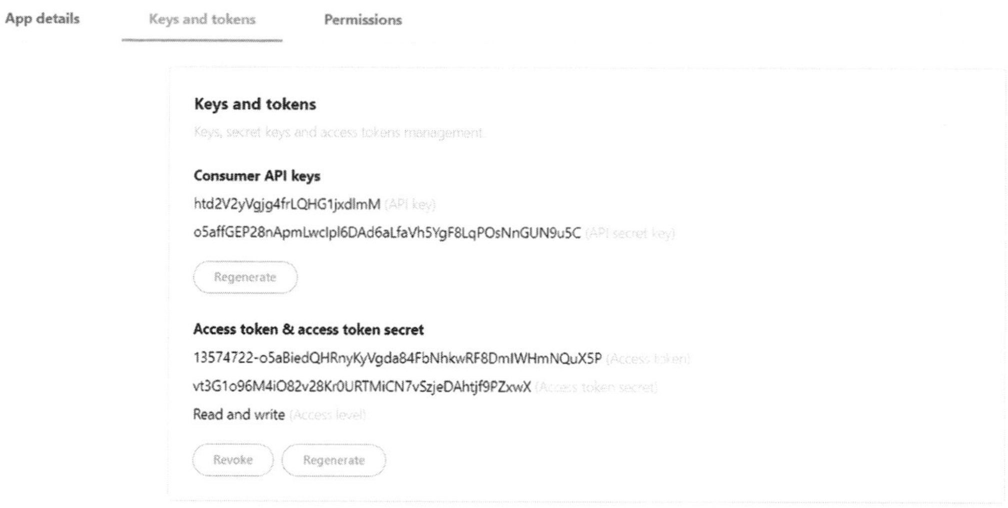
App details
Keys and tokens
Permissions
Keys and tokens
Keys, secret keys and access tokens management.
Consumer API keys
htd2V2yVgjg4frLQHG1jxdlmM (API key)
o5affGEP28nApmLwclpl6DAd6aLfaVh5YgF8LqPOsNnGUN9u5C (API secret key)
Regenerate
Access token & access token secret
13574722-o5aBiedQHRnyKyVgda84FbNhkwRF8DmIWHmNQuX5P (Access token)
vt3G1o96M4iO82v28Kr0URTMiCN7vSzjeDAhtjf9PZxwX (Access token secret)
Read and write (Access level)
Revoke
Regenerate

Figure 3.11 The "Keys and Tokens" tab in your Twitter developer account provides you with API keys, access tokens, and access secrets for your project.

python-twitter library. This is the library we just installed. It provides a whole host of convenient functions for working with the Twitter API. Before we can use any of those nice functions, however, we need to authenticate our app. We do so by initiating an `Api` class from the library. The class takes our application credentials, which we get from the Twitter developers website, and uses them when it makes calls to the Twitter API.

With this class ready to go, we can then create a function to return tweets from Twitter IDs. We'll need to pass our API object to this function so we can use it to make the requests to Twitter. Once we do that, we can use the API object's `.GetStatus` method to retrieve Tweets by their ID. Tweets retrieved in this way come back as Python objects, perfect for using in our script.

We'll use that fact in our next function, `tweet_to_text`, which takes the tweet object and returns its text. This function is very short. It calls the text property of our tweet object and returns that value. The text property of tweet objects that `python-twitter` returns contains, as we would expect, the text of the tweets.

With the tweet text ready, we can tokenize it. Tokenization is a process in which we break text up into smaller units that we can analyze. In some cases, this can be pretty complicated, but for our purpose, we'll split text wherever white space occurs to separate words from one another. For a sentence like `"This is a tweet"`, we would get a list containing each word: `["This", "is", "a", "tweet"]`. We'll use the built-in string `.split` method to do that.

Once we have our tokens, we need to score them. For that, we'll use our `score_text` function. This function will look up each token in a lexicon, retrieve its score, and then add all of those scores together to get an overall score for the tweet. To do that, we need a lexicon, a list of words and their associated scores. We'll use a `dict` to accomplish that here. To look up the scores for each word, we can map the `dict`'s `.get` method across the list of words.

The `dict .get` method allows us to look up a key and provide a default value in case we don't find it. This is useful in our case because we want words that we don't find in our lexicon to have a neutral value of zero.

To turn this method into a function, we use what's called a *lambda function*. The `lambda` keyword allows us to specify variables and how we want to transform them. For example, `lambda x: x+2` defines a function that adds two to whatever value is passed to it. The code `lambda x: lexicon.get(x, 0)` looks up whatever it is passed in our lexicon and returns either the value or 0 (if it doesn't find anything). We'll often use it for short functions.

Finally, with all of those helper functions written, we can construct our `score_tweet` pipeline. This pipeline will take a Tweet ID, pass it through all of these helper functions, and return the result. For this process, we'll use the `pipe` function from the toolz library. This pipeline represents the entirety of what we want to do at the tweet level. We can see all of the code needed in the following listing.

Listing 3.6 Tweet-level pipeline

```
from toolz import pipe                  # Imports the python-twitter library
import twitter

Twitter = twitter.Api(consumer_key="",          # Authenticates our app
                      consumer_secret="",
                      access_token_key="",
                      access_token_secret="")

# Uses our app to look up tweets by their ID
def get_tweet_from_id(tweet_id, api=Twitter):
    return api.GetStatus(tweet_id, trim_user=True)

def tweet_to_text(tweet):               # Gets the text from a tweet object
    return tweet.text

def tokenize_text(text):                # Splits text on white space so we can analyze words
    return text.split()

# Creates our score_text function
def score_text(tokens):
    lexicon = {"the":1, "to":1, "and":1,       # Creates a mini sample lexicon for scoring words
               "in":1, "have":1, "it":1,
               "be":-1, "of":-1, "a":-1,
               "that":-1, "i":-1, "for":-1}
    return sum(map(lambda x: lexicon.get(x, 0), tokens))   # Replaces each word with its point value

def score_tweet(tweet_id):              # Pipes a tweet through our pipeline
    return pipe(tweet_id, get_tweet_from_id, tweet_to_text,
                tokenize_text, score_text)
```

3.3.2 User-level pipeline

Having constructed our tweet-level pipeline, we're ready to construct our user-level pipeline. As we laid out previously, we'll need to do three things for our user-level pipeline:

1. Apply the tweet pipeline to all of the user's tweets
2. Take the average of the score of those tweets
3. Categorize the user based on that average

For conciseness, we'll collapse the first two actions into one function, and we'll let the third action be a function all its own. When all is said and done, our user-level helper functions will look like the following listing.

Listing 3.7 User-level helper functions

```
from toolz import compose

def score_user(tweets):
    N = len(tweets)
    total = sum(map(score_tweet, tweets))
    return total/N

def categorize_user(user_score):
    if user_score > 0:
        return {"score":user_score,
                "gender": "Male"}
    return {"score":user_score,
            "gender":"Female"}

pipeline = compose(categorize_user, score_user)
```

Averages the scores of all of a user's tweets

Finds the number of tweets

Finds the sum total of all of a user's individual tweet scores

Returns the sum total divided by the number of tweets

Takes the score and returns a predicted gender as well

If the user_score is greater than 0, we'll say that the user is male.

Otherwise, we'll say the user is female.

Composes these helper functions into a pipeline function

In our first user-level helper function, we need to accomplish two things: score all of the user's tweets, then find the average score. We already know how to score their tweets—we just built a pipeline for that exact purpose! To score the tweets, we'll map that pipeline across all the tweets. However, we don't need the scores themselves, we need the average score.

To find a simple average, we want to take the sum of the values and divide it by the number of values that we're summing. To find the sum, we can use Python's built-in `sum` function on the tweets. To find the number of tweets, we can find the length of the list with the `len` function. With those two values ready, we can calculate the average by dividing the sum by the length.

This will give us an average tweet score for each user. With that, we can categorize the user as being either `"Male"` or `"Female"`. To make that categorization, we'll create another small helper function: `categorize_user`. This function will check to see if the user's average score is greater than zero. If it is, it will return a `dict` with the score and a gender prediction of "Male". If their average score is zero or less, it will return a dict with the score and a gender prediction of "Female".

These two quick helper functions are all we'll need for our user-level pipeline. Now we can compose them, remembering to supply them in reverse order from how we want to apply them. That means we put our categorization function first, because we're using it last, and our scoring function last, because we're using it first. The result is a new function—gender_prediction_pipeline—that we can use to make gender predictions about a user.

3.3.3 *Applying the pipeline*

Now that we have both our user-level and tweet-level function chains ready, all that's left to do is apply the functions to our data. To do so, we can either use Tweet IDs with our full tweet-level function chain, or—if you decided not to sign up for a Twitter developer account—we can use just the text of the tweets. If you'll be using just the tweet text, make sure to create a tweet-level function chain (score_tweet) that omits the get_tweet_from_id and tweet_to_text functions.

APPLYING THE PIPELINE TO TWEET IDS

Applying our pipelines in the first instance might look something like listing 3.8. There, we start by initializing our data. The data we're starting with is four lists of five Tweet IDs. Each of the four lists represents a user. The Tweet IDs don't actually come from the same user; however, they are real tweets, randomly sampled from the internet.

Listing 3.8 Applying the gender prediction pipeline to Tweet IDs

```
users_tweets = [
[1056365937547534341, 1056310126255034368, 1055985345341251584,
 1056585873989394432, 1056585871623966720],
[1055986452612419584, 1056318330037002240, 1055957256162942977,
 1056585921154420736, 1056585896898805766],
[1056240773572771841, 1056184836900175874, 1056367465477951490,
 1056585972765224960, 1056585968155684864],
[1056452187897786368, 1056314736546115584, 1055172336062816258,
 1056585983175602176, 1056585980881207297]]

with Pool() as P:
    print(P.map(pipeline, users_tweets))
```

First, we need to initialize our data. Here, we're using four sets of Tweet IDs.

Then we can apply our pipeline to our data with map. Here, we're using a parallel map.

With our data initialized, we can now apply our gender_prediction_pipeline. We'll do that in a way we introduced last chapter: with a parallel map. We first call Pool to gather up some processors, then we use the .map method of that Pool to apply our prediction function in parallel.

If we were doing this in an industry setting, this would be an excellent opportunity to use a parallel map for two reasons:

1. We're doing what amounts to the same task for each user.
2. Both retrieving the data from the web and finding the scores of all those tweets are relatively time- and memory-consuming operations.

To the first point, whenever we find ourselves doing the same thing over and over again, we should think about using parallelization to speed up our work. This is especially true if we're working on a dedicated machine (like our personal laptop or a dedicated compute cluster) and don't need to concern ourselves with hoarding processing resources other people or applications may need.

To the second point, we're best off using parallel techniques in situations in which the calculations are at least somewhat difficult or time-consuming. If the work we're trying to do in parallel is too easy, we may spend more time dividing the work and reassembling the results than we would just doing it in a standard linear fashion.

APPLYING THE PIPELINE TO TWEET TEXT

Applying the pipeline to tweet text directly will look very similar to applying the pipeline to Tweet IDs, as shown in the following listing.

Listing 3.9 Applying the gender prediction pipeline to tweet text

First, we need to initialize our data. Here, we're using four sets of Tweet IDs.

```
user_tweets = [
    ["i think product x is so great", "i use product x for everything",
    "i couldn't be happier with product x"],
    ["i have to throw product x in the trash",
    "product x... the worst value for your money"],
    ["product x is mostly fine", "i have no opinion of product x"]]

with Pool() as P:
    print(P.map(gender_prediction_pipeline, users_tweets))
```

Then we can apply our pipeline to our data with map. Here, we're using a parallel map.

The only change in listing 3.9 versus listing 3.8 is our input data. Instead of having tweet IDs that we want to find on Twitter, retrieve, and score, we can score the tweet text directly. Because our `score_tweet` function chain removes the `get_tweet_from_id` and `tweet_to_text` helper functions, the `gender_prediction_pipeline` will work exactly as we want.

That it is so easy to modify our pipelines is one of the major reasons why we want to assemble them in the first place. When conditions change, as they often do, we can quickly and easily modify our code to respond to them. We could even create two function chains if we envisioned having to handle both situations. One function chain could be `score_tweet_from_text` and would work on tweets provided in text form. Another function chain could be `score_tweet_from_id` and would categorize tweets provided in Tweet ID form.

Looking back throughout this example, we created six helper functions and two pipelines. For those pipelines, we used both the `pipe` function and the `compose` function from the toolz package. We also used these functions with a parallel `map` to pull down tweets from the internet in parallel. Using helper functions and function chains makes our code easy to understand and modify and plays nicely with our parallel `map`, which wants to apply the same function over and over again.

3.4 Exercises

3.4.1 Helper functions and function pipelines

In this chapter, you've learned about the interrelated ideas of helper functions and function pipelines. In your own words, define both of those terms, then describe how they are related.

3.4.2 Math teacher trick

A classic math teacher trick has students perform a series of arithmetic operations on an "unknown" number, and at the end, the teacher guesses the number the students are thinking of. The trick is that the final number is always a constant the teacher knows in advance. One such example is doubling a number, adding 10, halving it, and subtracting the original number. Using a series of small helper functions chained together, map this process across all numbers between 1 and 100. How does the teacher always know what number you're thinking of?

EXAMPLE

```
map(teacher_trick, range(1,101))
>>> [?,?,?,?,...,?]
```

3.4.3 Caesar's cipher

Caesar's cipher is an old way of constructing secret codes in which one shifts the position of a letter by 13 places, so A becomes N, B becomes O, C becomes P, and so on. Chain three functions together to create this cypher: one to convert a letter to an integer, one to add 3 to a number, and one to convert a number to a letter. Apply this cypher to a word by mapping the chained functions of a string. Create one new function and a new pipeline to reverse your cypher.

EXAMPLE

```
map(caesars_cypher,["this","is","my",sentence"])
>>> ["wklv","lv","pb","vhqwhqfh"]
```

Summary

- Designing programs with small helper functions makes hard problems easy to solve by breaking them up into bite-sized pieces.
- When we pass a function through a function pipeline `pipe`, it expects the input data as its first argument and the functions in the order we want to apply them as the remaining arguments.
- When we create a function chain with `compose`, we pass the functions in our function chain as arguments in reverse order, and the resulting function applies that chain.

- Constructing function chains and pipelines is useful because they're modular, they play very nicely with `map`, and we can readily move them into parallel workflows, such as by using the `Pool()` technique we learned in chapter 2.
- We can simplify working with nested data structures by using nested function pipelines, which we can apply with `map`.

4 Processing large datasets with lazy workflows

> ***This chapter covers***
> - Writing lazy workflows for processing large datasets locally
> - Understanding the lazy behavior of `map`
> - Writing classes with generators for lazy simulations

In chapter 2 (section 2.1.2, to be exact), I introduced the idea that our beloved `map` function is *lazy* by default; that is, it only evaluates when the value is needed downstream. In this chapter, we'll look at a few of the benefits of laziness, including how we can use laziness to process big data on our laptop. We'll focus on the benefits of laziness in two contexts:

1. File processing
2. Simulations

With file processing, we'll see that laziness allows us to process much more data than could fit in memory without laziness. With simulations, we'll see how we can use laziness to run "infinite" simulations. Indeed, lazy functions allow us to work with an infinite amount of data just as easily as we could if we were working with a limited amount of data.

4.1 What is laziness?

Laziness, or *lazy evaluation*, is a strategy that programming languages use when deciding when to perform computations. Under lazy evaluation, the Python interpreter executes lazy Python code only when the program needs the results of that code.

For example, consider the `range` function in Python, which generates a sequence of numbers lazily. That is, we can call `range(10000)` and we won't get a list of 10,000 numbers back; we'll get an iterator that knows how to generate 10,000 numbers. This means we can make absurdly large `range` calls without being concerned that we'll use up all our memory storing integers. For example, `range(10000000000)` has the same size as `range(10)`. You can check this yourself with only two lines of code:

```
>>> from sys import getsizeof
>>> getsizeof(range(10000000000)) == getsizeof(range(10))
True
```

Lazy evaluation like this is the opposite of *eager* evaluation, where everything is evaluated when it's called. This is probably how you're used to thinking about programming. You write a piece of code, then when the computer gets to that point, it computes whatever it is you told it to compute. By contrast, with lazy evaluation, the computer takes in your instructions and files them away until it needs to use them. If you never ask the computer for a final result, it will never perform any of the intermediate steps.

In that way, lazy evaluation is a lot like a high school student with an assignment due far in the future. The teacher can tell the student how to write the assignment at the beginning of the year. They can even warn the student that the assignment will be coming due in a few weeks. But it's not until right before the deadline that the student actually begins to work on their assignment. The major difference: the computer will always complete the work.

Furthermore, just like the student is putting off doing their assignment so they can do other things—like work on other assignments due sooner or just hang out with their friends—our lazily evaluated program is doing other things too. Because our program lazily evaluates our instructions, it has more memory (time) to do the other things we ask of it (other assignments) or even run other processes altogether (hanging out with its friends maybe?).

4.2 Some lazy functions to know

We've already discussed how two functions you're familiar with—`map` and `range`—are lazy. In this section, we'll focus on three other lazy functions you should know about:

1. `filter`—A function for pruning sequences
2. `zip`—A function for merging sequences
3. `iglob`—A function for lazily reading from the filesystem

The `filter` function takes a sequence and restricts it to only the elements that meet a given condition. The `zip` function takes two sequences and returns a single sequence of tuples, each of which contains an element from each of the original sequences. And the iglob function is a lazy way of querying our filesystem.

4.2.1 Shrinking sequences with the filter function

The filter function does exactly what you expect it to: it acts as a filter. Specifically, it takes a conditional function and a sequence and returns a lazy iterable with all the elements of that sequence that satisfy that condition (figure 4.1). For example, in the following listing, we see how filter can take a function that checks if a number is even and return an iterable of only even numbers.

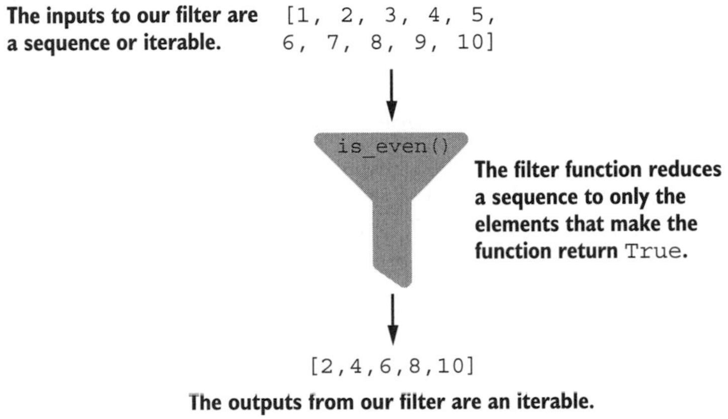
The inputs to our filter are a sequence or iterable.
[1, 2, 3, 4, 5, 6, 7, 8, 9, 10]
is_even()
The filter function reduces a sequence to only the elements that make the function return True.
[2,4,6,8,10]
The outputs from our filter are an iterable.

Figure 4.1 The filter function produces a new sequence that contains only elements that make the qualifier function return True.

Listing 4.1 Retrieving even numbers from a sequence

```
def is_even(x):
    if x%2 == 0: return True
    else: return False

print(list(filter(is_even, range(10))))
# [0,2,4,6,8]
```

In listing 4.1, we call list on our filter to get it to print nicely, just like we did with map. We have to call list in both cases because filter and map are both lazy and won't evaluate until we're interested in specific values. Because lists are not lazy, converting our lazy objects to a list lets us see the individual values.

The filter function is a valuable tool because we can use it to concisely define a common operation. Four related functions are also helpful to know about, all of which perform the same basic operation, with a twist:

1. filterfalse
2. keyfilter
3. valfilter
4. itemfilter

Just like filter, all of these functions just do what we expect them to do. We can use the `filterfalse` function when we want to get all the results that make a qualifier function return `False`. We can use the `keyfilter` function when we want to filter on the keys of a `dict`. We can use the `valfilter` function when we want to filter on the values of a `dict`. And we can use `itemfilter` when we want to filter on both the keys and the values of a `dict`. We can see examples of all of these in action in listing 4.2.

In listing 4.2, we use all four of these functions. The first, `filterfalse`, is from the `itertools` module that ships with Python. When we combine `iterfalse` with `is_even` from before, we get all the not-even (odd) numbers. For `keyfilter`, `valfilter`, and `itemfilter`, we need to input a `dict`. When we combine `keyfilter` with `is_even`, we get back all the items from the `dict` that have even keys. When we combine `valfilter` with `is_even`, we get back all the items from the `dict` that have even values. For `itemfilter`, we can evaluate both the keys and the values of the `dict`. In listing 4.2, we create a small function, `both_are_even`, that tests if both the key and the value of an item are even. As the listing shows, we do get back the items for which both the key and the value are even.

Listing 4.2 Testing variations of the `filter` function

```
from itertools import filterfalse
from toolz.dicttoolz import keyfilter, valfilter, itemfilter

def is_even(x):
    if x % 2 == 0: return True
    else: return False

def both_are_even(x):
    k,v = x
    if is_even(k) and is_even(v): return True
    else: return False

print(list(filterfalse(is_even, range(10))))
# [1, 3, 5, 7, 9]

print(list(keyfilter(is_even, {1:2, 2:3, 3:4, 4:5, 5:6})))
# [2, 4]

print(list(valfilter(is_even, {1:2, 2:3, 3:4, 4:5, 5:6})))
# [1, 3, 5]

print(list(itemfilter(both_are_even, {1:5, 2:4, 3:3, 4:2, 5:1})))
# [2, 4]
```

4.2.2 Combining sequences with zip

zip is another lazy function. We use zip when we have two iterables that we want to join together so that the items in the first position are together, the items in the second position are together, and so on. Naturally, it makes sense to think about the zip function like a zipper. When the zipper passes over each pair of teeth, it pulls them together into a pair (figure 4.2).

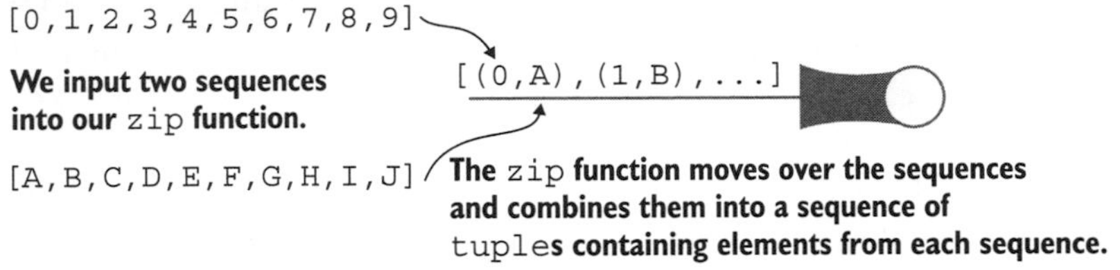
[0,1,2,3,4,5,6,7,8,9]
We input two sequences into our zip function.
[(0,A),(1,B),...]
[A,B,C,D,E,F,G,H,I,J]
The zip function moves over the sequences and combines them into a sequence of tuples containing elements from each sequence.

Figure 4.2 The zip function behaves like a zipper, but instead of interlocking metal teeth, it interlocks the values of Python iterables.

We use the zip function when we have related sequences that we want to bring together. For instance, if an ice cream vendor knows how many ice cream cones they've sold in the last two weeks, they may be interested in zipping that together with the temperature to analyze if there are any trends, as shown in the following listing.

Listing 4.3 Ice cream data and the zip function

```
ice_cream_sales = [27, 21, 39, 31, 12, 40, 11, 18, 30, 19, 24, 35, 31, 12]
temperatures = [75, 97, 88, 99, 81, 92, 91, 84, 84, 93, 100, 86, 90, 75]

ice_cream_data = zip(ice_cream_sales, temperatures)
print(list(ice_cream_data))
# [(27,75), (21,97), (39,88), ... (12,75)]
```

Having data paired in tuples like that is helpful because tuples can easily be passed to functions and unpacked. Because zip is lazy, the resulting iterator takes up hardly any memory. That means we can collect and move around massive amounts of data on our machine without holding it in memory.

The resulting single sequence is also the perfect target for mapping a function across because map takes a function and a sequence to which you want to apply that function. Because map is lazy as well, we can calculate all of these sales figures without much memory overhead. Indeed, all of our lazy functions, like map, filter, and zip, play nicely with one another. And because they all take sequences as inputs in one way or another, they can all be chained together and maintain their nice low-memory overhead laziness.

4.2.3 Lazy file searching with iglob

The last function we'll look at here is iglob. We can use the iglob function to find a sequence of files on our filesystem that match a given pattern. Specifically, the files match based on the standard Unix rules. For situations where filesystem-based storage is used, like in a lot of prototypes, this can be extremely helpful.

For example, if we have blog posts stored as JSON objects in files, we may be able to select all of the blog posts from June 2015 with a single line of code (the second line):

```
from glob import iglob

blog_posts = iglob("path/to/blog/posts/2015/06/*.json")
```

This type of statement would find all the JSON files in the 06 directory inside the 2015 directory inside the directory where we're storing all our blog posts.

For a single month, getting all the blog posts lazily may not be that big of a deal. But if we have several posts a day and several years of posts, then our list will be several thousand items long. Or if we've done some web scraping and stored each page as a .JSON object with metadata about when it was collected, we may have millions of these files. Holding that all in memory would be a burden on whatever processing we want to do.

In just a minute, we'll see an example where this lazy file processing can be useful, but first, let's take a second to talk about the nitty gritty details of sequence data types in Python.

4.3 Understanding iterators: The magic behind lazy Python

So far, we've talked about the benefits of laziness and about a couple functions that can take advantage of them. In this section, we'll dig into the details of iterators—objects that we can move through in sequence—and talk about generators—special functions for creating sequences. We touched on generators briefly in chapter 2, but this time we'll dive even deeper, including a look at small generator expressions.

It's important that we understand how iterators work because they are fundamental to our ability to process big data on our laptop or desktop computer. We use iterators to replace data with instructions about where to find data and to replace transformations with instructions for how to execute those transformations. This substitution means that the computer only has to concern itself with the data it is processing *right now*, as opposed to the data it just processed or has to process in the future.

4.3.1 The backbone of lazy Python: Iterators

Iterators are the base class of all the Python data types that can be iterated over. That is, we can loop over the items of an iterator, or we can map a function across one, like we learned how to do in chapter 2. The iteration process is defined by a special method called `.__iter__()`. If a class has this method and returns an object with a `.__next__()` method, then we can iterate over it.

THANK YOU, __NEXT__(): THE ONE-WAY NATURE OF ITERATORS.

The `.__next__()` method tells Python what the next object in the sequence is. We can call it directly with the `next()` function. For example, if we've filtered a list of words down to only the words that have the letter m in them, we can retrieve the next m word with `next()`.

Listing 4.4 demonstrates calling the `next` function on a lazy object. We create a small function to check if the string has an m in it. We then use that function with `filter` to winnow down our words to only the words containing m. Then, because the result of our filter is an iterable, we can call the next function on it to get an m word.

Listing 4.4 Retrieving m words with `next`

```
words = ["apple","mongoose","walk","mouse","good",
         "pineapple","yeti","minnesota","mars",
         "phone","cream","cucumber","coffee","elementary",
         "sinister","science","empire"]

def contains_m(s):
    if "m" in s.lower(): return True
    else: return False

m_words = filter(contains_m, words)

next(m_words)
next(m_words)
next(m_words)

print(list(m_words))
["mars","cream","cucumber","elementary", … ]
```

If you run this in the console, you'll be unsurprised to find that the `next()` function gets you the next item every time you call it. Something you might be surprised by, however, is that `filter` (and `map`, and all our lazy friends) are one-way streets; once we call `next`, the item returned to us is removed from the sequence. We can never back up and retrieve that item again. We can verify this by calling `list()` on the iterable after calling `next`. (See figure 4.3.)

Iterators work like this because they're optimized for bigger data, but they can cause us problems if we want to explore them element-by-element. They're not meant for by-hand inspection; they're meant for processing big data. Losing access to elements we've already seen can make iterators a little clumsier than lists if we're still tinkering with our code. However, when we're confident our code is working like expected, iterators use less memory and offer better performance.

```
>>> numbers = range(10)
>>> next(numbers)
0
>>> numbers.__next__()
1
>>> list(numbers
[2,3,4,5,6,7,8,9])
```

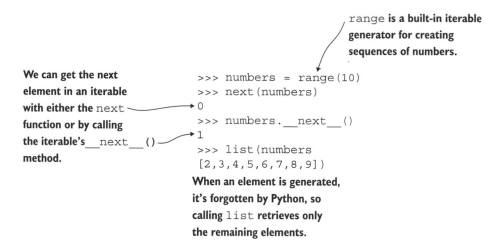

`range` is a built-in iterable generator for creating sequences of numbers.

We can get the next element in an iterable with either the `next` function or by calling the iterable's `__next__()` method.

When an element is generated, it's forgotten by Python, so calling `list` retrieves only the remaining elements.

Figure 4.3 When we call the `.__next__()` method or the `next()` function, we get the next item in the iterable.

4.3.2 Generators: Functions for creating data

Generators are a class of functions in Python that lazily produce values in a sequence. They're a simple way of implementing an iterator. In chapter 2, we used a generator function to produce URLs in a sequence. The benefit of that was we didn't have to spend memory on holding the list in place. Indeed, that's the primary advantage of generators and lazy functions: avoiding storing more in memory than we need to.

As we saw in chapter 2, one way of designing a generator is by defining a function that uses the `yield` statement. For example, if we wanted a function that would produce the first n even numbers, we could do that with a generator. That function would take a number, n, and yield the value of i*2 for every i between 1 and n, as demonstrated in listing 4.5.

GENERATOR EXPRESSIONS: INFINITE AMOUNTS OF DATA IN A SINGLE LINE OF CODE

If we're planning on doing that kind of generation multiple times, the `yield` statement is great. However, if we're only planning on using those numbers once, we can code this even more concisely with a *generator expression.* Generator expressions look like *list comprehensions*—short declarations of how to manipulate data into a new list—but instead of generating the list up front, they create a lazy iterator. This has the same advantage all our other lazy approaches have had: we can work with more data without incurring memory overhead.

A generator expression for the first 100 even numbers is shown at the end of listing 4.5. You'll note that the brackets around the expression are round instead of square. This is the syntactic distinction between a generator expression and a list comprehension.

Listing 4.5 Even numbers generator function

```
def even_numbers(n):
    i = 1
    while i <= n:
        yield i*2
        i += 1

first_100_even = (i*2 for i in range(1,101))
```

To get an intuitive understanding of the difference between generator expressions and list comprehensions, let's open up a Python console and run nearly identical commands: one with a generator expression and one with a list comprehension. For these statements, we'll use a function from the `itertools` module called `count`. The `count` function produces a lazy sequence of numbers, similar to `range`, but it's open-ended; the `count` function won't stop.

If we want an infinite string of even numbers, we can run a single command (after we've imported `count` from `itertools`):

```
from itertools import count
evens = (i*2 for i in count())
```

You'll notice that this command runs instantly. If we call `next()` on the `evens` object we just created, we'll get an even number. We also can take chunks from this sequence with the `islice` function from the `itertools` module (pronounced "i" "slice," not "is" "lice"):

```
from itertools import islice
islice(evens, 5,10)
```

Compare this with the same from a list comprehension.

> **WARNING** The following code is not going to finish running, so you may be better off running it in a web-based shell like https://repl.it.

Here's the list comprehension version:

```
evens = [i*2 for i in count()]
```

Our generator expression runs quickly and easily, but our list comprehension never finishes. That's because the list comprehension is attempting to generate all these numbers at once and store them in a list. That's nice if we want access to a specific element, or if we'll need repeated access to the sequence. Generators lose numbers that have been used, we can only access them once. But if we have to work with a large amount of data, our list comprehension is going to take quite a bit more time.

4.4 The poetry puzzle: Lazily processing a large dataset

Now that we've taken some time to review the ins and outs of iterators and lazy functions, let's take a look at two practical scenarios where we'd want to use these tools.

> **SCENARIO** A new poem has taken global culture by storm, but nobody can definitively identify the mysterious author. Two poets are claiming the poem and have provided you with terabytes of their unpublished poems so you can validate which poet is more likely to be the true author of the poem.

In this scenario, we need to process a large amount of data from two authors to confirm which one of them authored the popular mystery poem. We'll use a simple but powerful technique: comparing the frequencies of *function words*. Function words are words that have little content value but help sentences do things. Among other words, function words include the articles *a* and *the*. We'll use the ratio of those two words, *a* and *the*, to detect our true author (figure 4.4).

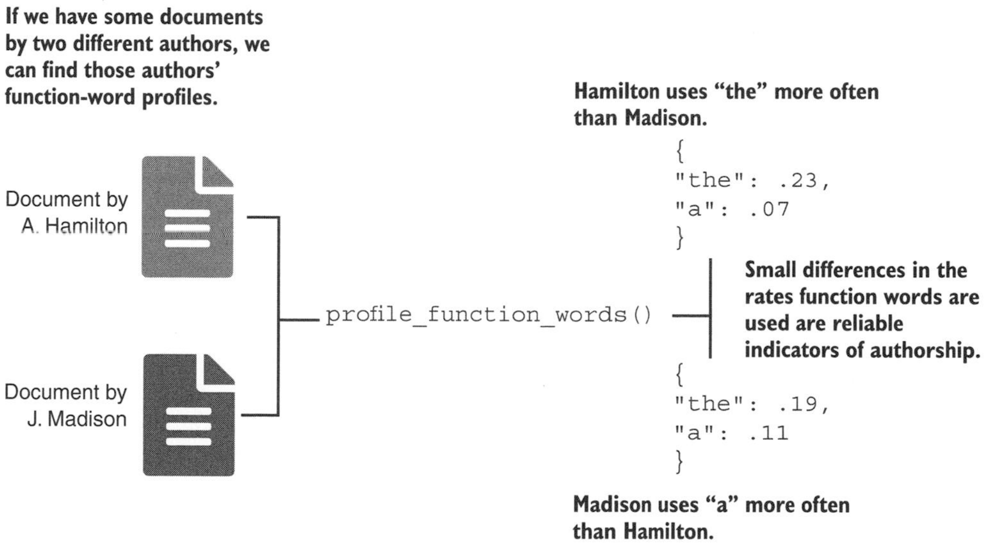
If we have some documents by two different authors, we can find those authors' function-word profiles.
Document by A. Hamilton
Document by J. Madison
profile_function_words()
Hamilton uses "the" more often than Madison.
{ "the": .23, "a": .07 }
Small differences in the rates function words are used are reliable indicators of authorship.
{ "the": .19, "a": .11 }
Madison uses "a" more often than Hamilton.

Figure 4.4 Counting function words can give us an idea of the true author of a document.

4.4.1 Generating data for this example

Because this scenario calls for a large dataset, large here being more than however much memory you have on the computer you're following along on, I've opted to provide a data generation script in the book's repository (https://github.com/jtwool/mastering-large-datasets). You can use that function to generate as much data as you want for this scenario. I suggest generating at least 100 MB if you can and then deleting it all after you've finished this section. That said, if you have a petabyte hard drive laying around, feel free to fill it up. The code in this section will be able to process it just fine—though it may take some time. Lazy functions are great at processing data, but hardware still limits how quickly we can work through it. Another great option: generate a tiny bit of data, finish the chapter, then generate more data and let the code process it overnight.

Unfortunately, because each author has provided us with so much information, we'll never be able to process it all in memory at once. So we'll have to use lazy functions to process it bit by bit. We'll also use some of the techniques we learned in chapter 3: breaking our large problem down into pieces we can solve with small, helper functions.

First, let's take a look at what we'll need to do.

1. We want to eventually compare the ratio of *a* and *the* for each author.
2. To do that, we need to read in each file for each author.
3. We'll also need a way to get word counts for *a* and *the.*
4. And to do that, we'll need to break the poems into words.

Ultimately, our process is going to look like figure 4.5. First, we'll read the files in. Then, we'll clean them so they're nice workable lists of words instead of unstructured poems. Then, we'll filter them down to just the words in which we're interested. Finally, we'll get counts and calculate a ratio.

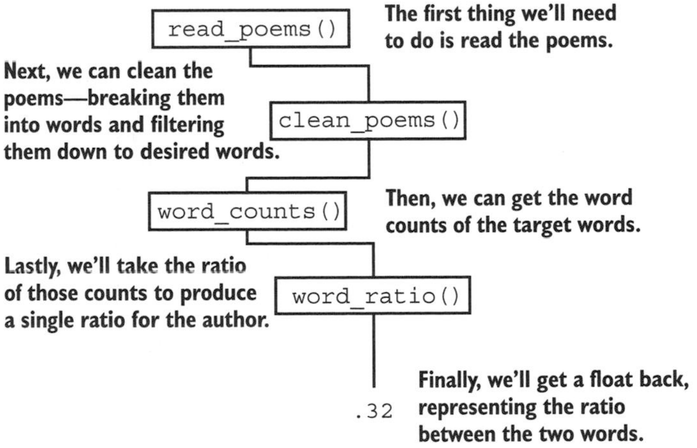
read_poems()
The first thing we'll need to do is read the poems.
Next, we can clean the poems—breaking them into words and filtering them down to desired words.
clean_poems()
word_counts()
Then, we can get the word counts of the target words.
Lastly, we'll take the ratio of those counts to produce a single ratio for the author.
word_ratio()
.32
Finally, we'll get a float back, representing the ratio between the two words.

Figure 4.5 Lots of small steps will add up to help us determine the author of the mystery poem.

4.4.2 *Reading poems in with iglob*

In section 4.2.3, we looked at `iglob`, a function for searching for files on a filesystem and returning a list of matching paths as an iterable. Because our poets were generous enough to provide us with reams of their unpublished works, we'll want to use this function to limit the overhead we need to spend storing these paths.

A straightforward step like this is also something that's good to get out of the way first. To read in the poems by each author, let's define two iterables using `iglob`: one for each author. This is a quick two-liner, as we can see in the following listing.

Listing 4.6 Listing the authors' poems using `iglob`

```
author1_poems = iglob("path/to/author_one/*.txt")
author2_poems = iglob("path/to/author_two/*.txt")
```

4.4.3 A poem-cleaning regular expression class

Now that we have the poems, we'll need a way to munge them into a workable data format. As we've done before with text data, we'll ultimately want to convert the long string of text data we get when we open and read the poem files into a list of words. Before that, however, we'll want to remove all the punctuation using a regular expression. For poems, this would be especially important because poets are known for distinctive use of punctuation.

Because we'll be using a regular expression, we'll want to create a class so that we can compile that regular expression once and use it as many times as we'd like. We'll give that class an attribute with a compiled regular expression that matches all the punctuation we want to remove and a method that uses that regular expression to remove the punctuation. Since we're using that method to make our text data easy to work with, it also makes sense to add lowercasing in there to normalize our text, and to split our words on whitespace.

We can see how that would play out in figure 4.6, where we transform a poem into our desired data structure. We start with the raw poem text, as the poet intended it, but after it's cleaned, the text is ready for us to analyze.

Ultimately, we should end up with a class that looks like the following listing. In the listing, I've chosen to remove all periods, commas, semicolons, colons, exclamation points, question marks, and hyphens with the regular expression.

Listing 4.7 A poem cleaner class

```
class PoemCleaner:
    def __init__(self):
        self.r = re.compile(r'[.,;:?!-]')        # Compiles the regular expression to match all punctuation

    def clean_poem(self, fp):
        with open(fp) as poem:
            no_punc = self.r.sub("",poem.read())     # Removes punctuation from the poem
            return no_punc.lower().split()       # Returns the no-punctuation poem lowercased and split into a list of tokens
```

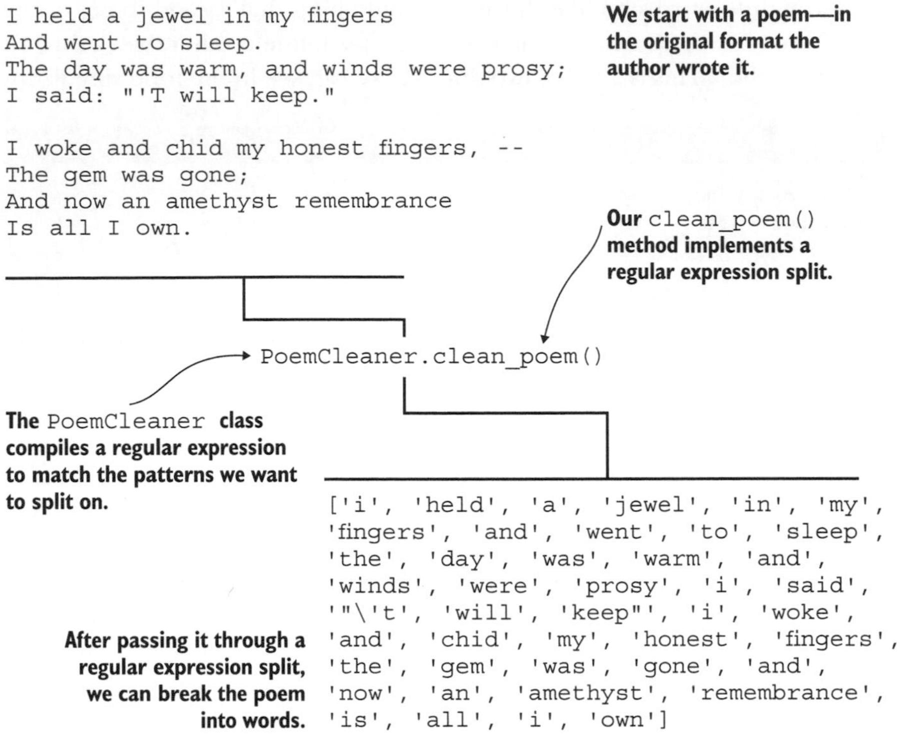
I held a jewel in my fingers
And went to sleep.
The day was warm, and winds were prosy;
I said: "'T will keep."
I woke and chid my honest fingers, --
The gem was gone;
And now an amethyst remembrance
Is all I own.
We start with a poem—in the original format the author wrote it.
Our clean_poem() method implements a regular expression split.
PoemCleaner.clean_poem()
The PoemCleaner class compiles a regular expression to match the patterns we want to split on.
['i', 'held', 'a', 'jewel', 'in', 'my', 'fingers', 'and', 'went', 'to', 'sleep', 'the', 'day', 'was', 'warm', 'and', 'winds', 'were', 'prosy', 'i', 'said', '"\'t', 'will', 'keep"', 'i', 'woke', 'and', 'chid', 'my', 'honest', 'fingers', 'the', 'gem', 'was', 'gone', 'and', 'now', 'an', 'amethyst', 'remembrance', 'is', 'all', 'i', 'own']
After passing it through a regular expression split, we can break the poem into words.

Figure 4.6 We can use a class containing a regular expression to transform a poem into a list of words.

4.4.4 *Calculating the ratio of articles*

The next step we'll work on, getting a ratio of articles, we'll solve with two custom functions: the `filter` function we've already looked at in this chapter and the `itertools.chain` function we looked at in chapter 3, plus a new function from the toolz library: `frequencies`. And all of this is going to be inside a wrapper function that we can use to pass in our `PoemCleaner` class (figure 4.7).

The first custom function we'll need is a function to determine if a word should be kept. We don't want to spend time or memory counting all the words, because we'll only use *a* and *the* to determine authorship. For this, we'll use a filter in conjunction with a helper function to narrow a lazy sequence of all the words down to just *a*'s and *the*'s. That helper function has to return `True` if a word is *a* or *the*, and `False` otherwise. That helper function will look like listing 4.8.

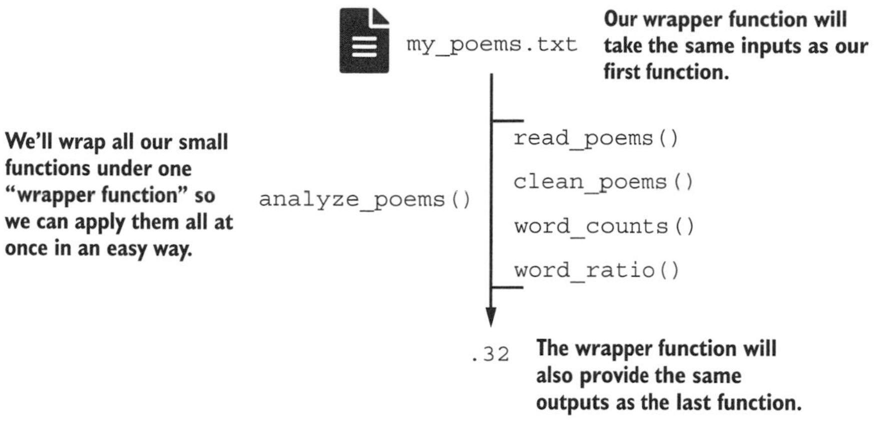
my_poems.txt
Our wrapper function will take the same inputs as our first function.
We'll wrap all our small functions under one "wrapper function" so we can apply them all at once in an easy way.
analyze_poems()
read_poems()
clean_poems()
word_counts()
word_ratio()
.32
The wrapper function will also provide the same outputs as the last function.

Figure 4.7 A large function will wrap all our smaller functions so we can readily apply our poem analysis pipeline.

NOTE The function word method for detecting the true author of a text may seem overly simplistic, but it's not far removed from a technique that was used in the most popular authorship analysis of all time: discovering the identity of the unattributed *Federalist Papers*. In that instance, a list of 30 function words was used to identify James Madison as the sole or primary author of the 12 disputed essays.

Listing 4.8 Function to test if a word is *a* or *the*

```
def word_is_desired(w):
    return w in ["a","the"]
```

We check if w is in the list containing "a" and "the" and return the result.

Once we've got that function built, we can use it as the condition part of our `filter` function. The input sequence for that filter is going to be our `.clean_poem` method mapped across the sequence of poem paths. We'll apply the `itertools.chain` function to the resulting sequences of words so we can treat them as one big sequence.

At this point, we've got a way to get a sequence for each author's uses of *a* and *the*. Now we need to count them and find a ratio between them. For the counting, the toolz library has a function `frequencies` that can do just that. It takes a sequence in and returns a `dict` of items that occurred in the sequence as keys with corresponding values equal to the number of times they occurred (figure 4.8). In other words: it provides the frequencies of items in our sequence.

From those counts, we can write another small function to calculate the ratios. That function needs to take a `dict` and return the value of the `"a"` key divided by the value of the `"the"` key. Because we're doing division, it's prudent to use the `.get` method of our `dict` with an ever-so-slightly larger than zero value so we don't risk

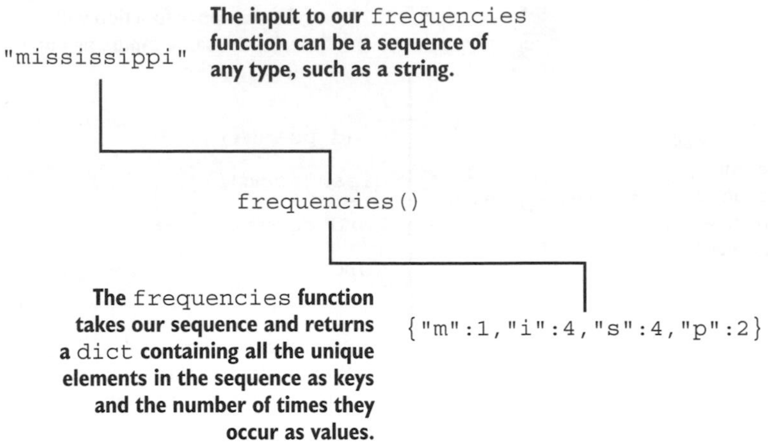
"mississippi"
The input to our frequencies function can be a sequence of any type, such as a string.
frequencies()
The frequencies function takes our sequence and returns a dict containing all the unique elements in the sequence as keys and the number of times they occur as values.
{"m":1,"i":4,"s":4,"p":2}

Figure 4.8 The `frequencies` function takes a sequence and turns it into a `dict` of items from the original sequence and the number of times they occur.

dividing by zero. That helper function and the combined poem analysis functions should look like the following listing.

Listing 4.9 Poem analysis function

```
def word_ratio(d):
    return float(d.get("a",0))/float(d.get("the",0.0001))

def analyze_poems(poems, cleaner):
    return word_ratio(
        toolz.frequencies(
            filter(word_is_desired,
                itertools.chain(*map(cleaner.clean_poem, poems)))))
```

To tie all of this together, we'll need to create an instance of our `PoemCleaner` class and apply our `analyze_poems` function to the iterables for each of our authors. Altogether, we'll have the code in the following listing. At the very end of the listing, I've added a `print` statement that'll show the authors' different tendencies, as well as the value found in the original poem. Running this script will tell you who the true author is!

Listing 4.10 Poem puzzle final script

```
import toolz
import re, itertools
from glob import iglob

def word_ratio(d):
    return float(d.get("a",0))/float(d.get("the",0.0001))
```

```
class PoemCleaner:
    def __init__(self):
        self.r = re.compile(r'[.,;:!-]')
    def clean_poem(self, fp):
        with open(fp) as poem:
            no_punc = self.r.sub("",poem.read())
            return no_punc.lower().split()

def word_is_desired(w):
    if w in ["a","the"]:
        return True
    else: return False

def analyze_poems(poems, cleaner):
    return word_ratio(
        toolz.frequencies(
            filter(word_is_desired,
                itertools.chain(*map(cleaner.clean_poem, poems)))))

if __name__ == "__main__":

    cleaner = PoemCleaner()
    author1_poems = iglob("path/to/author_one/*.txt")
    author2_poems = iglob("path/to/author_two/*.txt")

    author1_ratio = analyze_poems(author1_poems, cleaner)
    author2_ratio = analyze_poems(author2_poems, cleaner)

    print("""
    Original_Poem:  0.3
    Author One:     {:.2f}
    Author Two:     {:.2f}
    """.format(author1_ratio, author2_ratio))
```

With this script, we can parse a larger amount of data than we could handle in memory. Being able to do this is a key milestone in transitioning from a developer who can only work with small data to a developer who can work with big(ish) data. As we saw in this example with `iglob` and `filter`, laziness helps us a lot in this respect. Next, we'll see how laziness can help us in generating data.

4.5 Lazy simulations: Simulating fishing villages

The poetry puzzle covered in section 4.4 showed us how we can work with big data on our local machine; however, we also can use the tools in this chapter for producing big data.

> **SCENARIO** An environmental conservation group has commissioned you to design a simulation that illustrates the problem of overfishing. They have outlined a scenario involving four small villages and a lake. The people in each of those villages have agreed to take only one fish per person per year; however, some years a village will cheat and take twice as many fish as they're allowed. Each village has its own propensity for cheating, but if two villages get caught

cheating in the same year, each village increases its propensity for cheating. The villages will also grow each year. How many years can these villages survive?

For simulation problems like this, it's often useful to program in a slightly different way than we've been programming up to now. For simulations, we get a lot of value from writing classes, which we haven't talked about much outside of a way to compile regular expressions. Classes are great because they allow us to consolidate the data about each piece of the simulation (figure 4.9). In this specific simulation, we have two actors that need special attention and deserve their own class:

1. The simulation as a whole
2. The villages

Considering the simulation as a class will give us a place to keep track of what year we're in, how many fish are remaining, and which villages are associated with the simulation. It will give us an easy way to run lots of simulations in parallel, as we'll see later on.

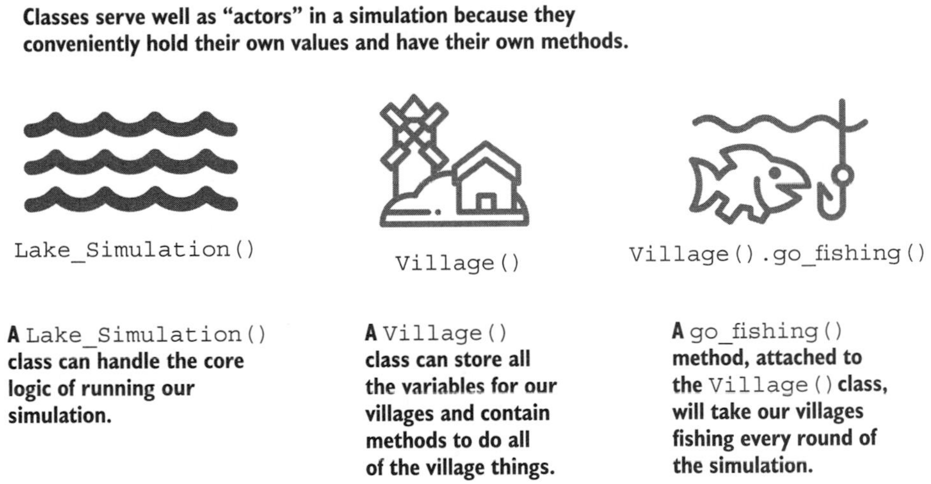
Classes serve well as "actors" in a simulation because they conveniently hold their own values and have their own methods.
Lake_Simulation()
Village()
Village().go_fishing()
A Lake_Simulation() class can handle the core logic of running our simulation.
A Village() class can store all the variables for our villages and contain methods to do all of the village things.
A go_fishing() method, attached to the Village() class, will take our villages fishing every round of the simulation.

Figure 4.9 We can use classes to represent actors in a complex simulation scenario, such as villages fishing a lake over time.

Considering the villages as a class is useful for many of the same reasons. The villages are all going to have their own unique bits of data, like a unique population and a unique inclination toward cheating. The villages also will need to do certain things, like increase population (and maybe increase their rate of cheating) each year.

You may notice that breaking the problem up into two classes is similar to how we were breaking large problems into chains of small helper functions in chapter 3. Indeed, we'll further break up the large simulation inside those two classes. The

`Lake_Simulation` class will get a method for handling the simulation itself, and the fishing villages will get methods for fishing and updating.

4.5.1 Creating a village class

Between the villages and the simulation, the village is a smaller chunk of work, so let's start there. For the villages, we'll create a class that has an attribute to store its population and an attribute to store its cheating rate (figure 4.10). Each of these two attributes will be unique to each village, and we don't want to have to set them ourselves for each simulation, so we'll use a random variable in their place. I'm going to keep the villages small—between 1,000 and 5,000—and the amount of cheating relatively low—between .05 and .15.

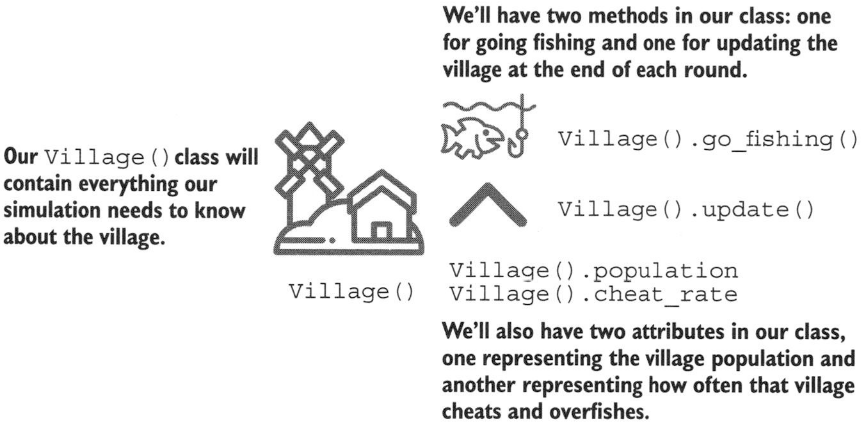
We'll have two methods in our class: one for going fishing and one for updating the village at the end of each round.
Our Village() class will contain everything our simulation needs to know about the village.
Village().go_fishing()
Village().update()
Village()
Village().population
Village().cheat_rate
We'll also have two attributes in our class, one representing the village population and another representing how often that village cheats and overfishes.

Figure 4.10 The `Village` class represents everything the village is and can do, including going fishing and growing.

To generate random numbers for the population and cheat rate, we'll need to import Python's `random` module and use its `uniform` function, which selects a value between two points with uniform likelihood. In other words, every number in that range has the same likelihood of occurring. We can call the `uniform` function for both population and cheat rate, as we see in the following listing.

Listing 4.11 The beginnings of a `Village` class

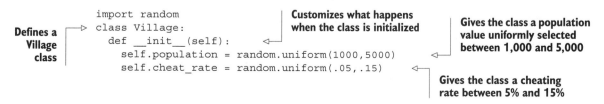

```
import random
class Village:
  def __init__(self):
    self.population = random.uniform(1000,5000)
    self.cheat_rate = random.uniform(.05,.15)
```

- **Defines a Village class** (class Village:)
- **Customizes what happens when the class is initialized** (def __init__(self):)
- **Gives the class a population value uniformly selected between 1,000 and 5,000** (self.population)
- **Gives the class a cheating rate between 5% and 15%** (self.cheat_rate)

This lays out the core of the Village class, and we can move on to some of the stuff the village will do: like going fishing and updating itself every round. Let's take a look at going fishing first.

GONE FISHING: A FIRST METHOD FOR OUR SIMULATION OBJECT

Every year, when a village goes fishing, it has the option to cheat, and all villages cheat at a different rate. To account for that, we'll generate a uniform random variable between 0 and 1. If that number is below the cheat rate, the village will cheat; otherwise, it'll play by the rules. When a village cheats, it'll take two fish per person. When it doesn't, it'll take only one fish. And then lastly, because our simulation will need to know if our village cheated and how many fish it took, we'll return the amount of fish taken and if the village cheated, as shown in the following listing.

Listing 4.12 A method for going fishing

```
def go_fishing(self):
  if random.uniform(0,1) < self.cheat_rate:
    cheat = 1
    fish_taken = self.population * 2
  else:
    cheat = 0
    fish_taken = self.population * 1
  return fish_taken, cheat
```

- Checks if the village will cheat; if it does, apply the cheat rules.
- If the village doesn't cheat, apply the standard rules.
- At the end, return the fish the village took and if they cheated or not.

A YEARLY UPDATE FUNCTION FOR THE VILLAGE CLASS

After going fishing, each village also will change a little each year. Every year, the population will grow, and, depending how many villages cheated that year, a given village may increase the rate at which it decides to cheat. To keep things simple, our villages will all grow at a rate of 2.5% each year.

To decide whether or not we increase the cheat rate, we'll need to know how many cheaters there were this year of the simulation. Because that information is contained inside the simulation class, we'll need to pass the simulation to the .update method, as shown in the following listing.

Listing 4.13 Updating our villages

```
def update(self, sim):
  if sim.cheaters >= 2:
    self.cheat_rate += .05
  self.population = int(self.population*1.025)
```

- If we find more than two cheaters, increase the cheat rate.
- Increase the population no matter what.

4.5.2 Designing the simulation class for our fishing simulation

Those two methods, .go_fishing and .update, round out our Village class. We'll use that class to represent villages in our simulation (figure 4.11). Additionally, as mentioned earlier, we'll need a class for the simulation itself. This class will keep track of the simulation-level variables, such as what year it is and how many fish remain.

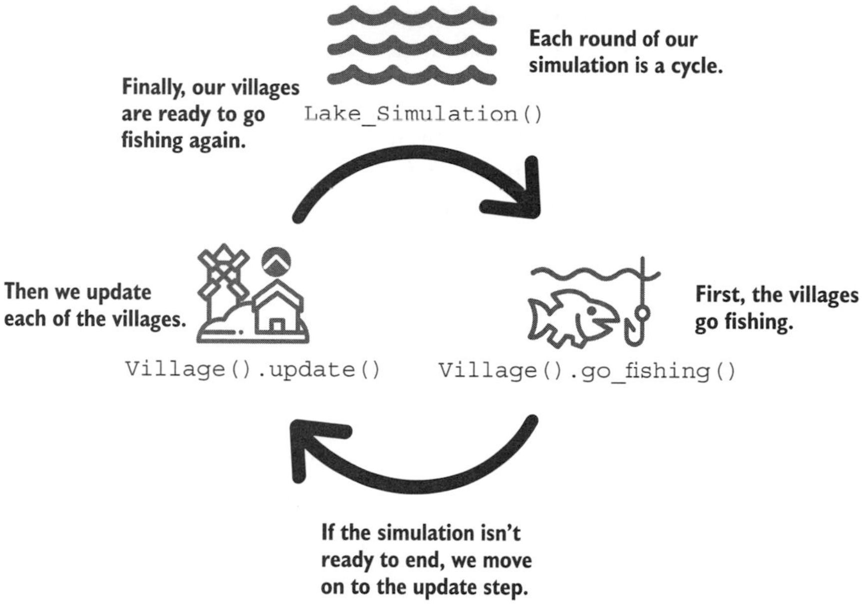
Each round of our simulation is a cycle.
Lake_Simulation()
Finally, our villages are ready to go fishing again.
First, the villages go fishing.
Village().go_fishing()
Then we update each of the villages.
Village().update()
If the simulation isn't ready to end, we move on to the update step.

Figure 4.11 Our simulation is a cyclical process in which we go fishing, check if we need to stop the simulation, update the simulation if we'll keep going, and then go fishing again.

Additionally, our simulation class will have a rather large method for running the simulation itself.

SETTING UP THE SIMULATION WITH THE .__INIT__ METHOD

The start of our simulation is its `.__init__` method, which will set up the simulation (listing 4.14). To set up the simulation, we only need four things:

1. *The villages*—Represented by a list of village objects, in our case 4
2. *The fish*—In this case, just the number of fish
3. *A start year*—Also a number, in our case 1
4. *The number of cheaters*—Again, an integer indicating the number of cheating villages

We'll assign each of these variables to the simulation class itself, so as our simulation changes, the variables will carry with it.

Listing 4.14 Setting up the simulation

```
class Lake_Simulation:
  def __init__(self):
    self.villages = [Village() for _ in range(4)]
    self.fish = 80000
    self.year = 1
    self.cheaters = 0
```

WRITING SIMULATION LOGIC IN OUR .SIMULATE METHOD

The simulation logic will go in the simulation class's `.simulate` method. That means this method will be responsible for

- finding the results of a year of fishing
- updating the simulation after each year
- ending the simulation if we run out of fish
- ending the simulation if we survive "long enough"

Because our simulation can go on forever if the lake never gets overfished, we'll start our `.simulate` method with an infinite loop; in this case, we'll use an infinite `for` loop:

```
for _ in itertools.count():
```

The `itertools.count()` function returns a generator that produces an infinite sequence of increasing numbers (1, 2, 3, 4, . . . 1000, 1001, 1002, . . . infinity). By using "_ " we tell Python to ignore the value returned by the `for` loop, since we won't be needing it.

VILLAGES GOING FISHING: INTRODUCING METHODCALLER FOR MAP AND CLASSES

With our loop set up, we can start finding the results of our year of fishing. For our simulation, each of our villages goes fishing individually. That's why we set up the village classes with a `.go_fishing` method. To have all the villages go fishing, we can map their `.go_fishing` method across the list of classes in our simulation's `.villages` attribute.

To do this, we'll need the `operator.methodcaller` function. `methodcaller` takes a string and returns a function that calls the method with the name of that string on any object passed to it. Because the map and reduce style of programming we're looking at in this book is so function-oriented, being able to call class methods using a function is extremely helpful This capability allows us to use functions like `map` and `filter` on them.

From there, because our `.go_fishing` method returns a `tuple` of fish caught and a number indicating if that village cheated or not, our output from mapping this function across a list of villages will look as if we used the `zip` function on a sequence of fish caught and a sequence of cheating indicators. Knowing this, we can unzip the sequence of `tuples` and take the sums of the individual sequences, which will give us the total number of fish caught and the total number of cheaters.

Unzipping is the opposite of zipping. Whereas zipping takes two sequences and returns a list of `tuples`, unzipping takes a single sequence and returns two. We can call unzip by putting a star in front of the list when we call the `zip` function: `zip(*my_sequence)`. We can see unzip and the rest of the first phase of our simulate step in the following listing.

Listing 4.15 All the villages go fishing

```
for _ in itertools.count():
    yearly_results = map(methodcaller("go_fishing"), self.villages)
    fishes, cheats = zip(*yearly_results)
    total_fished = sum(fishes)
    self.cheaters = sum(cheats)
```

Unzips the yearly_results into two lists: fishes and cheats

The fishes list contains the number of fish fished by each village, its sum being the total fish fished.

The cheats list contains a 1 for each village that cheated, its sum being the number of cheaters.

After we figure out how many cheaters there were and how many fish were caught, we'll check if the simulation should end or if we should keep going. For this, we'll use two `if` checks, each of which will break our infinite `for` loop.

1. The first `if` check will check if we've made it through 1,000 simulated years.
2. The second `if` check will check if all the fish have been fished.

If each of these conditions is triggered, we'll print a message to the screen explaining what happened. If we wanted to store the results of our simulation, this would be a good place to write our simulation results to a file. The following listing shows what this short bit of our code looks like.

Listing 4.16 Checking if the simulation should be over

```
if self.year > 1000:
    print("Wow! Your villages lasted 1000 years!")
    break
elif self.fish < total_fished:
    print("The lake was overfished in {} years.".format(self.year))
    break
```

FINAL CALCULATIONS: RESOLVING THE YEAR

If we make it past the year-end checks, we can update our simulation for the year. Updating the simulation involves removing the fished fish from the remaining fish, repopulating the fish some amount (fish do make more fish, after all), and updating all the villages. If you'd like, we also may want to add a `print` statement here so we can see what happens year over year.

To update the amount of fish remaining, we'll subtract `total_fished` from `self.fish` and then increase `self.fish` by 15%. To update all the villages, we'll again map `methodcaller` across all our villages. This time, however, we'll call for the `.update` method instead of `.go_fishing`. Lastly, for a `print` statement, I recommend including at least the year and the number of fish remaining. See the one shown in the following listing.

Listing 4.17 The `.simulate` method

```
else:
    self.fish = (self.fish-total_fished)* 1.15
    map(methodcaller("update"), self.villages)
    print("Year {:<5}   Fish: {}".format(self.year,
                                        int(self.fish)))
            self.year += 1
```

Updates the fish remaining

Updates the villages by mapping the "update" method across them

And with that, we've completed our fishing simulation! Initialize a `Lake_Simulation` class and call the `.simulate` method a few times to see what happens. You should get a different number of years survived each time you run the simulation. The following listing shows the full simulation code.

Listing 4.18 Full fishing simulation

```
import random, itertools
from operator import methodcaller

class Village:
  def __init__(self):
    self.population = random.uniform(1000,5000)
    self.cheat_rate = random.uniform(.05,.15)

  def update(self, sim):
    if sim.cheaters >= 2:
      self.cheat_rate += .05
    self.population = int(self.population*1.025)

  def go_fishing(self):
    if random.uniform(0,1) < self.cheat_rate:
      cheat = 1
      fish_taken = self.population * 2
    else:
      cheat = 0
      fish_taken = self.population * 1
    return fish_taken, cheat


class Lake_Simulation:
  def __init__(self):
    self.villages = [Village() for _ in range(4)]
    self.fish = 80000
    self.year = 1
    self.cheaters = 0

  def simulate(self):
    for _ in itertools.count():
        yearly_results = map(methodcaller("go_fishing"), self.villages)
        fishes, cheats = zip(*yearly_results)
        total_fished = sum(fishes)
        self.cheaters = sum(cheats)
```

```
        if self.year > 1000:
            print("Wow! Your villages lasted 1000 years!")
            break
        if self.fish < total_fished:
            print("The lake was overfished in {} years.".format(self.year))
            break
        else:
            self.fish -= total_fished
            self.fish = self.fish*1.15
            map(lambda x:x.update(self), self.villages)
            print("Year {:<5}   Fish: {}".format(self.year,
                                                 int(self.fish)))
            self.year += 1

if __name__ == "__main__":
    random.seed("map and reduce")
    Lake = Lake_Simulation()
    Lake.simulate()
    Lake.simulate()
    Lake.simulate()
    Lake.simulate()
```

We can run this simulation a few times (commenting out or changing the random seed each time) to see different results. The output of our simulation will be years, printed to the terminal, with the amount of fish remaining in that year. Usually, we'll see our simulation end after around 10 years, as shown in listing 4.19. Sometimes, though, it will go on for thousands of runs.

> **Simulations and random seeds**
> When we run simulations, we'll use lots of random number generators. Randomness in our code can cause confusion when we share it with others and they're expecting to get the same results we got. One way we can get around this is by using a *random seed*. By setting a seed, we can ensure that we'll get effectively random numbers, but that those numbers will be in the same sequence every time. Any other user running the same code with the same random seed will get the same results we do.

Listing 4.19 Fishing scenario output

```
Year 1       Fish: 77183
Year 2       Fish: 70035
Year 3       Fish: 65724
Year 4       Fish: 60766
Year 5       Fish: 49965
Year 6       Fish: 42644
Year 7       Fish: 30315
Year 8       Fish: 20046
Year 9       Fish: 8327
The lake was overfished in 10 years
```

In most runs of the scenario, the lake will be overfished in a dozen or so years.

These long runs represent the scenarios in which the villages avoid cheating during the early stages of the simulation. You can play around with the cheat rate, number of fish taken, and fish population growth rate to see how the simulation behaves under different assumptions.

4.6 Exercises

4.6.1 Lazy functions

Lazy functions are common when we use a map and reduce style in Python. Which of the following functions are lazy?

- `map`
- `reduce`
- `filter`
- `list`
- `zip`
- `sum`
- `range`
- `len`

4.6.2 Fizz buzz generator

A classic toy programming problem is the fizz buzz problem, where we want to replace any number divisible by 3 with fizz and any number divisible by 5 with buzz. If a number is divisible by both fizz and buzz, it should be replaced with fizz buzz. We implemented a version of this using classes in chapter 2. Create a generator that solves this problem. Hint: Remember, you can use the modulo operator (%) to check if division produces a remainder.

4.6.3 Repeat access

When we use a built-in generator function such as `range`, we can only iterate through it once. Why is that so?

4.6.4 Parallel simulations

There are many ways to run several simulations in parallel. One way is to map the `.simulate` method from our `Lake_Simulation` class over a sequence using the `with Pool() as P:` construction we introduced in chapter 2. Modify the code from listing 4.18 so you can run simulations in parallel.

4.6.5 Scrabble words

The popular game Scrabble involves spelling words by placing tiles on a board. Spelling long words and words with more rare letters in them earns you more points. In a simplified version, Z is worth 10 points; F, H, V, and W are worth 5; B, C, M, and P are worth three; and all other letters are worth one point. Using the functions `map` and `filter`, reduce this list of words to only the ones that are worth more than eight points: zebra, fever, charm, mouse, hair, brill, thorn.

Summary

- Lazy functions are those that evaluate only when we need the values they return—no sooner and no later. We can use lazy functions like `map`, `filter`, `zip`, and `iglob` to work with massive amounts of data on our laptops.
- Python implements laziness through iterators, which we can create ourselves, receive from functions, or build with convenient generator functions and statements.
- We can create generators with functions using `yield` statements or through concise and powerful list comprehension-like generator expressions.
- We can only go through iterators one way; once we've seen an element from an iterator, we never have access to that same element again.
- We can use the `filter` function to conveniently gather a subset of a list. There's a whole family of functions just like the filter function: `filterfalse`, `valfilter`, `keyfilter`, and `itemfilter`.
- We can use `zip` to combine two lists into a single sequence of `tuples`—a handy trick when combined with `map`.
- We can use `frequencies` from the toolz library to get counts of the unique elements of a sequence.
- We can apply lazy functions and generators toward solving data-intensive problems, such as text analysis and simulations.
- We can use `methodcaller` to map an object's method over a sequence of that object.

5 Accumulation operations with reduce

This chapter covers

- Recognizing the `reduce` pattern for N-to-X data transformations
- Writing helper functions for reductions
- Writing lambda functions for simple reductions
- Using `reduce` to summarize data

In chapter 2, we learned about the first part of the map and reduce style of programming: `map`. In this chapter, we introduce the second part: `reduce`. As we noted in chapter 2, `map` performs N-to-N transformations. That is, if we have a situation where we want to take a sequence and get a same-sized sequence back, `map` is our go-to function. Among the examples of this that we've reviewed are file processing (we have a list of files and we want to do something to all of them; discussed in chapter 4) and web scraping (we have a list of websites and we want to get the content for each of them; discussed in chapter 2).

In this chapter, we'll focus on `reduce` for N-to-X transformations; that is, situations where we have some sequence but we want to get something back besides another same-sized sequence, usually a sequence of a different size or possibly not even a sequence at all. Note, however, that situations do exist where we'll actually want to use reduce to get back a sequence of the same size. We'll look at all of these situations, learning about reduce and using it in some common transformations that you're already familiar with. Learning reduce will give us a handy tool to use in situations where map isn't appropriate, but where we still want to benefit from using a common programming pattern.

5.1 N-to-X with reduce

When we say that reduce is a function for N-to-X transformations, we mean that whenever we have a sequence and want to transform it into something that we can't use map for, we can happily use reduce. This is one of the reasons why map and reduce pair so neatly together: map can take care of most of the transformations in a very concise manner, whereas reduce can take care of the very final transformation, albeit in a somewhat less elegant fashion.

An example of an N-to-X transformation that you're already familiar with, and that we'll take a look at in more detail in section 5.2, is the summation function. In math, this is typically represented with a Σ. In Python, we have access to the sum function from the base library. The summation function takes a sequence of numbers (integers, floats, imaginary numbers) and returns a single number that is the total of all the numbers in the sequence added together (figure 5.1).

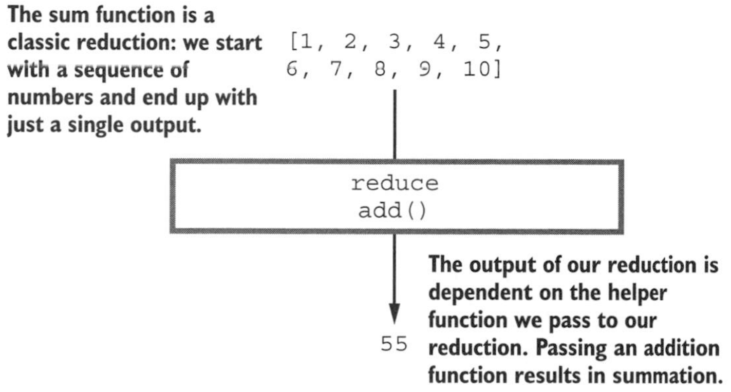
The sum function is a classic reduction: we start with a sequence of numbers and end up with just a single output.
[1, 2, 3, 4, 5,
6, 7, 8, 9, 10]
reduce
add()
55
The output of our reduction is dependent on the helper function we pass to our reduction. Passing an addition function results in summation.

Figure 5.1 The sum function is a common example of the reduce pattern that most people already know.

For example, if we had a sequence with the numbers 10, 5, 1, 19, 11, and 203, we could sum them up and get a single number back. This would take us from our six original numbers down to only one resulting number. We would have transformed our data from size N (6) down to X (1). This is the essence of the reduce pattern: taking a sequence and transforming it into something else.

5.2 The three parts of reduce

Summing a sequence of numbers with `reduce` is simple, but it will still require all three parts of a `reduce` function (figure 5.2):

1. An accumulator function
2. A sequence
3. An initializer

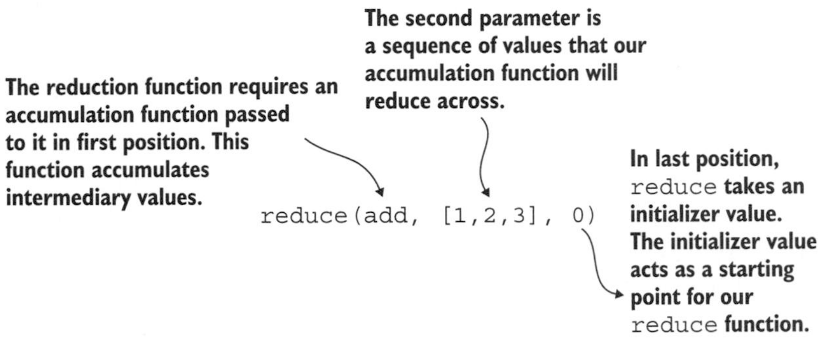
The second parameter is a sequence of values that our accumulation function will reduce across.
The reduction function requires an accumulation function passed to it in first position. This function accumulates intermediary values.
reduce(add, [1,2,3], 0)
In last position, reduce takes an initializer value. The initializer value acts as a starting point for our reduce function.

Figure 5.2 A `reduce` function has three parts: an accumulator, which specifies `reduce`'s behavior, a sequence, which we reduce over, and an initial value, which we use to start our `reduce` operation.

The accumulator function does the heavy lifting for `reduce`. It's a special type of helper function, like the ones we were using for `map` in chapters 2, 3, and 4. A sequence is an object that we can iterate through, such as lists, strings, and generators. And our initializer is the initial value to be passed to our accumulator. In most implementations of `reduce`, this parameter is optional.

If we were to sum up a sequence of numbers, we would want

1. to have our accumulator function be an addition function
2. our sequence to be the sequence of numbers we'd like to sum
3. our initial value to be 0 to start counting at zero

In Python, that may look something like the following listing. To run this code, you'll need to define an addition function—`my_add`. We'll do that in the next subsection on accumulation functions.

Listing 5.1 The three parts of `reduce`

```
from functools import reduce      # First, we need to import reduce from the functools library.

xs = [10,5,1,19,11,203]           # Then, we can set up our data to sum up.

reduce(my_add, xs, 0)             # When we call reduce, notice how the accumulator comes first, then the sequence, then the initial value.
```

Listing 5.1 provides an example of how summation with `reduce` may look. Two things are worth noting about this short bit of code. First, we need to `import reduce` from the functools library. The `reduce` function is not a default import like `map`, though it is available with any distribution of Python. In deprecated versions of Python (2.7 and below), `reduce` was available by default.

> **Removing the reduce function from base Python**
>
> In 2002, the creator of Python, Guido van Rossum, referred to including many of the approaches in this book as a mistake. He had the view that these approaches harmed readability and that the reduce method in particular was hard for most people to understand. I disagree. Reduce simply is not widely taught. Additionally, the rise of parallel and distributed computing makes these tools extremely valuable.
>
> In this chapter, you'll learn about a powerful, versatile tool that the Python language maintainers don't want you to know about.

Second, the order in which we place our parameters for `reduce` is specific. Like `map`, the accumulator or helper function comes first, then the sequence, and then our initializer comes last. The initializer comes last because it is an optional parameter.

5.2.1 Accumulation functions in reduce

Accumulator functions are all of a common prototype. They take an accumulated value and the next element in the sequence and return another object, typically of the same type as the accumulated value. For example, in our sum function, we're going to want to take in the sum up to that point as our accumulated value, and the next element in the sequence as our next value, and add them together. The code for that will look like the following listing.

Listing 5.2 An accumulator function for summation

```
def my_add(acc, nxt):          <- Our my_add function takes in an accumulated
                                  value (acc) and the next element (nxt).
    return acc + nxt           <- It returns those two values added together,
                                  which will be another number, just like acc.
```

The one thing you'll want to note about this one-line function is the variable names. My preferred convention labeling the variables to a `reduce` accumulator function is to use `acc` for the accumulated value and `nxt` for the next value; however, there are others. Some more concise teams like to use `a` to represent the accumulator and `b` to represent the next value. You also may see `left` used to represent the accumulator and `right` used to represent the next value. To understand why the accumulator function needs to take in an accumulated value and the next element, it helps to understand how `reduce` does its transformations.

How reduce works

In its simplest implementations, `reduce` loops over a sequence, processing each element in conjunction with an accumulated value. This accumulated value starts as either the initializer value, if we provide one, or the first element of the sequence if we do not. For example, when `reduce` is summing up 10, 5, 1, 19, 11, and 203, it's adding 10 to 0 to get 10, then adding 5 to the current total (10) to get 15, then adding 1 to that to get 16, then adding 19 to that to get 35, and so on until all the numbers are processed (figure 5.3). The total value is the accumulator value. The next value in the sequence is the next value.

> **Reducing from left to right**
>
> Because `reduce` loops over a sequence from left to right, some teams, as we just mentioned, will call the accumulated value in their accumulator helper functions `left` and the next value passed to those functions `right`. Versions of the `reduce` function in other programming languages can reduce from right to left instead. In these situations, teams can easily tell which functions were written for left-to-right reductions and which were written for right-to-left reductions.

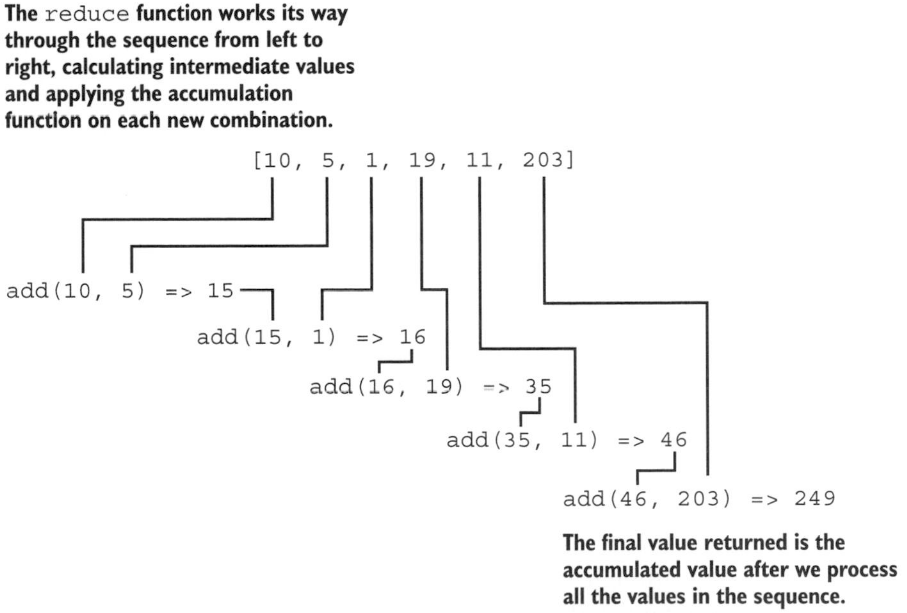
The reduce function works its way through the sequence from left to right, calculating intermediate values and applying the accumulation function on each new combination.
[10, 5, 1, 19, 11, 203]
add(10, 5) => 15
add(15, 1) => 16
add(16, 19) => 35
add(35, 11) => 46
add(46, 203) => 249
The final value returned is the accumulated value after we process all the values in the sequence.

Figure 5.3 The `reduce` function works by processing each element of a sequence and joining it with an accumulator value.

When these data structures and functions are simple, `reduce` can seem unnecessary; however, as the data structures, and the transformations we want to make of them, become more complex, we can use `reduce` to make our transformations more transparent. More sophisticated implementations of `reduce`, like we'll see in chapter 6, also allow for parallel reductions, which provide the same performance improvements we saw with parallel `map`, with little to no rewriting of our code.

TESTING OUR SUMMATION FUNCTION

At this point, we have a working summation reduction. Feel free to run the combined code from listings 5.1 and 5.2. If you wrap the `reduce` call in a `print` function, you should see an integer printed to your screen. Unlike `map` and the lazy data types we looked at in chapter 4, `reduce` evaluates when it's called.

5.2.2 Concise accumulations using lambda functions

As you may have been thinking while typing up the code for listing 5.2, sometimes it seems silly to create a whole function for a one-line statement like adding together two numbers. In cases like this, it's common to use a lambda function instead of defining a function.

Lambda functions are also known as anonymous functions because we don't save them to the name space. Although we're perfectly free to call our `my_add` function whenever and wherever we want, the anonymous function only exists inside of the `reduce` call and will not be available beyond the scope of that single command. For small operations, this is really nice. We don't even have to worry about naming these functions. For larger operations, we'd rather have a callable function.

Lambda functions in Python are defined in three parts (figure 5.4):

1. The lambda keyword
2. The parameters the function will take
3. A colon and the statement that the function will execute

For example, our `my_add` function could be a simple lambda function.

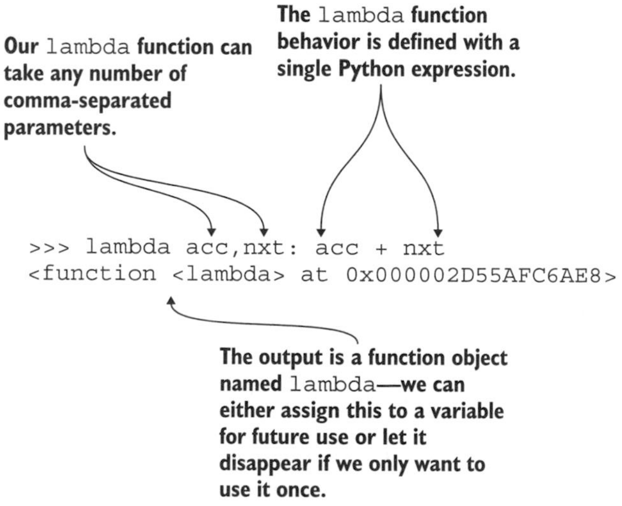

Our lambda function can take any number of comma-separated parameters.
The lambda function behavior is defined with a single Python expression.
>>> lambda acc,nxt: acc + nxt
<function <lambda> at 0x000002D55AFC6AE8>
The output is a function object named lambda—we can either assign this to a variable for future use or let it disappear if we only want to use it once.

Figure 5.4 We can use lambda functions in place of standard functions in `map` or `reduce` operations when we won't need to use the function's behavior again.

You'll notice the `lambda` keyword is the first thing in our statement, followed by our two parameters: `acc` and `nxt`. The two parameters are separated by a comma, just like they would be in a normal function declaration. Unlike a function declaration, however, we won't find any name for the function. Additionally, we declare the function's behavior immediately after the parameters on the same line, only separated by a colon and a space. Lastly, you'll notice that this lambda statement returns a function. We could assign this to a variable and use it like a normal function if we wanted to; however, usually we'll just want to be done with our anonymous, throwaway lambda function.

The best use for a lambda function is to declare it right inside our `reduce` call. To do that, we just write the lambda statement in the first position of our `reduce` function where the accumulator function goes, leaving the latter two positions for our sequence and our initializer. For example, we could simplify the code from listings 5.1 and 5.2 down to the code in the following listing using a lambda function.

Listing 5.3 Lambda function inside `reduce` for summation

```
from functools import reduce

xs = [10, 5, 1, 19, 11, 203]
print(reduce(lambda acc, nxt: acc+nxt, xs, 0))
```

Our lambda addition function goes in the first position of our reduce statement.

This code achieves the same end as our previous code. This time, though, we don't need to save space for our addition function. In this specific case, using the lambda function works great because our task at hand is small: we're adding two numbers. Other useful cases for using lambdas are when we want to expose class methods or attributes.

For example, we can use a lambda function to expose the `.get` method from the `dict` class and sum the price of several products. We can see this play out in the following listing.

Listing 5.4 Lambda functions can be used to expose class methods

```
from functools import reduce

my_products = [
    {"price": 9.99,
     "sn": '00231'},
    {"price": 59.99,
     "sn": '11010'},
    {"price": 74.99,
     "sn": '00013'},
    {"price": 19.99,      "sn": '00831'},
]

reduce(lambda acc, nxt: acc+nxt.get("price", 0), my_products, 0)
```

Our product data is stored in dicts, each containing a price and a serial number (sn).

We can call the .get method of each dict in the lambda function to add the prices.

Listing 5.4 shows a classic lambda function: we need to do something that's a bit nuanced, like getting the value of the price key of a `dict` and adding it to another value, but not something that we'll want to necessarily ever do again. Our lambda function is still very readable, and it would feel silly to create a whole function to get a value from a `dict` and add it to another value.

5.2.3 Initializers for complex start behavior in reduce

The last piece of the `reduce` puzzle is the initializer parameter. The initializer is the value that our `reduce` operation will use as the very first accumulated value. We can think of it as inserting that value at the head of our sequence and shifting all the other values to the right by 1 (figure 5.5).

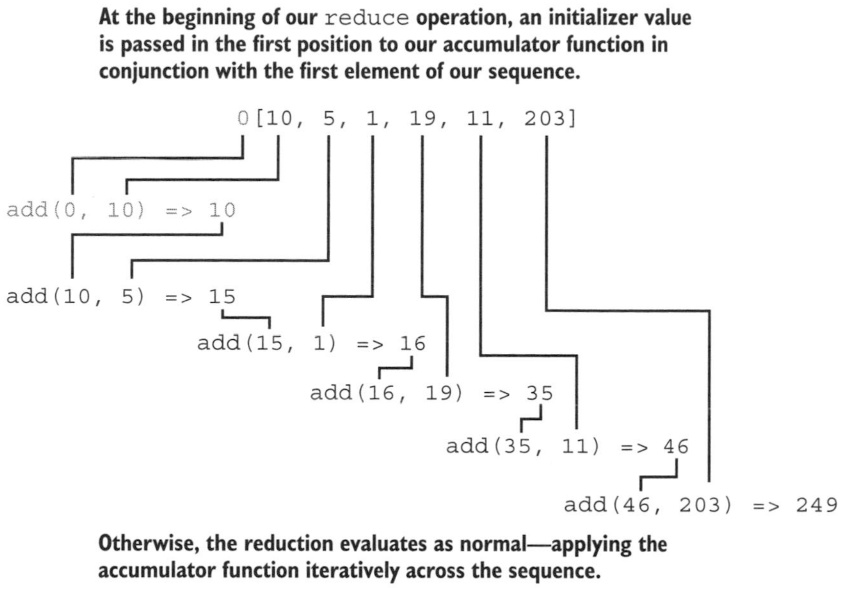
At the beginning of our reduce operation, an initializer value is passed in the first position to our accumulator function in conjunction with the first element of our sequence.
0 [10, 5, 1, 19, 11, 203]
add(0, 10) => 10
add(10, 5) => 15
add(15, 1) => 16
add(16, 19) => 35
add(35, 11) => 46
add(46, 203) => 249
Otherwise, the reduction evaluates as normal—applying the accumulator function iteratively across the sequence.

Figure 5.5 An initializer value shifts all the values to the right by 1, changing the start value of the `reduce` operation.

For our summation reduction, adding an initializer value of 10 would increase our entire `reduce` by 10. Instead of starting with the first value (the default) or with zero, we would start adding to 10. This might be useful if we wanted to add a $10 handling fee to all of the orders, for example.

Most often though, we'll want to use an initializer not when we want to change the *value* of our data but when we want to change the *type* of the data. By seeding our `reduce` with a value of a different type, our accumulator function can expect two different type parameters, even when we have a list in which all the values are of the same type. We can see this play out if we change the integer 0 in our summation reduction to a float 0, 0.0, as shown in the following listing.

Listing 5.5 Seeding a summation function with a float

```
from functools import reduce

xs = [10, 5, 1, 19, 11, 203]

print(reduce(lambda acc, nxt: acc+nxt, xs, 0.0))
```

Changing the last parameter from an integer (0) to a float (0.0) changes the output

Inserting a float into our summation reduction, as seen in listing 5.5, changes the eventual output type of our summation to a float. This happens because a float plus an integer always returns a float in Python. This effect cascades across our reduction because the accumulator function always has a float for its accumulator parameter (figure 5.6).

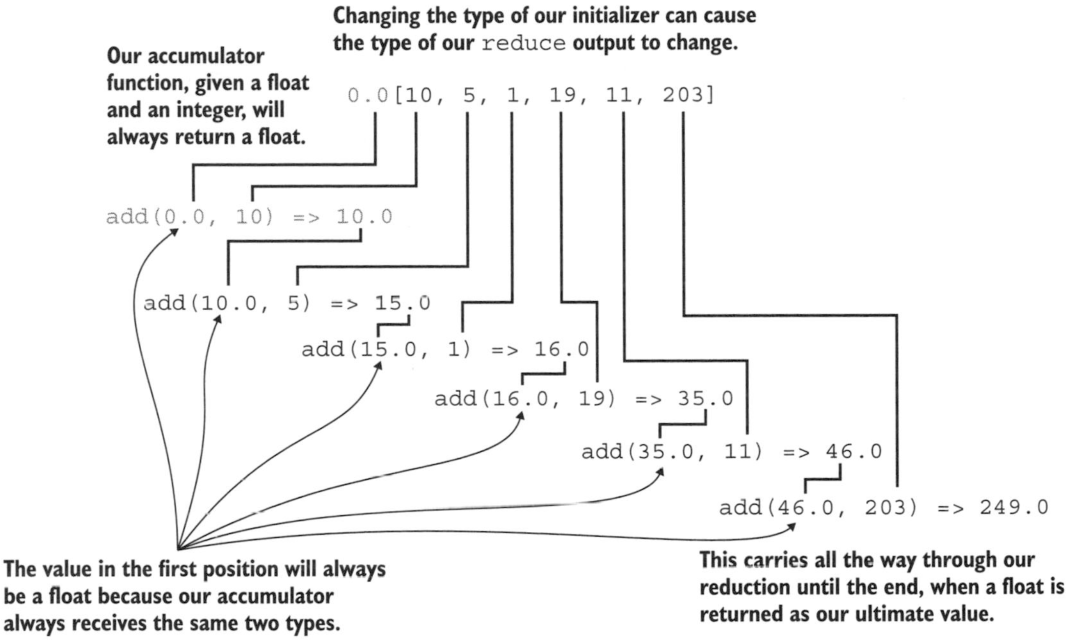

Changing the type of our initializer can cause the type of our reduce output to change.
Our accumulator function, given a float and an integer, will always return a float.
0.0[10, 5, 1, 19, 11, 203]
add(0.0, 10) => 10.0
add(10.0, 5) => 15.0
add(15.0, 1) => 16.0
add(16.0, 19) => 35.0
add(35.0, 11) => 46.0
add(46.0, 203) => 249.0
The value in the first position will always be a float because our accumulator always receives the same two types.
This carries all the way through our reduction until the end, when a float is returned as our ultimate value.

Figure 5.6 The type of the initializer often determines the behavior of our accumulator function.

This pattern, where we use the initializer to alter the type of our sequence, is going to be a common occurrence. We'll often want our accumulator to take and return a type that is different from the type of elements that are in our list. This represents a wider variety of transformations than we could achieve with just a single data type. We'll look at an example of that pattern shortly in section 5.3.2 and again later in this chapter.

5.3 Reductions you're familiar with

Having looked at the basics of reduce with the summation function, let's look at two more reductions that you've already seen in this book:

1 filter
2 frequencies

We explored both functions in chapter 4. The filter function returns a list of items that evaluate True for a given condition. The frequencies function returns a dict whose keys are the unique elements of a list and whose values are the counts of those items in the list.

5.3.1 Creating a filter with reduce

For our filter reduction, let's perform a filter operation that returns only even numbers. That way, we can compare this code to some of the examples we worked on in chapter 4. Before diving straight into the reduction, however, we should think about what this reduction is going to look like (figure 5.7).

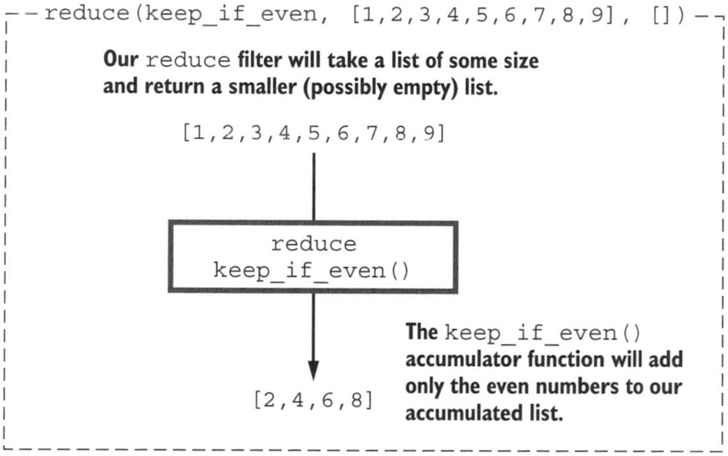
reduce(keep_if_even, [1,2,3,4,5,6,7,8,9], [])
Our reduce filter will take a list of some size and return a smaller (possibly empty) list.
[1,2,3,4,5,6,7,8,9]
reduce
keep_if_even()
The keep_if_even() accumulator function will add only the even numbers to our accumulated list.
[2,4,6,8]

Figure 5.7 The filter reduction is an N-to-X transformation from a list of some size to a list of some smaller or equal size.

The filter function starts with a sequence of some sort, so we know that it's a good candidate for reduction on that ground. Our output data in this instance is going to be a list of a length equal to or less than that of our previous sequence. For example, if we have a sequence where all the numbers are 2 (an even number), then our reduction should return the same sequence as a list. In contrast, if all the numbers are odd, our reduction should return an empty list.

Thinking this through gives us some sense of how our reduction needs to behave and how we need to set it up. We know we're going to need to be able to return an empty list in some cases, so it makes sense to initialize our reduction with an empty list. The rest of our reduction is going to depend on the accumulator function we design. Because we're attempting to filter down to just the even numbers, I'm going to call this function `keep_if_even`.

The `keep_if_even` function is going to need to take in two things:

1. An accumulated value (a list of even numbers)
2. The next value in our sequence

The function will also need to return either the original accumulated value, if the next value is not even, or the accumulated value plus the new value, if the next value is even. This function is implemented in the following listing.

Listing 5.6 An is it even? filter reduction

```
from functools import reduce

xs = [1, 2, 3, 4, 5, 6, 7, 8, 9]

def keep_if_even(acc, nxt):
    if nxt % 2 == 0:
        return acc + [nxt]
    else: return acc

print(reduce(keep_if_even, xs, []))
```

- Our accumulator function expects an accumulated value (a list) and the next item (a number).
- Checks if the next item is even
- If it is, we add it to our accumulator and return a new list.
- If it is not, we return the original accumulator.

Much of the code in listing 5.6 will be similar to code you've seen before, in either this chapter or chapter 4. One important thing to point out, however, is that we use the construction `acc + [nxt]` instead of `acc.append(nxt)`. We first used the `acc` and `nxt` parameter names in listing 5.2 of this chapter, with `acc` representing the accumulated value and `nxt` representing the next element in our sequence.

We don't use the `.append` method here because although `.append` is the preferred way of adding values to a list, our accumulator function will always need to return a value. By design, the `.append` method modifies the list in place and returns `None`. This forces us to use `acc + [nxt]`, which returns a new list.

You'll also note that this filter works as desired on the edge cases identified a few paragraphs ago. If we pass in a list of all 2s, we'll get the same-sized list back. If we pass in a list of all odd numbers (say, 3s), we'll get an empty list back.

5.3.2 Creating frequencies with reduce

The next type of reduction that we'll tackle is the frequency reduction. Frequency, which we saw in chapter 4 as `frequencies`, is a way of counting the elements of a sequence. Again, let's stop to think about the N-to-X transformation that's going on in this function. We'll start with a sequence (N), and we want to end up with a `dict` with some number of keys, each corresponding to a unique element in the sequence, and a value totaling their count within the sequence (figure 5.8).

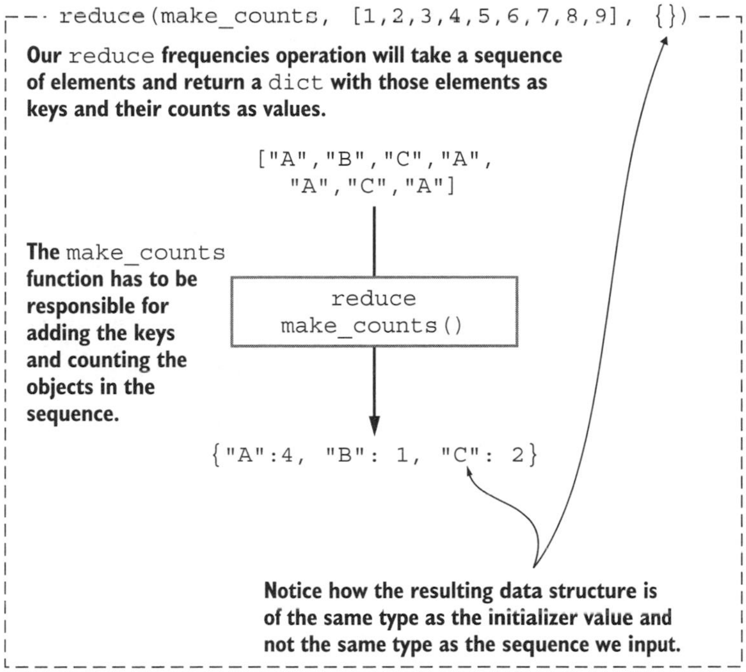
reduce(make_counts, [1,2,3,4,5,6,7,8,9], {})
Our reduce frequencies operation will take a sequence of elements and return a dict with those elements as keys and their counts as values.
["A","B","C","A", "A","C","A"]
The make_counts function has to be responsible for adding the keys and counting the objects in the sequence.
reduce
make_counts()
{"A":4, "B": 1, "C": 2}
Notice how the resulting data structure is of the same type as the initializer value and not the same type as the sequence we input.

Figure 5.8 Our frequency reduction transforms a list into a `dict` with keys for each unique element and values totaling their counts. We need to initialize with a `dict` because the accumulation function takes two parameters of different types.

The accumulator function for our frequency reduction will take a `dict` as an accumulated value and a miscellaneous element as our next value. It will have to return a `dict` as well so that, as we move through our sequence, we can ensure we always have a `dict` as our accumulated value. It also will have to count the element. To do this, we'll increment the value of that element as a key by 1. Also, this time, let's wrap our `reduce` operation in a function so we can reuse it.

Listing 5.7 provides the code for the accumulator and the reduction, along with test data and some print statements that demonstrate our function is working as desired. In those statements, we can see that our `frequencies` function can be used to count up sequences of all different types. We're able to do this because `reduce` doesn't care what type of objects we're iterating over and because our accumulation function doesn't rely on the objects in a sequence being of a specific type. We also see the importance of initializing our reduction with an empty dict so we can use the .get method from the start.

Listing 5.7 Finding frequencies using a reduction

```
from functools import reduce

def make_counts(acc, nxt):
    acc[nxt] = acc.get(nxt, 0) + 1
    return acc

def my_frequencies(xs):
    return reduce(make_counts, xs, {})

xs = ["A", "B", "C", "A", "A", "C", "A"]
ys = [1, 3, 6, 1, 2, 9, 3, 12]

print(my_frequencies(xs))
print(my_frequencies(ys))
print(my_frequencies("mississippi"))
```

Our make_counts function has the standard accumulator function parameters: acc and nxt.

For each element we come across, we increment the number of times we've seen that element by 1.

Returns the accumulated value at the end of the function

Our frequency reduction function will only need to take a sequence of some kind.

Our reduce statement uses the make_counts function we just made, as well as an empty dict as an initializer object.

5.4 Using map and reduce together

At this point, we've covered the basics of reduce. If you can decompose a problem into an N-to-X transformation, all that stands between you and a reduction that solves that problem is a well-crafted accumulation function. That said, I'd be remiss if we wrapped up our discussion of reduce without discussing how we can use it in conjunction with map in the eponymous map-reduce pattern.

So far, we've focused on situations where at least some of the data we want to end up with comes directly from our sequence.

1. In the sum reduction (listing 5.3), we needed the values in the list.
2. In the filter reduction (listing 5.6), we wanted to end up with the values that met a given condition.
3. In the frequency reduction (listing 5.7), we used the sequence elements as keys for our dict.

This is not always the case. Sometimes we don't want to work with the data in our sequence, only data that is somewhat related to our sequence. The classic example is that we have a sequence of file paths and want to open those files and do something with them. We saw that in chapter 4 in the poetry puzzle example. In that example, we had a bunch of files; however, it was the content of those files that was interesting to us, not the files themselves.

Another version of this problem could be a twist on the Scrabble exercise at the end of chapter 4. What if instead of filtering our list down to the words that met some point threshold, we summed all the points represented by the words in a list? In that example, the list may contain the words we've scored to date, and their sum would equal our total score. To find our total score, we want to convert the words to their scores (an N-to-N transformation) and then reduce those scores into a total score (an N-to-X transformation) (figure 5.9). Because this process represents both an N-to-N transformation and an N-to-X transformation, we can use both `map` and `reduce`: `map` to transform the words to scores and `reduce` to sum them up.

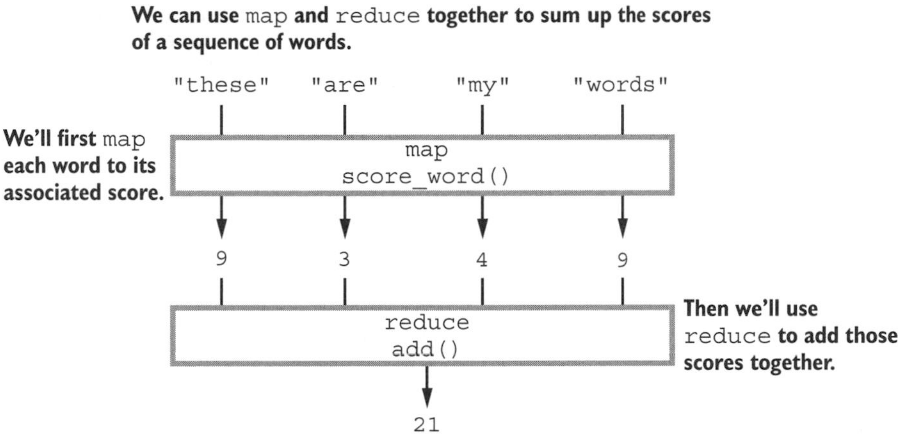
We can use map and reduce together to sum up the scores of a sequence of words.
"these"
"are"
"my"
"words"
We'll first map each word to its associated score.
map
score_word()
9
3
4
9
reduce
add()
Then we'll use reduce to add those scores together.
21

Figure 5.9 We can use the map and reduce pattern to transform words into scores and then calculate a sum of those scores.

To do this, we'll need to concoct two helper functions: one for `map` and one for `reduce`. If you completed exercise 4.6.5, you already have both of them on hand. (If you don't have them, you can either complete the exercise now or find the code in this book's source code repository at https://github.com/jtwool/mastering-large-datasets.) The helper function for `map` will need to take in a word and return a score. Just like in exercise 4.6.5, we'll use the simplified scoring scheme: Z is worth 10 points; F, H, V, and W are worth 5; B, C, M, and P are worth 3; and all other letters are worth 1 point. The helper function for `reduce` will be either the helper function from listing 5.2 or the lambda expression from listing 5.3—either will work.

With those two helper functions in place, to find our total score we `map` the scoring function across our words and `reduce` over the results of that `map`. We can see this entire process in the following listing.

Listing 5.8 Scoring words with `map` and `reduce`

```
from functools import reduce


def score_word(word):
    points = 0
    for char in word:
        if char == "z": points += 10
```

```
        elif char in ["f", "h", "v", "w"]: points += 5
        elif char in ["b", "c", "m", "p"]: points += 3
        else: points += 1
    return points


words = ["these", "are", "my", "words"]

total_score = reduce(lambda acc,nxt: acc+nxt,
                     map(score_word, words))
print(total_score)
```

This reduction is identical to the summation reduction we used at the beginning of the chapter, except instead of passing reduce a sequence of numbers, we pass it the result of our map operation.

The power of map and reduce is in the simplicity of its execution. When we actually go to execute our `reduce` and `map` statements, we do so in a single line of code, though this one line implements complex behavior through the invoked helper functions. We can use the map and reduce pattern to decouple the transformation logic—the things we want to do to our data—from the actual transformation itself. This permits simplicity and leads to highly reusable code. When working with large datasets, keeping our functions simple becomes paramount because we may have to wait a long time to discover we made a small error.

5.5 Analyzing car trends with reduce

Before we move on from chapter 5 and start looking at `reduce` in parallel, let's try our hand at a more complex reduction scenario.

> **SCENARIO** Your customer is a used car dealer. They have data on cars that they've bought and sold in the last six months and are hoping you can help them find what type of used cars they make the most profit on. One salesman believes that highly fuel-efficient cars (those that get more than 35 miles per gallon (mpg)) make the most money, while another believes that medium-mileage cars (with odometers at 60,000 to 100,000 miles) result in the highest average profit on resale. Given a CSV file with a variety of attributes about some used cars, write a script to find the average profit on cars of low (<18 mpg), medium (18–35 mpg), and high (>35 mpg) fuel efficiency, as well as low (<60,000 miles), medium (60,000–100,000 miles), and high mileage (>100,000 miles), to settle the debate.

Before we dig into the details of the problem, let's take a look at its fundamentals: the data transformations. We'll start with a series of `dicts`, each of which represents a vehicle. By default, these `dicts` will have a lot of information we're not interested in and won't have some of the information we do want, so it'll be a good idea to transform the data into a better format for analysis. We'll tackle that with a `map` because we want to clean up each `dict`. From there, we want to roll that data up into a `dict` that can help us understand the profit that each type of car produces. This will require a reduction.

Overall, the whole problem will look something like figure 5.10. On the left, we start with the data our customer hands us. We'll concoct a function to clean up each record and `map` that across our data. Then, we'll pass that into `reduce`, which itself has an accumulator function we've designed to collect the necessary information. For this, we'll want to gather both sum and count by group—the two figures necessary to calculate an average.

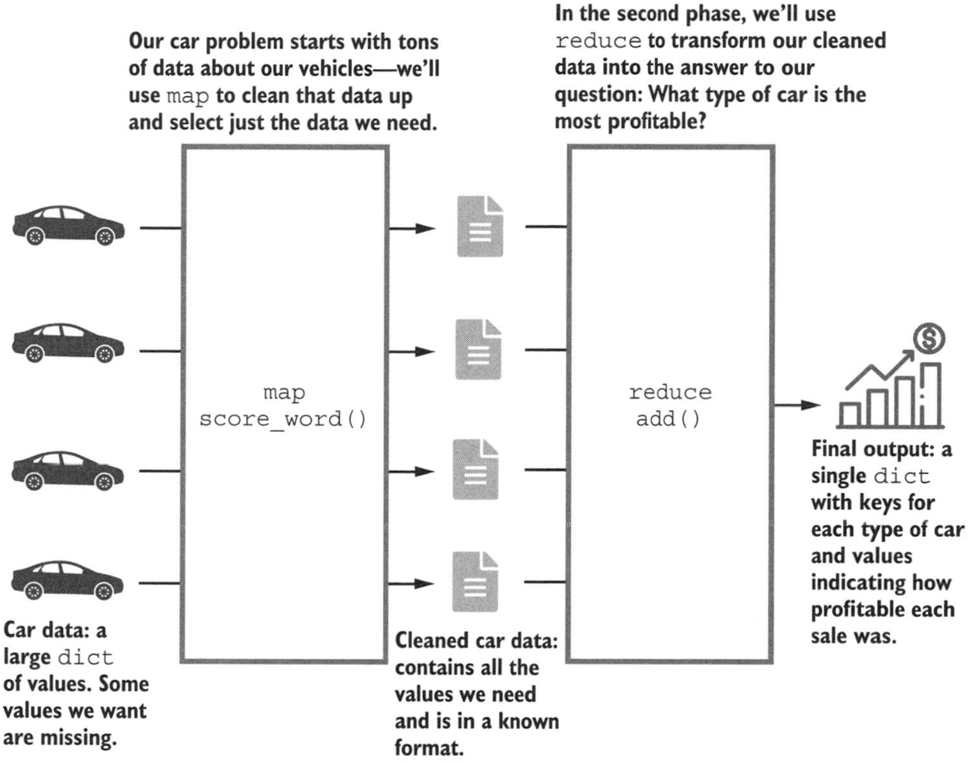
In the second phase, we'll use reduce to transform our cleaned data into the answer to our question: What type of car is the most profitable?
Our car problem starts with tons of data about our vehicles—we'll use map to clean that data up and select just the data we need.
map
score_word()
reduce
add()
Final output: a single dict with keys for each type of car and values indicating how profitable each sale was.
Car data: a large dict of values. Some values we want are missing.
Cleaned car data: contains all the values we need and is in a known format.

Figure 5.10 We can solve our car data analysis task using a `map` step that cleans up car data and a `reduce` step that accumulates the data into one data structure that answers our question.

5.5.1 *Using map to clean our car data*

To design our cleaning helper function, let's first take a closer look at the individual elements with which we'll be working. Each car in our dataset is going to look something like figure 5.11.

For each entry, we'll have a `dict` with lots of attributes we're not particularly interested in, along with the four that we are interested in: `price-buy`, `price-sell`, `mpg`, and `odo`. These four keys in our `dict` represent the price the car was bought at, the price the car was sold at, the manufacturer-listed miles per gallon of the vehicle, and

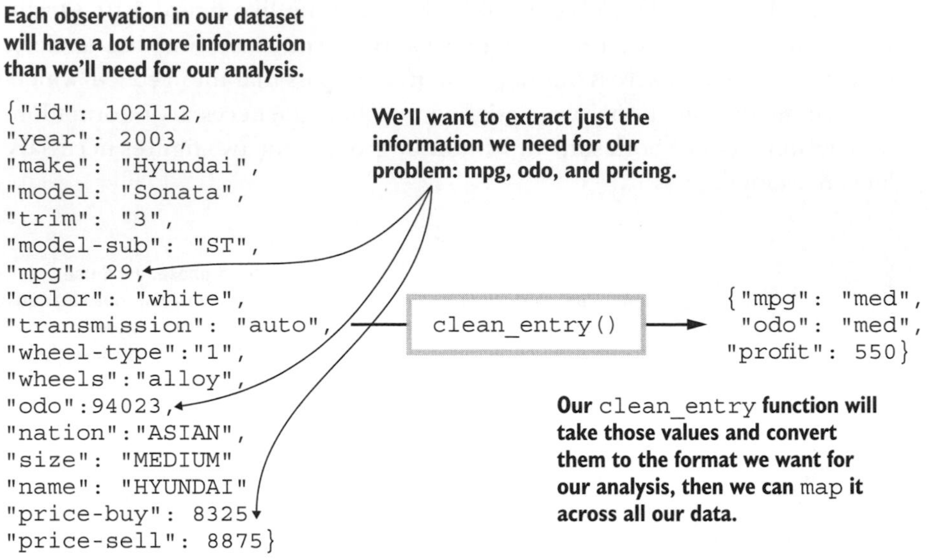
Each observation in our dataset will have a lot more information than we'll need for our analysis.
{"id": 102112,
"year": 2003,
"make": "Hyundai",
"model: "Sonata",
"trim": "3",
"model-sub": "ST",
"mpg": 29,
"color": "white",
"transmission": "auto",
"wheel-type":"1",
"wheels":"alloy",
"odo":94023,
"nation":"ASIAN",
"size": "MEDIUM"
"name": "HYUNDAI"
"price-buy": 8325
"price-sell": 8875}
We'll want to extract just the information we need for our problem: mpg, odo, and pricing.
clean_entry()
{"mpg": "med",
"odo": "med",
"profit": 550}
Our clean_entry function will take those values and convert them to the format we want for our analysis, then we can map it across all our data.

Figure 5.11 Each car in our dataset will have many attributes, only four of which we really care about: price-buy, price-sell, mpg, and odo. We'll use `map` plus a helper function to transform those numerical variables into categorical variables for easier comparison.

the number of miles on the car. However, we're not actually interested in the values of any of these variables directly. Rather, we're interested in values that we can calculate from them.

- Instead of price bought and sold, we're interested in total profit.
- Instead of absolute miles per gallon, we're interested in low, medium, and high mpg.
- Instead of absolute number of miles, we're interested in low, medium, and high mileage.

To that end, to clean each data entry, we'll want to do three things:

1. Calculate profit on the vehicle from price bought and sold
2. Sort the vehicle into low, medium, and high mpg
3. Sort the vehicle into low, medium, and high mileage

To do this, we'll create three separate functions that each handle a piece of the problem and wrap them in a single function we can map across all our data. Let's design each of these three helper functions now, starting with calculating profit.

The profit calculation function is only a small change from a basic operation: arithmetic. In other conditions, this might be a good case for a lambda function; however, because we're planning on using this function inside another function, we'll want to give it a name. Our `get_profit` function will find the difference between the price the car was sold at and the price the car was bought at. We can see it in the following listing.

Listing 5.9 Lambda function for calculating price differences

```
def get_profit(d):
    return d.get("price-sell",0) - d.get("price-buy",0)
```

One thing to note about listing 5.9 is that we use the .get method of the dict instead of the [<key>] syntax because with get we can provide a default value. We do this to preempt the errors that a missing value would throw (though there are no missing values in the data you've been provided).

Next up, we have two helper functions that provide similar functionality: one that buckets mpg into three categories—low, medium, and high—and one that buckets mileage into three categories—low, medium, and high. Because these functions are so similar, let's work on them at the same time.

Both of these functions share a common behavior: comparing a value to a series of break points and then assigning them to either low, medium, or high. We can write a general function that takes a dict, a key, and two break points and returns low when the value of the dict at the key specified is below the first break point, medium when it's below the second, and high when it's above both. That function will look like the code in the following listing.

Listing 5.10 A generic low-medium-high function

```
def low_med_hi(d, k, low, high):
    if d[k] < low:
        return "low"
    elif d[k] < high:
        return "med"
     return "high"
```

- If the value of the dict at the key of interest is below our first break, we return low.
- If that value is below the second break, we return medium.
- If it's not lower than either break, we return high.

With this function written, we can start to assemble all of the pieces together. We'll want to do three things:

1. Take in a dict
2. Clean the dict with our select_keys function
3. Return a dict that has three keys
   - a. A profit key indicating the profit made on the vehicle
   - b. An mpg key indicating the vehicle's mpg category
   - c. An odo key indicating the vehicle's mileage

A wrapper function for that process may look like the following listing.

Listing 5.11 Wrapping our car helpers into a single function

```
def clean_entry(d):
    r = {}
    r['profit'] = get_profit(d)
    r['mpg'] = low_med_hi(d,'mpg',(18,35))
    r['odo'] = low_med_hi(d,'odo',(60000,100000))
    return r
```

Initializes a new dict for our output data

Uses our profit function to get the profit

Uses the low-medium-high function twice to get our mpg and odo categories

Each use takes different parameters corresponding to the specifics of those variables.

5.5.2 Using reduce for sums and counts

With our map wrapper function written, it's time to move on to our reduction (figure 5.12). Knowing what our map will begin returning, we can use reduce to convert those items into our desired output data. What we want is a dict with six keys: one each for high, medium, and low mpg and one each for high, medium, and low mileage. The values of each of these keys should contain the average profit on vehicles of that type. Because we'll need the total profit and the total number of cars sold to calculate average profit, we'll keep track of those values as well. For readability, it makes sense to throw those values into a dict too. This will leave us with a dict with six keys—one for each of the categories, each of which points to another dict with three keys: one for average profit and two for the values necessary to calculate the average profit.

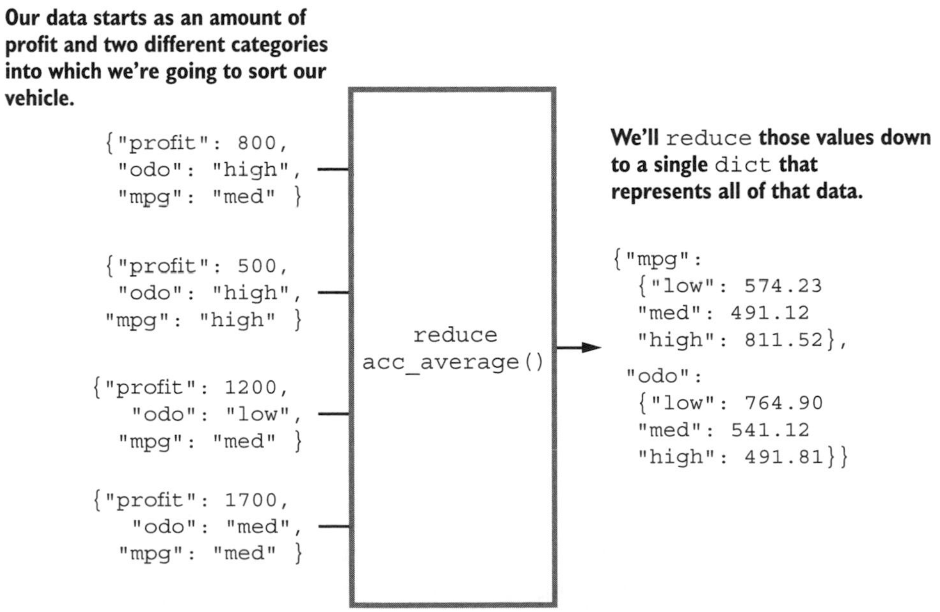
Our data starts as an amount of profit and two different categories into which we're going to sort our vehicle.
{"profit": 800, "odo": "high", "mpg": "med" }
{"profit": 500, "odo": "high", "mpg": "high" }
{"profit": 1200, "odo": "low", "mpg": "med" }
{"profit": 1700, "odo": "med", "mpg": "med" }
reduce
acc_average()
We'll reduce those values down to a single dict that represents all of that data.
{"mpg": {"low": 574.23 "med": 491.12 "high": 811.52},
"odo": {"low": 764.90 "med": 541.12 "high": 491.81}}

Figure 5.12 We'll reduce over the profit and vehicle category data to produce a single dict that contains the total, count, and average for each category.

To do this, our accumulator function will roll the profit of each observation of our dataset into keys of our accumulated value: one based on its mileage category and one based on its mpg category. Because calculating the total profit, count, and average is a little involved—more than we can accomplish with a single expression—let's wrap this behavior in a helper function. That helper function will take the accumulated total, count, and average of the category of car and mix in the profit for the new car, while also incrementing the count and calculating a new average. We can see these two functions together in the following listing.

Listing 5.12 Profit average accumulator and helper function

```
def acc_average(acc, profit):                        <-- Defines a helper function that calculates averages
    acc['total'] = acc.get('total',0) + profit       <-- Uses the .get method in case we find an empty dict
    acc['count'] = acc.get('count',0) + 1
    acc['average'] = acc['total']/acc['count']       <-- Our average value will be the profit divided by the count.
    return acc

def sort_and_add(acc, nxt):                          <-- Again, our accumulator function will take an acc and a nxt.
    profit = nxt['profit']                           <-- Because we'll use profit twice, we'll store it in a variable for easy access.
    nxt_mpg = acc['mpg'].get(nxt['mpg'],{})
    nxt_odo = acc['odo'].get(nxt['odo'],{})
    acc['mpg'][nxt['mpg']] = acc_average(nxt_mpg,
                                         profit)     <-- We'll modify the accumulated value for each of the two categories in which the car belongs.
    acc['odo'][nxt['odo']] = acc_average(nxt_odo,, profit)
    return acc
```

Again, in listing 5.12, as occurred several times previously in this chapter, we're using the dict .get method to access the key of a dict and provide a default value. In each of these cases, we want to have a default value that provides the expected type of data to the function using the resulting data. In our `acc_average` function, we use `get` because our addition operation needs a number. In this case, we specify the integer 0 if we don't have the key in question. In our `sort_and_add` accumulator function, we specify an empty `dict` because our `acc_average` function expects a `dict` in its first position. Because we use the `.get` method in both places, we can go from having no data to having a fully populated data structure without making any assumptions about what categories are in the underlying data. This is the same trick we used in our `frequencies` reduction example, just on a bigger scale.

5.5.3 Applying the map and reduce pattern to cars data

With all of our helper functions written, including the data transformation for `map` and the accumulator for `reduce`, we're ready to process our data. One of the great things about using a map and reduce style is that this takes only a single line of code:

```
reduce(sort_and_add, map(clean_entry, cars_data), {})
```

We use map to apply the clean_entry function to each entry in our cars data, resulting in a cleaned sequence of data that is ready for us to reduce through. Then we call reduce with its three parameters: the accumulator function, the data, and an optional initializer. For the accumulator function, we use the accumulator we designed: sort_and_add. For the data, we use the results from our map operation. For the initializer, we use an empty dict.

Altogether, our code will look like the following listing. Run the code and settle the debate between the two car salesmen: Which car category makes the most profit?

Listing 5.13 Map and reduce to find average used car profit

```
from functools import reduce

def low_med_hi(d,k,breaks):
    if float(d[k]) < breaks[0]:
        return "low"
    elif float(d[k]) < breaks[1]:
        return "medium"
    else:
        return "high"

def clean_entry(d):
    r = {'profit':None, 'mpg':None, 'odo':None}
    r['profit'] = float(d.get("price-sell",0)) - float(d.get("price-buy",0))
    r['mpg'] = low_med_hi(d,'mpg',(18,35))
    r['odo'] = low_med_hi(d,'odo',(60000,100000))
    return r

def acc_average(acc, profit):
    acc['total'] = acc.get('total',0) + profit
    acc['count'] = acc.get('count',0) + 1
    acc['average'] = acc['total']/acc['count']
    return acc

def sort_and_add(acc,nxt):
    p = nxt['profit']
    acc['mpg'][nxt['mpg']] = acc_average(acc['mpg'].get(nxt['mpg'],{}), p)
    acc['odo'][nxt['odo']] = acc_average(acc['odo'].get(nxt['odo'],{}), p)
    return acc

if __name__ == "__main__":
    import json
    with open("cars.json") as f:
        xs = json.load(f)
    results = reduce(sort_and_add, map(clean_entry, xs), {"mpg":{},"odo":{}})
    print(json.dumps(results, indent=4))
```

5.6 Speeding up map and reduce

Looking back on the exercise from section 5.5, we can see that we didn't do anything to make our map and reduce operation any faster. From the techniques we've covered so far in this book, we might think about using a parallel map from chapter 2 to speed up this process. Unfortunately, using a parallel map will counterintuitively make our work slower—not faster.

A parallel `map` will slow down our map and reduce workflow because it will force us to iterate over the dataset twice, incurring the associated costs of storing and retrieving data from memory. This happens because `map`, as we've mentioned before, is naturally lazy. It stores instructions; it doesn't evaluate. That means that we don't evaluate our lazy `map` until we're in the `reduce` loop. Our parallel `map`, on the other hand, is eager: it evaluates immediately. This means that by the time we're reducing, we've already looped through our data once (figure 5.13).

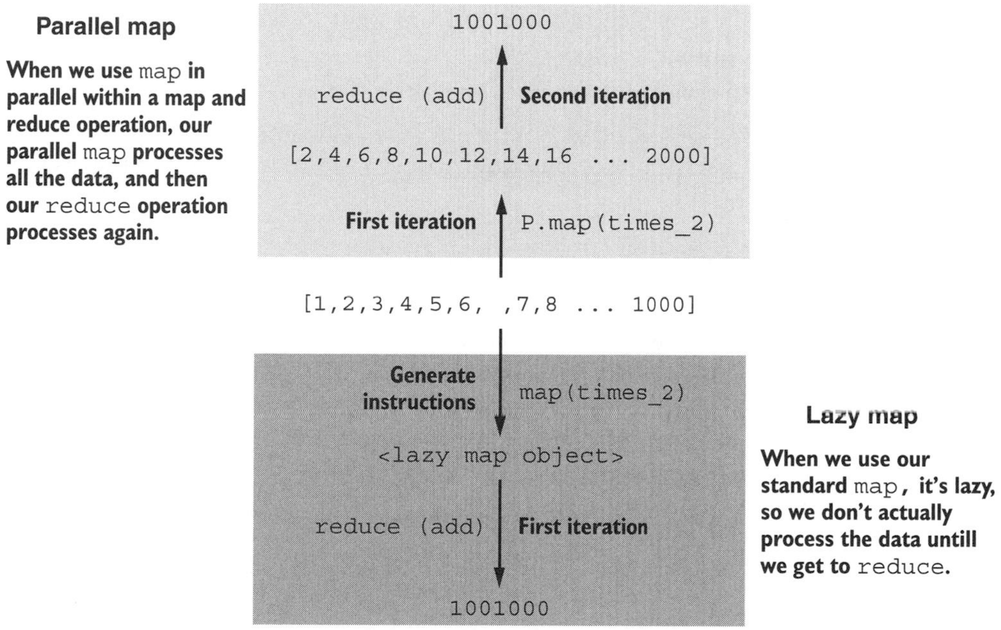
Parallel map
When we use map in parallel within a map and reduce operation, our parallel map processes all the data, and then our reduce operation processes again.
1001000
reduce (add)
Second iteration
[2,4,6,8,10,12,14,16 ... 2000]
First iteration
P.map(times_2)
[1,2,3,4,5,6, ,7,8 ... 1000]
Generate instructions
map(times_2)
<lazy map object>
reduce (add)
First iteration
1001000
Lazy map
When we use our standard map, it's lazy, so we don't actually process the data untill we get to reduce.

Figure 5.13 Using a parallel `map` can counterintuitively be slower than using a lazy `map` in map and reduce scenarios—we'll want to choose the right combination of map and reduce for the best performance.

That we're prevented from using parallelization here is a pretty undesirable side effect. After all, one of the big reasons we're exploring these techniques is that they're supposed to be good for big datasets. If we can't use parallelization, we can't scale our processing with our data and we'll ultimately be limited in the size of data we can use. Fortunately for us, we can always use parallelization at the `reduce` level instead of at the `map` level. We'll take a look at that in the next chapter, on parallel `reduce`.

5.7 Exercises

These exercises test your knowledge of `reduce` and accumulator functions and reinforce the material in this chapter.

5.7.1 Situations to use reduce

The `reduce` function is a powerful and flexible tool. In which of the following situations would you use `reduce`, and in which should you use another tool we've covered in this book?

- You have a long sequence of words and you return only a sequence containing the letter *A*.
- You have a sequence of users and you want to transform them into just their User ID number.
- You have a series of users and you want to find the five who have purchased the most from you.
- You have a sequence of purchase orders and you want to find the average price of a purchase.

5.7.2 Lambda functions

We can use lambda functions for simple functions that we are only planning on using once; however, there is no difference at bytecode level between these functions and normal Python functions. Replicate the following functions with lambda functions.

```
def my_addition(a, b):
    return a+b

def is_odd(a):
     return a % 2 == 1

def contains(a, b):
    return b in a

def reverse(s):
     return s[::-1]
```

5.7.3 Largest numbers

In Python, we can use the `max` function to find the maximum value in a sequence and the `min` function to find the minimum value in a sequence. However, sometimes we don't want just the largest or smallest value, we want the largest or smallest several values. Use `reduce` to write a function that gets the five largest (or smallest) values from a sequence.

Once you have it written, try extending the function to collect the largest (or smallest) N values.

EXAMPLE

```
five_largest([10,7,3,1,9,8,11,21,15,72])
>>> [72,21,15,11,10]

n_largest([10,7,3,1,9,8,11,21,15,72], n=3)
>>> [72,21,15]
```

5.7.4 Group words by length

Group by is a useful reduction where we take the elements of a sequence and group them based on the results of some function applied to them. Use `reduce` to write a version of this function that can group words based on their length.

EXAMPLE

```
group_words(["these", "are", "some", "words", "for", "grouping"])
>>> {3: ["are","for"],
     4: ["some"],
     5: ["these","words"],
     8: ["grouping"]}
```

Summary

- The `reduce` function accumulates a sequence of data (N) into something else (X), with the help of an accumulator function and an initializer.
- Accumulator functions take two variables: one for the accumulated data (often designated as `acc`, `left`, or `a`), and one for the next element in the sequence (designated `nxt`, `right`, or `b`).
- `reduce` is useful in situations where you have a sequence of data and want something other than a sequence back.
- `reduce`'s behavior is heavily customizable based on the accumulator function we pass to it.
- Anonymous lambda functions can be useful when our accumulation function is concise, clear, and unlikely to be reused.
- We can use `map` and `reduce` together to break complex transformations up into small contingent parts.
- `map`, counterintuitively, provides better performance than parallel `map` when we're using both `map` and `reduce`.

6 Speeding up map and reduce with advanced parallelization

This chapter covers

- Advanced parallelization with `map` and `starmap`
- Writing parallel `reduce` and `map reduce` patterns
- Accumulation and combination functions

We ended chapter 5 with a paradoxical situation: using a parallel method and more compute resources was slower than a linear approach with fewer compute resources. Intuitively, we know this is wrong. If we're using more resources, we should at the very least be as fast as our low-resource effort—hopefully we're faster. We never want to be slower.

In this chapter, we'll take a look at how to get the most out of parallelization in two ways:

1. By optimizing our use of parallel `map`
2. By using a parallel `reduce`

Parallel `map`, which I introduced in section 2.2, is a great technique for transforming a large amount of data quickly. However, we did gloss over some nuances when we were learning the basics. We'll dig into those nuances in this chapter. Parallel `reduce` is parallelization that occurs at the `reduce` step of our map and reduce pattern.

That is, we've already called `map`, and now we're ready to accumulate the results of all those transformations. With parallel `reduce`, we use parallelization in the accumulation process instead of the transformation process.

6.1 Getting the most out of parallel map

Back in chapter 2, when we introduced parallel `map`, we covered a few of its shortfalls:

- Python's parallel `map` uses pickling, a method of saving Python objects to the disk, to share work; this causes problems when working with some data types.
- Parallel `map` sometimes can result in unintended consequences when we're working with stateful objects, such as classes.
- The results of a parallel `map` operation are not always evaluated in the order that we would expect.

Ultimately, however, we concluded that there were more situations in which we could live with those constraints than those in which we couldn't. Indeed, up until chapter 5, we hadn't seen a scenario where we needed to worry about parallel `map`. And then we came across the first of two situations where parallel `map` is slower than the lazy `map`. Parallel `map` will be slower than lazy `map` when

1. we're going to iterate through the sequence a second time later in our workflow
2. the size of the work done in each parallel instance is small compared to the overhead that parallelization imposes

In the first situation, when we're going to iterate through the sequence a second time—that is, we're going to `map` over a sequence and then do something later with all of its elements—using lazy `map` allows us to sidestep the first iteration. Instead of iterating through our sequence to transform all the elements, with lazy `map` we can perform the transformations in what would have been the second iteration. We visualized this in figure 5.13, shown again in figure 6.1.

Figure 6.1 shows how the lazy `map` outputs a lazy `map` object, no iteration involved, whereas the parallel `map` iterates through the entire sequence. We'll look at solving this problem using parallel `reduce` in section 6.2.

6.1.1 Chunk sizes and getting the most out of parallel map

The second situation—when the sequence is split into a large number of chunks whose overhead is large compared to the amount of work being done on those chunks—is one we haven't encountered yet. In these instances, parallel `map` will be slower than lazy because we're adding overhead to the task.

If we imagine our programs as a software project, we can imagine parallelization as the contractor. The contractor wants to get the job done with as few workers as possible because every new worker added requires the contractor to explain the task to them (which costs time) and pay them (which costs money). Around the margins, this might not matter. But if the contractor has workers sitting around not doing

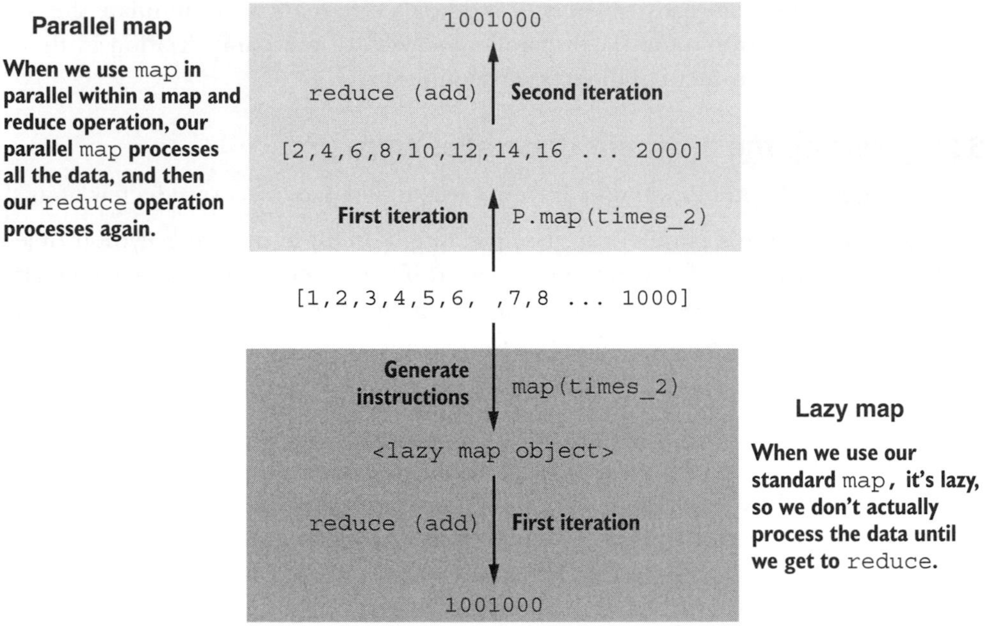
Parallel map
When we use map in parallel within a map and reduce operation, our parallel map processes all the data, and then our reduce operation processes again.
1001000
reduce (add)
Second iteration
[2,4,6,8,10,12,14,16 ... 2000]
First iteration
P.map(times_2)
[1,2,3,4,5,6, ,7,8 ... 1000]
Generate instructions
map(times_2)
<lazy map object>
reduce (add)
First iteration
1001000
Lazy map
When we use our standard map, it's lazy, so we don't actually process the data until we get to reduce.

Figure 6.1 Lazy `map` can be faster than parallel `map` when we'll follow up our `map` statement by iterating over the results.

work but getting paid, or they're spending so much time explaining the project to new workers that they can't oversee it, the contractor would be better off with a smaller team.

The same is true for our parallel processing. For example, imagine we have 100 seconds of work to do, and each time we add a new parallel worker, we need to spend 1 second communicating with that worker. If we have

- 2 workers working 50 seconds each, we can get the job done in 52 seconds
- 4 workers working 25 seconds each, we can get the job done in 29 seconds
- 25 workers working 4 seconds each, we'll complete the task in 29 seconds
- 100 workers working 1 second each, we'll take 101 seconds

After a point, the amount of work being done is too small to justify the cost of communicating it. We need to ensure that when we assign work to our parallel jobs, we're assigning enough work that the processors spend a large enough amount of time doing the work to justify taking the time to communicate it to them. The way we do that is by specifying a *chunk size*.

Chunk size refers to the size of the different pieces into which we break our tasks for parallel processing. Larger chunk size tasks will require the processors to spend more time working on them, whereas smaller chunk size tasks will be finished more quickly.

NOTE It's ideal to pick a chunk size that's large—we'll learn how to pick the right size later in this chapter—but that still allows all the processors to finish their final task at approximately the same time. If we choose a chunk size that's too small, we end up in the situation described at the beginning of the chapter: communicating the instructions takes longer than processing our jobs. If we choose a chunk size that's too large, we'll end up in a position where only one processor is working the final chunk, while the others are waiting.

We can intuitively understand these limit behaviors by thinking about their extremes. If we ask each of our processors to handle only a single element at a time, we then have to

- transfer that element and the instructions for processing it,
- process it,
- and transfer that element back.

Then we have to repeat those steps for every single element. Assuming a reasonable-sized task, this is certainly more work than just processing each element one-by-one. In linear processing, we don't have the added communication steps we have in parallel processing.

For the large chunk size problem, it helps to first think about an infinitely large chunk size. Well, that's the same as using just a single processor, because we'll only have one chunk. If our chunk size is half the size of our sequence, we'll only be using two processors. If it's a third of our sequence, we'll only use three. It may seem like this might not be a problem, especially if we have a computer with only a few processors, but think about what happens when our second processor gets all the easy work and the first processor gets all the hard work. Our first processor will continue to work long after the second processor has stopped.

The optimal chunk size is somewhere in between these two extremes. Unfortunately, beyond this general notion that chunking too small and chunking too large are bad, giving advice about specific chunk sizes is hard. The very reason why Python makes `chunksize` available as an option is because we'll want to vary it according to the task at hand. I recommend starting with the default value, then increasing your chunk size until you see runtime start to decrease.

6.1.2 Parallel map runtime with variable sequence and chunk size

Now that we know more about chunk size and differences in the behavior of parallel `map` and lazy `map`, let's look at some code. We'll start by seeing how lazy and parallel `map` behave over different-sized sequences, and how, for simple operations on small data, there's really no benefit to parallelization. Then we'll test out parallel `map` with a few different chunk sizes and see how that impacts our performance.

SEQUENCE SIZE AND PARALLEL MAP RUNTIME

What's the optimal size at which we should start thinking about parallelization? Well, a lot of that depends on how complex our task is.

> **TIP** When our tasks are complex, we benefit quickly from parallelization. When our tasks are simple, we benefit only when there's a large amount of data.

Consider the example at the end of chapter 2 when we were scraping data from the web and there was web-related latency with every request. In these situations, parallelization is almost always going to make sense.

But what about when our tasks are small, such as doing arithmetic or calling methods of Python data types? Here, the situation is murky and depends on the size of the sequence. We can prove this to ourselves if we run a lazy `map` and a parallel `map`. The following listing shows how this can be done, using a `times_two` function as a simple operation and comparing parallel `map` and lazy `map` on sequences with between 1 and 1 million elements.

Listing 6.1 Comparing parallel `map` and lazy `map` on different-sized sequences

```
from time import clock
from multiprocessing import Pool

def times_two(x):
  return x*2

def lazy_map(xs):
  return list(map(times_two, xs))

def parallel_map(xs, chunk=8500):
  with Pool(2) as P:
    x =  P.map(times_two, xs, chunk)
  return x

for i in range(0,7):
  N = 10**i
  t1 = clock()
  lazy_map(range(N))
  lm_time = clock() - t1

  t1 = clock()
  parallel_map(range(N))
  par_time = clock() - t1
  print("""
-- N = {} --
Lazy map time:      {}
Parallel map time:  {}
""".format(N,lm_time, par_time))
```

In the output of that code, we can see a pattern appear.

```
-- N = 100 --
Lazy map time:      6.0999999999991616e-05
Parallel map time:  0.007081000000000004
```

```
-- N = 1000 --
Lazy map time:       0.00035899999999999982
Parallel map time:   0.007041999999999993

-- N = 100000 --
Lazy map time:       0.03779999999999986
Parallel map time:   0.019601000000000007
```

For small sequence sizes or processes that complete quickly, not only is it not beneficial to use parallel `map`, it's counterproductive. Lazy `map` is actually faster. However, when we start to notice that our code is taking a while to run—when we start facing delays of seconds or minutes—using parallel map is faster.

CHUNK SIZE AND PARALLEL MAP RUNTIME

We can run the same experiment with chunk size as well. For this experiment, instead of varying the size of the sequence, we'll hold the sequence constant and only vary the size of the chunks our parallelization approach uses. We'll have to use a large enough sequence that we'll see some variation, but not so long that we'll be waiting forever for our results. Based on our previous experiment, about 10 million will do. The code for this experiment appears in the following listing.

Listing 6.2 Comparing the effect of chunk size on parallel `map` runtime

```
from time import clock
from multiprocessing import Pool

def times_two(x):
  return x*2+7

def parallel_map(xs, chunk=8500):
  with Pool(2) as P:
    x =  P.map(times_two, xs, chunk)
  return x

print("""
{:<10}  |  {}
-------------------------""".format("chunksize","runtime"))

for i in range(0,9):
  N = 10000000
  chunk_size = 5 * (10**i)

  t1 = clock()
  parallel_map(range(N), chunk_size)
  parallel_time = clock() - t1

  print("""{:<10}  |   {:>0.3f}""".format(chunk_size, par_time))
```

The results of this code appear in the following output snippet. We can see that for small chunk sizes, our runtime is high. This is because the amount of time spent on communicating between all the workers is high, relative to the performance gained.

By splitting the problem up into too many pieces, we make it inefficient. With too large of a chunk size, though, we get the reverse problem: we're not using enough workers to solve the problem efficiently. Most of the sizes in the middle, however, give us reasonably good performance when compared to the two extremes.

```
chunksize    |  runtime
-------------------------
5            4.849
50           0.753
500          0.192
5000         0.188
50000        0.195
500000       0.146
5000000      0.167
50000000     0.171
500000000    0.168
```

6.1.3 More parallel maps: .imap and starmap

We should be familiar with two more types of parallel maps in Python:

1. `.imap` for lazy(ish) parallel mapping
2. `starmap` for parallel mapping over sequences of `tuples`

We can use the `.imap` method to work in parallel on very large sequences efficiently and `starmap` to work with complex iterables, especially those we're likely to create using the `zip` function.

Using .imap and .imap_unordered for large sequences

We discussed the benefits to laziness in chapter 4, and when working in parallel there's no reason we have to give them up. If we want to be lazy and parallel, we can use the `.imap` and `.imap_unordered` methods of `Pool()`. These methods both return iterators instead of lists, as shown in the following listing. Other than that, `.imap` behaves just like parallel `map`.

Listing 6.3 Variations of parallel `map`

```
from multiprocessing import Pool

def increase(x):
  return x+1

with Pool() as P:
  a = P.map(increase, range(100))

with Pool() as P:
  b = P.imap(increase, range(100))

with Pool() as P:
  c = P.imap_unordered(increase, range(100))

print(a)                    <-- Our standard parallel map returns a list.
# [1, 2, 3, ... 100]
```

```
print(b)
# <multiprocessing.pool.IMapIterator object at
➥ 0x7f53207b3be0>
print(c)
# <multiprocessing.pool.IMapUnorderedIterator object at
➥ 0x7fbe36ed2828>
```

Both lazy parallel maps return iterator objects.

`.imap_unordered` behaves the same, except it doesn't necessarily put the sequence in the right order for our iterator. That's why it's called unordered: the values are placed in the iterator in the exact order our processor processes them. When we're dealing with big datasets, the laziness of these two methods can mean a big decrease in runtime for our programs.

USING STARMAP FOR WORKING WITH ZIP IN PARALLEL

We've seen how useful `map` can be for transforming data and how we can use it in parallel to speed up operations on large datasets; however, `map` has a disappointing shortcoming: it can only be used on functions that take a single parameter. Sometimes, this isn't enough. We'll want to use functions that take two or more parameters. We can use `starmap` in those situations to get the same benefits.

The `starmap` function unpacks `tuples` as positional parameters to the function with which we're mapping, and we can use it as a lazy function (from `itertools.starmap`) or a parallel function (as a method of a `Pool()` object, typically `P.starmap`). If we `zip` two sequences together, as we learned how to do in chapter 4, then we've got an iterable primed and ready to go for use with `starmap`.

For example, we might want to find the largest element at each position in two sequences. Instead of looping through the sequences and comparing them, we could `zip` the sequences together and `map` over them. Listing 6.4 shows a comparison between these two methods. In the first, we use a list comprehension and an enumerate to compare the elements in the same places. In the second, with `starmap`, we `zip` together our parameters and then `map` the relevant function across them.

Listing 6.4 Using `starmap` to use `map` with multiple variables

```
from itertools import starmap
xs = [7, 3, 1, 19, 11]
ys = [8, 1, -3, 14, 22]

loop_maxes = [max(ys[i], x) for i,x in enumerate(xs)]
map_maxes = list(starmap(max, zip(xs, ys)))

print(loop_maxes)
# [8, 3, 1, 19, 22]
print(map_maxes)
# [8, 3, 1, 19, 22]
```

To use starmap, we need to import it from itertools.

First, let's create some testing data.

A list comprehension to show how this could be done without map

Uses starmap and zip to achieve the same effect

In addition to simplifying the code and bringing it into a pattern we're familiar with by now, `starmap` brings along all the benefits we've grown to expect from `map`. Both `zip` and `starmap` are lazy, so we can work with big datasets with greater piece of mind that we're only holding the data we need in memory. We can also quickly convert our `starmap` to work in parallel by making it a method call to a `Pool()` object.

6.2 Solving the parallel map and reduce paradox

At the end of chapter 5, we noticed a problem—our parallel `map` and `reduce` was slower than our lazy `map` and `reduce`. Then in section 6.1, we explored the behavior of parallel `map` in more depth. Although that helps us understand the problem better, it doesn't necessarily help us solve it. To solve the problem, we'll have to do something different: use a parallel `reduce`. In this section, we'll take a look at implementing parallel `reduce` to speed up our reduction operations.

6.2.1 Parallel reduce for faster reductions

The easiest way to think of parallel `reduce` is as a cross between our parallel `map` and our linear `reduce`. Parallel `reduce` will share the costs and benefits of parallel `map`, while having the signature of linear `reduce`. Just like with parallel `map`, parallel `reduce` will

- break a problem up into chunks
- make no guarantees about order
- need to pickle data
- be finicky about stateful objects
- run slower than its linear counterpart on small datasets
- run faster than its linear counterpart on big datasets

Like linear `reduce`, parallel `reduce` will

- require an accumulator function, some data, and an initial value
- perform N-to-X transformations

All things considered, we can use parallel `reduce` to solve the problem we faced at the end of chapter 5. We can perform transformations and accumulate the results in a time-friendly way.

BREAKING DOWN THE PARALLEL REDUCE PARAMETERS

When we first looked at `reduce` in chapter 5, one of the graphics we looked at showed the parts of our `reduce` function. We saw that `reduce` had three parts:

1. An accumulation function
2. A sequence
3. An initializer value

That figure, shown here again in figure 6.2, lays out what we need to be able to use `reduce`. In comparison to `map`, `reduce` is a little more complex—`map` has two parts, whereas `reduce` has three—but not overly so. Parallel `reduce` ups the ante.

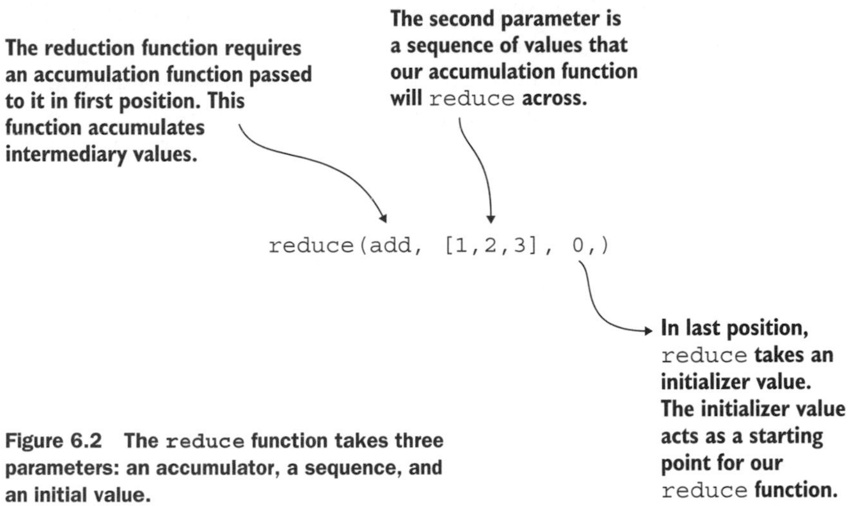
The reduction function requires an accumulation function passed to it in first position. This function accumulates intermediary values.
The second parameter is a sequence of values that our accumulation function will reduce across.
reduce(add, [1,2,3], 0,)
In last position, reduce takes an initializer value. The initializer value acts as a starting point for our reduce function.

Figure 6.2 The `reduce` function takes three parameters: an accumulator, a sequence, and an initial value.

The implementation of parallel `reduce` we'll be looking at has six parts:

1. An accumulation function
2. A sequence
3. An initializer value
4. A `map`
5. A `chunksize`
6. A combination function

You should recognize most of these six parts, which are diagrammed in figure 6.3. The first three—the accumulation function, sequence, and initializer value—come directly

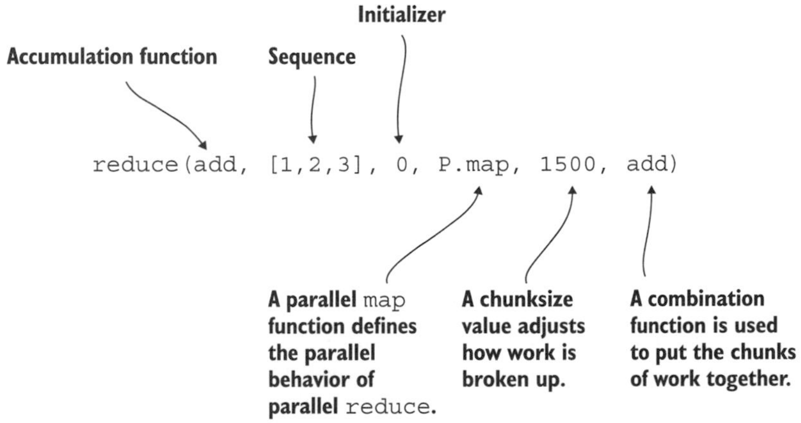
Accumulation function
Sequence
Initializer
reduce(add, [1,2,3], 0, P.map, 1500, add)
A parallel map function defines the parallel behavior of parallel reduce.
A chunksize value adjusts how work is broken up.
A combination function is used to put the chunks of work together.

Figure 6.3 Parallel `reduce` has six parameters: an accumulation function, a sequence, an initializer value, a map, a `chunksize`, and a combination function—three more than the standard `reduce` function.

from `reduce`. We just finished talking about `chunksize` in section 6.1.2. That leaves us with two new parameters, and even these two are only new-ish.

The `map` parameter to parallel `reduce` is exactly what we would expect it to be, given its name: it's a `map` function. The parallel `reduce` implementation we'll use piggybacks off the parallelism we implemented in our parallel `map`. That's why our parallel `reduce` will share all of its benefits and drawbacks—a lot of the behavior is directly inherited.

That being said, we don't have to pass our parallel `reduce` a parallel `map`. We are free to pass it a lazy `map`. For example, we could pass it the lazy `map` that comes standard with Python. If we do this, we won't have a parallel `reduce`, we'll have a lazy `reduce`. This is much less useful than a lazy `map`, however, because `reduce` only results in a single accumulated value—even if that value is a complex data structure—and we have to operate on the entire sequence to know what it is.

The last parameter is a combination function. The combination function is like an accumulation function, except for the parts of our parallel reduction problem. To understand how combination functions work, let's take a look at the parallel `reduce` workflow in greater depth.

6.2.2 *Combination functions and the parallel reduce workflow*

Because parallel `reduce` is based on parallel `map`, the parallel `reduce` workflow has the same primary parts that our parallel `map` workflow does (figure 6.4). We will

1. break our problem into pieces
2. do some work
3. combine the work
4. return a result

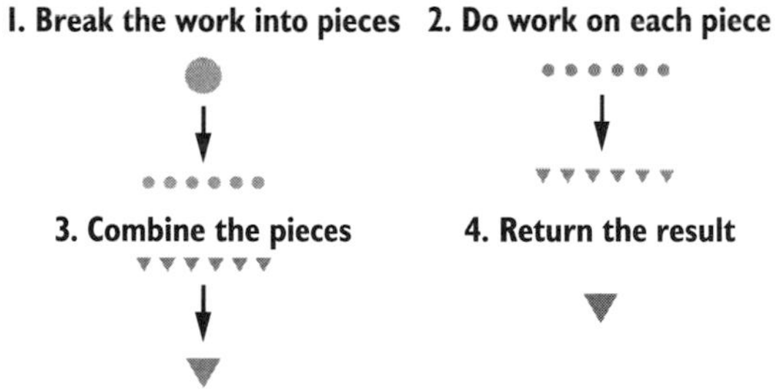
1. Break the work into pieces
2. Do work on each piece
3. Combine the pieces
4. Return the result

Figure 6.4 Parallel `reduce` workflows involve doing one operation in parallel on chunks of our original sequence with an aggregation function and another operation on the data that results from the aggregation (combination).

For parallel `map`, we need to understand all of these steps, but most of our code writing effort will go into the second step: doing the work of transforming our data. In some situations—when we're specifying the chunk size—we'll be concerning ourselves with the first step as well: breaking the problem into pieces. With parallel `reduce`, we also need to consider the third step: combining the work. This is where our combination function comes into play.

THE IMPLICIT COMBINATION FUNCTION IN PARALLEL MAP

In parallel `map`, we don't need to call a combination function because the data is always joined in the same way. As a result, the combination function is hardcoded into the parallel `map` operation itself. Because `map` is performing an N-to-N transformation of data—a concept introduced in chapter 2, which describes how `map` transforms sequences into sequences of the same size with different elements—we know that our combination function will always be some form of adding two sequences together.

For any two pieces of work that our parallel `map` function completes, the master can reassemble those pieces by combining them in the right order. The piece that corresponds to the earlier elements of the sequence goes first, and the piece that corresponds to the later elements of the sequence goes next. We can imagine this function as both the image in figure 6.5 and the code in the following listing.

Listing 6.5 The implicit combination function in parallel `map`

```
def map_combination(left, right):
  return left + right

xs = [1, 2, 3]
ys = [4, 5, 6]
print(map_combination(xs, ys))
# [1,2,3,4,5,6]
```

Notice how the signature of the function looks like the signature of our accumulators—it takes a left and a right object and returns an object of the same type as the left. (annotation on `def map_combination(left, right):`)

In listing 6.5, we can see what a `map` combination function would look like if we had to write it ourselves. We can imagine that two sequences—in this case `xs` and `ys`—are the parts returned by our parallel `map` operation, and we can use the `map_combination` function to combine them. We also see that the `map_combination` function is similar to an accumulation function. We're even using two of the variant parameter names for accumulation functions: left and right.

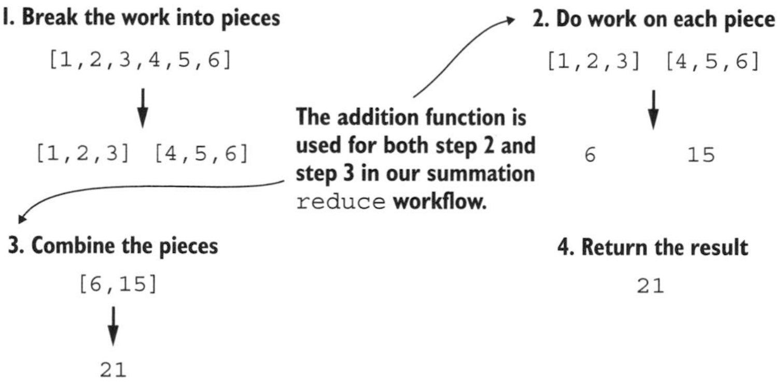
1. Break the work into pieces
[1,2,3,4,5,6]
[1,2,3] [4,5,6]
2. Do work on each piece
[1,2,3] [4,5,6]
6
15
The addition function is used for both step 2 and step 3 in our summation reduce workflow.
3. Combine the pieces
[6,15]
21
4. Return the result
21

Figure 6.5 A parallel `reduce` summation workflow is a simple case where we have the same function for the accumulation step and combination step.

CUSTOM COMBINATION FUNCTIONS FOR PARALLEL REDUCE

With parallel `reduce`, however, we trade the simplicity of always having the same combination function for the flexibility of more possible transformations. Let's consider three cases and see how we would handle the combination function in each case:

1. Summation
2. `filter`
3. `frequencies`

We implemented summation with `reduce` in section 5.2—the purpose of this function is to add a sequence of numbers. When we use `reduce` for summation, we accumulate a partial sum and continuously add new values to this partial sum until there are no more elements in our sequence. Combining this with our parallel workflow, we get a process that looks like figure 6.5.

The process follows the basic parallel workflow steps we outlined at the beginning of section 6.2.2. We first break the problem into pieces, turning our sequence into several smaller sequences, then do some work:

- First, we sum each of the smaller sequences.
- Then, we combine our results. Combining the partial sums requires us to take the sum of sums.
- Finally, we can return this value as our result.

In summation, we get lucky because the combination function is the same as the accumulation function. The accumulation function takes two values—both of which are numerical—adds them together, and returns their result to get an intermediary sum. Combining our subsequence sums is the same process: we add together pairs of the sums, each of which is a numerical value. The following listing approximates this process and shows how we can use the accumulation function to our `reduce` again to combine our partial results.

Listing 6.6 Approximation of parallel `reduce` summation

```
from functools import reduce

def my_add(left, right):          # Our accumulation function
  return left+right               # is simple addition.

xs = [1,2,3,4]                    # We break our long
ys = [5,6,7,8]                    # sequence into three parts.
zs = [9,10,11,12]

sum_x = reduce(my_add, xs)        # We work each
sum_y = reduce(my_add, ys)        # of those parts
sum_z = reduce(my_add, zs)        # independently.

print(my_add(my_add(sum_x, sum_y), sum_z))
# 78
```

Then, finally, we combine those parts—notice how we use my_add in both of the final two steps.

We're not always lucky enough that we get to use the same function, however. Next, we'll explore the parallel `reduce` workflow for the `filter` function. We first saw `filter` in chapter 4, and we implemented a `reduce`-based version of it in section 5.3.1. The idea behind `filter` is that we have a large sequence and we want to create a subsequence that contains only the elements of that sequence that cause a function to return `True`.

Our standard `filter` workflow is to start with an empty sequence and move through our sequence element by element, adding only the elements that make our condition function return `True` to our accumulated sequence. To make this parallel, we will

1. break our sequence into smaller sequences
2. accumulate the elements of those small sequences that make our condition return `True` in a new sequence
3. join those new sequences together
4. return the composite sequence

We can see this entire process in figure 6.6. Notice that the function for step 2, which takes a sequence and produces a subsequence, is different from our function for step 3, which joins the sequences together. The function for taking sequences and returning subsequences is our accumulation function for our `filter` reduction from chapter 5. The function for joining the sequences is actually the implicit combination function from `map`.

We can modify our example approximating parallel summation from listing 6.6 to approximate a parallel `filter` to see this in action. First, we'll have to create a new accumulation function. Here we'll use the `keep_if_even` function we wrote in section 5.3.1.

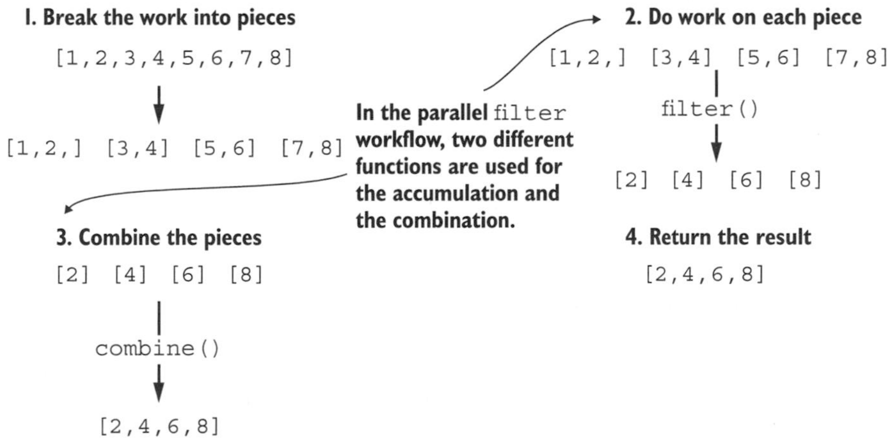

1. Break the work into pieces
[1,2,3,4,5,6,7,8]
[1,2,] [3,4] [5,6] [7,8]
2. Do work on each piece
[1,2,] [3,4] [5,6] [7,8]
filter()
[2] [4] [6] [8]
In the parallel filter workflow, two different functions are used for the accumulation and the combination.
3. Combine the pieces
[2] [4] [6] [8]
combine()
[2,4,6,8]
4. Return the result
[2,4,6,8]

Figure 6.6 In our workflow for the parallel `filter`, we need to use a different function for our accumulation step than for the combination step. This makes the operation more complex than our parallel summation.

We'll also need to add a combination function. Because we already identified this function to be the same function from parallel map's implicit combination step, let's use the function we wrote in listing 6.5. We can see the combination of the two, approximating a `filter` function using parallel `reduce`, in the following listing.

Listing 6.7 Parallel `filter` using different accumulation and combination functions

```
from functools import reduce

def map_combination(left, right):          <-- Creates our combination function
  return left + right

def keep_if_even(acc, nxt):                <-- Creates our accumulation function from filter
    if nxt % 2 == 0:
        return acc + [nxt]
    else: return acc

xs = [1,2,3,4]
ys = [5,6,7,8]
zs = [9,10,11,12]

f_acc = keep_if_even                       <-- Assigns our accumulation and combination functions
f_com = map_combination                        to differentiate them

res_x = reduce(f_acc, xs, [])              Uses the accumulation function
res_y = reduce(f_acc, ys, [])              on our broken-up sequences,
res_z = reduce(f_acc, zs, [])              returning intermediate results

print(f_com(f_com(res_x, res_y), res_z))   <-- Uses our combination function on those results,
# [2, 4, 6, 8, 10, 12]                         returning a final result
```

In listing 6.7, we can see that our accumulation function (represented by `f_acc`) and our combination function (represented by `f_com`) are different. Like we mentioned earlier, the accumulation function is `keep_if_even`, from chapter 5, and the combination function is `map_combination` from listing 6.5. We need both of these functions to take our broken-up work and achieve the desired result.

It's important to notice that these functions expect different types of parameters. The `keep_if_even` function takes a list in first position and a numerical value in second position. The `map_combination` function expects lists in both positions. In our case with `filter`, we know that the accumulation step always results in a list, so our combination function takes two lists.

NOTE Combination functions always take two parameters of the same type because each parameter is the result of the same process.

We can see this rule in our `frequencies` example as well. We first implemented the `frequencies` function, which returns a `dict` of elements and their counts when provided with a sequence, in section 5.3.2. In its linear form, we went through each element of the sequence and incremented the count of each element by one every time we saw it. In parallel, we're going to need to do four things:

1. Break up our sequence into smaller sequences
2. Obtain counts from those smaller sequences
3. Combine the counts together
4. Return our combined counts

Figure 6.7 shows that, like `filter`, the `frequencies` process will use different functions for the accumulation and combination steps. For the accumulation step, we'll use the `make_counts` function from listing 5.7. For the combination step, we'll have to write an entirely new function. This function will have to go through the unique keys of our two `dict`s and add the values of those keys together in a new `dict`. We can see that even though our `frequencies` process can take iterables with any number of types of elements, we'll always be passing `dict`s to our combination function because that's the type that our `make_counts` accumulation function returns.

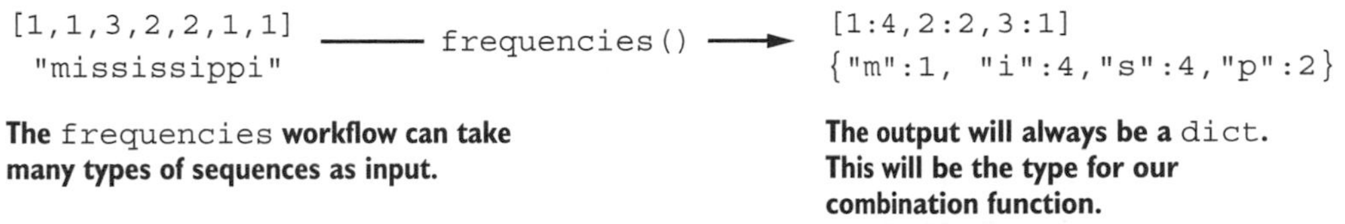
[1,1,3,2,2,1,1]
"mississippi"
frequencies()
[1:4,2:2,3:1]
{"m":1, "i":4,"s":4,"p":2}
The frequencies workflow can take many types of sequences as input.
The output will always be a dict. This will be the type for our combination function.

Figure 6.7 The parallel `frequencies` reduction workflow can take a number of types as its input, but it will always pass `dicts` into its combination step and return `dicts` as a result.

Listing 6.8 shows an approximation of the parallel `reduce` version of `filter`. We can see the original `make_counts` accumulation function and our new combination function, in the same general pattern we saw with both our summation example and our `filter` example. Again, we see one of the major benefits of adopting a map and reduce style: we can use the same patterns of programming to solve a diverse set of problems.

Listing 6.8 Approximating a parallel `reduce frequencies`

```
from functools import reduce

def combine_counts(left, right):
  unique_keys = set(left.keys()).\
                union(set(right.keys()))
  return {k:left.get(k,0)+right.get(k,0)
          for k in unique_keys}

def make_counts(acc, nxt):
    acc[nxt] = acc.get(nxt,0) + 1
    return acc
```

Creates a unique sequence of keys by finding a set that represents the union of both sets of keys

Because dict keys are of the keys type, we'll have to use explicit set conversion.

Loops through the keys and returns a dict mapping keys to the sum of its value in each dict

The make_counts function is our old accumulator from chapter 5.

```
xs = "miss"
ys = "iss"
zs = "ippi"

f_acc = make_counts
f_com = combine_counts

res_x = reduce(f_acc, xs, {})
res_y = reduce(f_acc, ys, {})
res_z = reduce(f_acc, zs, {})

print(f_com(f_com(res_x, res_y), res_z))
# {'i': 4, 'm': 1, 's': 4, 'p': 2}
```

Assigns make_counts as the accumulation function and combine_counts as the combination function

Works on the split-up sequences using our accumulation functions

Combines the intermediate results using our combination function

We can see this reusable pattern in how similar listings 6.7 and 6.8 are. Having abstracted the combination and accumulation into `f_acc` and `f_com`, all we needed to change to get from one to the other was how those functions resolve. Now that we've seen how summation, `filter`, and `frequencies` will work in parallel, let's take a look at how we can actually implement these three functions with parallel `reduce`.

6.2.3 Implementing parallel summation, filter, and frequencies with fold

So far in this chapter, we've looked at implementation nuances of parallelism. Specifically, we've looked at when we should use parallel workflows and how the parallel `reduce` workflow differs from the parallel `map` workflow with which we were already familiar. Now that we've got that down, we can finally solve the problem we noticed at the end of chapter 5 of `reduce` working more slowly in parallel. We're finally ready to use parallel `reduce`.

Like our standard `map` and our parallel `map`, the moving from standard `reduce` to parallel `reduce` is a little anticlimactic. Assuming that we have our accumulation and combination functions in place, implementing parallel `reduce` requires only three steps:

1. Importing the proper classes and functions
2. Rounding up some processors
3. Passing our `reduce` function the right helper functions and variables

For the first of these three steps, we have to move beyond what base Python gives us. Python doesn't natively support parallel `reduce`. One of the libraries we'll need for this is the pathos library, which we discussed in chapter 2 when we first introduced parallelism and discussed some problems related to pickling. We can use pathos to get around Python's weaknesses in pickling and chunk up our problem up for parallel `reduce`.

We'll also need to reach into the toolz library for an implementation of parallel `reduce`. We used the toolz library before in chapters 2 and 4 when we borrowed handy functions that fit the map and reduce style of programming. The parallel `reduce` implementation in the toolz library is called `fold`. `fold` is an alternative name for reduce, which is useful as a metaphor for reduce: folding each element into the accumulator, one at a time, until only the accumulator is left.

> **The toolz library**
>
> The toolz library is intended to be the functional utility library that Python never came with. Many functional programming languages—Scala, Clojure, Haskell, and OCaml—come with handy utilities for common sequence transformation patterns. Python does not, and toolz fills in those convenience functions. A high-performance version of the library is available as CyToolz. You can install CyToolz with `pip install cytoolz`.

Once we have these imports, all we need to do is call Pool to round up some processors and call our parallel reduce with all the right parameters. With summation, for example, we'll need to make our imports, call Pool, and pass our parallel reduce (fold) our addition function. We can see this all in action in the following listing.

Listing 6.9 Summation in parallel with reduce

```
import dill as pickle
from pathos.multiprocessing
    import ProcessingPool as Pool
from toolz.sandbox.parallel import fold
from functools import reduce

def my_add(left, right):
  return left+right

with Pool() as P:
    fold(my_add, range(500000), map=P.imap)

print(reduce(my_add, range(500)))
# 124750
```

- We'll need features of the dill, pathos, and toolz libraries to perform a parallel reduce.
- Creates our accumulation and combination function, which are the same for summation
- Rounds up the processors we want to use
- Passes the parameters to our parallel reduce function: fold
- Includes a linear reduce for comparison

Listing 6.9 shows that, just like calling map in parallel versus calling our regular lazy map, calling reduce in parallel requires almost no modification to our base code. We need to import some capabilities that are not included in base Python, sure, but there are no substantial changes to the workflow. Importantly, we use exactly the same accumulation function in each case.

TIP Listing 6.9 also shows how we call parallel map as a parameter to parallel reduce. This is because the parallel reduce implementation in the toolz library does not actually implement parallelism. This function has to sit on top of a parallel map to do its parallel magic. If we wanted to, we could pass our normal lazy map function to the fold function and we would get a linear reduce back. This can be useful if we're testing our code on a small subset of a larger dataset because we can use the fold function without parallelism and then add the parallelism later when we're working with a big dataset.

For a parallel filter, we see that the process is mostly the same, except that now we need to add our combination function and an initializer. We can see this process in the following listing.

Listing 6.10 filter in parallel with reduce

```
import dill as pickle
from pathos.multiprocessing import ProcessingPool as Pool
from toolz.sandbox.parallel import fold
from functools import reduce

def map_combination(left, right):
  return left + right

def keep_if_even(acc, nxt):
    if nxt % 2 == 0:
        return acc + [nxt]
    else: return acc

with Pool() as P:
    fold(keep_if_even, range(500000), [],
         map=P.imap, combine=map_combination)

print(reduce(keep_if_even, range(500), []))
# [0, 2, 4, 6, 8, 10, 12, ... 484, 486, 488, 490, 492, 494, 496, 498]
```

- Our parallel reduce implementation requires the same imports as before.
- As in listing 6.7, map_combination is our combination function.
- keep_if_even, from chapter 5, is our accumulation function.
- Notice the empty list being used as an initializer and the combination function map_combination.
- Our standard reduce workflow for comparison

Listing 6.10 shows how the parallel filter workflow incorporates the combination function and the initializer. Just like our linear filter, we put the initializer—an empty list—in third position. Again, we use an empty list for filter because we want to return a list. Also, we can see how the combination function is passed to our parallel reduce function in final position as a named parameter. This combination function and the parallel map parameter are the only things that distinguish our linear reduce from our parallel reduce.

We can see the same limited changes between linear and parallel frequencies, as shown in the following listing. Again, what's important is that we pass the combination function and the parallel map.

Listing 6.11 Implementing frequencies in parallel with parallel reduce

```
import dill as pickle
from pathos.multiprocessing import ProcessingPool as Pool
from toolz.sandbox.parallel import fold
from random import choice
from functools import reduce
```

- Uses the same three imports: dill, ProcessingPool, and fold
- Implements choice to generate some example data

```
def combine_counts(left, right):
  unique_keys = set(left.keys()).union(set(right.keys()))
  return {k:left.get(k, 0)+right.get(k, 0) for k in unique_keys}

def make_counts(acc, nxt):
    acc[nxt] = acc.get(nxt,0) + 1
    return acc

xs = (choice([1, 2, 3, 4, 5, 6]) for _ in range(500000))

with Pool() as P:
    fold(make_counts, xs, {},
         map=P.imap, combine=combine_counts)
rand_nums = (choice([1, 2, 3, 4, 5, 6]) for _ in range(500))
reduce(make_counts, rand_nums, {})
# {6: 87, 1: 59, 5: 88, 4: 85, 3: 93, 2: 88}
```

combine_counts will be our combination function.

make_counts will be our accumulation function.

Uses a generator expression to create a lot of dummy data

Calls our parallel reduce on this data, passing our accumulation function, the data, a dict as an initializer, our parallel map, and the combination function

Includes a linear reduce for comparison

We can see again how similar the parallel `reduce` and the linear `reduce` are. With the key exception of the combination function and the parallel `map`, they both use the same parameters: the same accumulation function, the same data inputs, and the same initializer. Across all three examples—parallel `reduce` summation, parallel `reduce filter`, and parallel `reduce frequencies`—we have seen our combination functions increase in complexity. Getting this combination function right is the key to successfully using parallel `reduce`.

Summary

- Sometimes, parallel `map` can be slower than a lazy `map`, especially when the amount of data is small or the work to be done is easy.
- There are several variations of `map`, such as `starmap` and `.imap`, that can be useful in the right situation.
- We can use parallel `reduce` in conjunction with lazy `maps` for a fast map and reduce workflow.
- Parallel `reduce` takes five parameters: an accumulator function, a sequence, an initializer, a parallel `map` function, and an optional combiner.
- The parallel `map` function tells parallel `reduce` how to split up the workload.
- The optional combiner tells `reduce` how to join chunks of work completed in parallel whose data type may be different from that of items in the sequence.
- To use parallel `reduce`, we need to design a combine function that can combine the different accumulated chunks.

Part 2

Part 2 teaches how to use two popular open source distributed computing frameworks: Hadoop and Spark. Hadoop is the originator and foundation of contemporary distributed computing. We'll explore how to use Hadoop streaming and how to write Hadoop jobs with the mrjob library. We'll also learn Spark, a modern distributed computing framework that can take full advantage of the latest, high-memory compute resources. You can use the tools and techniques in this part for large data in categories 2 and 3: tasks that needs parallelization to finish in a reasonable amount of time.

7 Processing truly big datasets with Hadoop and Spark

This chapter covers

- Recognizing the `reduce` pattern for N-to-X data transformations
- Writing helper functions for reductions
- Writing lambda functions for simple reductions
- Using `reduce` to summarize data

In the previous chapters of the book, we've focused on developing a foundational set of programming patterns—in the map and reduce style—that allow us to scale our programming. We can use the techniques we've covered so far to make the most of our laptop's hardware. I've shown you how to work on large datasets using techniques like `map` (chapter 2), `reduce` (chapter 5), parallelism (chapter 2), and lazy programming (chapter 4). In this chapter, we begin to look at working on big datasets beyond our laptop.

In this chapter, we introduce distributed computing—that is, computing that occurs on more than one computer—and two technologies we'll use to do distributed computing: Apache Hadoop and Apache Spark. Hadoop is a set of tools that support distributed map and reduce style programming through Hadoop MapReduce. Spark is an analytics toolkit designed to modernize Hadoop. We'll focus on Hadoop for batch processing of big datasets and focus on applying Spark in analytics and machine learning use cases.

7.1 Distributed computing

In this chapter, we'll review the basics of distributed computing—a method of computing where we share not just a single workflow, but tasks and data long-term across a network of computers. Computing in this way has challenges, such as keeping track of all our data and coordinating our work, but offers large benefits in speed when we can parallelize our work.

In chapter 1, I laid out three sizes of datasets. Those that are

1. small enough to work with in memory on a single computer
2. too big to work with in memory on a single computer but small enough that we can process them with a single computer
3. both too big to fit into memory on a single computer and too big to process on a single computer

The first dataset size poses no inherent challenges: most developers can work with these datasets just fine. Somewhere between the second size—too big for memory, but we can still process it locally—and the third size, however, most people will start to say they're working with *big datasets.* In other words, they're starting to have problems doing what they want to do with the datasets, and sometimes rightfully so—if we have a dataset of the third size and only a single computer, we're out of luck.

Distributed computing solves that problem (figure 7.1). It's the act of writing and running programs not for a single computer, but for a cluster of them. This cluster of

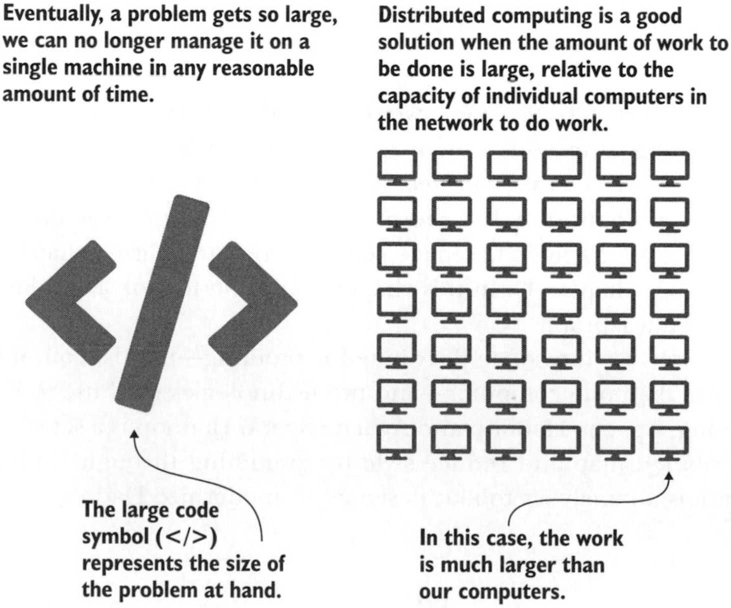
Eventually, a problem gets so large, we can no longer manage it on a single machine in any reasonable amount of time.
Distributed computing is a good solution when the amount of work to be done is large, relative to the capacity of individual computers in the network to do work.
The large code symbol (</>) represents the size of the problem at hand.
In this case, the work is much larger than our computers.

Figure 7.1 Distributed computing involves several computers working together to execute a single task.

computers works together to execute a task or solve a problem. We can use distributed computing to great effect when we pair it with parallel programming.

If we think back to our discussions of parallel programming, the main advantage we talked about was that parallel programming allowed us to do lots of different bits of work all at once. We split the task at hand up into pieces and worked it several pieces at a time. For small problems, this had few, if any, benefits. As tasks got larger, however, we saw the value of parallelization rise. By using distributed computing, we can multiply this effect (figure 7.2).

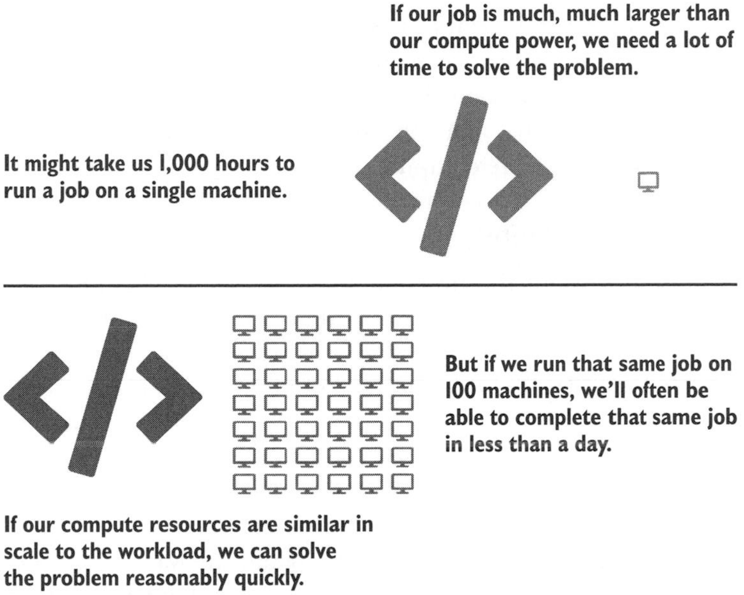
If our job is much, much larger than our compute power, we need a lot of time to solve the problem.
It might take us 1,000 hours to run a job on a single machine.
But if we run that same job on 100 machines, we'll often be able to complete that same job in less than a day.
If our compute resources are similar in scale to the workload, we can solve the problem reasonably quickly.

Figure 7.2 Distributed computing allows us to reduce our compute time by parallelizing our work across multiple machines. We can use distributed computing to solve problems in days, hours, or minutes that would have taken weeks.

When we add computers to our workflow, we're adding all the processing power of those computers. For example, if each computer we add has four cores, every time we add a new machine to our cluster, we'll add four additional cores. If we started with a four-core machine, running in parallel might cut our processing time down to one-fourth, but with two machines, we could be down to one-eighth. Adding two more machines might bring us down to one-sixteenth of the time it originally took to process our data in linear time.

And although there is a physical limit to how many processors we can reasonably have on a single machine, there's no limit to how many processors we can have in a distributed network. Dedicated *supercomputers* might have hundreds of thousands of processors across tens of thousands of machines, whereas *scientific computing networks* make hundreds of thousands of computers available to researchers engaged in serious number crunching. More commonly, companies, government entities, not-for-profits, and researchers are all turning to the cloud for on-demand cluster computing. We'll talk more about that in chapter 12.

Of course, distributed computing is not without its drawbacks. The curse of communication pops up again. If we distribute our work prematurely, we'll end up losing performance spending too much time talking between computers and processors. A lot of performance improvements at the high-performance limits of distributed computing revolve around optimizing communication between machines.

For most use cases, however, we can rest assured that by the time we're considering a distributed workflow, our problem is so time-consuming that distributing work is sure to speed things up. One indicator is that distributed workflows tend to be measured in minutes or hours, rather than the seconds, milliseconds, or microseconds that we traditionally use to measure compute processes.

7.2 Hadoop for batch processing

In this section, we'll talk about the fundamentals of Apache Hadoop. Hadoop is a prominent distributed computing framework and one that you can use to tackle even the largest datasets. We'll first review the different parts of the Hadoop framework, then we'll write a Hadoop MapReduce job to see the framework in action.

The Hadoop framework focuses specifically on the processing of big datasets on distributed clusters. Hadoop's basic premise is that we can combine the map and reduce techniques we've seen so far, along with the idea of moving our code (not our data), to solve problems with small and large datasets alike.

We can find a lot of similarities between Hadoop and the way we've been thinking about computing so far in this book. I've been preaching that we should start small (and local) and then scale up as we need more resources. Hadoop promises the same thing. You can develop and test on a single local machine and then scale out to a thousand-machine cluster hosted in the cloud. Hadoop advocates for this in much the same way we do, through a map and reduce style of programming.

7.2.1 Getting to know the five Hadoop modules

The Hadoop framework includes five modules for big dataset processing and cluster computing (figure 7.3):

1. *MapReduce*—A way of dividing work into parallelizable chunks
2. *YARN*—A scheduler and resource manager
3. *HDFS*—The file system for Hadoop
4. *Ozone*—A Hadoop extension for object storage and semantic computing
5. *Common*—A set of utilities that are shared across the previous four modules

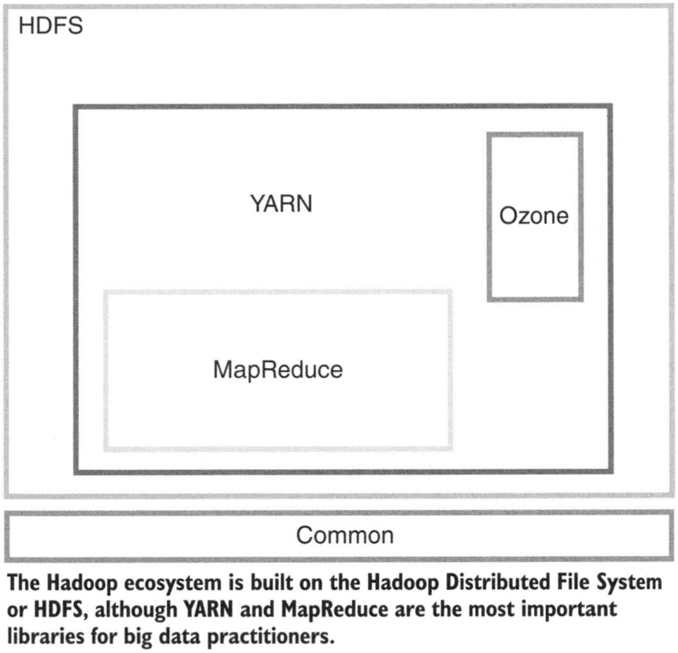
HDFS
YARN
Ozone
MapReduce
Common
The Hadoop ecosystem is built on the Hadoop Distributed File System or HDFS, although YARN and MapReduce are the most important libraries for big data practitioners.

Figure 7.3 The Hadoop framework is made up of five pieces of software, each of which tackles a different big dataset processing problem.

MapReduce is an implementation of the map and reduce steps you've already seen in this book that is designed to work in parallel on distributed clusters. YARN is a job scheduling service with cluster management features. HDFS—or Hadoop Distributed File System—is the data storage system of Hadoop. Ozone is a new (version 0.3.0 as I'm writing this) Hadoop project that provides for semantic object store capabilities. Common is a set of utilities common to all the Hadoop libraries.

We'll touch on the first three—MapReduce, YARN, and HDFS—now. These three libraries are the classic Hadoop stack. The Hadoop Distributed File System manages the data, YARN manages tasks, and MapReduce defines the data processing logic (figure 7.4).

HADOOP'S TWIST ON MAP AND REDUCE

The main aspect of Hadoop with which we'll concern ourselves in this book is the MapReduce library. Hadoop MapReduce is a massive data processing library that we can use to scale the map and reduce style of programming up to tens of terabytes or even petabytes by extending it across tens, hundreds, or thousands of worker machines. MapReduce divides programming tasks into two tasks: a `map` task and a `reduce` task—just like we saw at the end of chapter 5.

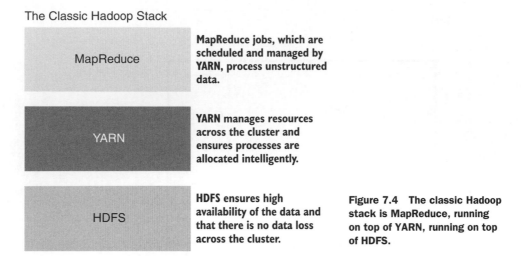

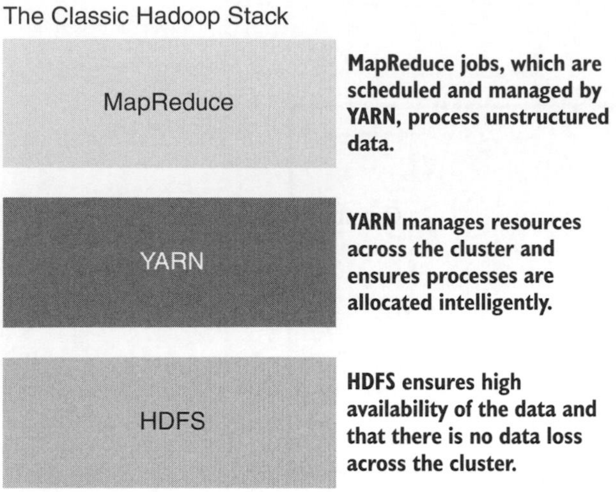
The Classic Hadoop Stack
MapReduce
MapReduce jobs, which are scheduled and managed by YARN, process unstructured data.
YARN
YARN manages resources across the cluster and ensures processes are allocated intelligently.
HDFS
HDFS ensures high availability of the data and that there is no data loss across the cluster.

Figure 7.4 The classic Hadoop stack is MapReduce, running on top of YARN, running on top of HDFS.

YARN FOR JOB SCHEDULING

YARN is a job scheduler and resource manager that splits resource and job management into two components: scheduling and application management. The scheduler, or *resource manager*, oversees all of the work that is being done and acts as a final decision maker in terms of how resources should be allocated across the cluster. Application managers, or *node managers*, work at the node (single-machine) level to determine how resources should be allocated within that machine (figure 7.5). Application managers also monitor what's going on within their node and report that information back to the scheduler.

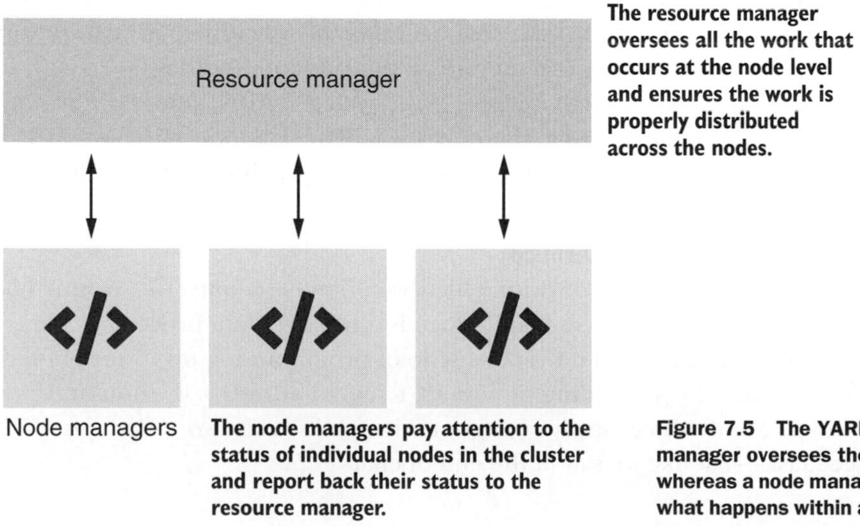
Resource manager
The resource manager oversees all the work that occurs at the node level and ensures the work is properly distributed across the nodes.
</>
</>
</>
Node managers
The node managers pay attention to the status of individual nodes in the cluster and report back their status to the resource manager.

Figure 7.5 The YARN resource manager oversees the entire job, whereas a node manager oversees what happens within a single node.

We can tie together resource managers in extremely high demand use cases where thousands of nodes are not sufficient. This process is called *federation.* When we federate YARN resource managers together, we can treat several YARN resource managers as a single resource manager and run them in parallel across multiple subclusters as if they were a single massive cluster.

THE DATA STORAGE BACKBONE OF HADOOP: HDFS

The foundation of the Hadoop framework is its distributed file system abstraction, aptly named Hadoop Distributed File System. The Hadoop authors designed HDFS to work for cases where users want to

- process big datasets (several terabytes and up; too big for local processing)
- be flexible in their choice of hardware
- be protected against hardware failure—a common cluster computing problem

Additionally, HDFS operates based on another key observation: that moving code is faster than moving data. When we introduced parallelization in chapter 2, we talked about how Python's base map moves both code and data. This is effective up to a point, but eventually the cost of moving data around—especially if the data files are large or numerous—becomes too much to justify parallelization. We run into the same problem we saw at the end of chapter 5: the act of parallelization costs more than the benefits of doing the work in parallel.

By distributing the data across the cluster and moving the code to the data, we avoid this problem. Code—even in its lengthiest, most obtuse forms—will be small and cheaper to move than the data it needs to work on. In the typical case, our data is large and our code is small.

> **Distributed file systems**
>
> HDFS is a reliable, performant foundation for high-performance distributed computing, but with that comes complexity. Because this book is not focused on data engineering, I've chosen to omit the details of HDFS. The book *Hadoop in Action* (Manning, 2010) goes into HDFS in more depth and includes cookbook-style recipes for common HDFS operations. Chuck Lam, the book's author, introduces Hadoop's Distributed File System in section 3.1 and does a deep dive into HDFS in chapter 8.

7.3 Using Hadoop to find high-scoring words

Now that we've covered the fundamentals of Hadoop, let's dive into some code to really see how it works. Consider the following scenario. (You can find the data for the scenario in the book's code repository online: https://github.com/jtwool/mastering-large-datasets.)

SCENARIO Two of your friends—one a nurse and the other a pop culture critic—have been arguing for days about a peculiar topic: the relative sophistication of the two seemingly unrelated figures Florence and the Machine (a contemporary English rock band) and Florence Nightingale (a legendary English nurse). To settle their dispute, you've been asked to count the frequencies of words longer than six letters occurring in songs by Florence and the Machine and the writings of Florence Nightingale.

To do this we'll need to do a few things:

1. Install Hadoop
2. Prepare a mapper—a Python script to do our `map` transformation
3. Prepare a reducer—a Python script to do our reduction
4. Call the mapper and reducer from the command line

7.3.1 MapReduce jobs using Python and Hadoop Streaming

Before we get into the details of implementation, though, let's take a look at what Hadoop's MapReduce does. Hadoop's MapReduce is a piece of software, written in Java, that we can use to execute MapReduce on distributed systems. When we talk about running Hadoop MapReduce with Python, we are (generally speaking) talking about running Hadoop Streaming, a Hadoop utility for using Hadoop MapReduce with programming languages besides Java.

To run that utility, we'll call it from the command line along with options such as

- the mapper
- the reducer
- input data files
- output data location

Hadoop provides an example code snippet demonstrating this command. An annotated version of this snippet appears in figure 7.6.

Hadoop's streaming utility makes it easy for us to use the Java software with any executables, for example, Unix tools.

```
mapred streaming \
    -input myInputDirs \
    -output myOutputDir \
    -mapper /bin/cat \
    -reducer /usr/bin/wc
```

All we need to do is specify the input and output locations. (pointing to `-input myInputDirs`)

It also makes it easy for us to use the executables we want to for the map and reduce steps of the workflow. (pointing to `-mapper /bin/cat`)

Figure 7.6 A word count example in Hadoop, using Hadoop Streaming and Unix tools.

The code snippet in figure 7.6 calls on two Unix commands to serve as its mapper and reducer. `/bin/cat` refers to the Unix concatenate software, and `/bin/wc` refers to the Unix word count software. Used together like this, `cat` will print the text and `wc` will count the words. Hadoop will ensure that these actions are performed in parallel on the documents in the directory located at the input location and the results are written to the output directory.

Once run, the result will be that we can go into whatever directory we pointed output to and retrieve the count of the words. Before we move on to a full-scope example, let's implement the word count mappers and reducers in Python. To emulate the `cat` capability in Python, let's print each word to a new line. To emulate the `wc` capability, we'll increment a counter for each word we come across. We'll need to wrap both of these capabilities in solo, executable scripts.

The mapper might look like listing 7.1, and the reducer might look like listing 7.2.

Listing 7.1 Word count mapper in Python

```
#!/usr/bin/env python3
"""Print words to lines"""
import sys

for line in sys.stdin:
  for word in line.split():
    print(word)
```

Listing 7.2 Word count reducer in Python

```
#!/usr/bin/env python3
"""Count words"""
import sys
from functools import reduce

print(reduce(lambda x, _:x+1, os.stdin, 0))
```

In these two examples, some strange new things are going on. First, we're reading from `stdin`. This is because Hadoop handles the opening of files for us, along with chopping up extra-large files into smaller bits. Hadoop is designed to be used with massive files, so having the ability to split a big file across several processors is important. We also can use Hadoop to work with compressed data—it natively supports compression formats such as .gz, .bz2, and .snappy (as shown in table 7.1).

Table 7.1 A comparison of compression formats available for use out of the box with Hadoop

Format	Description	Use case	Hadoop Codec
.bz2	Slow compression, but shrinks files more than older algorithms	Semi-long-term storage, file transfer between people	`BZip2Codec`
.gz	Fast, well-supported compression algorithm	Transfer of files between processes (such as Hadoop steps)	`GzipCodec`
.snappy	New, fast compression algorithm; less support than .gz but better compression	Transfer of files between processes (such as Hadoop steps)	`SnappyCodec`

Second, both of our scripts print their output to the terminal. Again, this is because of how Hadoop is oriented. Hadoop will capture what's printed to `stdout` and use that later on in the workflow. This creates an additional step on top of our standard workflow and can cause us to have to convert strings into Python objects.

Lastly, both scripts start with the Python shebang. This line tells the computer to use these scripts as executables. Hadoop will try to call these scripts using the program at the designated shebang path, in this case, Python.

If you haven't already tried, replacing the mapper and reducer from before with our two scripts will let us run our MapReduce job. This is shown in the following listing.

Listing 7.3 Running a Streaming MapReduce with Python

```
$HADOOP_HOME/bin/hadoop  jar $HADOOP_HOME/hadoop-streaming.jar \
    -input myInputDirs \
    -output myOutputDir2 \
    -file ./wc_mapper.py \
    -mapper ./wc_mapper.py \
    -file ./wc_reducer.py
    -reducer ./wc_reducer.py \
```

The output of this command will be in myOutputDir2 inside a file called results. The result should be the same as the second number that the command we called in figure 7.6 returns.

7.3.2 Scoring words using Hadoop Streaming

Let's turn back to our example of finding the counts of long words. For Hadoop, we'll focus only on the words by Florence and the Machine. (We'll save the texts of Florence Nightingale for Spark later in this chapter.) To get counts of specific words with Hadoop—instead of simply an overall count of words—we'll have to modify our mapper and our reducer. Before we jump right into the code, let's take a look at how this process will compare with our word counting example. I've diagrammed both processes, step by step, in figure 7.7.

With our word count mapper, we had to extract the words from the document and print them to the terminal. We'll do something very similar for our long word frequency example; however, we'll want to add a check to ensure we're only printing out long words. Note that this behavior—doing our filtering and breaking our documents into sequences of words—is very similar to how the workflow might execute in Python. As we iterated through the sequence, both the transformation and the filter would lazily be called on the lines of a document.

For our word count reducer, we had a counter that we incremented every time we saw a word. This time, we'll need more complex behavior. Luckily, we already have this behavior on hand. We've implemented a frequency reduction several times and can reuse that reduction code here. Let's modify our reducer from listing 7.2 so it uses the

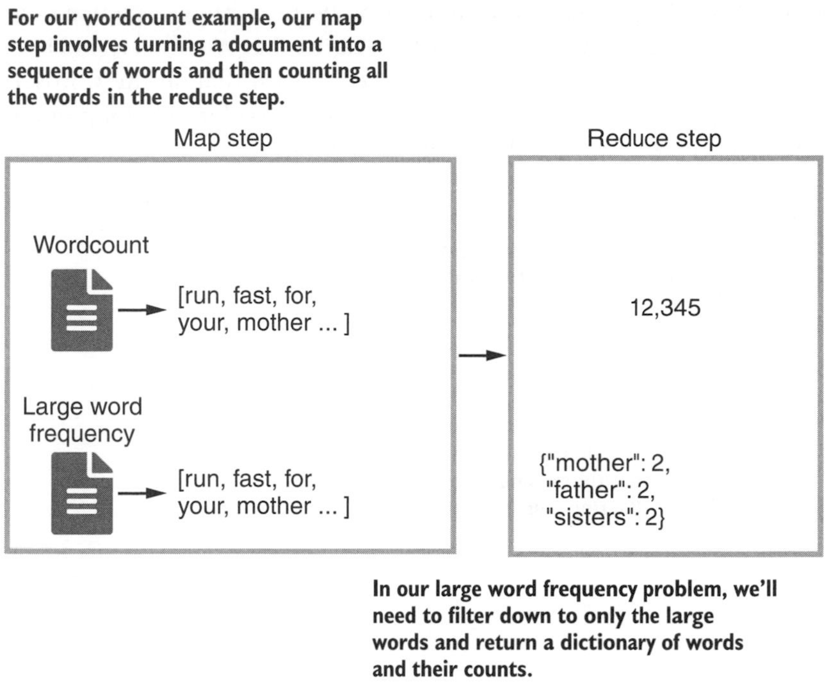
For our wordcount example, our map step involves turning a document into a sequence of words and then counting all the words in the reduce step.
Map step
Reduce step
Wordcount
[run, fast, for, your, mother ...]
12,345
Large word frequency
[run, fast, for, your, mother ...]
{"mother": 2, "father": 2, "sisters": 2}
In our large word frequency problem, we'll need to filter down to only the large words and return a dictionary of words and their counts.

Figure 7.7 Counting words and getting the frequencies of a subset of words have similar forms but require different mappers and reducers.

`make_counts` function we first wrote back in chapter 5. Our mapper will look like listing 7.4, and our reducer will look like listing 7.5.

Listing 7.4 Hadoop mapper script to get and filter words

```
#!/usr/bin/env python3
import sys

for line in sys.stdin:
  for word in line.split():
    if len(word)>6: print(word)
```

Listing 7.5 Hadoop reducer script to accumulate counts

```
#!/usr/bin/env python3
import sys
from functools import reduce

def make_counts(acc, nxt):                          <-- This is our make_counts function from chapter 5.
    acc[nxt] = acc.get(nxt,0) + 1
    return acc

for w in reduce(make_counts, sys.stdin, {}):        <-- We apply it to the sys.stdin stream, which is where our data will come in.
    print(w)
```

The output of our MapReduce job will be a single file with a sequence of words and their counts in it. The results should look like figure 7.8. We also should see some log text printed to the screen. We can quickly check to see that all the words are longer than six letters, just as we'd hoped. In chapter 8, we'll explore Hadoop in more depth and tackle scenarios beyond word filtering and counting.

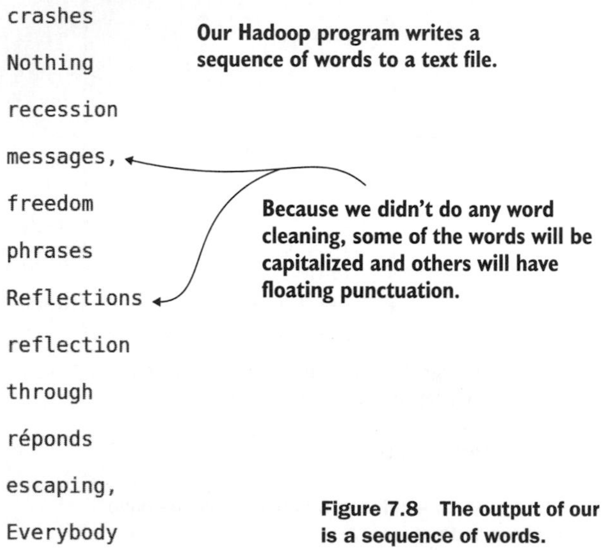
crashes
Nothing
recession
messages,
freedom
phrases
Reflections
reflection
through
réponds
escaping,
Everybody
Our Hadoop program writes a sequence of words to a text file.
Because we didn't do any word cleaning, some of the words will be capitalized and others will have floating punctuation.

Figure 7.8 The output of our MapReduce job is a sequence of words.

7.4 Spark for interactive workflows

So far in this chapter, we've been talking about the Hadoop framework for working with big datasets. In this section, we'll turn our attention to another popular framework for big dataset processing: Apache Spark. Spark is an analytics-oriented data processing framework designed to take advantage of higher-RAM compute clusters that are now available.

Spark offers several other advantages, from the perspective of most Python programmers:

- Spark has a direct Python interface—PySpark.
- Spark can query SQL databases directly.
- Spark has a `DataFrame` API—a rows-and-columns data structure that should feel familiar to Python programmers with experience in `pandas`.

7.4.1 Big datasets in memory with Spark

As we touched on briefly in the introduction to section 7.3, Spark processes data in memory on the distributed network instead of storing intermediate data to a filesystem. This can lead to up to 100 times improvements in processing speed versus Hadoop on some workflows, to say nothing about the difference between a Spark task and a linear Python task. The caveat to this is that Spark requires machines with greater memory capacity.

CHOOSING SPARK VERSUS HADOOP

Because Spark makes full use of a cluster's RAM, we should favor Spark over Hadoop when we

- are processing streaming data
- need to get the task completed nearly instantaneously
- are willing to pay for high-RAM compute clusters

Spark's use of in-memory processing means we don't necessarily have to save the data anywhere. This makes Spark ideal for streaming data—one aspect of the conventional definition of big data. We should reserve Hadoop for batch processing.

Because Spark can be so much faster than Hadoop, we should use Spark when we need near instant processing of data. Of course, this is only really feasible up to a certain point. Eventually the data will be too big to process immediately, unless we throw an unjustifiable amount of resources at the problem.

That situation is directly tied to the last factor in our list: if money is of no concern, we can freely choose Spark. Because Spark runs faster when it has access to many high-RAM machines, if we can afford to assemble a cluster of high-RAM machines, then Spark is the obvious choice. Hadoop is designed to make the most out of low-cost computing clusters.

As you can imagine, the answer to which distributed computing framework to use is not always clear cut; however, the map and reduce style we've developed throughout this book will serve you well working with big datasets in either one.

7.4.2 *PySpark for mixing Python and Spark*

Spark was designed for data analytics, and one way we can see that is in the Spark design team's commitment to developing APIs for both Python and R. Like Hadoop, Spark is written to run on the Java Virtual Machine (JVM), which would normally make it hard for scientists, researchers, data scientists, or business analysts, who most often use languages like Python, R, and Matlab. We saw this problem in Hadoop. We were not able to interact directly with Hadoop through Python. Instead, we had to call our Python functions through Hadoop Streaming, and we had to use somewhat clumsy workarounds to work with Python data beyond strings. When we're working with Spark, we can use its Python API, PySpark, to get around that issue.

With PySpark, we can call Spark's Scala methods through Python just like we would a normal Python library, by importing the modules and functions we need. For example, we'll often be using the `SparkConf` and `SparkContext` functions to set up our Spark jobs. We'll talk more about these functions in chapter 9 when we dive into Spark. For now, we can work with them in Python by importing them from PySpark, as shown in the following listing.

Listing 7.6 Importing from Spark into Python

```
from pyspark import SparkConf, SparkContext

config = SparkConf().setAppName("MyApp")
context = SparkContext(conf=config)
```

We'll see this in full force later in this chapter when we dive into PySpark in section 7.5.

7.4.3 Enterprise data analytics using Spark SQL

A significant benefit of Spark is its support for SQL databases through Spark SQL. Built on top of the widespread Java Database Connectivity—which you'll often see abbreviated as JDBC—Spark SQL makes it easy to work with structured data. This is especially important if we're working with *enterprise data*. Enterprise data refers to common business data—HR or employee data, financial or payroll data, and sales order or operational data—and the most common means of storing that data—relational databases, especially Oracle DB or Microsoft SQL Server.

Because Spark is designed first and foremost for Scala, the Spark SQL Python API is not compliant with the PEP 249 specification for Python database connections. Nonetheless, its core functionality makes intuitive sense, and we can use it with any database that has a JDBC connection, including popular free and open source databases such as MySQL, PostgreSQL, and MariaDB. In its simplest form, querying databases with Spark is as easy as passing our SQL query into the `.sql` method of a `SparkSession` object.

7.4.4 Columns of data with Spark DataFrame

When we've queried data using Spark, our data will end up in what's known as a `DataFrame`, a Spark class that we can think of as being equivalent to a SQL table or a `pandas.DataFrame`. Unlike either a SQL table or a `DataFrame` from `pandas` though, the `DataFrame` in Spark is optimized for distributed computing workflows.

Like SQL and `pandas`, Spark `DataFrames` are organized around columns with names. This is helpful if we want to make conditional subsets of our data for machine learning or statistical summary. For example, if we wanted to get the average purchase size of customers with more than 20 orders, we could use the `DataFrame .filter` and `.agg` methods, combined with Spark's knowledge of our column names, to get that information. We can see this example in figure 7.9.

`DataFrame`'s version of `.filter` has a use similar to that of the `filter` function we saw in chapters 4–6. In fact, a lot of the map and reduce-oriented data processing functions make their way into the `pyspark.sql.functions` library, including `zip` as `arrays_zip`. The `DataFrame` API is a more general API that provides a convenience layer on top of the core Spark data object: the `RDD` or Resilient Distributed Dataset. `RDDs` are the Hadoop-abstraction that powers Spark's in-memory distributed processing, and the PySpark `RDD` API provides access to all the functions we've become

`DataFrame`s in Spark have built-in methods for common operations.

```
DF.filter(orders>20).agg(avg)
```

The `.filter` method works just like the `filter` function we've used in this book.

The `.agg` method takes a function and uses that function to aggregate results based on other variables.

Figure 7.9 Spark `DataFrames` have a `.filter` method that we can use to quickly take subsets of our big datasets.

familiar with, including `map`, `reduce`, `filter`, and `zip`. We'll see an example of these functions in the next section.

7.5 Document word scores in Spark

Now that we've covered the fundamentals of Spark, let's dive into some code. In the previous example in this chapter, we found all the words with more than six letters from the songs of the band Florence and the Machine. This served as evidence of their lyrical sophistication and also helped introduce us to Hadoop. In this section, we'll complete the comparison between Florence and the Machine and Florence Nightingale by running the same process on a document by Florence Nightingale in Spark.

As in section 7.3, we'll break this process down into three areas:

1. A mapper
2. A reducer
3. Running the code in Spark

Our mapper will be responsible for taking the files and turning them into sequences of words with more than six characters, and the reducer will be responsible for counting up the words we find. Running the code in Spark parallelizes the workflow for us. We can see this process play out in figure 7.10.

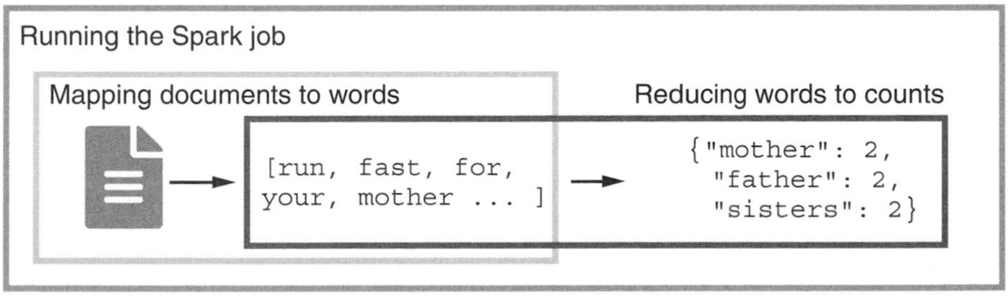

Running the Spark job
Mapping documents to words
Reducing words to counts
[run, fast, for, your, mother ...]
{"mother": 2, "father": 2, "sisters": 2}

We'll write the map and reduce parts of the workflow in Python and then pass a script off to Spark for parallelization.

Figure 7.10 Counting up the big words used by Florence Nightingale involves three steps in Spark.

7.5.1 Setting up Spark

Before we can jump into our Spark job, let's take a second to set up Spark. Unlike setting up Hadoop—which may have been a hairy process if you weren't familiar with Java—installing Spark is pretty straightforward. Go to https://spark.apache.org/downloads.html and follow the download instructions on the page, and that's it! You've got everything you need to use Spark.

> **Spark clusters**
>
> Just like we didn't do a deep dive into setting up a Hadoop cluster in this book, we also won't do a deep dive into setting up a Spark cluster—though we will show you how to provision cloud resources for these technologies in chapter 12. If you're interested in a full Spark book after the two and a half chapters we'll spend on it here, Manning has several books dedicated to Spark, including *Spark in Action* (2016) and *Spark GraphX in Action* (2016).

Now that we have Spark installed, we can run Spark jobs and interact with Spark using PySpark. The easiest way to take either of these actions is through the utilities that Spark provides. Just like Hadoop provided us the Hadoop Streaming utility, Spark provides two utilities: one that sets up an interactive Python shell called `pyspark` and one that allows us to run Spark jobs—similar to Hadoop streaming—called `spark-submit`.

EXPLORING BIG DATA INTERACTIVELY

One of the reasons why Spark is so popular is that it allows for us to interactively explore big data through a PySpark shell REPL. This more playful style of development, where we iterate through our problem line by line, is more familiar to a lot of data scientists than writing out extended chunks of code all at once. It also allows us to see what our intermediate results are or consult the Python documentation as we develop.

We kick this process off by running the utility `pyspark`. That process brings up a screen—like figure 7.11—where we can enter Python commands. Right off the bat, we

```
      ____              __
     / __/__  ___ _____/ /__
    _\ \/ _ \/ _ `/ __/  '_/
   /__ / .__/\_,_/_/ /_/\_\   version 2.4.0
      /_/

Using Python version 2.7.13 (default, Nov 24 2017 17:33:09)
SparkSession available as 'spark'.
>>> sc
<SparkContext master=local[*] appName=PySparkShell>
>>> spark
<pyspark.sql.session.SparkSession object at 0x7ff4b9d95950>
>>> 
```

Figure 7.11 Spark provides an interactive terminal where we can run Python commands with all the power of a Spark cluster behind them.

have access to `SparkContext` and `SparkSession` instances as `sc` and `spark`. (The `pyspark` utility imports them for us; when we write our own Spark scripts, we'll need to import them ourselves.) The `sc` variable has methods for building the Resilient Distributed Dataset instances we mentioned in section 7.4.4. We can use the `spark` variable to bring data into `DataFrames`—the parallel optimized tabular data abstractions we also mentioned in section 7.4.4. If we run python's `help` command on these variables in the interactive session, we'll see a list of methods available for each one. We'll go into some of them in this book, but a full list of methods for each variable is available in the online documentation.

Running jobs

When we're not working with Spark interactively, we'll work with it by running Spark jobs. This is a similar process to how we ran MapReduce jobs in Hadoop. We write some code, and then we pass it as an argument to a utility. In the case of Spark, we'll use the `spark-submit` utility and we'll pass it a single Python script.

In that Python script, we can create instances of any of the Spark objects we need. We'll have access to them once we import the `pyspark` module. Let's take a look at this method of working with Spark in action.

7.5.2 MapReduce Spark jobs with spark-submit

Turning our attention back to the question at hand—the lexical excellence of Florence Nightingale—we'll break our work into three steps:

1. Turning a document into a sequence of words
2. Filtering those words down to those having more than six characters
3. Gathering counts of the rest

When we worked through this process in Hadoop, we accomplished step 1, turning a document into a sequence of words, and step 2, filtering out the small words, together in the mapper. With Spark, the three steps will all stand apart.

To accomplish this process in Spark, the first thing we'll want to do is bring our data into an `RDD`—Spark's powerful parallel data structure. This is a good starting point for most work in Spark. To do that, we'll need a `SparkContext`, so we'll have to instantiate a `SparkContext` instance. Then we can use the `SparkContext` method `.textFile` to read in text files from our filesystem. This method creates an `RDD` with the lines of those documents as elements.

We can turn this dataset into a sequence of words by calling the `.flatMap` method of the `RDD`. The `.flatMap` method is like `map` but results in a flat sequence, not a nested sequence. `.flatMap` also returns an `RDD`, so we can use the `.filter` method of the `RDD` to filter down to only the large words, and then the `.countByValue` method of that resulting `RDD` to gather the counts. We can see this whole process in just a few lines in the following listing.

Listing 7.7 Counting words of six letters or more in Spark

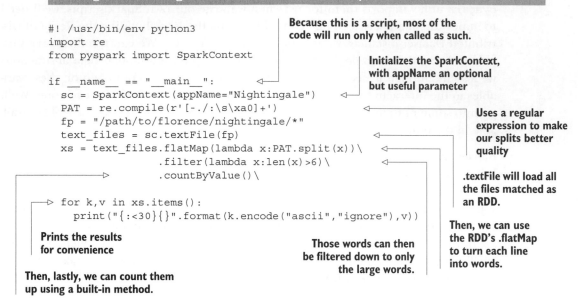

```
#! /usr/bin/env python3
import re
from pyspark import SparkContext

if __name__ == "__main__":
  sc = SparkContext(appName="Nightingale")
  PAT = re.compile(r'[-./:\s\xa0]+')
  fp = "/path/to/florence/nightingale/*"
  text_files = sc.textFile(fp)
  xs = text_files.flatMap(lambda x:PAT.split(x))\
                .filter(lambda x:len(x)>6)\
                .countByValue()\

  for k,v in xs.items():
    print("{:<30}{}".format(k.encode("ascii","ignore"),v))
```

Because this is a script, most of the code will run only when called as such.

Initializes the SparkContext, with appName an optional but useful parameter

Uses a regular expression to make our splits better quality

.textFile will load all the files matched as an RDD.

Then, we can use the RDD's .flatMap to turn each line into words.

Those words can then be filtered down to only the large words.

Then, lastly, we can count them up using a built-in method.

Prints the results for convenience

When you're done running the code, you should see a long list of large words output. If all's right, the words should all be over six letters in length. There will also be a bunch of output related to the Spark job that was run to process this code. The final result will look something like the following listing.

Listing 7.8 Code output from Spark, counting up large words

```
hurting                   10
Englishman                1
Conceit                   1
contain                   1
deficient                 1
especially                9
weekend                   2
pretend                   1
weaknesses,               1
servants                  1
suppose                   2
forever                   4
stagnant                  2
```

Unlike Hadoop, where we're free to print our results to get them to write to the output file, with Spark, we'll typically want to write our results directly to a file. That way, we won't have to dig them out of a mass of terminal messages. In the next three chapters, we'll touch on some more best practices for using Hadoop and Spark by working through more in-depth examples.

7.6 Exercises

7.6.1 Hadoop streaming scripts

What are the scripts called that we write for a Hadoop Streaming job? (Choose one.)

- Mapper and Reducer
- Applier and Accumulator
- Functor and Folder

7.6.2 Spark interface

When we interact with Spark, we'll do it through PySpark, which is a Python wrapper around the Spark code written in which programming language? (Choose one.)

- Clojure
- Scala
- Java
- Kotlin
- Groovy

7.6.3 RDDs

Spark's innovations center around a data structure called an `RDD`. What does `RDD` stand for? (Choose one.)

- Resilient Distributed Dataset
- Reliable Defined Data
- Reduceable Durable Definition

7.6.4 Passing data between steps

With Hadoop Streaming, we need to manually ensure that the data can pass between the map and reduce steps. What do we need to call at the end of each step? (Choose one.)

- `return`
- `yield`
- `print`
- `pass`

Summary

- Hadoop is a Java framework that we can use to run code on data across distributed clusters.
- When writing Python for Hadoop MapReduce jobs, we write one script for the mapper and one for the reducer.
- Both the Python mapper script and the Python reducer script need to `print` their results to the console.

- In Spark, we can write a single Python script that handles both the map and reduce portions of our problem.
- We interact with Spark through Python using the `pyspark` API.
- We can work with Spark in interactive mode or by running jobs—this gives us flexibility in our development workflow.
- Spark has two high-performance data structures: `RDDs`, which are excellent for any type of data, and `DataFrames`, which are optimized for tabular data.

8 Best practices for large data with Apache Streaming and mrjob

This chapter covers

- Using JSON to transfer complex data structures between Apache Streaming steps
- Writing mrjob scripts to interact with Hadoop without Apache Streaming
- Thinking about mappers and reducers as key-value consumers and producers
- Analyzing web traffic logs and tennis match logs with Apache Hadoop

In chapter 7, we learned about two distributed frameworks for processing large datasets: Hadoop and Spark. In this chapter, we'll dive deep into Hadoop—the Java-based large dataset processing framework. As we touched on last chapter, Hadoop has a lot of benefits. We can use Hadoop to process

- lots of data fast—distributed parallelization
- data that's important—low data loss
- absolutely enormous amounts of data—petabyte scale

Unfortunately, we also saw some drawbacks to working with Hadoop:

- To use Hadoop with Python, we need to use the Hadoop Streaming utility.
- We need to repeatedly read in strings from `stdin`.
- The error messages for Java are not super helpful.

In this chapter, we'll look at how we can deal with those issues by working through some scenarios. We'll analyze the skill of tennis players over time and find the most talented players in the sport.

8.1 Unstructured data: Logs and documents

The Hadoop creators designed Hadoop to work on *unstructured data*—a term that refers to data in the form of documents. Though they will often contain useful, interpretable metadata—for example, author or date—the important content is typically unrestricted in form. A classic example of unstructured data is a web page.

The web page is written in HTML and has some general formatting requirements:

- The page starts with a head tag.
- Inside the head tag are CSS and JavaScript imports.
- There should also be some metadata inside the head tag—maybe a description of the page or the page's title.
- Then there's the body tag, which is the main content of the page.

The web page has useful metadata—we could quickly write up some code to find the title of any web page and even its keywords and description, if they're listed as metadata—however, none of these aspects of the page is why anyone goes to it. What users are interested in is entirely in the body section. And, of course, the body of the web page can contain anything its author pleases, such as text, images, videos, music, and so on.

Compare this to other common forms of unstructured data, such as social media content, text or office documents, spreadsheets, and logs. If we think about a social media post, we know that these posts have required or imputed fields (such as time of post), but, more importantly, they also have freeform fields, such as the text of a tweet or a Facebook status. If we think about an office document, we know that our office software will record information like time last saved and the names of the users who have edited the document, but the main body of the document can be anything from a love letter to a business report. If we think about log data, we typically have more structure—machines do more logging than people—however, logs are often saved in file formats that are considered unstructured, such as plain text, and fall into this category for that reason.

Unstructured data is notoriously unwieldly. It's not amenable to the kind of tabular analysis that most data analysts cut their teeth on. This makes problems that involve unstructured data more frustrating for analysts, because their standard bag of tricks doesn't typically work, and less satisfying for customers, because the analysis takes longer and may be less fruitful.

At the same time, unstructured data is one of the most common forms of data around. Companies that have made an effort to assess how much data they have in structured versus unstructured formats have consistently found unstructured data makes up more than 80%, sometimes even as much as 95%, of their data. This makes sense when we consider that technologies such as personal web pages, social media, email, blogs, and other self-publishing platforms all produce unstructured data.

Keeping data in an unstructured format does have some advantages, chiefly that it's loosely coupled with the systems that rely on it. If the format of the data is not under your control (for example, it comes from a system owned by another group or another company), or you're working with data in several different formats, keeping that data unstructured provides an advantage because you will never need to restructure a datastore to accommodate changes. These facts about unstructured data—especially its prevalence—make it important to have a tool like Hadoop, which is designed for unstructured data, in one's belt.

8.2 Tennis analytics with Hadoop

To demonstrate the power of Hadoop—and how we can use it to turn log-style data into usable information—we'll tackle an example from the world of tennis.

> **SCENARIO** A new professional tennis league is forming, and they have hired you to come up with skill estimates for professional tennis players so that they can direct their efforts for recruiting players to the new league. They have provided you with data for several years of matches and would like you to return to them with a list of players and their corresponding skills.

Solving this problem will involve three steps. We need to

1. read in the data for each match
2. update the rankings of the winner and loser of each match
3. sort the rankings when all of our work is done

We'll break each of these steps up into a Hadoop MapReduce job in the streaming style we learned in chapter 7. Thinking back to chapter 7, we know we'll need a mapper script and a reducer script. Our mapper script will handle step 1, and our reducer script will handle steps 2 and 3 (figure 8.1).

Figure 8.1 shows what data will look like as it flows through this process. We'll start with our input datafiles, we'll read the matches from those files, then we'll reduce the matches into ratings for each tennis player. Finally, we'll sort the matches to return the players in order. As the data moves, you'll notice it changes from a comma-separated string into key-pairs into a sequence of key-value pairs.

8.2.1 A mapper for reading match data

Because step 1 is neatly contained within our mapper script, let's start our process there. We'll start by inspecting how the matches are contained within a file, part of which is previewed in figure 8.2.

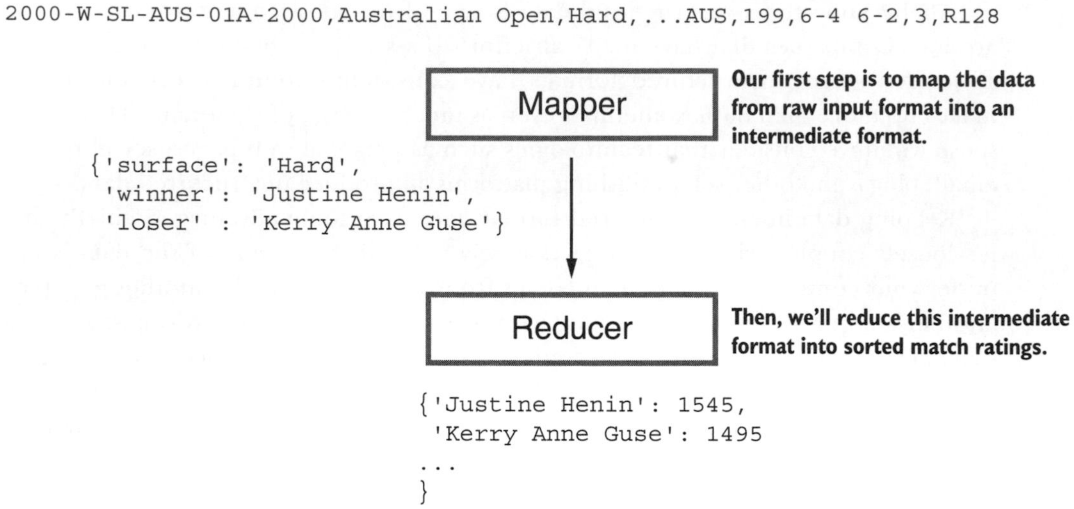
2000-W-SL-AUS-01A-2000,Australian Open,Hard,...AUS,199,6-4 6-2,3,R128
Mapper
Our first step is to map the data from raw input format into an intermediate format.
{'surface': 'Hard',
'winner': 'Justine Henin',
'loser' : 'Kerry Anne Guse'}
Reducer
Then, we'll reduce this intermediate format into sorted match ratings.
{'Justine Henin': 1545,
'Kerry Anne Guse': 1495
...
}

Figure 8.1 The tennis analytics problem requires three steps broken up between mapper and reducer scripts. In the mapper, we assemble the information we need, and in the reducer, we rank and sort the players.

The women's tennis match data contains a description of each match, with values separated by commas.

```
2001-W-SL-AUS-01A-2001 ... Martina Hingis ... Katalin Marosi ... 6-1 6-1,3,R128
2001-W-SL-AUS-01A-2001 ... Els Callens ... Rachel Mcquillan ... 6-3 6-1,3,R128
2001-W-SL-AUS-01A-2001 ... Anne Kremer ... Iroda Tulyaganova ... 6-4 2-6 6-4,3,R128
2001-W-SL-AUS-01A-2001 ... Virginie Razzano ... Tatiana Panova ... 7-6(6) 6-3,3,R128
```

Some values included are tournament ID, tournament name, surface, size of the draw, level of the tournament, date, and match number, and the ID, seed, name, handedness, height, country, age, and rank of both players.

Figure 8.2 The tennis match logs contain matches as comma-separated strings.

In the file, we can see that each match is a single line—just like we'll need it for Hadoop—and that each line contains a number of attributes describing the match, such as the winner, the loser, the surface, and more. For our purposes, we can concern ourselves with these three elements: winner, loser, and surface.

To access these elements of each match, we'll need to split each line on the commas and then call the elements we want by number: the surface is in the 2nd position, the winner is in the 10th position, and the loser is in the 20th position. This isn't especially clear to someone else reading our script, so we'll pass the data on to our reducer function using key-value pairs. Key-value pairs provide much greater interpretability than comma-separated value data, at the cost of being bulkier to store. Key-value pairs are more costly to store because the keys must be stored in addition to the values, whereas a comma-separated value string needs no keys.

JSON FOR PASSING DATA BETWEEN MAPPER AND REDUCER

To pass the key-value pair between our mapper and reducer, we'll use a data interchange format known as JSON. JSON—or JavaScript Object Notation—is a data format used for moving data in plain text between one place (typically a computer) and another (again, typically a computer). Modern web developers are fond of JSON because it

- is easy for humans and machines to read
- provides a number of useful basic data types (such as string, numeric, and array)
- has an emphasis on key-value pairs that aids the loose coupling of systems

As a Python developer, you can use Python's built-in `JSON` module for converting Python objects into JSON data and back. We'll use the `json.dumps` (dump string) function to turn a Python `dict` into a JSON string that we can print to the `stdout` with our mapper. Then we'll use the `json.loads` (load string) function for reading it in with our reducer.

Altogether, our mapper script looks like the following listing.

Listing 8.1 Mapper for analyzing tennis scores

```
#! /usr/bin/python3
import json
from sys import stdin


def clean_match(match):
  ms = match.split(',')
  match_data = {'winner': ms[10],
                'loser': ms[20],
                'surface': ms[2]}
  return match_data


if __name__ == "__main__":
  for line in stdin:
    print(json.dumps(clean_match(line)))
```

We bring each line in and process it with a helper function called `clean_match`. This is the function that we would map across all our data. To process each match, we split it on the comma and select the 10th, 20th, and 2nd elements of the line. These are the positions of the winner, loser, and surface respectively. We then populate a `dict` with those three elements, labeling each with an appropriate key. Finally, our `clean_match` function returns the `dict`.

If we were working in Python alone, this would be enough; however, we have to move our data across the terminal as a string to use Hadoop streaming. For this reason, we pass our data into the `json.dumps` function, which converts our Python `dict` into a corresponding JSON format—in this case, an object.

The other elements of the script are identical to the Hadoop Streaming scripts you've already written. We use a Python3 shebang to declare how the script should be executed, and we read data in from `stdin`. The shebang, `#! /usr/bin/python3`, tells your machine to process the script using Python.

8.2.2 Reducer for calculating tennis player ratings

With our mapper finished, we're ready to tackle the reducer. The reducer is responsible for turning matches into assessments of players' skill. To do that, we'll rely on a simplified version of a formula that was originally developed to rate chess players: the Elo rating system.

RATING PLAYERS BASED ON MATCH PERFORMANCE

The Elo rating system has a simple goal: take match results and use them to update the ratings of the players who participated in that match. To do this, the system makes statements about how often players of one rating beat players of another rating when they compete head-to-head. Typically, a 200-point rating difference between two players corresponds to the higher-rated player having a 75% chance to beat the lower-rated player.

Mathematically, we'll update players' ratings using a simplified Elo formula that calculates the expected chance of winning for each player and then grants the winner the number of points staked by their opponent. Each player must stake a number of points proportional to their likelihood of winning the match, so the higher rated player is risking more but is also expected to win more often. We'll also use a common heuristic for calculating the Elo rating, such as starting off never-before-seen players at 1,400 points. We can see the concept of Elo rating illustrated in figure 8.3.

Figure 8.3 shows how in a match between a player with a 1600 rating and a player with a 1550 rating, the 1550 player has more to gain and less to lose. That's because the rating system expects the 1550 player to lose to the 1600 player more often than not. When the 1600 player wins, they'll still gain points, but it will be a modest amount.

Using the techniques we learned in chapter 5, we'll structure the score accumulation in a reduce pattern. We'll bring in new matches and use their results to adjust the ratings for each player, which are being stored in a `dict` that we're holding onto throughout the reduce step. We can see this process in figure 8.4.

In figure 8.4, we can see how the accumulation of player scores occurs.

- We bring in the data for the next match.
- We calculate the impact that match had on each player's rating.
- We give the match winner the points they won.
- We deduct from the match loser the points they lost.
- If either the winner or loser are new observations, we start them at 1,400 points.
- We return the `dict` to be used for the next match.

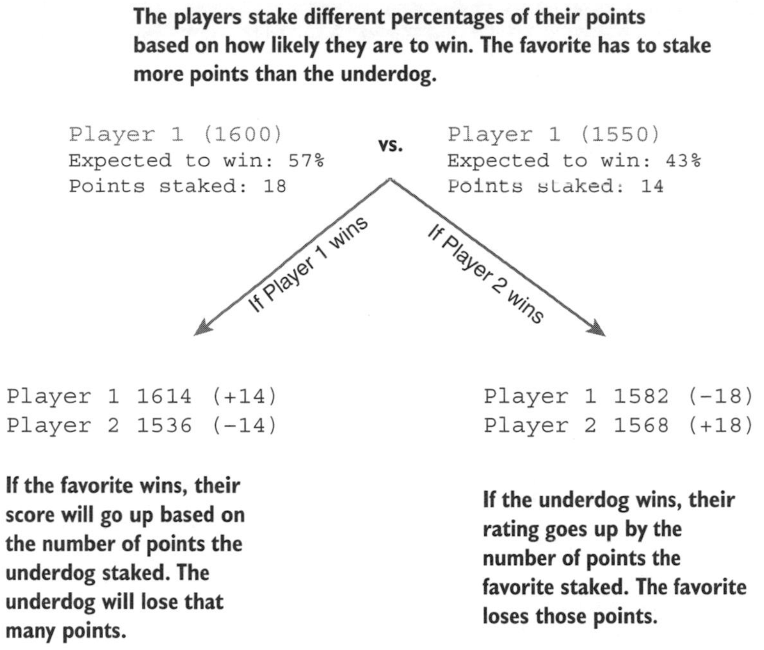
The players stake different percentages of their points based on how likely they are to win. The favorite has to stake more points than the underdog.
Player 1 (1600)
Expected to win: 57%
Points staked: 18
vs.
Player 1 (1550)
Expected to win: 43%
Points staked: 14
If Player 1 wins
If Player 2 wins
Player 1 1614 (+14)
Player 2 1536 (-14)
Player 1 1582 (-18)
Player 2 1568 (+18)
If the favorite wins, their score will go up based on the number of points the underdog staked. The underdog will lose that many points.
If the underdog wins, their rating goes up by the number of points the favorite staked. The favorite loses those points.

Figure 8.3 The Elo rating approach works by adjusting players' rankings after each match they play, with their ratings going up in a win or down in a loss. Underdogs are set to gain more points in a win than they would lose in a loss.

This process occurs for each match until we've reduced all the matches to a single `dict`: our N (many matches) to X (a single `dict` of ratings) transformation. Lastly, when we're done, we can print our `dict` to the screen as a JSON object so we can easily use it for further analysis down the road. The code for this process appears in listing 8.2.

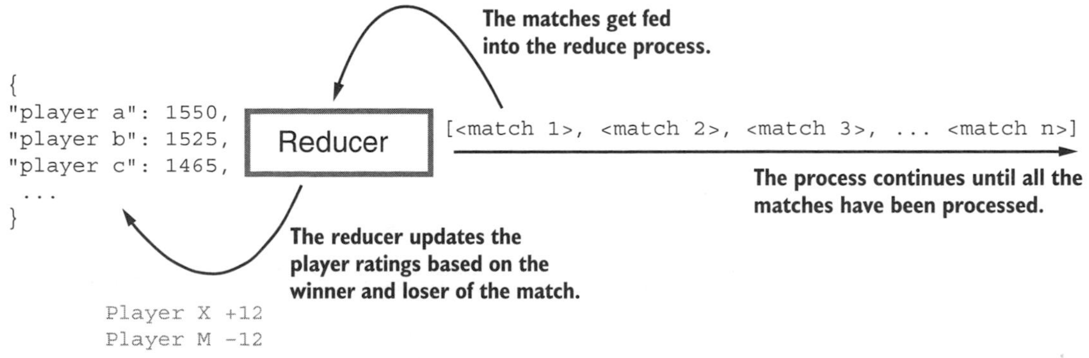
The matches get fed into the reduce process.
{
"player a": 1550,
"player b": 1525,
"player c": 1465,
...
}
Reducer
[<match 1>, <match 2>, <match 3>, ... <match n>]
The process continues until all the matches have been processed.
The reducer updates the player ratings based on the winner and loser of the match.
Player X +12
Player M -12

Figure 8.4 To calculate player ratings, we can reduce over matches, awarding them points for wins and taking points away for losses.

Listing 8.2 Reducing over matches to calculate player ratings

```
#! /usr/bin/python3
import json
from sys import stdin
from functools import reduce

def round5(x):
  return 5*int(x/5)

def elo_acc(acc,nxt):
  match_info = json.loads(nxt)
  w_elo = acc.get(match_info['winner'], 1400)
  l_elo = acc.get(match_info['loser'], 1400)
  Qw = 10**(w_elo/400)
  Ql = 10**(l_elo/400)
  Qt = Qw+Ql
  acc[match['winner']] = round5(w_elo + 100*(1-(Qw/Qt)))
  acc[match['loser']] = round5(l_elo - 100*(Ql/Qt))
  return acc

if __name__ == "__main__":
  xs = reduce(elo_acc, stdin, {})
  for player, rtg in xs.items():
    print(rtg, player)
```

In listing 8.2, we're reducing over the matches with a function we've called `elo_acc`. The first thing to notice about the `elo_acc` function is that we're reading the line in as a JSON string with `json.loads`. Because we output our `dicts` representing the matches as JSON strings, we can reconstitute them using a JSON string reader. This gives us `match_info`, a `dict` that contains the data we want about the match. Furthermore, because we've already done the work of creating keys for `winner` and `loser`, we can quickly retrieve the values by their corresponding keys.

From there, we can use this information to calculate the adjustments to the players' ratings. In short, this process involves taking each player's rating, dividing it by 400, and comparing those two values to come up with the amount of points that each player has at stake during the match. I round this number off to the nearest five-point interval out of personal preference. You can omit this step or round off to a larger number, like 10, 25, or even 100, if you'd like. Lastly, we'll print the players and their ratings by unpacking the `tuples` that `reduce` created.

Finally, we can set these two scripts as executables and run them from the command line. The command will look like the following listing.

Listing 8.3 The Hadoop streaming command to run our rating calculator

```
$HADOOP/bin/hadoop jar /home/<user>/bin/hadoop/hadoop-streaming-3.2.0.jar \
  -file ./elo-mapper.py -mapper ./elo-mapper.py \
  -file ./elo-reducer.py -reducer ./elo-reducer.py \
  -input '/path/to/wta/files/wta_matches_200*.csv' \
  -output ./tennis_ratings
```

After it finishes running, which should only be a few seconds, you should be able to open the results file included in the `tennis_ratings` directory and see output like this:

```
{
  "Julia Helbet": 1360,
  "Glenny Cepeda": 1400,
  "Hana Sromova": 1075,
  "Sophie Ferguson": 1130,
  "Anne Mall": 1360,
  "Nuria Llagostera Vives": 1120,
  "Maria Vento Kabchi": 1050,
  "Roxana Abdurakhmonova": 1380,
  "Zarina Diyas": 1405,
  "Stephanie Vogt": 1430,
  "Soumia Islami": 1390,
  "Pei Ling Tong": 1380,
  "Shikha Uberoi": 1160,
  "Amani Khalifa": 1410,
...
}
```

As we had planned, our output is a map of players and their corresponding Elo ratings, reflecting how skillful those players are estimated to have been during the period we analyzed. Before we move on, there is a caveat to this analysis that we've seen a few times throughout this book (including chapters 2 and 6). You'll note that if you run this analysis several times, you'll receive different results each time. That's because the order in which the matches are played affects the ratings each player (and their opponents) accumulates, altering the number of points they have at stake in each match. This was one of the problems we saw with parallel processing back when we first learned about it in chapter 2. For a real Elo rating, we would want to process the matches in order.

8.3 mrjob for Pythonic Hadoop streaming

Assurances about order aside, perhaps the most striking thing about working with Hadoop streaming is that it doesn't really feel like writing Python. Sure, we write two Python scripts, but we keep needing to print our data to `stdout` instead of passing it around inside the code. We have to resort to tricks like `json.loads` and `json.dumps` to work with complex file formats in any way. What we really want is a Pythonic way of working with Hadoop. For this, we can turn to mrjob—a Python library for Hadoop Streaming that focuses on cloud compatibility for truly scalable analysis.

Yelp originally created the mrjob library for its own Hadoop MapReduce needs, including several high-importance recommendation systems that power the eatery review site:

- "People who viewed this also viewed" recommendations
- Review highlights
- Text autocomplete
- Restaurant search
- Advertisements

The company developed the mrjob framework because the framework allowed its engineers to use Python—a quick to write, easy to debug language—to work with massive, distributed data through Hadoop. And, indeed, massive is the operative word. Yelp's data systems were processing more than 100 GB of data each day when it developed the framework. The scalability is important—that's why we want to use Hadoop and distributed computing in the first place—but here we'll focus on the Python.

8.3.1 The Pythonic structure of a mrjob job

A chief benefit of mrjob is that we get to write more Python. Indeed, instead of writing two scripts and calling them from the command line (and getting weird Java-based errors back when we make a mistake), with mrjob we can write our entire Hadoop Streaming job in Python. The mrjob library removes the need to interact directly with Hadoop at all.

Yelp created mrjob to analyze web logs, and we'll do the same to get used to the mrjob syntax. For example, let's consider the problem of finding the pages on a website that throw a 404 error the most. The 404 error represents a page that can't be found, so the presence of these errors in our logs is a direct reflection of inconvenience for our users. In a standard map and reduce workflow, we'd break this task up into two steps (figure 8.5):

1. A `map` step where we turn each line of a log into the error we're interested in
2. A `reduce` step where we count up the errors and find the offending pages

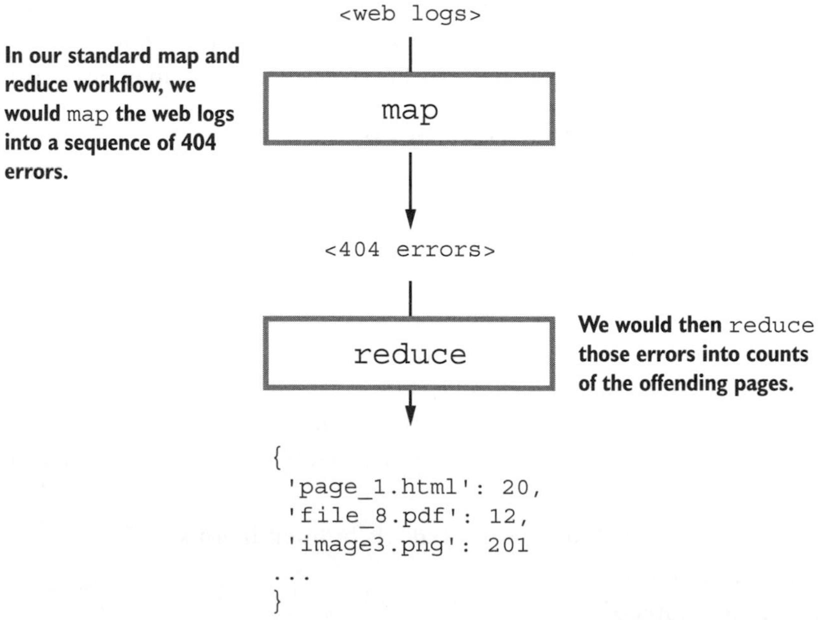
<web logs>
In our standard map and reduce workflow, we would map the web logs into a sequence of 404 errors.
map
<404 errors>
reduce
We would then reduce those errors into counts of the offending pages.
{
'page_1.html': 20,
'file_8.pdf': 12,
'image3.png': 201
...
}

Figure 8.5 To find 404 error offenders, we'd break the task up in a standard map and reduce style.

As shown in the figure, we'd start by ingesting our log files with a `map`. Then we would transform each of those files into a sequence of errors and offending pages. And finally, we'd `reduce` over this sequence and count up the error messages.

To do this with mrjob, we'll have to use a slightly different approach. mrjob keeps the mapper and reducer steps but wraps them up in a single worker class named `mrjob`. The methods of `mrjob` correspond directly to the steps we're used to: there's a `.mapper` method for the `map` step and a `.reducer` method for the `reduce` step. The required parameters for these two methods, though, are a little different from the `map` and `reduce` functions we've come to know. In `mrjob`, all the methods take a key and value parameter as input and return `tuples` of a key and a value as output (figure 8.6).

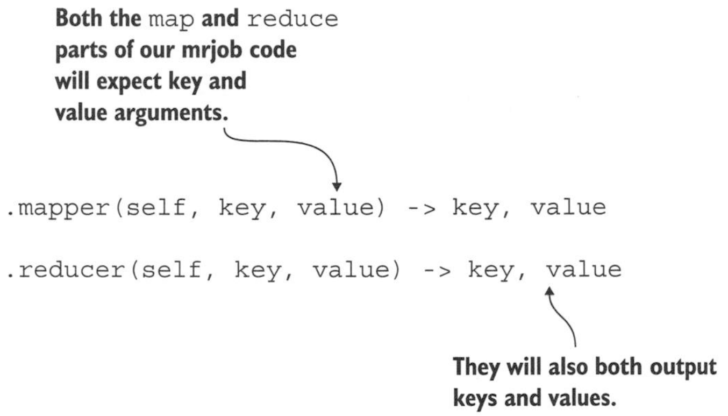
Both the map and reduce parts of our mrjob code will expect key and value arguments.
.mapper(self, key, value) -> key, value
.reducer(self, key, value) -> key, value
They will also both output keys and values.

Figure 8.6 The mrjob versions of `map` and `reduce` share the same type signature, taking in keys and values and outputting keys and values.

At first, thinking about `map` and `reduce` as consumers and producers of key-value pairs might be a little confusing, especially because we've been talking about both of these processes working on sequences of any form, not just on those that take the shape of key-value pairs. Under the hood, however, this is how Hadoop treats `map` and `reduce`.

The key-value method of map and reduce

In Hadoop, `map` and `reduce` are implemented as two methods: `.mapper` and `.reducer`. Each method takes a sequence of key-value pairs and produces key-value pairs in return. The `.mapper` method produces *intermediate key-value pairs.* In other words, it takes in data as keys and values and outputs them for the `.reducer`. Because the `.reducer` is expecting a key-value pair, this is perfect. In fact, a hidden step between the `map` and `reduce` steps in Hadoop sorts the keys and values Hadoop consumes by key. This makes the `.reducer` job even easier.

Using keys allows Hadoop to make good use of our compute resources as it allocates work. Intermediate records output by `map` with like keys will tend to go to the same location for processing.

For our .mapper step in a standard MapReduce job, the key to our .mapper will be None, and the value will be the lines we consume. Because of this, our thinking about map and .mapper doesn't have to change dramatically. We can ignore the key-value expectation of .mapper by simply ignoring the first parameter.

For the .reducer though, we will want to be aware of the key-value structure. Hadoop, through mrjob, does a lot of the organizing of keys and values for us. We can take advantage of that by considering the .mapper output not as a sequence but as a dict populated with keys and sequences. In our error analysis example, we'll set these keys to the page URLs so we can quickly count the number of 404 errors associated with those pages. We can see this play out in listing 8.4.

8.3.2 Counting errors with mrjob

Listing 8.4 is a small example, but because this is the first time we've seen mrjob code in the book, we'll want to look at it pretty closely. On the first line, we're importing a class MRJob, from the mrjob library's job module This class contains all the core MapReduce capability that we'll need to interact with Hadoop. The primary thing we'll do when working with the mrjob library is create new classes that inherit from the MRJob class.

Listing 8.4 MRJob script for finding 404 error messages in a traffic log

```
from mrjob.job import MRJob

class ErrorCounter(MRJob):

  def mapper(self, _, line):
    fields = line.split(',')
    if fields[7] == '404.0':
      yield fields[6], 1

  def reducer(self, key, vals):
    num_404s = sum(vals)
    if num_404s >5:
      yield key, num_404s

if __name__ == "__main__":
  ErrorCounter.run()
```

Not surprisingly, the next thing we do is create a new class ErrorCounter that inherits from the MRJob class. We're also going to define .mapper and .reducer methods for this class. As discussed in section 8.3.1, both of these methods expect keys and values, and you can see that they both use three parameters: self, a key, and a value.

For our .mapper, we'll ignore the first of these parameters (the key), as suggested in the previous section. To do that, we'll use the underscore variable, which is our way of saying we won't do anything with this variable. We'll name the second parameter line because the value of our input is going to be each line of our log file. Coming from working directly with Hadoop Streaming, this should feel pretty familiar. We're receiving the data just as if it came from `stdin`.

Because the data we're getting comes in as a comma-separated string, we'll use Python's `.split` method to split the input line into fields. We'll check the HTTP response code field, which happens to be in 7th position, to see if it is a 404 error, and if it is, we'll return the page name—which is in 6th position—and a 1. We can visualize that process as shown in figure 8.7.

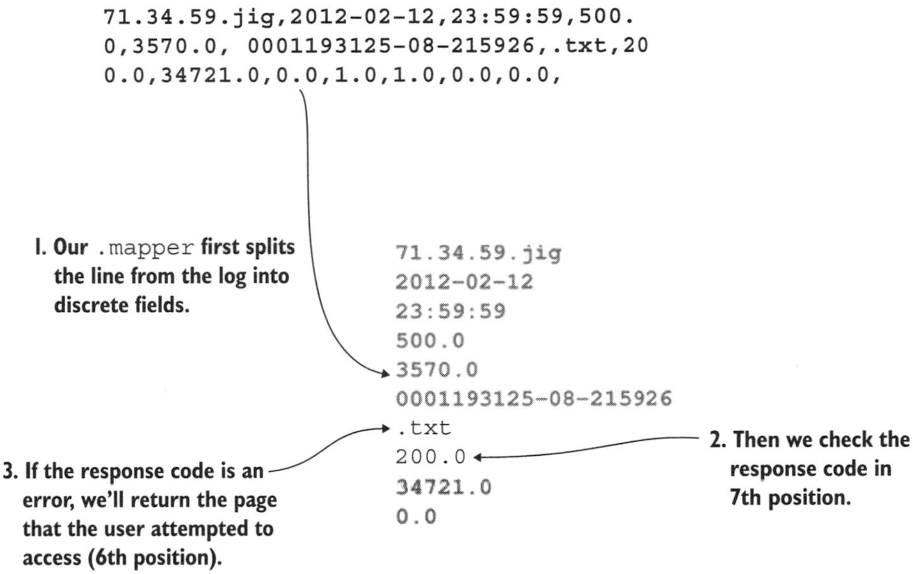
71.34.59.jig,2012-02-12,23:59:59,500.
0,3570.0, 0001193125-08-215926,.txt,20
0.0,34721.0,0.0,1.0,1.0,0.0,0.0,
1. Our .mapper first splits the line from the log into discrete fields.
71.34.59.jig
2012-02-12
23:59:59
500.0
3570.0
0001193125-08-215926
.txt
200.0
34721.0
0.0
2. Then we check the response code in 7th position.
3. If the response code is an error, we'll return the page that the user attempted to access (6th position).

Figure 8.7 Our `.mapper` consumes lines, splits them into fields, checks the value of the error message field, and then returns the page name and a 1.

> **The return values of mrjob methods**
>
> Earlier in this chapter, we discussed how when working with complex data structures, it is often helpful to pass our data around as JSON so that we can quickly and easily reconstitute it from strings. The mrjob library authors thought this was such a good idea that they require every `.mapper` and `.reducer` output to be JSON serializable. This means that you'll be best served by using simple Python data structures when you can, such as `floats`, `ints`, `strings`, `lists`, and `dicts`. These data structures are serializable in base Python. That said, you can turn any Python data structure into JSON by implementing your own method.

With our `.mapper` sending out data as keys (page names) and values (indicator counts of those pages), we're ready to move on to our `.reducer`. For our `.reducer`, we'll sum up the number of 404s our `.mapper` reported and return that value along with the original key. I'm restricting this to only pages that have more than five 404 errors because I'm personally only interested in high-frequency offenders, but you can omit this step if you'd like.

This `.reducer` is the first place we really see how the key-value expectation changes how we think about our map and reduce steps. We can still think about `reduce` moving through a sequence, but this time we're moving through a sequence of key-value pairs. And the value for each key is a sequence. In this specific situation, our key will be a page name, like `index.html`, and our value will be a list of indicators of 404 errors, such as `[1, 1, 1, 1]`. Figure 8.8 shows what this looks like.

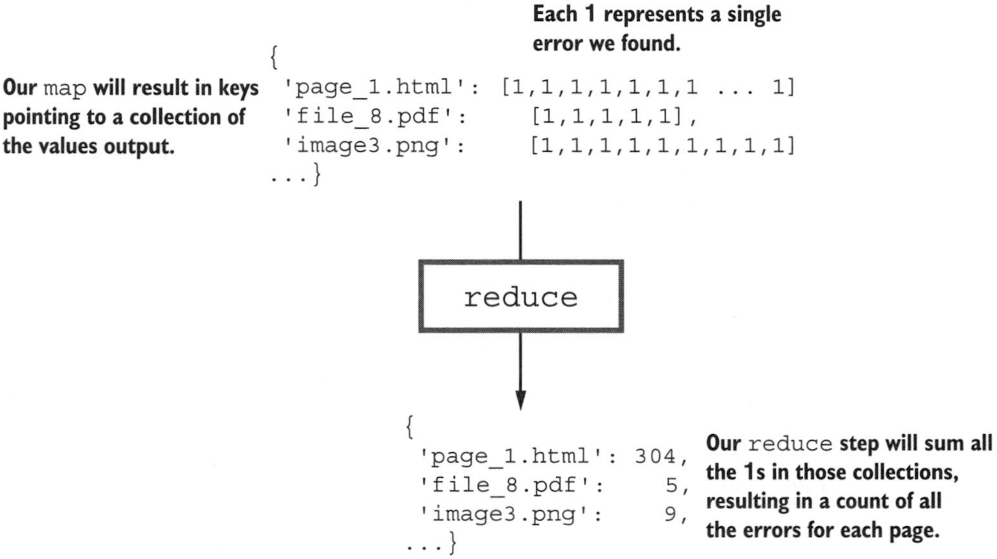
Each 1 represents a single error we found.
Our map will result in keys pointing to a collection of the values output.
{
'page_1.html': [1,1,1,1,1,1,1 ... 1]
'file_8.pdf': [1,1,1,1,1],
'image3.png': [1,1,1,1,1,1,1,1,1]
...}
reduce
{
'page_1.html': 304,
'file_8.pdf': 5,
'image3.png': 9,
...}
Our reduce step will sum all the 1s in those collections, resulting in a count of all the errors for each page.

Figure 8.8 Our `.mapper` produces key-value pairs that our `.reducer` then iterates through, operating on the key and its associated values.

When we think about the line `num_404s = sum(vals)` from listing 8.4, this line works because Hadoop has already sorted our data into a format where the key is the page and the `vals` variable contains a sequence of all the indicators (`1`). Summing up all those 1s then gives us a count of the number of 404 errors. Then we can return this value along with the key to get a count of the errors associated with each page.

Lastly, also in listing 8.4, we see the Pythonic `main` call at the end of our script. To run our mrjob MapReduce job, we'll call this script from the command line, adding our input data as an additional parameter. We'll need to have Hadoop still installed from chapter 7 to run the mrjob operation:

```
python3 common_errors.py traffic-logs.txt
```

After that, we should see pages and their corresponding error counts printed to the screen:

```
Using configs in /etc/mrjob.conf
No configs specified for inline runner
Creating temp directory /tmp/common-errors.jt-w.20191108.012559.032175
Running step 1 of 1...
job output is in /tmp/common-errors.jt-w.20191108.012559.032175/output
Streaming final output from /tmp/common-errors.jt-
     w.20191108.012559.032175/output...
".hdr.sgml"    2
".txt"    191
"form448073_20120210093319-.xml"    1
Removing temp directory /tmp/common-errors.jt-w.20191108.012559.032175...
```

From this output, we can see that most of the errors on our site are coming from links pointing to a file called ".txt".

8.4 Tennis match analysis with mrjob

Having seen a small mrjob MapReduce workflow, let's return to our tennis match data and dive into two more examples, each revolving around one of the greatest tennis players in history: Serena Williams.

8.4.1 Counting Serena's dominance by court type

In this scenario, we'll analyze Serena Williams' historical dominance and learn to think in the key-value style that mrjob expects.

> **SCENARIO** One of the most interesting things about tennis is that it's one of the few sports where the playing surface changes. Successful professionals learn to play on courts made of grass, clay, and concrete. Regardless of court, Serena Williams has been one of the most impressive tennis players in history. A sports writer has asked us to analyze the match logs and count her wins and losses on each court type.

If we were to think about this process in our old map and reduce way of thinking, we could imagine mapping each file into `dicts` that contained the information we'd be interested in and then reducing over that information to get the counts (figure 8.9). To use mrjob, though, we want to be thinking about keys and values. What data do we want to end up as keys in our final output, and what data should be in the values?

Well, we know we want to have the data organized by surface, so that makes sense as a key. As a value, we want Serena's record: a count of her wins and a count of her losses. We can accumulate those counts in our `.reducer` by using our `frequencies` function—the same one we wrote back in chapter 5 when we introduced `reduce`—if we have a list of wins and losses. What we'll want to output from our `.mapper` is the surface and either a `W` for a win or an `L` for a loss. Consider how this compares to our traditional map and reduce style approach in figure 8.9.

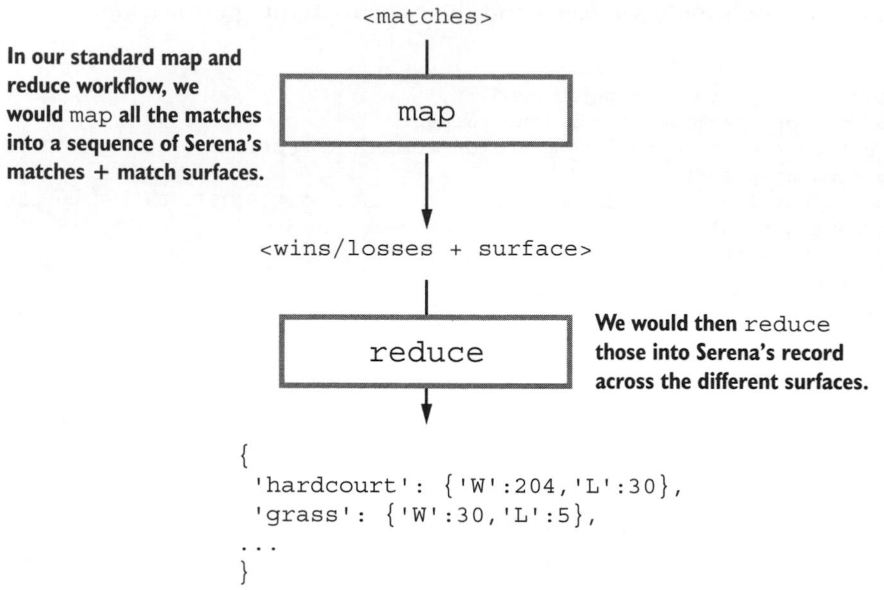
<matches>
In our standard map and reduce workflow, we would map all the matches into a sequence of Serena's matches + match surfaces.
map
<wins/losses + surface>
reduce
We would then reduce those into Serena's record across the different surfaces.
{
'hardcourt': {'W':204,'L':30},
'grass': {'W':30,'L':5},
...
}

Figure 8.9 A traditional map and reduce solution would map information into `dicts` to allow us to count Serena's wins.

To implement this arrangement, we'll make a new class that inherits from `MRJob` called `SerenaCounter` with a `.mapper` method that returns either the surface and a `W` or the surface and an `L`. That class also will need to have a `.reducer` method that gets the frequencies of her results for each surface. To do that, we'll bring back our `frequencies` code from chapter 5. We can see what this process looks like in the following listing.

Listing 8.5 Counting Serena Williams' wins and losses by surface with `MRJob`

```
from mrjob.job import MRJob
from functools import reduce

def make_counts(acc, nxt):
    acc[nxt] = acc.get(nxt,0) + 1
    return acc

def my_frequencies(xs):
    return reduce(make_counts, xs, {})

class SerenaCounter(MRJob):

  def mapper(self, _, line):
    fields = line.split(',')
    if fields[10] == 'Serena Williams':
        yield fields[2], 'W'
```

```
    elif fields[20] == 'Serena Williams':
        yield fields[2], 'L'

  def reducer(self, surface, results):
    counts = my_frequencies(results)
    yield surface, counts

if __name__ == "__main__":
  SerenaCounter.run()
```

Our `.mapper` method ingests the lines from our match logs and checks the winner and loser fields for Serena's name. If we find her in the winner field, we'll output the court type and a `W`. If we find her in the loser field, we'll output the court type and an `L`. If we don't find her in either field, we won't output anything.

The `.reducer` method receives that information by key, which we take in through the `surface` parameter, and value, which we take in through the `results` parameter. Because we passed the court type out in first position in our `.mapper`, that value will be read as the key. The results will be accessible for each court type as a sequence, like `['W', 'L', 'W', 'W', . . . ]`. We can use our `frequencies` function to get a `dict` of the counts of each unique element. We'll output the surface and counts at the end of our `.reducer` to see the court type with which each grouping of wins and losses is associated.

When we're ready to run the script, we can run it from the command line:

```
python3 serena_counter.py '/path/to/tennis/matches/wta_*.txt'
```

Shortly after, we should see something like the following printed to the screen.

```
"Carpet"  {"W": 15, "L": 3}
"Clay"    {"L": 34, "W": 145}
"Hard"    {"W": 418, "L": 67}
"Grass"   {"W": 84, "L": 10}
```

`MRJob` combs through each record in all the match log files and sums up all of Serena's wins and losses, providing us her record by court type. From this, we can see that she's a dominant grass court player, winning more than eight matches for every loss. On clay comparatively, she's the most human, winning just shy of 75% (67 wins in 90 matches) of her matches. On hard courts, where she plays most of her matches, she has racked up more than 240 wins, claiming victory more than 80% (243 wins in 290 matches) of the time.

8.4.2 *Sibling rivalry for the ages*

Serena Williams is not alone in the Williams family when it comes to dominance in the sport of tennis.

SCENARIO Serena Williams' story is made all the more interesting by her rivalry with another tennis great, her sister: Venus Williams, an Olympic gold

> medalist and five-time Wimbledon winner. Coming to terms with the fact that a story about Serena's dominance across court types is not going to be very interesting—she's amazing, we get it—the same sports writer has asked us to assess which sister has the advantage over the other on each type of court.

We'll attack this scenario just like the last one: working our way backwards from the results we want to the transformations we need to make. We know we'll need our data organized by court type—that's what the reporter wants to see—and we'll also need counts of each sister's victories on those courts. Sounds like our court types should be the keys, and the winners and wins should be our values.

Because we know that both Williams sisters will play in all the matches they play against each other, it's enough to count the winner—the loser of the match will be whoever doesn't win. Our `.mapper`, then, will check to see if it's a match between the sisters, and if it is, it'll output the surface and the winner. Our `.reducer` will count up the wins for each sister by surface type. This process is illustrated in figure 8.10.

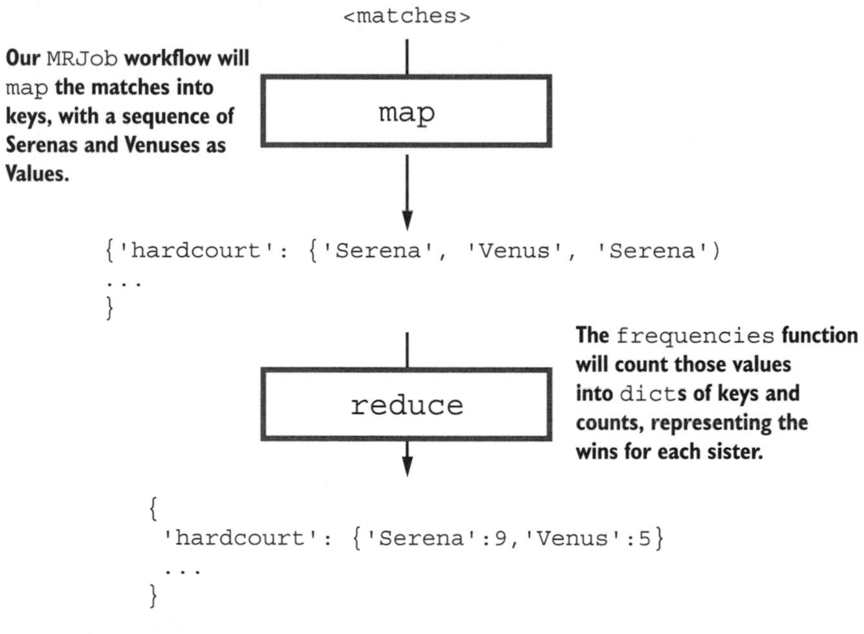
<matches>
Our MRJob workflow will map the matches into keys, with a sequence of Serenas and Venuses as Values.
map
{'hardcourt': {'Serena', 'Venus', 'Serena')
...
}
The frequencies function will count those values into dicts of keys and counts, representing the wins for each sister.
reduce
{
'hardcourt': {'Serena':9,'Venus':5}
...
}

Figure 8.10 The `MRJob` workflow uses keys and values to count up wins for the Williams sisters by surface.

Programmatically, we'll have to create another class inheriting from the `MRJob` class. This one we'll call `WilliamsRivalry`. The `WilliamsRivalry` class will need two methods: a `.mapper` and a `.reducer`. The `.mapper` will split the lines up into fields, check that both Venus and Serena Williams are playing, and output the winning sister and the surface they played on. The `.reducer` will need to count up each sister's victories on the different types of courts. The code will look like the following listing.

Listing 8.6 Evaluating the Williams sisters' rivalry with `MRJob`

```
from mrjob.job import MRJob
from functools import reduce

def make_counts(acc, nxt):
    acc[nxt] = acc.get(nxt,0) + 1
    return acc

def my_frequencies(xs):
    return reduce(make_counts, xs, {})

class WilliamsRivalry(MRJob):

  def mapper(self, _, line):
    fields = line.split(',')
    players = [fields[10], fields[20]]
    if 'Serena Williams' in players and 'Venus Williams' in players:
      yield fields[2], fields[10]

  def reducer(self, surface, results):
    counts = my_frequencies(results)
    yield surface, counts

if __name__ == "__main__":
  WilliamsRivalry.run()
```

A lot of the code in listing 8.6 is similar to the code in listing 8.5. In fact, the only substantive change is in the `.mapper` method. The new `.mapper` method breaks each line up into fields like our old `.mapper`, then creates a `players` variable—a string that holds the names of the winning and losing players. We use this to check that each of the Williams sisters is playing. If we find both sisters' names in the `players` variable, we can then output the surface type, which is stored in the 2nd position, and the winner, which is stored in the 10th position.

Then, because our `my_frequencies` function counts up whatever is passed to it, we can achieve the desired results without changing our `.reducer` at all. Instead of counting up wins and losses by surface type, the counter will count up the winners by surface type. Ultimately, the `.reducer` will output the surface type and a `dict` containing each sister's name and the number of times they bested the other on that surface.

We can run this code from the command line, remembering to pass the path to the data as an argument, and we should see output like this:

```
"Clay"    {"Serena Williams": 2}
"Grass"   {"Venus Williams": 2, "Serena Williams": 4}
"Hard"    {"Serena Williams": 10, "Venus Williams": 6}
```

From the output, we can see that the siblings are competitive across both grass and hard courts. Venus won two of the grass-court matches, and Serena won four (66%). In hard-court matches, Serena is besting her sister in a similar percentage of the matches they play (64%). For Serena, winning 64% of the matches is a poor showing—remember that she won nearly 80% of her matches against the professional circuit at large on hard courts and nearly 90% of her matches on grass.

8.5 Exercises

8.5.1 Hadoop data formats

Which data format does `MRJob` use to share data between the `map` step and the `reduce` step? (Choose one.)

- Binary
- Raw text
- JSON
- Pickle

8.5.2 More Hadoop data formats

True or **False**: Parallel processes like Hadoop MapReduce jobs are deterministic—their outputs are always produced in the same order.

8.5.3 Hadoop's native tongue

Which of the following languages is Hadoop written in? (Choose one.)

- Haskell
- C++
- JavaScript
- Java

8.5.4 Designing common patterns in MRJob

When working with `MRJob`, we'll achieve better performance if we attempt to code in an `MRJob` style—using keys and values along with `mappers` and `reducers`. Implement some of the common map and reduce style patterns we've seen so far.

> **NOTE** The code snippets here illustrate the functionality of the desired functions. You'll want to implement the `MRJob` class for each snippet.

- *Filter*—Take a sequence and return a subset of that sequence.

```
>>> filter(is_even, [1,2,3,4,5]) # [2,4]
```

- *Frequencies*—Take a sequence and count the things in that sequence.

```
>>> frequencies([1,2,1,1,2])  # {1:3, 2:2}
```

- *GroupBy*—Group a sequence by values resulting from a function.

```
>>> group_by(is_even, [1,2,3,4,5])  # {True: [2,4], False: [1,3,5]}
```

- *CountBy*—Get counts of keys resulting from a function.

```
>>> count_by(is_even, [1,2,3,4,5])  # {True: 2, False: 3}
```

Summary

- JSON is a data format that we can use to pass complex data structures between the `mapper` and `reducer` steps of an Apache Hadoop Streaming MapReduce job.
- We use the `json.dumps()` and `json.loads()` functions from Python's json library to achieve this transfer.
- We can use the mrjob library to write MapReduce jobs without having to interact directly with Hadoop.
- The mrjob library forces us to think about our `map` and `reduce` steps as taking in and spitting out key-value pairs.
- Hadoop uses these keys under the hood to allocate data to the proper location.
- The mrjob library enforces JSON data exchange between the `mapper` and `reducer` phases, so we need to ensure that our output data is JSON serializable.
- The mrjob library was designed for big data processing in the cloud—it has excellent support for Amazon Web Services' Elastic MapReduce, which we will cover in chapter 12.

9 PageRank with map and reduce in PySpark

This chapter covers

- Options for parallel map and reduce routines in PySpark
- Convenience methods of PySpark's `RDD` class for common operations
- Implementing the historic PageRank algorithm in PySpark

In chapter 7, we learned about Hadoop and Spark, two frameworks for distributed computing. In chapter 8, we dove into the weeds of Hadoop, taking a close look at how we might use it to parallelize our Python work for large datasets. In this chapter, we'll become familiar with PySpark—the Scala-based, in-memory, large dataset processing framework.

As mentioned in chapter 7, Spark has some advantages:

- Spark can be very, very fast.
- Spark programs use all the same map and reduce techniques we learned about in chapters 2 through 6.
- We can code our Spark programs entirely in Python, taking advantage of the thorough PySpark API.

In this chapter, we'll take a look at how we can make the most of PySpark by focusing on its foundational class: the `RDD`—Resilient Distributed Dataset. We'll explore the map and reduce-like methods of the `RDD` that we can use to perform familiar map and reduce workflows in parallel. We'll learn about some of the `RDD` class's convenience methods that make our lives easier. And we'll learn all this by implementing the PageRank algorithm—the simple but elegant ranking algorithm that once formed the backbone of Google's search.

9.1 A closer look at PySpark

In chapter 7, we introduced Spark and saw that we could use it to write Python code and have that code translated into fast parallel map and reduce programs. This process of translation—from Python into Scala—was reflected in the style of our Python code. In this chapter, we'll take a look at the map and reduce style utilities available to us through PySpark's `RDD` class.

The `RDD` class has methods that we can group into three categories:

1. `map`-*like methods*—Methods we can use to replicate the function of `map`
2. `reduce`-*like methods*—Methods we can use to replicate the function of `reduce`
3. *Convenience methods*—Methods that solve common problems

We've seen functions throughout this book that fall into each of these categories; for example, the map variations (`imap`, `starmap`) all fall into `map`-like methods, and functions like `filter` and `frequencies` fall into the convenience methods. PySpark has its own tools that offer similar convenience as well as PySpark `RDD`-based parallelization.

9.1.1 Map-like methods in PySpark

We'll start our closer look at PySpark by examining `map`-like methods: `.map`, `.flatMap`, `.mapValues`, `.flatMapValues`, `.mapPartitions`, and `.mapPartitionsWithIndex`. You're already familiar with the first two—we've seen them in previous chapters. The second two are unique to Spark and require us to dive a little more into how Spark works. In this section, we'll take a look at how we can use these methods to replicate the `map` behaviors we've seen in previous chapters.

> **REFRESHER** Resilient Distributed Dataset objects are the foundation of Spark's power. They are an abstraction that allows programmers to use high-level methods (like `.map` and `.reduce`) to execute parallel operations in-memory across a distributed system. Because `RDD`s hold as much data in memory as possible, Spark can be much, much faster than Hadoop. In PySpark, most of the parallel operations we'll want to take advantage of are implemented as methods to an `RDD` class. This class represents the Resilient Distributed Dataset we're operating on.

The `RDD`'s `.map` method, as we would expect, takes a function and applies it to each of the elements of our `RDD`. For example, if we open some text files with `SparkContext`'s `.textFile` method (which we introduced in chapter 7), we would map a function over the resulting strings. We can imagine a function `make_words` that splits a string into words and would turn our list of text strings into a list of word lists, with one word list for each string. We can see this process in figure 9.1.

Like we saw in listing 7.7, though, sometimes we'll want one big sequence instead of a sequences of sequences. For that, we can use the `RDD` `.flatMap` method. `.flatMap` is equivalent to `map`, but it returns a flattened sequence of the elements. Using the same example from figure 9.1, `.flatMap` would return a single long sequence of words, disregarding the information about which string they came from. Figure 9.2 shows an example of this.

The `.mapValues` and `.flatMapValues` methods are like `.map` and `.flatMap`, except they operate only on the values of key-value pairs. For example, we may have data about web pages on our site and the IP addresses that visited them, and we're interested

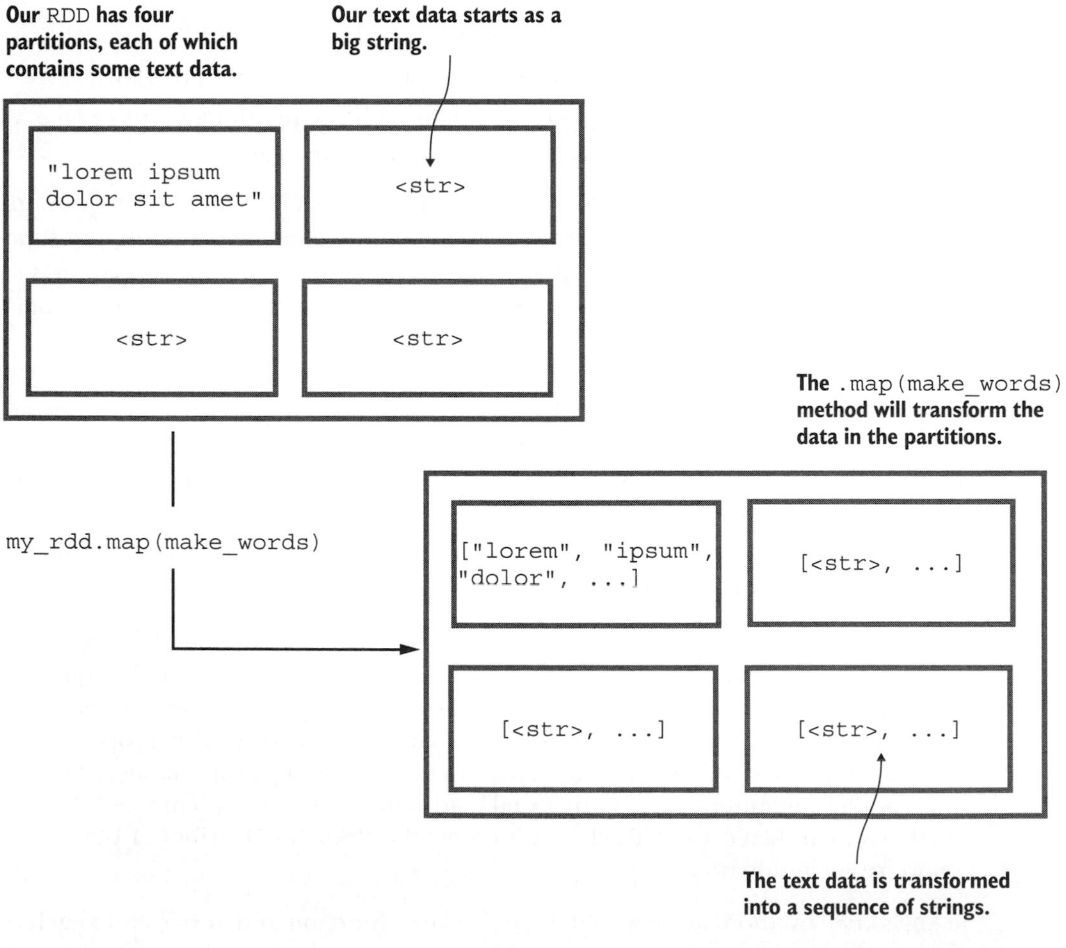
Our RDD has four partitions, each of which contains some text data.
Our text data starts as a big string.
"lorem ipsum dolor sit amet"
<str>
<str>
<str>
The .map(make_words) method will transform the data in the partitions.
my_rdd.map(make_words)
["lorem", "ipsum", "dolor", ...]
[<str>, ...]
[<str>, ...]
[<str>, ...]
The text data is transformed into a sequence of strings.

Figure 9.1 The `RDD` `.map` method maps across the `RDD`, in this case turning words in each string into a list of strings.

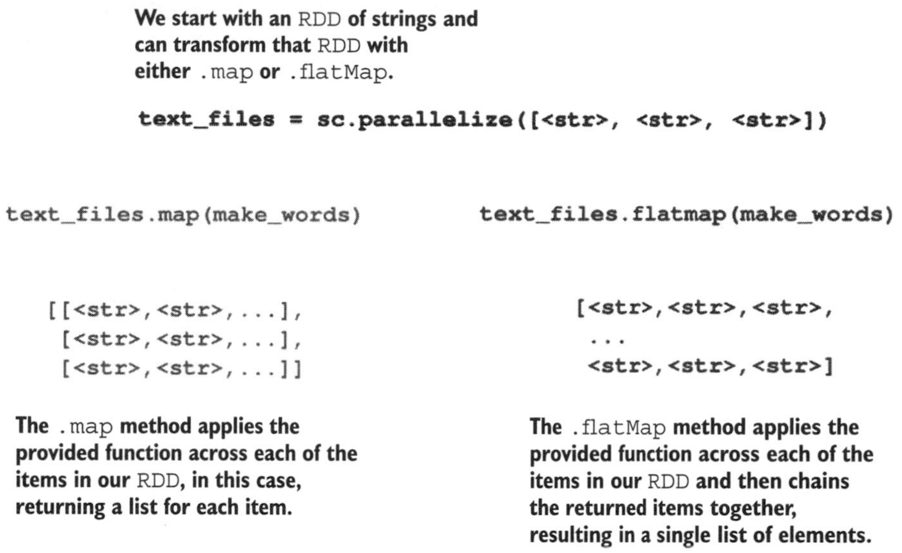
We start with an RDD of strings and can transform that RDD with either .map or .flatMap.
text_files = sc.parallelize([<str>, <str>, <str>])
text_files.map(make_words)
text_files.flatmap(make_words)
[[<str>,<str>,...],
[<str>,<str>,...],
[<str>,<str>,...]]
[<str>,<str>,<str>,
...
<str>,<str>,<str>]
The .map method applies the provided function across each of the items in our RDD, in this case, returning a list for each item.
The .flatMap method applies the provided function across each of the items in our RDD and then chains the returned items together, resulting in a single list of elements.

Figure 9.2 The RDD .flatMap method returns a flattened sequence and is useful when we're interested in the elements of each partition all together.

in the number of unique visitors for each page. Assuming we had this data stored as key-value pairs, we could then use `.mapValues` to retain the information in the key (the web page) but alter each value, transforming a list of IP addresses into a count. We can see this example in figure 9.3.

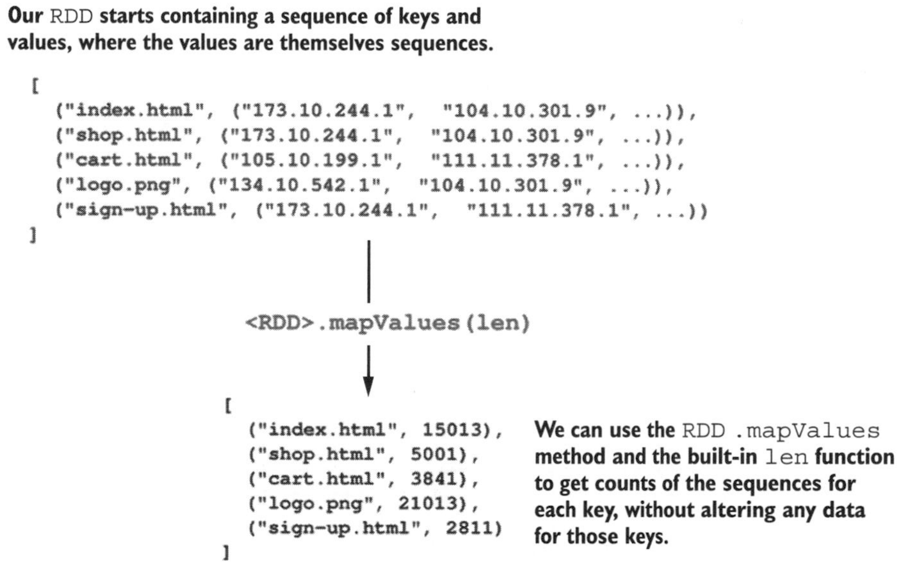
Our RDD starts containing a sequence of keys and values, where the values are themselves sequences.
[
("index.html", ("173.10.244.1", "104.10.301.9", ...)),
("shop.html", ("173.10.244.1", "104.10.301.9", ...)),
("cart.html", ("105.10.199.1", "111.11.378.1", ...)),
("logo.png", ("134.10.542.1", "104.10.301.9", ...)),
("sign-up.html", ("173.10.244.1", "111.11.378.1", ...))
]
<RDD>.mapValues(len)
[
("index.html", 15013),
("shop.html", 5001),
("cart.html", 3841),
("logo.png", 21013),
("sign-up.html", 2811)
]
We can use the RDD .mapValues method and the built-in len function to get counts of the sequences for each key, without altering any data for those keys.

Figure 9.3 You can use the RDD's .mapValues method to retain the keys while altering the values.

Lastly, the `.mapPartions` and the `.mapPartionsWithIndex` methods of the `RDD` class are variations of `map` that are *partition aware*—they know which partition of our `RDD` the data being processed resides on. Partitions, as we mentioned in chapter 7, are the abstraction that `RDD`s use to implement parallelization. The data in an `RDD` is split up across different partitions, and each partition is handled in memory. It is common in (very) large data tasks to partition an `RDD` by a key. For example, if we have an enormously popular web page—going back to the example we just discussed in figure 9.3—we may partition the website by page using the `RDD`'s `.partitionBy` method. Using this partitioning strategy, we could perform operations on each page in memory in a single partition (in other words, we'd perform those operations quickly). `.mapPartitions` and `.mapPartitionsWithIndex` are the `.map` and `.mapValues` equivalents for partitions. An example of this is shown in figure 9.4.

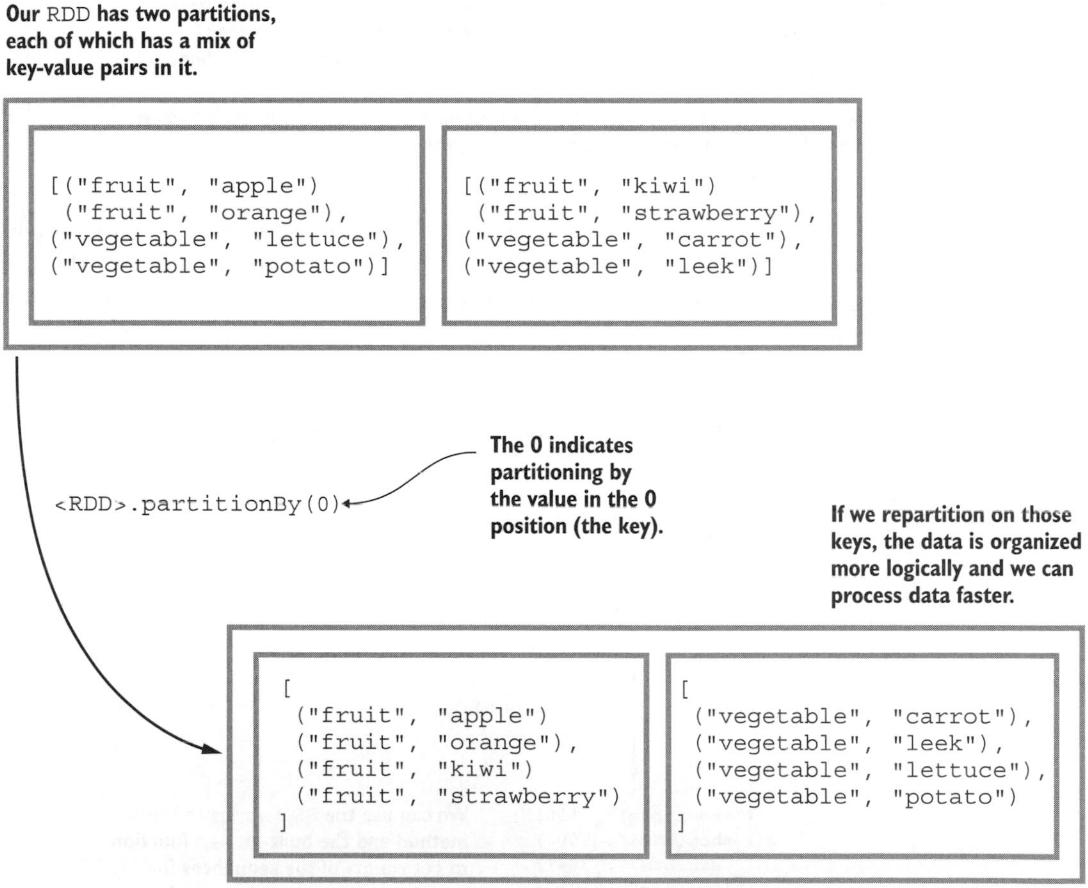
Our RDD has two partitions, each of which has a mix of key-value pairs in it.
[("fruit", "apple")
("fruit", "orange"),
("vegetable", "lettuce"),
("vegetable", "potato")]
[("fruit", "kiwi")
("fruit", "strawberry"),
("vegetable", "carrot"),
("vegetable", "leek")]
<RDD>.partitionBy(0)
The 0 indicates partitioning by the value in the 0 position (the key).
If we repartition on those keys, the data is organized more logically and we can process data faster.
[
("fruit", "apple")
("fruit", "orange"),
("fruit", "kiwi")
("fruit", "strawberry")
]
[
("vegetable", "carrot"),
("vegetable", "leek"),
("vegetable", "lettuce"),
("vegetable", "potato")
]

Figure 9.4 Partitioning a large dataset by logical keys optimizes our compute processes and makes future join operations easier.

9.1.2 Reduce-like methods in PySpark

Of course, while we need `map` to do our data transformation, we also need `reduce` to summarize our data. The `RDD` class has three methods that I consider `reduce`-like:

- `.reduce`
- `.fold`
- `.aggregate`

Each of these methods has a `byKey` variation:

- `.reduceByKey`
- `.foldByKey`
- `.aggregateByKey`

The methods `.reduce`, `.fold`, and `.aggregate` are all similar to Python's `reduce` function you've gotten to know, except that they each have differing levels of assumptions—with `.reduce` being the most presumptive, `.aggregate` being the most flexible, and `.fold` falling in between.

The `RDD` `.reduce` method provides `reduce` functionality—taking a sequence and accumulating it into some other data structure—however, we can't provide either an initializer value or a combination function to `RDD`'s `.reduce` method. This means that to use the `RDD` `.reduce` method, we'll expect to have the same data type all the way through the operation—including our ultimate data structure. A good example of the type of operation this would be suited for is summation. In summation, all of our elements will be numeric data types, and our output value will be a numeric data type.

Slightly more nuanced, the `.fold` method allows us to provide an initializer value in addition to an aggregation operation. This makes `.fold` suitable in situations where we may want to have a guaranteed value that doesn't exist in our sequence. For example, if we wanted to find the minimum value of a sequence of numbers but we wanted to ensure that it would be at least as small as one, we could use `.fold` with the `min` function and 1 as an initializer.

The `.aggregate` method provides all the functionality of a parallel `reduce`. We can provide an initializer value, an aggregation function, and a combination function. (We introduced combination functions in chapter 6 on parallel `reduce`. They provide the instructions for how to join work accumulated in parallel by the accumulation functions and may be different from the accumulation functions in complex workflows.) We can use this method for anything `.reduce` and `.fold` can do, and anything else we may want to use a parallel `reduce` for. Table 9.1 summarizes the differences between the methods.

Table 9.1 Differences between the `RDD`'s `.reduce`, `.fold`, and `.aggregate` methods

Method	Aggregate	Initialize	Combine
`RDD.reduce()`	Yes	No	No
`RDD.fold()`	Yes	Yes	No
`RDD.aggregate()`	Yes	Yes	Yes

As mentioned, each of the three methods we just looked at—`.reduce`, `.fold`, and `.aggregate`—also has a `byKey` variation: `.reduceByKey`, `.foldByKey`, and `.aggregateByKey`. Each of these methods works like the previous methods, but they operate on the values of a sequence of key-value pairs and only accumulate one value per key. For example, if we had a sequence of keys and values indicating pages and the number of seconds a user spent on a page during a single visit to it, we could get totals for each page using the `.reduceByKey` method. This is illustrated in figure 9.5 and shown in listing 9.1.

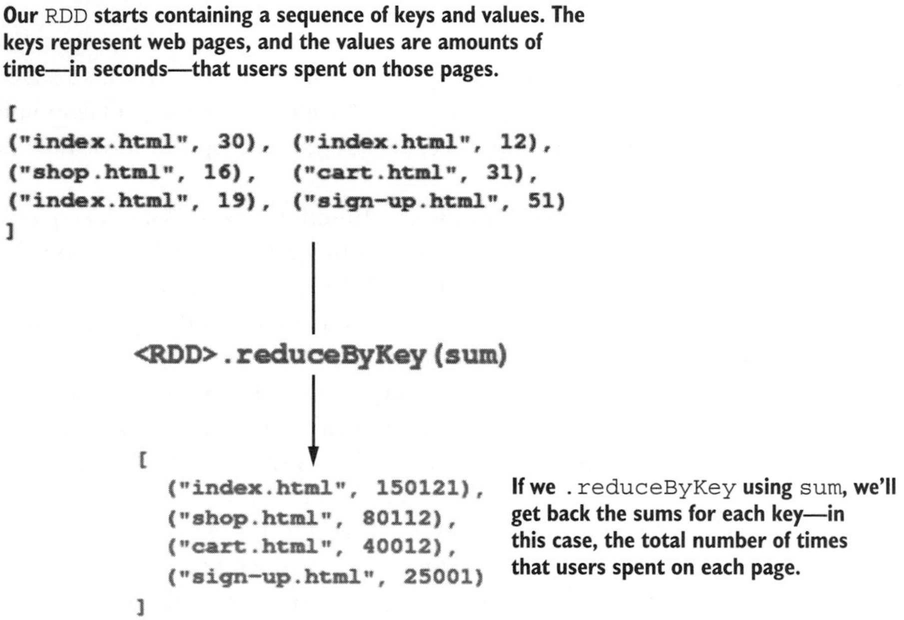
Our RDD starts containing a sequence of keys and values. The keys represent web pages, and the values are amounts of time—in seconds—that users spent on those pages.
[
("index.html", 30), ("index.html", 12),
("shop.html", 16), ("cart.html", 31),
("index.html", 19), ("sign-up.html", 51)
]
<RDD>.reduceByKey(sum)
[
("index.html", 150121),
("shop.html", 80112),
("cart.html", 40012),
("sign-up.html", 25001)
]
If we .reduceByKey using sum, we'll get back the sums for each key—in this case, the total number of times that users spent on each page.

Figure 9.5 You can use the `.reduceByKey` method (as well as `.foldByKey` and `.aggregateByKey`) to accumulate values specifically for each key in a sequence of key-value pairs.

Listing 9.1 Counting page visit time with `.reduceByKey`

```
>>> page_visits = sc.parallelize([("index.html", 3), ("cart.html", 11),
                                  ("checkout.php", 2), ("index.html", 6),
                                  ("search.html", 2), ("cart.html", 3)])
>>>> page_vists.reduceByKey(sum)
("index.html", 9)
("cart.html", 14)
. . .
```

9.1.3 *Convenience methods in PySpark*

Lastly, PySpark provides a number of convenience methods for manipulating RDDs. Many of these mirror the convenience functions in the functools, itertools, and toolz libraries we've seen already in chapters 4 and 6. Others are Python mirrors of methods that exist in Scala—the language in which Spark is written. Methods you should be aware of include

- `.countByKey()`
- `.countByValue()`
- `.distinct()`
- `.countApproxDistinct()`
- `.filter()`
- `.first()`
- `.groupBy()`
- `.groupByKey()`
- `.saveAsTextFile()`
- `.take()`

THE .FILTER, .FIRST, AND .TAKE METHODS OF SPARK'S RDD

Let's start with the ones that have direct mirrors in previous chapters: `.filter`, `.first`, and `.take`. The `RDD` class's `.filter` method behaves like Python's `filter` function: it uses a function to return a new sequence with only elements that pass the filter by making the function return `True`. The `RDD` class's `.first` method returns the first value in the sequence. And the `.take` method, like `take` from toolz, allows us to retrieve the first however many elements of a sequence.

COUNTING ELEMENTS OF AN RDD WITH .COUNTBYKEY AND .COUNTBYVALUE

Next, we have `.countByKey` and `.countByValue`. These methods behave like the `frequencies` function—both the one we built ourselves and the one implemented in toolz. We can use these methods to get a key-value sequence of things and their counts. `.countByKey` returns counts of the keys in the `RDD`, whereas `.countByValue` returns counts of the values. We can see an example of how the two differ in the following listing.

Listing 9.2 PySpark RDD's .countByKey and .countByValue methods

```
>>> xs = sc.paralellize(["Spark", "is", "great"])
>>> xs.map(lambda x:(x, len(x))).countByKey()
[("Spark", 1), ("is", 1), ("great", 1)]

>>> xs.map(lambda x:(x, len(x)).countByValue()
[(5, 2), (2, 1)]
```

Listing 9.2 shows that if we have an `RDD` of words and their lengths as `tuples`, we can use the `.countByKey` method to get a count of all the unique words and the `.countByValue` method to get a count of the unique lengths. In this case, the words are acting as the keys because they're in first position, and the lengths are acting as the values because they're in second position.

Counting unique things with RDD's .countApproxDistinct

Another counting method that's useful—especially when working with large datasets—is the `.countApproxDistinct` method. Often, we want to know how many unique elements are in our dataset. How many unique words were used in a document collection? How many unique IP addresses are in our logs? How many unique sessions visited our site? Spark provides the `.distinct` method for when we have a small enough dataset that it's fine to calculate an exact number. The problem when we have large datasets is that these counts are time expensive; they require a full pass of often very long sequences. `.countApproxDistinct` allows that process to be sped up and parallelized, if a small window of error is allowable. It uses an approximation algorithm that is parallelizable, allowing us to benefit from the time savings of parallelization

Collecting elements of an RDD with .groupBy and .groupByKey.

Another category of convenience methods we'll want to know about are two methods—`.groupBy` and `.groupByKey`—we can use for restructuring our `RDD`. Each of these methods collects all the instances of items in our `RDD` and returns an `RDD` of key-value `tuples`. For `.groupByKey`, the items are organized using the keys of the existing key-value `tuples`. For `.groupBy`, the items are organized under new keys resulting from a function (that we get to provide) applied to each element of the `RDD`.

For example, if we had a sequence of words and wanted to collect them based on their first letter, we would pass a function to `.groupBy` that returned the first character of a string.

```
>>> xs = sc.parallelize(["apple", "banana", "cantaloupe"])
>>> xs.groupBy(getFirstLetter)
[("a",["apple"]), ("b", ["banana"]), ("c", ["cantaloupe"])]
```

If we had a sequence where we already had key-value `tuples`, we could use `.groupByKey`, similarly, to obtain groupings of the elements that shared a key.

```
>>> xs = sc.parallelize([("pet", "dog"), ("pet", "cat"),
                         ("farm", "horse"), "farm", "cow")])
>>> xs.groupByKey()
[("pet", ["dog", "cat"]), ("farm", ["horse", "cow"])]
```

Somewhat counterintuitively, `.groupBy` is a special implementation of the `.groupByKey` method, so whenever you're given a choice between the two, it's better to use `.groupByKey`.

Saving RDDs to text files

Lastly, there's the `.saveAsTextFile` method, which does what its name implies it does: it saves an `RDD` to a text file. Each element of the `RDD` will be written in string form to a text file, separated from the next element by a newline. This is excellent for a few reasons:

1 The data is in a human-readable, persistent format.
2 We can easily read this data back into Spark with the `.textFile` method of `SparkContext`.
3 The data is well structured for other parallel tools, such as Hadoop's MapReduce.
4 We can specify a compression format for efficient data storage or transfer.

First, having the data in a persistent, human-readable format puts us in a good position to have high-quality data for a long time. Because the data is human readable, it can be manually inspected—even by nonprogrammers—to ensure that it's free from errors. Because the data is in plain text and not bytecode, we have some security that changes to our operating system or our runtime environment won't render the data obsolete.

Second, we can quickly read the data back in using the `.textFile` method of `SparkContext`. This is excellent if we have textual data where we want to be working with strings, or if we have simply structured data. If our data is complex, we may not want to store the data in this format; the process of reconstituting it could be painful. Most of the work we'll do in Spark will use straightforward data structures.

Third, this format is excellent for Hadoop's MapReduce, which expects a file with lines to process. If you have MapReduce code that you like and you're doing work in Spark as well, this can be a great way to share data between the two processes. This is a common use case, with lots of teams having legacy MapReduce jobs they like but starting to incorporate more and more Spark into their work.

Fourth, and finally, we can specify a compression format for the text file so it's saved in a space-efficient way. A wide range of codecs are available for this, including two common codecs: bz2 and gzip. Between bz2 and gzip, bz2 is the slower, more compressed format, and gzip is the faster, less compressed format. Specifying a compression format will make the data unreadable by a human until it is decompressed. However, we don't need to decompress the data before using it again in Spark or Hadoop jobs.

To specify a compression format, we have to call the format's full Hadoop codec name. The full name for bz2 is `org.apache.hadoop.io.compress.BZip2Codec`, and the full name for gzip is `org.apache.hadoop.io.compress.GzipCodec`.

```
>>> my_rdd.saveToText("./path/to/file.bz2",
                      "org.apache.hadoop.io.compress.BZip2Codec")

>>> my_rdd.saveToText("./path/to/file.gz",
                      "org.apache.hadoop.io.compress.GzipCodec")
```

It's convention to save a bz2 compressed file with a .bz2 ending and a gzip compressed file with a .gz ending.

9.2 Tennis rankings with Elo and PageRank in PySpark

Now that we have the basics of Spark under us, let's use it to build one of the classic large dataset algorithms: PageRank. Consider the scenario from chapter 8.

> **SCENARIO** A new professional tennis league is forming, and they have hired you to come up with skill estimates for professional tennis players so that they can direct their efforts for recruiting players to the new league. They have provided you with data for several years of matches and would like you to return to them with a list of players and their corresponding skills.

9.2.1 Revisiting Elo ratings with PySpark

We looked at how we could solve this problem using Elo ratings—a ranking system that iteratively adjusts players' scores after each win and loss—with Hadoop MapReduce. We can implement this solution in Spark as well, using Spark's `reduce` capabilities. To do that, we'll need to

1. write Spark code to bring in the data
2. copy the `elo_acc` accumulator function from listing 8.2
3. call the `elo_acc` function with the right Spark `reduce`-like method

We can see what this will look like in the following listing.

Listing 9.3 Elo rating reduction in Spark

```
#! /usr/bin/env python3

import re
from pyspark import SparkContext

def round5(x):
  return 5*int(x/5)

def clean_match(match):
  ms = match.split(",")
  match_data = {"winner": ms[10],
                "loser": ms[20],
                "surface": ms[2]}
  return match_data

def elo_acc(acc,nxt):
    w_elo = acc.get(nxt["winner"],1600)
    l_elo = acc.get(nxt["loser"],1600)
    Qw = 10**(w_elo/400)
    Ql = 10**(l_elo/400)
    Qt = Qw+Ql
    acc[nxt["winner"]] = round5(w_elo + 25*(1-(Qw/Qt)))
    acc[nxt["loser"]] = round5(l_elo - 25*(Ql/Qt))
    return acc

def elo_comb(a,b):
    a.update(b)
    return a
```

```
if __name__ == "__main__":
  sc = SparkContext(appName="TennisElos ")
  text_files = sc.textFile("/path/to/my/data/wta_matches*")
  xs = text_files.map(clean_match) \
              .aggregate({},elo_acc, elo_comb)

  for x in sorted(xs.items(), key=lambda x:x[1], reverse=True)[:20]:
      print("{:<30}{}".format(*x))
```

The majority of the code in the listing comes from chapter 8 and needs little further explanation. We reviewed the `clean_match` and `elo_acc` functions in section 8.2.2. These are the two major differences between the code in listing 9.3—written for PySpark—and the code from listing 8.2:

1. This code does without any of the `stdin`/`stdout` and JSON we had to concern ourselves with using MapReduce.
2. We use Spark methods to read in the data, clean the data, and aggregate over the data.

The thing that we're probably most happy with about the PySpark version of our Elo rating code is that the code is entirely in Python—without any need to interact with the terminal through `stdout` or `stdin` and without any need to translate our data types into JSON. By using PySpark, we use Python data types everywhere, and we don't even need to import the `JSON` module. This is a pretty big advantage in terms of convenience, especially if we're dealing with more sophisticated data structures that may not convert neatly into JSON.

It's also important that we can use Spark methods to handle all our data processing:

1. The first method we call, `.textFile`, brings in the text data.
2. The `.textFile` method returns an `RDD`, which has a `.map` method we can use to clean the data with our `clean_matches` function, so we do that next.
3. Then, lastly, we use the `.aggregate` method with our `elo_acc` function and a new `elo_comb` function to score the players.

We use the `.aggregate` method in this instance because it's the simplest `reduce`-like method that meets our needs. We need an empty `dict` to start with, so we can't use the `.reduce` method because that has no space for an initializer. And we also need a different combine function than the `aggregate` function, so we can't use `.fold`—`.fold` has no room for a combine function. The only `reduce`-like method left is `.aggregate`, which gives us the opportunity to specify all three pieces of our parallel `reduce`.

That covers the substantive changes to the code; however, you may have noticed one cosmetic change in listing 9.3. It's subtle, but in the middle of our map and reduce workflow, we insert a backslash character and move to the next line. This is a PySpark convention and an aspect of the Scala programming language adapted for Python. In Scala, you can chain methods, with each method on a new line by default. If we do that in Python, Python will throw an error. That's because Python is famously white-space aware. We can get around this error by adding a backslash after our method call, as shown in the following listing. The backslash character is Python's manual line wrap character.

Listing 9.4 Method chaining in Scala, and two ways in Python

```
# Example Scala code
my_dataset.map(foo)
          .reduce(bar)

# Example Python code (no wrap)
my_dataset.map(foo).reduce(bar)

# Example Python code (with wrap)
my_dataset.map(foo)\
          .reduce(bar)
```

If you're working with other PySpark developers, they're more likely than not going to be aware of this convention. For traditional Python developers, however, this convention might seem strange or even incorrect.

Ultimately, though, we'll run our script and receive Elo ratings for our tennis players that look something like figure 9.6. Here, we can see a sorted collection of players and their rankings.

The players' names → (Kim Clijsters) **And the players' ratings** → (1840)

```
Kim Clijsters           1840
Justine Henin           1815
Serena Williams         1795
Amelie Mauresmo         1740
Venus Williams          1720
Maria Fernanda Alves    1715
Lindsay Davenport       1710
Lisa Mcshea             1690
Monique Adamczak        1685
Jennifer Capriati       1685
Elena Dementieva        1675
Martina Hingis          1665
Caroline Wozniacki      1665
Maria Sharapova         1655
```

Figure 9.6 When we calculate the Elo ratings of tennis players using PySpark, our output will be a sequence of players and their ratings—the higher the rating, the better the player.

9.2.2 *Introducing the PageRank algorithm*

Now we can rank players based on their Elo rating with both MapReduce and Spark, but what if we didn't want to use Elo ratings? What if we wanted a system that didn't punish players for losing matches but only rewarded players for beating opponents? What if we wanted to reward players extra for beating high-quality opponents, encouraging top-ranked players to play competitive matches against one another? We can design a system like that using a variation of the PageRank algorithm.

PageRank is famous as the former backbone to Google's ranking system. Websites that had a higher PageRank score would show up higher in the Google search results, and websites with low PageRank scores may not show up at all. Over time, this process has changed, but the algorithm's simple and powerful assumptions have led to its longevity, and it's still used outside of Google searches (including in a variety of capacities related to sports analytics).

> **PageRank and Google search**
>
> The PageRank algorithm was the result of a research project by then Stanford PhD students Larry Page (who named the algorithm after himself) and Sergey Brin. The two would go on to use the algorithm as the backbone of Google's search engine. Historians credit Google's success to the ease of distributing the algorithm, which allowed Google to scale, and the way the algorithm naturally aligns with human assessments of importance.
>
> Over time, Google's search engine has become more complex. The search algorithm now uses hundreds of features. Google still uses a version of PageRank to assess the reliability and authority of websites. The Google Knowledge Graph and Google's preference for mobile-friendly and social-friendly content are the most evident forces in contemporary Google search.

The basic premise of PageRank was to treat website rankings like an election, with somewhat unique rules. The general rules are as follows:

1. Every page has a number of points: its PageRank score.
2. Every page votes for the pages that it links to, distributing to each page a number of points equal to the linking page's PageRank score divided by the number of pages it links to.
3. Each page then receives a new PageRank score, based on the sum of all the votes it received.
4. The process is repeated until the scores are "good enough."

Of course, tennis players don't link to other tennis players. We can, however, use players' losses as a vote for the players who are better than them. For example, if Venus Williams defeats her sister Serena at tennis, then Serena will vote for Venus with some of her points. A small-scale example of the PageRank algorithm for tennis rankings is shown in figure 9.7.

In the figure, we see five tennis players, each with 100 points to distribute.

- Player 1 lost to players 2, 3, and 5 (3 total).
- Player 2 lost to players 1 and 4 (2 total).
- Player 3 lost to players 1 and 2 (2 total).
- Player 4 lost to players 2 and 3 (2 total).
- Player 5 lost to everyone (4 total).

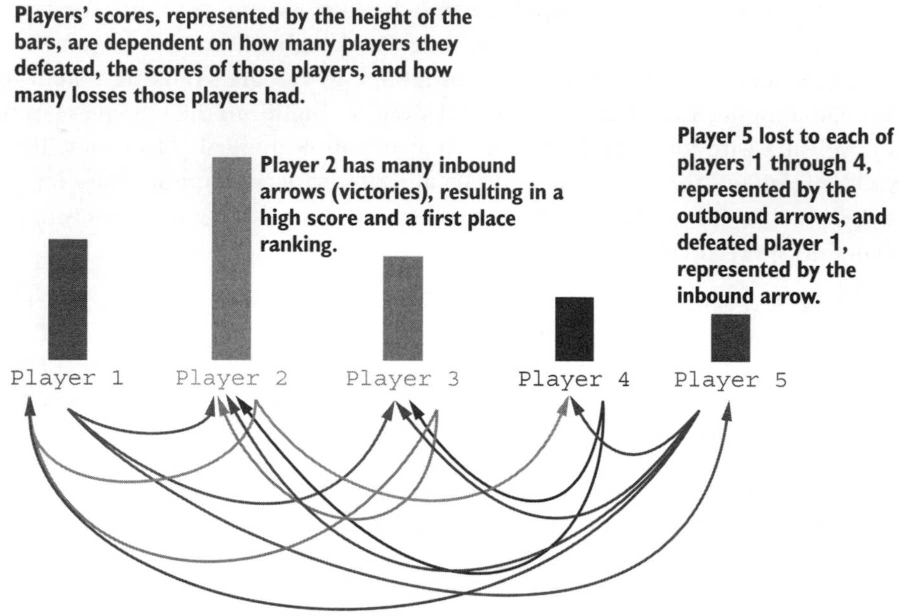
Players' scores, represented by the height of the bars, are dependent on how many players they defeated, the scores of those players, and how many losses those players had.
Player 2 has many inbound arrows (victories), resulting in a high score and a first place ranking.
Player 5 lost to each of players 1 through 4, represented by the outbound arrows, and defeated player 1, represented by the inbound arrow.
Player 1
Player 2
Player 3
Player 4
Player 5

Figure 9.7 We can apply the PageRank algorithm to tennis players, where each player contributes points to the players who are better than them.

Because three players have two losses, it's hard to tell immediately who's the best, but PageRank will help us figure it out. Player 1 distributes 33 (1/3) of their 100 points to players 2, 3, and 5. Players 2, 3, and 4 each vote with 50 points to the players to whom they lost. And player 5 votes with 25 points to each other player.

Next, we would add up all the votes. Player 2 ends up with the most points at 158 (50+50+25+33), followed by player 1 with 125 (50+50+25), followed by player 3 at 108 (50+33+25), player 4 at 75 (50+25), and player 5 at 33, from their lone victory over player 1. In a more robust example, we would then repeat this process a few times so that victories over higher rated players would be worth more. For example, players 1 and 4 should get lots of points for their victory over player 2—who is the best player—whereas beating player 5, who lost to everyone, should adjust the ratings much less. After three iterations, the players would be rated as follows:

1. Player 2—145 points
2. Player 1—125 points
3. Player 3—101 points
4. Player 4—81 points
5. Player 5—47 points

One of the largest advantages of the PageRank algorithm, which we'll see in the next section, is that it's naturally parallelizable. We can do all the point giving and point summing in parallel with our most strict assumptions about parallelization. This is one of the reasons why it worked so well for Google—they were able to parallelize their problem and scale it to the massive dataset they were working with. In the next section, we'll implement a parallel PageRank algorithm with PySpark.

9.2.3 Ranking tennis players with PageRank

Now that we have an idea of how PageRank works, how should we go about implementing it in PySpark? Well, we know our implementation will need to have five steps:

1. Read in the data.
2. Structure the data in the right way.
3. Do an initial point allocation.
4. Do several rounds of point allocation until we're satisfied with the results.
5. Return some ratings.

Figure 9.8 illustrates the first four steps.

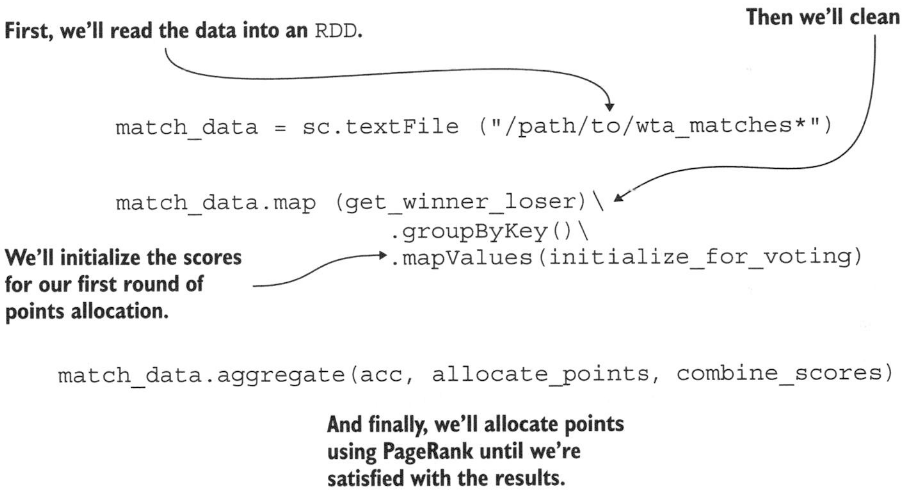
First, we'll read the data into an RDD.
Then we'll clean the data.
match_data = sc.textFile ("/path/to/wta_matches*")
match_data.map (get_winner_loser)\
.groupByKey()\
.mapValues(initialize_for_voting)
We'll initialize the scores for our first round of points allocation.
match_data.aggregate(acc, allocate_points, combine_scores)
And finally, we'll allocate points using PageRank until we're satisfied with the results.

Figure 9.8 Using the PageRank algorithm for rating tennis players in PySpark requires both custom Python functions and parallel PySpark methods.

To read in the data, we'll use the same method we've been using so far in this book: the `.textFiles` method from `SparkContext`. This method returns an `RDD`, which is the Spark class that has all the nice parallel map and reduce options we'll want to use to build our programs.

Next, we'll move on to structuring the data. For that, we'll use the `RDD`'s `.map` method to retrieve the winners and losers of each match, and we'll use the `RDD`'s

`.groupByKey` method to get a list of defeats for each player. To ensure that `.groupByKey` does what we want, we'll return winners and losers as a `tuple` in the form of: `(<loser>, <winner>)`. From there, we'll use another `.map` statement to add some metadata that will be helpful when calculating the PageRank scores.

With the data in the right format, we'll reduce over our data several times. Each time, we'll calculate the PageRank scores for each player, based on who defeated who, by looping through the losing players and giving a fraction of their score to each player who defeated them. Every new round, we'll use the latest score of the player.

Lastly, after a few rounds, we can sort our players, return their scores, and call it a day. All in all, the solution we'll draw up for this problem will be a pretty large program. You can find the full script in the code repository for this book (https://github.com/jtwool/mastering-large-datasets). Here, I think it's worth focusing our attention on three major areas:

1. The data preparation process with `.groupByKey` and `.mapValues`
2. The allocate points aggregator function and the `combine_scores` combiner
3. The iterative score calculations and the partial application of the allocate points function

Preparing the tennis match data with .groupByKey and .mapValues

The first section, data preparation, revolves around this bit of code:

```
xs = match_data.map(get_winner_loser)\
               .groupByKey()\
               .mapValues(initialize_for_voting)
```

In this section, we've already read the data into a variable called `match_data`, so we're working with an `RDD` of strings. We know that what we want to have is an `RDD` of keys (player names) with `dicts` as their values. Each of those `dicts` must have the information we need to calculate PageRank scores later on. To that end, they'll need the players the player lost to, the number of those players, and the player's current page rank score.

To get from a match string to this value will be a three-step process:

1. We'll map the match data into `tuples` of losers and winners.
2. We'll group the matches by the losing player.
3. We'll map a transformation across the keys and values to prepare our data for PageRank.

Altogether, this process will look like figure 9.9.

As we can see in figure 9.9, our first map step involves taking a subset of the match data and arranging it into `tuples`. This will return an `RDD` of `tuples`, which we can use `.groupByKey` on to return an `RDD` of keys and values. The keys in these

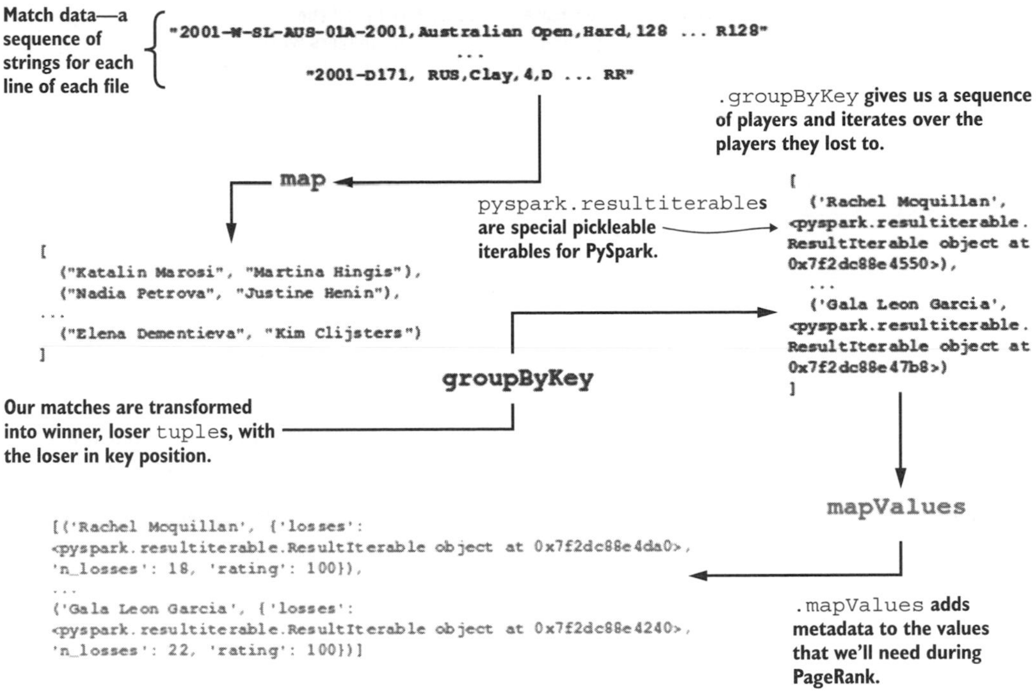
Match data—a sequence of strings for each line of each file
"2001-W-SL-AUS-01A-2001,Australian Open,Hard,128 ... R128"
...
"2001-D171, RUS,Clay,4,D ... RR"
map
[
("Katalin Marosi", "Martina Hingis"),
("Nadia Petrova", "Justine Henin"),
...
("Elena Dementieva", "Kim Clijsters")
]
Our matches are transformed into winner, loser tuples, with the loser in key position.
groupByKey
pyspark.resultiterables are special pickleable iterables for PySpark.
.groupByKey gives us a sequence of players and iterates over the players they lost to.
[
('Rachel Mcquillan', <pyspark.resultiterable.ResultIterable object at 0x7f2dc88e4550>),
...
('Gala Leon Garcia', <pyspark.resultiterable.ResultIterable object at 0x7f2dc88e47b8>)
]
mapValues
[('Rachel Mcquillan', {'losses': <pyspark.resultiterable.ResultIterable object at 0x7f2dc88e4da0>, 'n_losses': 18, 'rating': 100}),
...
('Gala Leon Garcia', {'losses': <pyspark.resultiterable.ResultIterable object at 0x7f2dc88e4240>, 'n_losses': 22, 'rating': 100})]
.mapValues adds metadata to the values that we'll need during PageRank.

Figure 9.9 We prepare tennis match data for PageRank in PySpark with `.map`, `.groupByKey`, and `.mapValues`.

instances represent the losing players, whereas the values are a sequence of players to whom the losing player lost. Lastly, we can use the `initialize_for_voting` function to add metadata and convert the list into a `dict` for a clearer workflow down the road.

ALLOCATING POINTS AND COMBINING THE SCORES

The next two parts of the process we'll want to pay extra attention to are the aggregation and combination functions. These are the functions we call during the `reduce` step that constitute the heavy lifting of our program. These functions are how we implement PageRank, and we can see them in figure 9.10.

Our aggregation function—`allocate_points`–is responsible for taking in a new player, their losses, and associated metadata, and assigning points to the players who defeated them. The points are then stored in a `dict`, with players' names as keys and players' PageRank scores as values. We can see this process in figure 9.11.

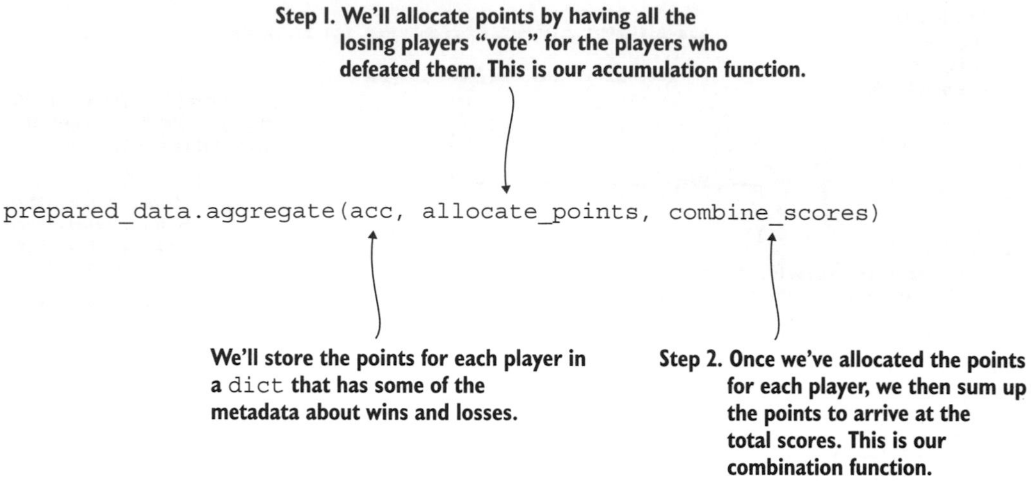
Step I. We'll allocate points by having all the losing players "vote" for the players who defeated them. This is our accumulation function.
prepared_data.aggregate(acc, allocate_points, combine_scores)
We'll store the points for each player in a dict that has some of the metadata about wins and losses.
Step 2. Once we've allocated the points for each player, we then sum up the points to arrive at the total scores. This is our combination function.

Figure 9.10 We can parallelize the ranking step of PageRank into a two-step parallel reduce workflow.

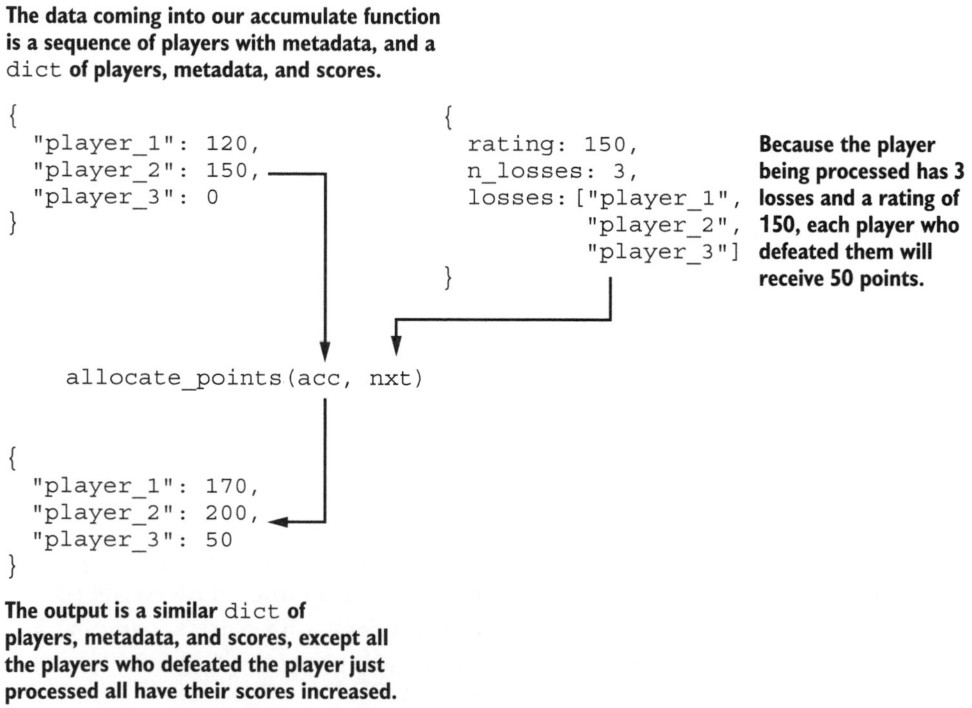
The data coming into our accumulate function is a sequence of players with metadata, and a dict of players, metadata, and scores.
{
"player_1": 120,
"player_2": 150,
"player_3": 0
}
{
rating: 150,
n_losses: 3,
losses: ["player_1",
"player_2",
"player_3"]
}
Because the player being processed has 3 losses and a rating of 150, each player who defeated them will receive 50 points.
allocate_points(acc, nxt)
{
"player_1": 170,
"player_2": 200,
"player_3": 50
}
The output is a similar dict of players, metadata, and scores, except all the players who defeated the player just processed all have their scores increased.

Figure 9.11 The `allocate_points` function takes in players' information and updates the accumulation variable to reflect the players' updated scores.

Taking a look at the code for the allocate_points function, we can see precisely how this works. We split the player into a key and value because we had the player data stored as a two-tuple coming out of our .mapValues step from the previous subsection.

```
def allocate_points(acc, nxt):
  k,v = nxt
  boost = v['rating'] / (v['n_losses'] + .01)
  for loss in v['losses']:
    if loss not in acc.keys():
      acc[loss] = {'losses':[], 'n_losses': 0}
    opp_rating = acc.get(loss,{}).get('rating',0)
    acc[loss]['rating'] = opp_rating + boost
  return acc
```

Next, we calculate the boost that each player who defeated the current player will receive. Each player allocates their entire rating uniformly to all those who defeated them. This means that the amount of the boost a player receives by beating our current player is equal to that player's rating divided by their number of losses. To prevent a divide by zero error, I add a small value to the number of losses a player has, in the event they're undefeated.

Then, we allocate those points to each player who has defeated our current player—updating the accumulation variable. We do this by setting the opposing player's rating equal to their current rating plus the boost factor. After this, we return the accumulator and move on to the next player.

This takes care of the accumulation step of our parallel reduce. As we know from chapter 6, though, parallel reduce has two parts: the parallel accumulation and the combination. In our combination step, we have to join together all the values we accumulated in parallel. Typically, this is the challenging part of parallel reduce because we'll concoct complex data structures—no such problems here.

Coming out of our reduce step, we'll want to join dicts with keys as strings and values that are integers, such that the resulting dict has all the keys of both dicts and the values are the sums of the values. We can see this process in figure 9.12.

In Python, we'll implement this process by looping through all the elements of one dict and attempting to add the values to the current value for that key in the other dict. As we do that, we'll update the dict that we aren't looping through. If we don't find a key from the dict we are looping through in the other, we'll update the other so that key is equal to the value from our looping dict. Finally, we'll return the dict we didn't loop through, since that's the dict we've been updating. Here's how that looks:

```
def combine_scores(a, b):
  for k,v in b.items():
    if k in a:
      a[k]['rating'] = a[k]['rating'] + b[k]['rating']
    else:
      a[k] = v
  return a
```

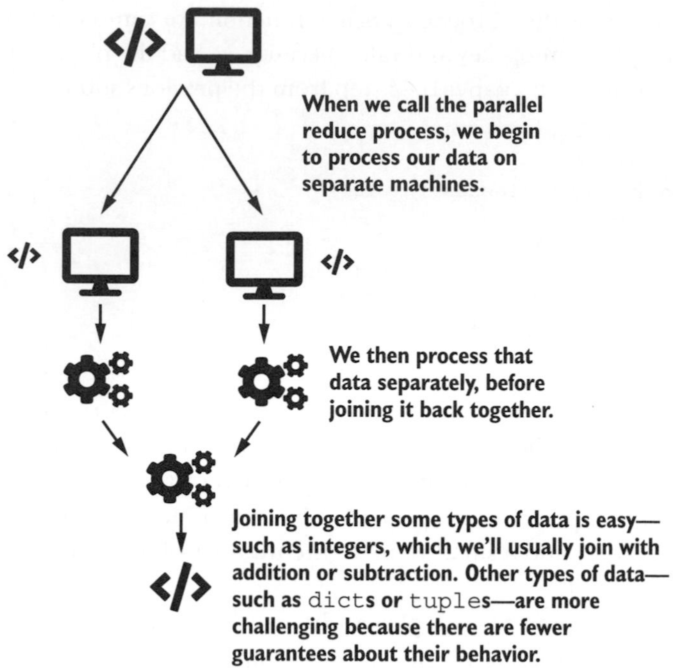
When we call the parallel reduce process, we begin to process our data on separate machines.
We then process that data separately, before joining it back together.
Joining together some types of data is easy—such as integers, which we'll usually join with addition or subtraction. Other types of data—such as dicts or tuples—are more challenging because there are fewer guarantees about their behavior.

Figure 9.12 Combining the players' PageRank ratings together requires joining `dicts` into a single `dict`.

Together, these two steps represent a single round of PageRank. One of the beauties of the PageRank algorithm is that we can do the entire process in parallel. We can take advantage of this fact if we need to rank large amounts of information quickly. By increasing our compute capacity, we can decrease the time we spend ranking.

ITERATIVELY CALCULATING SCORES

The last step we'll want to pay extra attention to is the way we iteratively calculate these scores. In the first round of a PageRank process, each of the *pages*—in our case, tennis players—are rated evenly. I decided to start everyone with 100 points, but any number of points will do. Having a uniform number of points, however, doesn't reflect reality. Some web pages are more important than others, and some tennis players are better than others. A link from the *New York Times* web page will mean more traffic than a link from a high school newspaper's web page, and a victory over Serena Williams is more notable than a victory over a career journeywoman.

To resolve this problem, we run the PageRank process several times. Each time we do the same thing, but we'll use the scores from the previous round to inform our ratings. This way, wins over Serena or links from the *New York Times* become more important in each subsequent round.

To do this, we'll insert our `reduce` step inside a `for` loop and bookend it with some code to set up the next round of the reduction:

```
for i in range(7):
  if i > 0:
    xs = sc.parallelize(zs.items())
  acc = dict(xs.mapValues(empty_ratings).collect())
  zs = xs.aggregate(acc, allocate_points, combine_scores)
```

Before we start our `reduce` step, we need to set up our accumulation variable: `acc`. This is the variable that holds all the players and their updated ratings. To get this variable, we'll empty the ratings of all the keys from our `dict` of `dicts`.. This will give each player a fresh new rating of 0 at the beginning of each PageRank step. From there, we can `reduce`.

Then, after each `reduce` step beyond the first, we'll create a new sequence of players to `reduce` over. This sequence will have all the metadata from our initialization, plus the new ratings that we can use in the next PageRank iteration.

Importantly, though, our `reduce` process—which we call using the `RDD .aggregate` method—returns a `dict`. We need an `RDD` so that we can take advantage of Spark's parallelization. To get an `RDD`, we'll need to explicitly convert the items of that `dict` into an `RDD` using the `.parallelize` method from our SparkContext: `sc`.

Once our iteration is complete, we'll have a `dict` with the players as keys and their scores as values. When you run this script, remember to run it with the `spark-submit` utility to take advantage of Spark's parallelization. You can run it with your local Python runtime as well, but it won't take advantage of the full power of Spark. We can see the script's output in figure 9.13.

After running our `spark-page-rank.py` script with the `spark-submit` utility, we'll get back a list of players in rank order based on their PageRank scores.

```
>>> spark-submit spark-page-rank.py

Justine Henin           12.0 4150
Serena Williams         12.0 4010
Venus Williams          12.0 3985
Kim Clijsters           11.9 3875
Amelie Mauresmo         11.9 3760
Lindsay Davenport       11.8 3685
Elena Dementieva        11.7 3360
Svetlana Kuznetsova     11.3 2585
Maria Sharapova         11.3 2540
Patty Schnyder          11.2 2395
```

Players' names

Players' PageRank scores

The log of players' PageRank scores

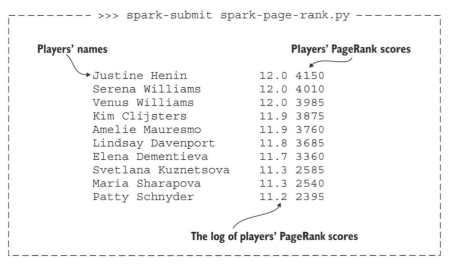

Figure 9.13 The output of our PageRank process shows the top players and their PageRank scores.

Note that in addition to the PageRank scores, we also include the log of the players' PageRank scores. Taking the log of each player's scores groups players whose scores are similar. When Google released the PageRank toolbar, they revealed a log-scaled version of their PageRank scores instead of the PageRank scores themselves. The log-scaled scores may be better representations of PageRank scores, as the difference between 4100 and 3990 is quite small.

9.3 Exercises

9.3.1 sumByKey

A common situation in which you'll find yourself in Spark will be having an `RDD` of keys and values in two-`tuples`. A common operation on those keys and values will be summing all the values by key. This operation can be called `sumByKey`. Use the right `reduce`-like method of the `RDD` to sum the values in an `RDD` by key.

```
>>> xs = sc.parallelize([("A", 1), ("A", 1), ("A", 2),
...                      ("B", 2), ("A", 1),
...                      ("C", 1),
...                      ("D", 7), ("D", -2)])
>>> sumByKey(xs)
[("A", 4), ("B", 3), ("C", 1), ("D", 5)]
```

9.3.2 sumByKey with toolz

The toolz library has a `reduceBy` function that takes a key function, an operation, and a sequence to achieve the same effect as the Spark `reduceByKey`. Implement `sumByKey` using the toolz `reduceBy` function for use in non-Spark workflows.

9.3.3 Spark and toolz

One of the great things about Spark is that it has many of the same convenience methods that we've already learned to love from the toolz library. In Scala, replicate the following transaction written using toolz. Bonus: Use Spark-style method chaining for added readability.

```
>>> import toolz
>>> xs = [("orange", "O"), ("apple", "A"), ("tomato", "T"),
          ("kiwi", "K"), ("lemon", "L")]
>>> toolz.take(toolz.frequencies((filter(lambda x: "a" in x[0], xs)), 10)
[{"O":1}, {"A": 1}, {"T": 1}]
```

9.3.4 Wikipedia PageRank

PageRank works for ranking tennis players, but it was designed to rank web pages in a network. Modify the code we wrote in this chapter to perform a PageRank of the pages from the Wikipedia network we collected in chapter 2. A dataset for this exercise is provided for your convenience in the code repository for this book (https://github.com/jtwool/mastering-large-datasets).

Summary

- The `RDD` class has three different `reduce`-like methods: `.reduce`, for operations where the data is the same all the way through, `.fold`, for when we want to specify an initializer value, and `.aggregate`, for when we want an initializer and a custom combiner function.
- The `RDD` class's `.saveAsTextFile` method is an excellent way to persist an `RDD` on-disk for long-term storage or for sharing with others—we can even use it to save our data in a compressed format!
- To take advantage of Spark's parallelization, we need to ensure that our data is in the `RDD` class. We can turn data into an `RDD` with the `SparkContext` class's `.parallelize` method.
- Spark programs often use \ characters in their method chaining to increase their readability.
- Using the `byKey` variations of methods in PySpark often results in significant speed-ups because like data is worked on by the same distributed compute worker.

10 Faster decision-making with machine learning and PySpark

This chapter covers

- An introduction to machine learning
- Training and applying decision tree classifiers in parallel with PySpark
- Matching problems and appropriate machine learning algorithms
- Training and applying random forest regressors with PySpark

Chapter 9 showed how we can write Python and take advantage of Spark, one of the most popular distributed computing frameworks. We saw some of Spark's raw data transformation options, and we used Spark in the map and reduce style we've been exploring throughout the book. However, one of the reasons why Spark is so popular is its built-in machine learning capabilities.

Machine learning refers to the design, training, application, and study of judgmental algorithms that adjust themselves based on input data. A familiar example of machine learning is the spam filter. Spam filter designers feed spam into their spam filter algorithms, which either are or contain machine learning algorithms.

Then the spam filter algorithm learns to make judgments about whether or not an email is spam (figure 10.1).

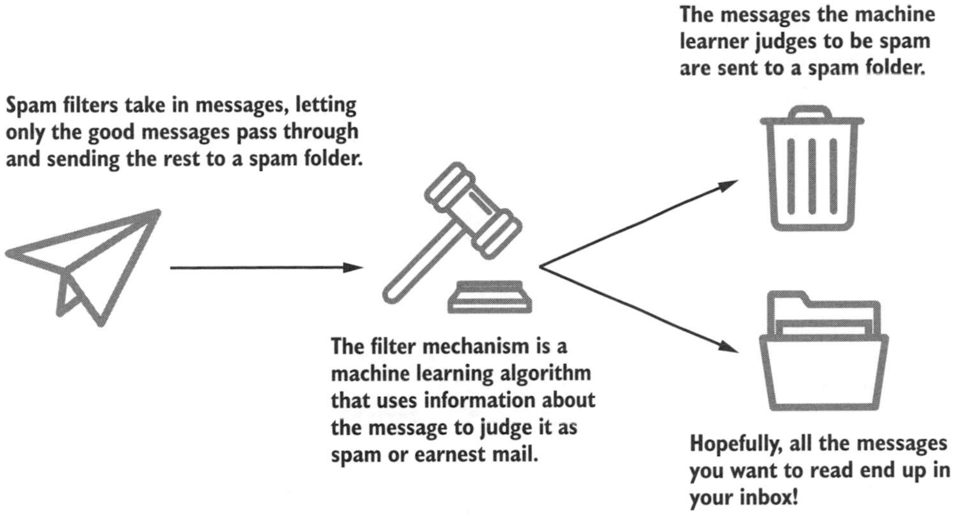
The messages the machine learner judges to be spam are sent to a spam folder.
Spam filters take in messages, letting only the good messages pass through and sending the rest to a spam folder.
The filter mechanism is a machine learning algorithm that uses information about the message to judge it as spam or earnest mail.
Hopefully, all the messages you want to read end up in your inbox!

Figure 10.1 Spam filters are machine learning algorithms that learn how to judge emails as spam or not by looking at lots of spam emails and nonspam emails.

In this chapter, we'll look at how to use PySpark for machine learning. First, we'll explore what machine learning is in greater depth. Then we'll build two machine learners in PySpark:

1. One that uses PySpark's decision tree classifier—a classifier that makes judgements by following learned yes/no rules
2. One that uses the random forest classifier—a classifier that has multiple decision trees vote on an outcome

10.1 What is machine learning?

Before we look at implementing machine learning algorithms in the later sections of this chapter, it makes sense to delve deeper into what machine learning is. I've offered a definition of machine learning:

> **DEFINITION** Machine learning refers to the design, training, application, and study of judgmental algorithms that adjust themselves based on input data.

In this section, we'll examine that definition in greater depth and take a look at some machine learning applications with which you may already be familiar.

10.1.1 Machine learning as self-adjusting judgmental algorithms

Let's examine a few examples to better understand our definition, which has four core components (figure 10.2):

1. There must be an algorithm involved.
2. That algorithm must make judgments.
3. The algorithm must adjust itself.
4. That adjustment must take place based on data.

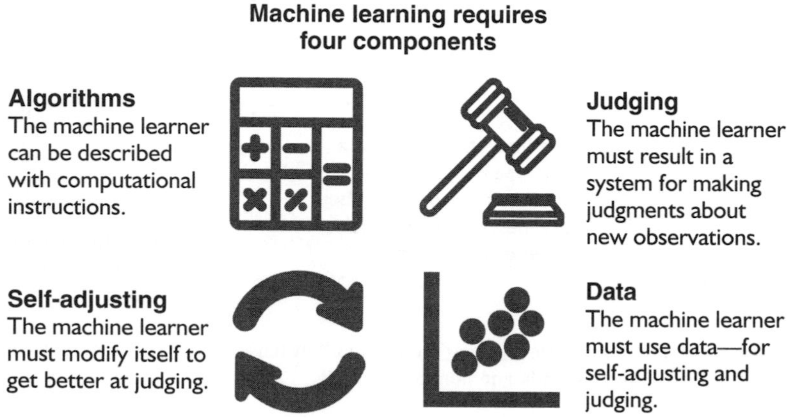
Machine learning requires four components
Algorithms
The machine learner can be described with computational instructions.
Judging
The machine learner must result in a system for making judgments about new observations.
Self-adjusting
The machine learner must modify itself to get better at judging.
Data
The machine learner must use data—for self-adjusting and judging.

Figure 10.2 Machine learning has four components: algorithms, judging, self-adjusting, and data.

The first of these components insists that all machine learning must involve at least one algorithm: a sequence of computations that we can use to solve a problem. This is good because it means that any type of machine learning we'll want to do can be solved using computers.

Second, I consider only algorithms that make judgments to be machine learning algorithms. That means that algorithms that describe data, such as summation, or algorithms that simply transform data, such as a doubling algorithm, are not machine learning. However, that doesn't mean the judgments have to be important, true, or difficult. Silly, wrong, and simple judgments count too.

> **More on machine learning from Manning Publications**
>
> Machine learning is a complex and rapidly evolving topic. Though we don't need to go into mathematical proofs to understand the big picture of machine learning, I suspect many readers of this book will be interested in the finer details. Manning has some excellent and accessible books and other resources geared toward the topic of machine learning. I'd recommend three in particular.

> First, for someone looking to get an overview of machine learning, is *Grokking Machine Learning*, by Luis G. Serrano (2020). This book teaches machine learning with an emphasis on conceptual understanding instead of mathematical proofs. It's a great entry point into the material. Chapter 5 covers decision trees.
>
> *Machine Learning in Action*, by Peter Harrington (2012), has an entire chapter—chapter 3—dedicated to decision trees in Python. This chapter would be a good starting point for anyone interested in more detail on decision trees than I go into here. The rest of the book is solid as well.
>
> *AWS Machine Learning in Motion*, a Manning LiveVideo by Kesha Williams, covers implementing machine learning on AWS. That course expands on the overlap between concepts introduced in this chapter, as well as the next two chapters on cloud computing.

Third, machine learning algorithms must be self-adjusting. This is what makes them *machine learning* algorithms instead of just *machine judging* algorithms. The algorithms must define rules for them to get better at judging. Consider the Elo rating example from chapters 8 and 9 (figure 10.3): we defined some rules, then the algorithm applied those rules to judge who the best players were and make judgments about how likely they were to beat one another. We didn't tell the algorithm anything about the players, it learned all that itself.

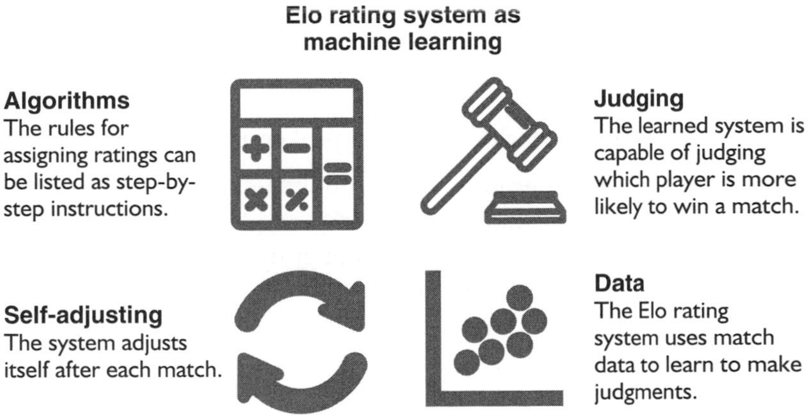
Elo rating system as machine learning
Algorithms
The rules for assigning ratings can be listed as step-by-step instructions.
Judging
The learned system is capable of judging which player is more likely to win a match.
Self-adjusting
The system adjusts itself after each match.
Data
The Elo rating system uses match data to learn to make judgments.

Figure 10.3 We can consider calculating Elo ratings to be machine learning: the rating rules define a learning process, and the algorithm can use the output ratings to judge future match win likelihoods.

Fourth and finally, the algorithm must adjust itself based on data. Again, looking at our Elo rating example from chapters 8 and 9, the match data was necessary to obtain ratings for the players. We didn't go in and encode player ratings based on how we felt about the players personally. This last component gives machine learning algorithms their mystique. Business, science, and government are all interested in the hidden insights that algorithms can find that humans would typically overlook. If these algorithms learn differently than humans, the theory goes, perhaps they're capable of learning better than humans.

This interest becomes especially great when we take machine learning into the realm of large datasets. One of the hallmarks of large datasets—those you can process but not store on your laptop, and larger—is that manually they're almost impenetrable. People have a variety of cognitive biases and shortcuts that make them ill-suited at assessing large datasets. Computers, which excel at repeating simple behaviors again and again, doing exactly what they are told and nothing else, excel at assessing large datasets.

10.1.2 Common applications of machine learning

Because machine learning goes so neatly hand-in-hand with large datasets, many common machine learning applications are large dataset applications. Consider a few:

- *Media content recommendations*—Judging what new songs, videos, or clips you might like based on what you've listened to or watched in the past
- *Online review summarization*—Judging what words best encapsulate the meaning of a restaurant, video, or other product review
- *Website feature testing*—Judging what features of web pages best improve user experience
- *Image recognition*—Adding metadata to images or identifying objects in images
- *Medical diagnoses*—Judging which diseases are most likely to be causing the symptoms of a patient
- *Voice recognition*—Judging which words a speaker intended

Most of these areas are only a decade and a half old. Media content recommendation, for example, is perhaps most famously recognized on platforms like Netflix and YouTube, which both have recommendations prominently featured in their applications. These organizations didn't come into their own until the mid-2000s, when Google purchased YouTube and Netflix launched its video streaming service. Let's look at these five applications of machine learning and identify the four components of machine learning involved in each application.

MEDIA CONTENT RECOMMENDATIONS

Media organizations use machine learning to recommend new content to their audience based on information that the organizations accumulate about the tastes and interests of viewers. The primary goal of these machine learning algorithms is to recommend new content that the media consumer would like to continue consuming (typically to sell more advertising).

These algorithms learn to judge what a user will like from logs that indicate which users have consumed which media (figure 10.4). For example, in the case of YouTube,

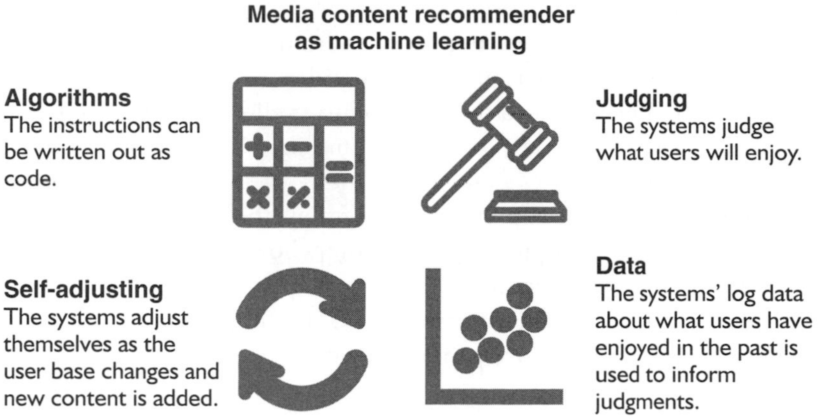
Media content recommender as machine learning
Algorithms
The instructions can be written out as code.
Judging
The systems judge what users will enjoy.
Self-adjusting
The systems adjust themselves as the user base changes and new content is added.
Data
The systems' log data about what users have enjoyed in the past is used to inform judgments.

Figure 10.4 Media content recommendation algorithms are an example of machine learning, where an algorithm learns to judge which content a user would like based on what previous, similar users have liked.

its algorithm would compare the videos you've watched there against the site's records of which videos all of its users have watched. The algorithm would judge videos that users similar to you liked, but you haven't yet seen, as good videos for you to watch.

ONLINE REVIEW SUMMARIZATION

Another area where machine learning overlaps with large datasets is when online retailers, like Amazon, summarize reviews of their products. The goal of these machine learning algorithms is to judge which reviews are related and how to best describe those review groupings. Shoppers can then use the groupings to look for specific product information.

Amazon developers write programs to learn which words best describe which reviews (figure 10.5). These programs—machine learning algorithms—take in a large dataset of product reviews and adjust themselves until they can accurately group and summarize reviews. Then, once these programs have learned enough, developers can incorporate them into the product page for customers to interact with.

Read reviews that mention
cup of coffee
touch screen
water reservoir
easy to use
stopped working
hot water
hot chocolate
coffee grounds
green mountain
error message
waste your money
save your money

Figure 10.5 Amazon uses machine learning to find short phrases that best encapsulate product reviews on its website. Those summaries help shoppers learn about the products from other shoppers.

WEBSITE FEATURE TESTING

In the pursuit of constantly improving user experience, many websites will show subsets of their visitors features that are under development. For example, a company may want to test whether making a purchase button yellow, red, or green results in the most purchases. Developers can write programs that learn users' favorite features from what users do on the site.

Like the media content recommender programs, these programs also learn from user log data. Instead of grouping users together, however, these programs learn to judge which features make users more likely to engage in behaviors that the website designers value, such as spending more time on the site, adding more items to their shopping cart, or purchasing more products from the website.

IMAGE RECOGNITION

An area in machine learning where advances are being rapidly made is in image recognition. The goal of this subfield is to identify objects in images, or otherwise generate metadata about the image (such as where it was taken), based on visual cues alone. Facebook is famous for using image recognition on all the photos uploaded to its site. For example, when I upload my author photo to Facebook, it provides these tags: photo of one person, smiling, beard, close-up (figure 10.6).

We can see another example of object detection in figure 10.6. This form of image recognition attempts to put boxes around items that the algorithm identifies. In this case, our algorithm recognized three boats in the picture. Amazon is using this

Some image recognition systems, like one used by Facebook, are tasked with detecting "traits" of images and applying metadata corresponding to those traits.
{"metadata":
["person", "smiling",
"beard", "close up"
]
}
Others are tasked with identifying objects in photos, such as this system, which identifies boats.

Figure 10.6 These photos demonstrate two examples of image recognition: metadata tagging of images (top) and object detection (bottom).

technology—along with others—in an attempt to create point-of-sale-free stores where machine learning technology identifies what you've placed in your bag.

Medical diagnoses

Yet another place where machine learning is being used is in the arena of medical diagnoses. There, programmers, doctors, and scientists are collaborating to improve how we judge which illness someone has based on their symptoms, medical history, and test results. For example, machine learning allows radiologists to work on lower quality images than they previously could, because the machine learning algorithms can learn to judge unclear or blurry images better than humans can.

These algorithms learn from large datasets of electronic health information to judge health outcomes, much like doctors themselves learn diagnostics during medical school. However, unlike medical students, who are taught by experienced doctors, these algorithms teach themselves. And sometimes they'll learn patterns that are entirely different from what trained experts expect.

Voice recognition

The last machine learning example is voice recognition. In voice recognition, programmers are attempting to write code that can take in sound from a person's voice and judge which words the speaker intended (figure 10.7). You may be familiar with this technology from voice-to-text capabilities on your smartphone or an Amazon Alexa, Google Home, or Facebook Portal device.

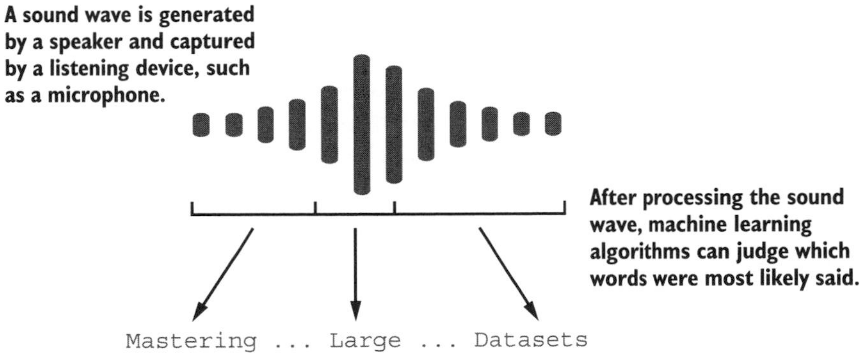
A sound wave is generated by a speaker and captured by a listening device, such as a microphone.
After processing the sound wave, machine learning algorithms can judge which words were most likely said.
Mastering ... Large ... Datasets

Figure 10.7 Voice recognition machine learning attempts to judge which words a speaker meant by analyzing sound waves produced by their speech.

Programmers write these programs to learn which sounds suggest which words by processing large datasets of sound files with corresponding transcripts. The often lackluster performance of these programs compared to the relative ease with which people are able to understand one another's voices highlights a difference in how algorithms learn versus how people learn. Even the best voice recognition algorithms have not taught themselves how to understand words as well as most elementary school children do.

Now that we've gone over five (plus two) examples of machine learning and how to think about them as self-learning judgment algorithms, we're ready to try our hand at some machine learning. In the next section, we'll take a look at using PySpark's decision tree classifier, a type of machine learning algorithm that learns to judge alternative outcomes by learning yes/no rules from the data.

10.2 Machine learning basics with decision tree classifiers

For our introduction to machine learning, we'll be looking at decision tree classifiers. Decision tree classifiers are an excellent choice of machine learning algorithm when we want interpretable results, because the yes/no rules are intuitively simple. Even the mathematically uninclined can usually trace their way down a decision tree to see how the algorithm arrived at its judgment. Because of this, they're a great way to solve the scenario we'll be approaching in this chapter.

SCENARIO A group of hikers is tired of having to bring snacks on the trail. They've collected a bunch of data about mushrooms—such as the mushrooms' size, color, and cap shape—and they want you to use that data and come up with a way to judge whether or not a mushroom is safe to eat. Design a machine learning algorithm that can provide the hikers rules for choosing which mushrooms are edible and which are poisonous.

WARNING The information on mushrooms in this section is for learning purposes only and is **not** to be used for identifying mushrooms. Eating wild mushrooms can have serious and possibly fatal consequences.

With this setup, we know we're in a good situation to use machine learning. We have a judgment problem—judging which mushrooms are poisonous and which are safe to eat—and we have historical data from which we can learn. That takes care of two of the criteria. The two remaining can be met by writing some code to learn to make judgments from the data. That part is up to us.

10.2.1 Designing decision tree classifiers

Before we write our decision tree classifier code, let's take a look at how decision tree classifiers work. Table 10.1 shows what a subset of the mushroom data might look like.

Table 10.1 A subset of mushroom data for a small decision tree classifier

Is it edible?	Cap color	Odor	Habitat
Poison	Brown	Almond	Meadow
Poison	Red	Spicy	Meadow
Poison	Purple	Musty	Woods
Edible	Brown	Musty	Meadow
Edible	Grey	Musty	Woods

The decision tree classifier we'll write works by learning a series of rules against which to judge new mushrooms. For example, for the data in table 10.1, our decision tree classifier may learn to ask three questions (figure 10.8):

1. Does that mushroom smell musty?
2. Was the mushroom found in the woods?
3. Is the mushroom purple?

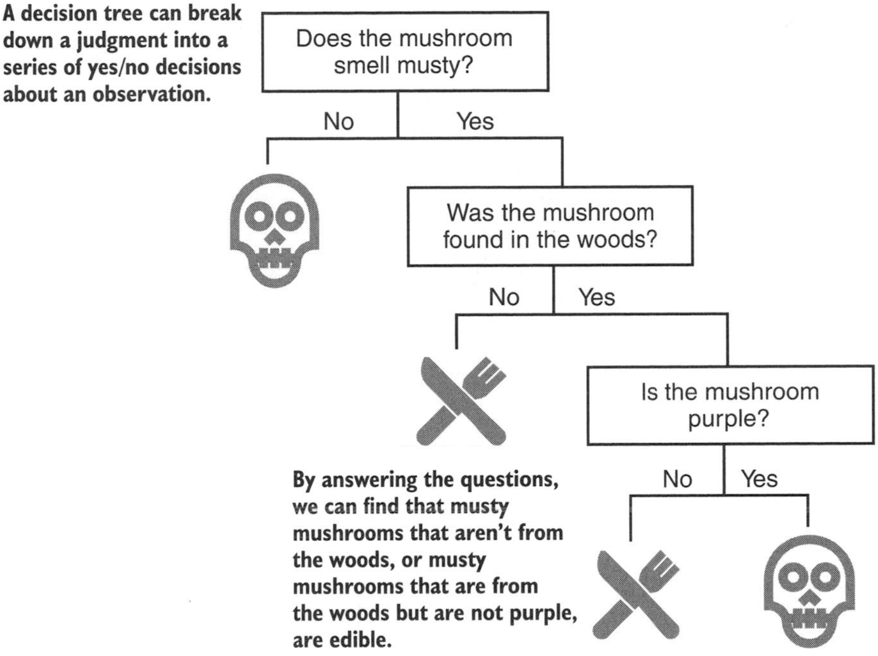
A decision tree can break down a judgment into a series of yes/no decisions about an observation.
Does the mushroom smell musty?
No
Yes
Was the mushroom found in the woods?
No
Yes
Is the mushroom purple?
No
Yes
By answering the questions, we can find that musty mushrooms that aren't from the woods, or musty mushrooms that are from the woods but are not purple, are edible.

Figure 10.8 Decision tree algorithms learn to construct binary rules against which they can judge new data.

By answering these three questions, we can judge all of the five mushrooms in our dataset. We can represent these rules as a series of `if-else` statements or a tree of yes/no questions. In fact, the decision tree algorithm gets its name from the fact that these rules can be represented in a flowchart-like tree diagram.

For the miniature example in this section, the process of learning these rules would be fast. There are only three variables to test and only a few options for each variable. As noted, our self-adjusting algorithm would need to learn to judge based on only two rules. With more data, there are more calculations to make, and the process takes longer.

At each step in the rule-making process, the decision tree algorithm learns to create rules that optimally separate the group into maximally similar categories. In our case, the algorithm will learn to maximally separate edible and poisonous mushrooms at each step. This is why smell would be the first question our algorithm would learn to ask. If the mushroom is musty smelling, then it will be safe to eat 2 times out of 3. We can see that in table 10.1. Indeed, none of the mushrooms in our small dataset that don't smell musty are edible.

Compare this to if we had chosen to split on color. If we split on color first, we would have almost no new information. Each of the mushrooms is a different color! Sure, we could go through each of the colors one by one, but we prefer to ask the questions in an order such that the groups separate more quickly.

We can refer to this process of sorting data into groups of similar classification items as maximizing homogeneity. As users of decision trees, we'll often face the choice of which measurement to use for this process. The two common metrics you'll hear of are called *Gini impurity* and *information gain*. I won't go into detail on either of these terms—for the purposes of an introduction to PySpark's machine learning capabilities, it's enough to know they're both measures of the differences in a grouping of data.

Figure 10.9 shows how our algorithm may judge a new observation. We can see that first, it checks the smell. The smell is musty, so we move on to the second rule. The mushroom was found in the woods, so we move on to the final question. Indeed, this mushroom was purple, so we put it aside: our decision tree expects this mushroom to be poisonous.

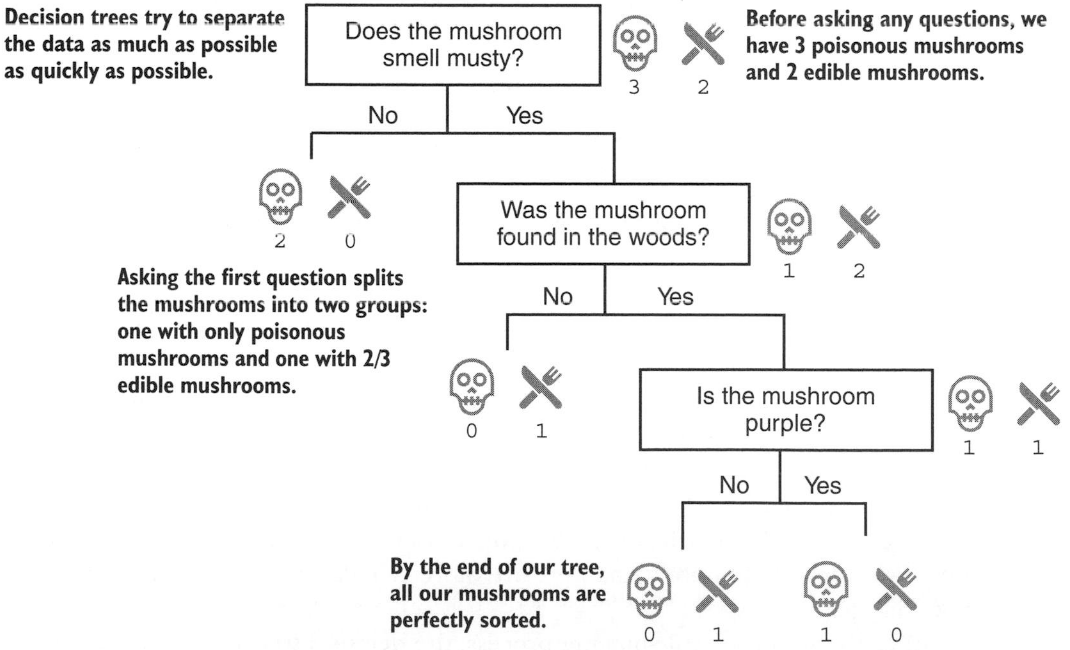
Decision trees try to separate the data as much as possible as quickly as possible.
Does the mushroom smell musty?
3
2
Before asking any questions, we have 3 poisonous mushrooms and 2 edible mushrooms.
No
Yes
2
0
Was the mushroom found in the woods?
1
2
Asking the first question splits the mushrooms into two groups: one with only poisonous mushrooms and one with 2/3 edible mushrooms.
No
Yes
0
1
Is the mushroom purple?
1
1
No
Yes
By the end of our tree, all our mushrooms are perfectly sorted.
0
1
1
0

Figure 10.9 Decision tree algorithms work by learning to group the data into the most similar chunks. The algorithm will judge new data based on the grouping that data would end up in if it was applied against the tree.

Now that we've taken a look at how our decision tree algorithms work, let's take a look at using them in PySpark.

10.2.2 *Implementing a decision tree in PySpark*

PySpark's machine learning capabilities live in a package called `ml`. This package itself contains a few different modules categorizing some of the core machine learning capabilities, including

- `pyspark.ml.feature`—For feature transformation and creation
- `pyspark.ml.classification`—Algorithms for judging the category in which a data point belongs
- `pyspark.ml.tuning`—Algorithms for improving our machine learners
- `pyspark.ml.evaluation`—Algorithms for evaluating machine leaners
- `pyspark.ml.util`—Methods of saving and loading machine learners

All of these modules are similar in style to the PySpark methods we looked at in chapters 7 and 9. However, all of PySpark's machine learning features expect us to have our data in a PySpark `DataFrame` object—not an `RDD`, as we've been using. The `RDD` is an abstract parallelizable data structure at the core of Spark, whereas the `DataFrame` is a layer on top of the `RDD` that provides a notion of rows and columns. If you remember, back in chapter 7 when we introduced PySpark, I mentioned that PySpark `DataFrames` are Spark's preferred data type for interacting with SQL databases. This is because the Spark `DataFrame` provides a tabular interface to data stored in an `RDD`, just like SQL databases provide tabular storage and retrieval.

Bringing the data into a `DataFrame` will be the first step in our machine learning process. The other steps include running our decision tree learner and evaluating the decision tree we've built.

BRINING DATA INTO A DATAFRAME

The first step in our machine learning process is getting the data ready for our analysis. This step includes any preprocessing we might want to do—such as changing formats of the variables and data cleaning. In this case, we're lucky: our data is coming in clean.

For `RDD`s, Spark provided a simple method—`.textFile`—that we could use to read in text data and process it. Similarly, for `DataFrames`, we have several convenient options. If the data is already in an `RDD`, we can call `DataFrame` on the `RDD` and convert it. If the data is in a database, we can use `SparkSession`'s `.sql` method to return a `DataFrame` representation of the results of a SQL query.

For our example, we have our data in a flat file (which you can find on this book's repository online: https://www.manning.com/downloads/1961). To handle that format, PySpark has a method called `.csv` that returns a `DataFrameReader`. We can turn a CSV file into a PySpark `DataFrame` by calling `SparkSession.read.csv` and passing in the name of our file. The method has options for just about anything you would need to ensure your tabular flat-file data is coming in properly. One of my favorites is `inferSchema`, which is used in the following listing.

Listing 10.1 Reading in text data

```
from pyspark import sql

spark = sql.SparkSession.builder \
                        .master("local") \
                        .appName("Decision Trees") \
                        .getOrCreate()

df = spark.read.csv("mushrooms.data", header=True, inferSchema=True)
```

The `inferSchema` option of the `.csv` method tells Spark to make a guess at the type of the variables in our data. If you remember, in the last two chapters, unless the data was coming in as JSON, we had to explicitly cast our data to the types we wanted it to be. For small datasets, this isn't a challenge, but if we have hundreds of variables, this can be a tiresome process. In these cases, `inferSchema` can be a real time saver.

ORGANIZING THE DATA FOR LEARNING

Now that we have data in a `DataFrame`, we're one step closer to feeding it into a Spark machine learner. Before we can do that, however, we have to get the data into the specific type of `DataFrame` format that Spark insists on.

Spark's machine learning classifiers look for two columns in a `DataFrame`:

1. A `label` column that indicates the correct classification of the data
2. A `features` column that contains the features we're going to use to predict the label

Your `DataFrame` can contain as many columns as you would like, with whatever names you'd like, but these two columns are the ones that Spark will use for its machine learning. The `label` column is what Spark's machine learning classifiers learn to judge—is the data the algorithm sees more like this label or that label? The `features` column is the data about each observation that the machine learning algorithm will learn to use to make that judgment.

Furthermore, Spark expects specific data types for these columns. For our numerical data—data that would be represented as floats and integers in Python—Spark knows what to do. For categorical data, we'll have some choices to make. The simplest way to handle such data is to use PySpark's `StringIndexer`. The `StringIndexer` transforms categorical data stored as category names (using strings) and indexes the names as numerical variables. `StringIndexer` indexes categories in order of frequency—from most common to least common—not in order observed. The most common category will be 0, the second most common category 1, and so on (figure 10.10).

When we use `StringIndexer`, Spark returns a new `DataFrame`, with our old columns and our new indexed column (figure 10.11). Spark has to return a new `DataFrame` because most data structures in Spark are immutable—they can't be changed

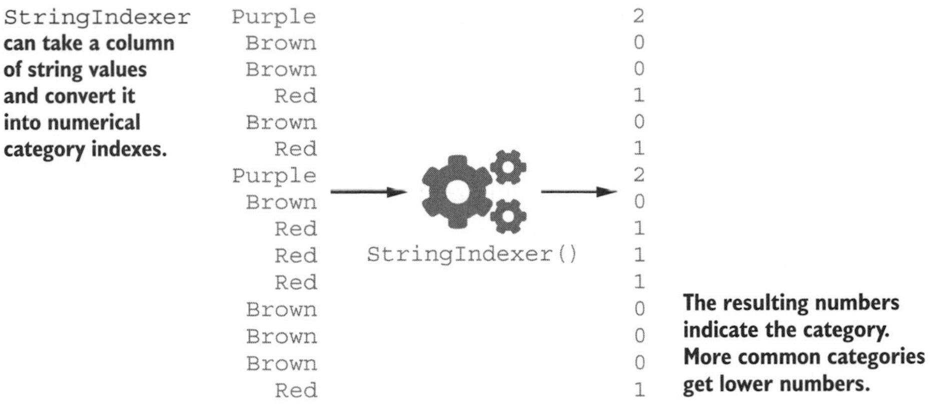
StringIndexer can take a column of string values and convert it into numerical category indexes.
Purple
Brown
Brown
Red
Brown
Red
Purple
Brown
Red
Red
Red
Brown
Brown
Brown
Red
StringIndexer()
2
0
0
1
0
1
2
0
1
1
1
0
0
0
1
The resulting numbers indicate the category. More common categories get lower numbers.

Figure 10.10 Spark's `StringIndexer` transforms categorical variables as strings into numerical categories. More common categories have lower indexes.

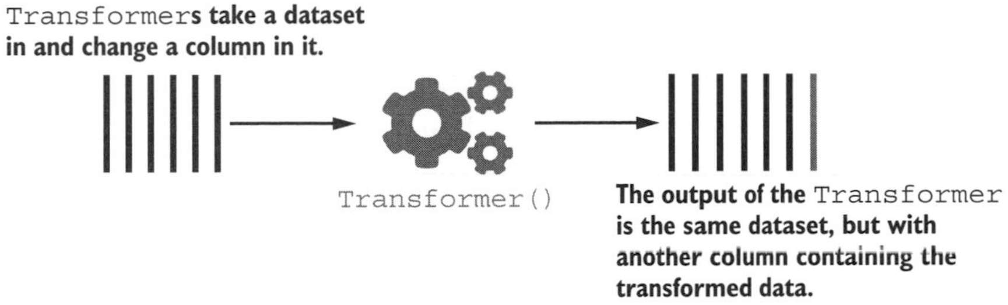
Transformers take a dataset in and change a column in it.
Transformer()
The output of the Transformer is the same dataset, but with another column containing the transformed data.

Figure 10.11 `Transformers` in PySpark, such as `StringIndexer`, return a `DataFrame` that contains all the columns of the original, plus a new column, specified by the transformation.

once they're created. That's a property of the Scala programming language in which Spark is written. For our purposes, this is great because it means we can write a small reduce statement and update our `DataFrame`, as we can see in the following listing.

Listing 10.2 Transforming strings to indexed categorical variables with `StringIndexer`

```
from pyspark.ml.feature import StringIndexer

def string_to_index(label, df):
    return StringIndexer(inputCol=label,
              outputCol="i-"+label).fit(df) \
              .transform(df)
```

- Defines a helper function for our reduce statement—instead of acc—and next we'll use label and df
- Takes column labels—input and output—as parameters and appends to the DataFrame a transformed version of the input column with the new label
- The .fit and .transform methods apply the changes and return a new DataFrame.

```
categories = ['cap-shape', 'cap-surface', 'cap-color']
df = reduce(string_to_index, categories, df)
```

We'll need a sequence of columns to transform—this is what we'll reduce over.

Lastly, we'll call reduce and transform our data frame.

Listing 10.2 shows this process in action. We first write a helper function that will apply the `StringIndexer` to a given column. The helper function calls `StringIndexer` and passes it an input label, which is specified by the parameter in first position, and an output label, in this case, that variable preceded by an `"i-"`. Our transformed columns will be added into the `DataFrame`, so they need to have unique names. All columns in a `DataFrame` must have unique names.

Then, we select some categories we want to transform. In listing 10.2, I've chosen to use cap-shape, cap-surface, and cap-color. I'm hoping that mushroom caps can tell me something about whether a mushroom is poisonous or not. We can then call `reduce`, passing it our helper function, our categories, and our `DataFrame`.

This process results in a `DataFrame` with three additional columns:

1. `i-cap-shape`—An indexed transformation of cap-shape
2. `i-cap-surface`—An indexed transformation of cap-surface
3. `i-cap-color`—An indexed transformation of cap-color

Spark's machine learning classifiers, though, only want one column named `features`. To use these three columns as features, we'll have to gather them up in another column. Conveniently, PySpark has a class for this as well: `VectorAssembler`. `VectorAssembler` is a `Transformer` like `StringIndexer`—it takes some input column names and an output column name and has methods to return a new `DataFrame` that has all the columns of the original, plus the new column we want to add (figure 10.12).

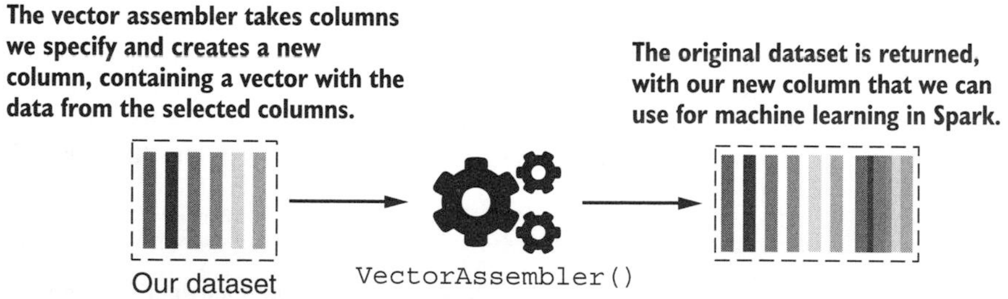
The vector assembler takes columns we specify and creates a new column, containing a vector with the data from the selected columns.
The original dataset is returned, with our new column that we can use for machine learning in Spark.
Our dataset
VectorAssembler()

Figure 10.12 **`VectorAssembler` is a `Transformer` that can take several columns and gather them up as a vector in a single column. This class is especially useful for preparing features for machine learning.**

Unlike `StringIndexer`, which expects to work on one column at a time, `VectorAssembler` expects to round up a host of columns. For our transformation, we only need a single call to `VectorAssembler`, as shown in the following listing.

Listing 10.3 Gathering features for machine learning with `VectorAssembler`

```
from pyspark.ml.feature import VectorAssembler
df = VectorAssembler(inputCols=["i-cap-shape",
                                "i-cap-surface",
                                "i-cap-color"],
      outputCol="features").transform(df)
```

We initialize VectorAssembler with the names of the columns we want to assemble and the desired output column name.

Calling .transform on a DataFrame returns a new DataFrame with an additional column.

In listing 10.3, we can see an example of how `VectorAssembler` works. We can see that we're passing the three columns we want to use as features to the `inputCols` parameter as a list, and the `outputCol` parameter is set to `"features"`. This tells `VectorAssembler` to gather those three columns up and make a new column called `features`. At the end of this step, our `DataFrame` will contain all the columns of the original `DataFrame`, plus four new columns—one for each categorical variable we indexed and one containing all of them together.

At this point, the only thing we need before we can move on to machine learning is the labels. Our labels are contained in a column called `edible?`, which has two labels—`edible` or `poisonous`—both represented as strings. Again, we can use `StringTransformer`. Instead of looping through a sequence of column names though, we only need to worry about one column: `edible?`, as shown in the following code.

```
df = StringIndexer(inputCol="edible?",
                   outputCol='label').fit(df) \
                                     .transform(df)
```

In listing 10.4, you can see that we specify the `edible?` column as we initialize `StringIndexer`, along with the name `label`, which Spark's machine learning classifier will be looking for. Just like when we transformed our feature columns, we call `.fit` and `.transform` and then assign this `DataFrame` back on top of our original variable.

Label names and data frames

Because Spark's `DataFrames` are immutable and we'll usually want to transform our `label` column before using it with Spark's machine learning, we can run into problems if the original column name is `"label"`. When this happens, we'll need to rename the column when we transform it. Spark will not let you overwrite columns in a `DataFrame`. We can, however, pick an alternate column name by specifying the `labelCol` parameter of our machine learning function, such as `DecisionTreeClassifier(labelCol="my-column-name")`.

With these transformations complete, we have our `DataFrame` prepared just like Spark needs. We have a `label` column, which contains the labels the algorithm will learn to judge, and we have a `features` column, which has the features the algorithm will use to do the judging. Finally, we're ready to learn.

RUNNING OUR DECISION TREE LEARNER

Running the machine learning classifier in Spark will feel similar to transforming the data. We'll use a class from Spark's ml.classifier library called `DecisionTreeClassifier`, and we'll call its `.fit` method on the `DataFrame` we have prepared. For the amount of math that's going on behind the scenes, you would think that this process would be more difficult than two short lines:

```
tree = DecisionTreeClassifier()
model = tree.fit(df)
```

However, these two lines show all the code that's necessary to run a decision tree classifier on our `DataFrame`. The first line initializes the classifier with the default parameters, and the second fits the classifier to the data. The classifier's `.fit` method returns a model—this is the tree that has learned to judge our label based on our data. In our case, the model is a type of `DecisionTreeClassificationModel` object. Each classifier in PySpark has a `.fit` method that produces a corresponding model object. These models describe the model that's been learned and have convenient functions for inspecting them.

> **`.fit` and `.transform` in Spark**
>
> You may have noticed a lot of `.fit` and `.transform` floating around in this chapter. That's because the classes upon which much of the Spark machine learning capability is built share these methods. `.fit` is inherited from Spark's `Estimator` class. This class is used for learning information about data, such as when we learn how to index a dataset or how to make judgments about data with a decision tree. The `.fit` method returns a `Model`. A `Model` inherits from a `Transformer`, which provides a `.transform` method. This method executes the transformation that we learn with the `Estimator`.

For example, `DecisionTreeClassificationModel` has a method called `.toDebugString` that shows us all the rules that the model uses to make judgments. We can print that string to the screen to see the rules by using `print(model.toDebugString)`.

In the following code lines, we can see these rules written as `if-else` statements. You'll notice that none of the feature names are included. This is because the `features` column we assembled with `VectorAssembler` doesn't hold onto the names of the inputs. To use this decision tree manually, you would have to remember the order in which you placed the variables. If we're writing a script and not working in the terminal interactively, we can usually find this in our script.

```
If (feature 1 in {2.0,3.0})
 If (feature 2 in {0.0,2.0,4.0,6.0,7.0})
  If (feature 2 in {0.0,2.0,7.0})
   If (feature 0 in {0.0,1.0,2.0,4.0})
    Predict: 0.0
   Else (feature 0 not in {0.0,1.0,2.0,4.0})
    Predict: 1.0
```

```
  Else (feature 2 not in {0.0,2.0,7.0})
   If (feature 2 in {6.0})
    Predict: 1.0
   Else (feature 2 not in {6.0})
    Predict: 0.0
 Else (feature 2 not in {0.0,2.0,4.0,6.0,7.0})
  If (feature 2 in {3.0})
   Predict: 1.0
  Else (feature 2 not in {3.0})
   Predict: 0.0
```

For example, we can see in the following listing the order of our variables. The first column label we specified, in this case, `i-cap-shape`, will be variable `0`; the second, `i-cap-surface`, will be variable `1`; and so on.

Listing 10.4 Gathering features for machine learning with `VectorAssembler`

```
from pyspark.ml.feature import VectorAssembler
df = VectorAssembler(inputCols=["i-cap-shape",
                                "i-cap-surface",
                                "i-cap-color"],
                     outputCol="features").transform(df)
```

i-cap-shape will be feature 0, i-cap-surface will be feature 1, and i-cap-color will be feature 2

EVALUATING THE JUDGMENTS OF A DECISION TREE

After the machine learning algorithm is trained, a good question to ask is: How good is the algorithm at actually making judgments? This is the question that PySpark's `ml.evaluation` module is designed to answer. The `evaluation` module contains classes that compute different evaluation metrics for different machine learners:

- `BinaryClassificationEvaluator`—For evaluating cases learners with two possible outcomes
- `RegressionEvaluator`—For evaluating continuous value judgments
- `MulticlassClassificationEvaluator`—For evaluating multiple label judgments

Because in our case we only have two options—`poisonous` or `edible`—we want to use the `BinaryClassificationEvaluator`. Using this `Evaluator` should feel similar to using our machine learner or our `Transformers`. We'll first initialize the `Evaluator`, then we'll call its `.evaluate` method on a modeled version of our `DataFrame`:

```
bce = BinaryClassificationEvaluator()
bce.evaluate(model.transform(df))
# 0.633318
```

When we initialize the `BinaryClassificationEvaluator`, we have the opportunity to pick an evaluation metric. The area under the receiver operating characteristic (confusingly known by two acronyms: AUC and ROC) curve is the default choice and the one I recommend using for most problems (figure 10.13). This metric is one way of evaluating the trade-off between false-positive and false-negative assessments.

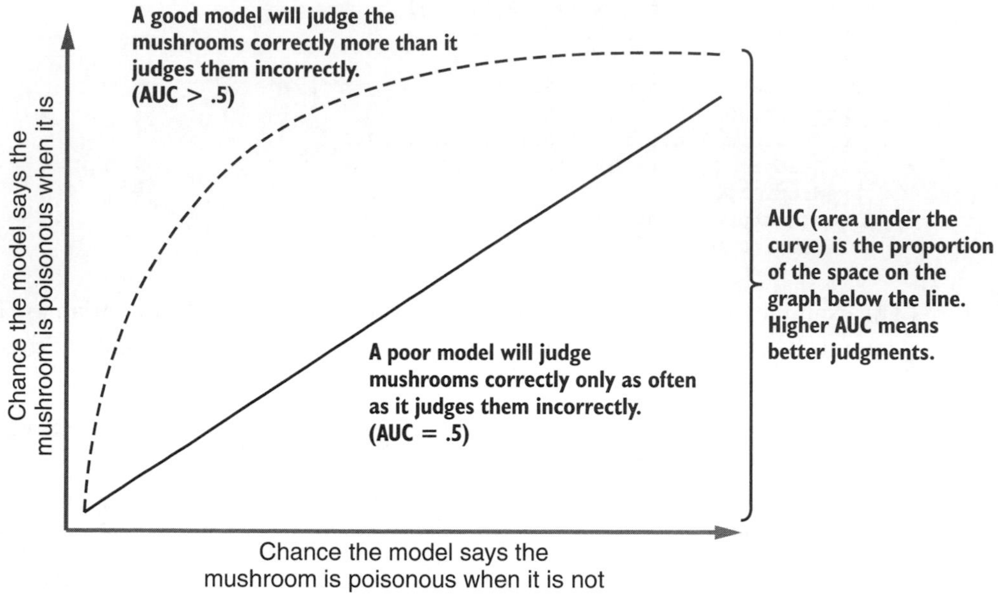
A good model will judge the mushrooms correctly more than it judges them incorrectly. (AUC > .5)
AUC (area under the curve) is the proportion of the space on the graph below the line. Higher AUC means better judgments.
A poor model will judge mushrooms correctly only as often as it judges them incorrectly. (AUC = .5)
Chance the model says the mushroom is poisonous when it is
Chance the model says the mushroom is poisonous when it is not

Figure 10.13 The receiver operating characteristic (ROC) curve allows us to balance making cautious judgments about poisonous mushrooms, while judging a reasonable number of mushrooms as safe.

The curve represents the balance between making true positive and false positive judgments. In our case, it represents how good we are at judging poisonous mushrooms to be poisonous, without misidentifying edible mushrooms as poisonous. The model is a curve because the more we favor identifying mushrooms as poisonous—to prevent people from dying—the more we will misjudge edible mushrooms as poisonous. The curve helps us find an acceptable point.

With both metrics—area under the receiver operating characteristic curve and area under the precision-recall curve—we're hoping to have as large a number as possible. If we have an area under the receiver operating characteristic curve value of 1, that means we can correctly judge all poisonous mushrooms as poisonous, without judging a single edible mushroom to be inedible. Anything less than 1, and there's some room for improvement. A 0.63 area under the receiver operating characteristic curve is not great, but it's acceptable for an early pass. Next, we'll take a look at some ways we can improve our model.

10.3 Fast random forest classifications in PySpark

In the previous section, we built a decision tree to judge whether a mushroom was poisonous or not. However, the area under the receiver operating characteristic curve suggests that we can do better. One way we can try to do better is to use a random forest classifier—a machine learning algorithm that's closely related to the decision tree.

In this section, we'll look at random forests and implement one in PySpark to achieve better results.

10.3.1 Understanding random forest classifiers

Random forest classifiers work by growing lots of different decision trees and then taking a poll of them. During the learning phase, they grow a diverse selection of trees by randomly selecting features to use. During the judgment phase, each tree classifies the observation based on its rules and votes for the classification that results from those rules—the random forest judges the observation to belong to the category with the most votes (figure 10.14).

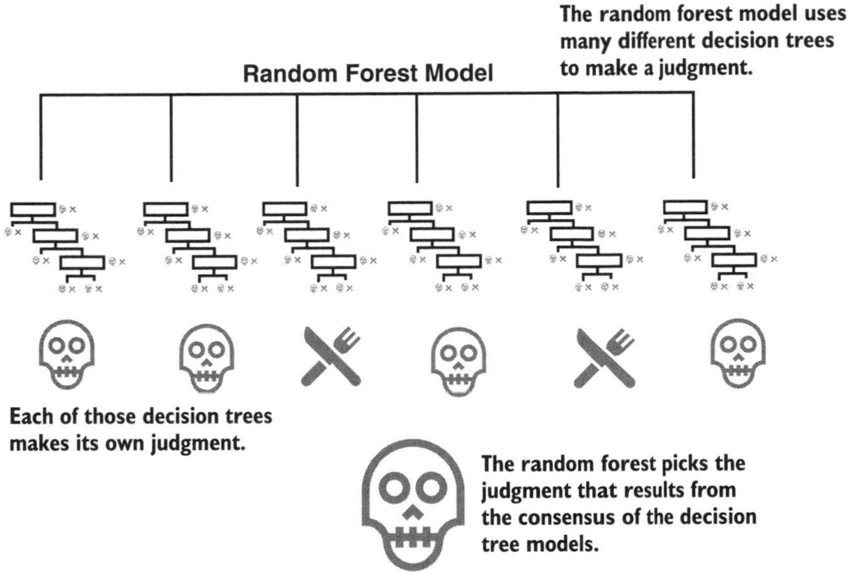
The random forest model uses many different decision trees to make a judgment.
Random Forest Model
Each of those decision trees makes its own judgment.
The random forest picks the judgment that results from the consensus of the decision tree models.

Figure 10.14 A random forest classifier relies on growing different decision trees, each seeded with different randomly selected features. Those trees then vote to classify new observations.

As an example, consider a reduced version of the mushrooms dataset that only has seven features related to the mushroom's caps and gills:

1. Cap shape
2. Cap surface
3. Cap color
4. Gill attachment
5. Gill spacing
6. Gill size
7. Gill color

A simple random forest might grow five classifiers from these. The first might contain cap shape, gill spacing, gill size, and gill color; the second might contain cap surface, gill attachment, gill color, and gill size; and so on (table 10.2). Each tree has the features it can use randomly selected.

Table 10.2 Five randomly seeded decision trees for an example random forest

Tree 1	Tree 2	Tree 3	Tree 4	Tree 5
Cap shape	Gill spacing	Gill size	Gill color	Cap surface
Gill attachment	Gill color	Gill size	Cap surface	Cap color
Gill attachment	Gill color	Cap shape	Cap color	Gill attachment
Gill size	Cap color	Gill attachment	Gill spacing	Gill size

When we have a new observation we want to label, we can pass it to the random forest, and the random forest will poll each tree in it. For example, trees 1, 2, and 4 might judge the observation to be edible, whereas trees 3 and 5 might say that it's poisonous. Between the five of them, the vote is 3 to 2 in favor of edible. That would be the class that the random forest would ultimately judge the new observation to be.

This process works because the randomization of features available to the decision trees makes random forests resilient to overfitting: a problem in machine learning where the algorithms disproportionately use one feature to make judgments. The improved resilience, high performance, and overall versatility of random forest models—which can be used for any type of judgment problem: binary classification, multiclass classification, and regression—makes random forest models a popular machine learning tool.

10.3.2 Implementing a random forest classifier

To build our random forest classifier, we'll start off the same way we started with our decision tree: by bringing in the data and arranging it into a `label` column and a `features` column. Unlike our previous attempt with decision trees, this time we won't make any assumptions about which features will be useful and which won't be. This time, we'll select all the features and let the random forest sort it out.

To use all the features, we'll use the same reduce strategy as before. This time, though, instead of passing in a list where we name every feature we want, we'll create the list from the `DataFrame`'s columns attribute and pop the label off, as shown in listing 10.5 We'll also need to construct a list that has the new labels. To do this, I like to use a list comprehension that prepends the feature indicator to the feature name.

Listing 10.5 Reading and preparing data for random forest classification

```
df = spark.read.csv("mushrooms.data", header=True, inferSchema=True)
categories = df.columns
categories.pop(categories.index('edible?'))
df = reduce(string_to_index, categories, df)
indexes = ["i-"+c for c in categories]

df = VectorAssembler(inputCols=indexes,
                     outputCol="features").transform(df)
df = StringIndexer(inputCol='edible?',
                   outputCol='label').fit(df).transform(df)
```

Our categories will include all the columns in our DataFrame.

The only category we don't want is the label, so we'll pop that out.

Transforms all these strings into indexes

We can use a list comprehension to get a list of index names—we'll need this to assemble the indexes.

With the `DataFrame` in good shape, we're ready to start building our random forest. We'll build the random forest similarly to how we built the decision tree earlier in this chapter:

- First, we'll import the `RandomForestClassifier` class.
- Then, we'll instantiate the class using the default settings.

But we'll also do some things a little differently:

- We'll use a parameter grid to optimize hyperparameters.
- We'll use a cross validator to ensure our results are more robust.

In the decision tree example, you may have noticed that we evaluated our decision tree on the same dataset that we learned it from. This is fine for getting used to writing PySpark machine learning code, but the results will not be reliable. To get a better assessment of how well our machine learners judge new observations, we should always cross-validate our models by testing them on data that we've held out from the learning process.

Two types of cross-validation are worth knowing about:

1. K-fold cross-validation
2. Train-test-evaluate validation

As shown in figure 10.15, in k-fold cross-validation we split the dataset up into K chunks, then we rotate through the chunks, considering one chunk the evaluation data and all the other chunks the test data. This process can be time-consuming if both K and your dataset are large, because you'll end up training a machine learning model many times on a large dataset. Common values of K include 5, 10, 100, and the total number of observations in your dataset.

In train-test-evaluate validation, the dataset is split into three chunks: a large training chunk, a small testing chunk, and an even smaller evaluation chunk. The training chunk is used for training the model. The testing chunk is used during an iterative training

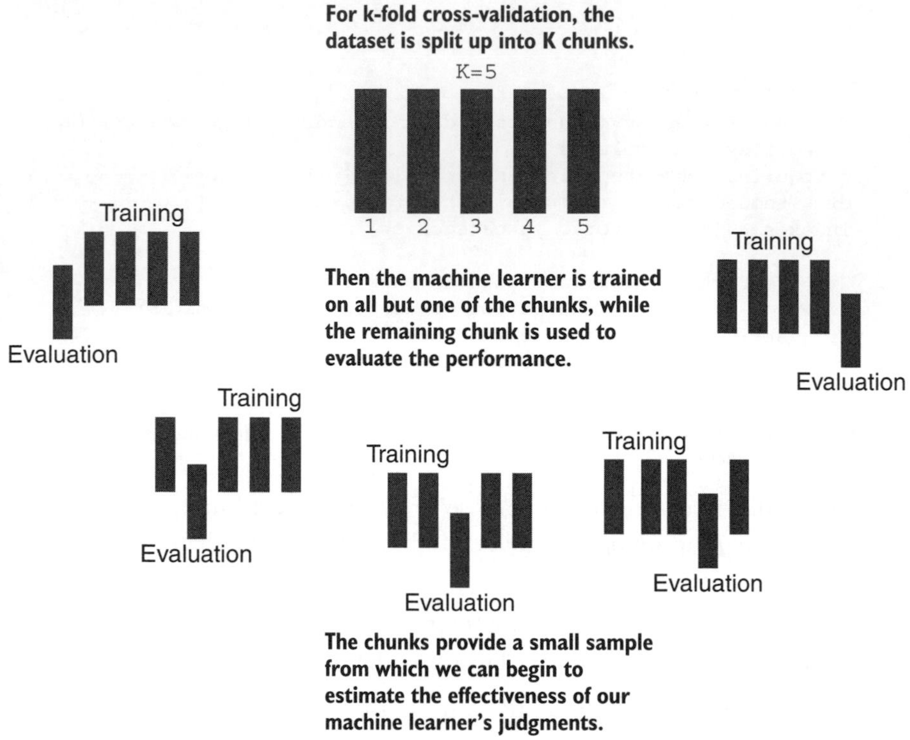
For k-fold cross-validation, the dataset is split up into K chunks.
K=5
1 2 3 4 5
Then the machine learner is trained on all but one of the chunks, while the remaining chunk is used to evaluate the performance.
Training
Evaluation
Training
Evaluation
Training
Evaluation
Training
Evaluation
Training
Evaluation
Training
Evaluation
The chunks provide a small sample from which we can begin to estimate the effectiveness of our machine learner's judgments.

Figure 10.15 K-fold cross-validation splits the data into K groups and then learns a model from all the other groups to judge the selected group.

cycle, as shown in figure 10.16. Whenever we have an idea about how to improve the algorithm, we make the improvement, relearn from the training chunk, and test on the testing chunk. Then, when we're happy with the model we have, we can judge the evaluation data and use that to assess our model. The trick here is to keep the evaluation set removed from the process as much as possible. If you can stick to rarely judging the evaluation chunk, train-test-evaluation may work for you. Otherwise, you may be better off using k-fold cross-validation. With the train-test-evaluate approach, it's common to use 70% of the dataset as training data, 20% as testing data, and 10% as evaluation data.

To implement cross-validation in PySpark, we'll use the `CrossValidator` class, which we can use to do k-fold cross-validation. The `CrossValidator` needs to be initialized with

- *An estimator*—The classifier we want to use
- *A parameter estimator*—A `ParamGridBuilder` object
- *An evaluator*—We'll use the `BinaryClassificationEvaluator` we used in our decision tree example. I like to do 10-fold validation unless I have a compelling reason not to—we also pass this choice into the `CrossValidator` class as we initialize it.

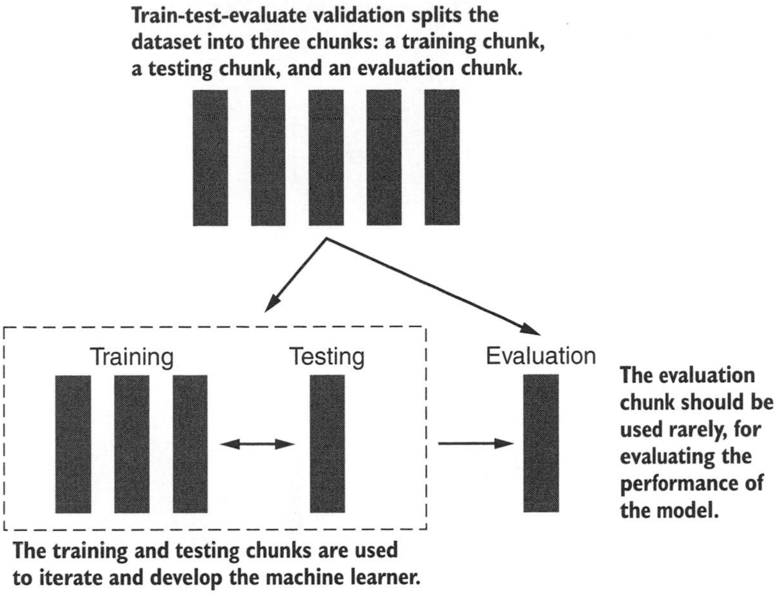
Train-test-evaluate validation splits the dataset into three chunks: a training chunk, a testing chunk, and an evaluation chunk.
Training
Testing
Evaluation
The evaluation chunk should be used rarely, for evaluating the performance of the model.
The training and testing chunks are used to iterate and develop the machine learner.

Figure 10.16 Train-test-evaluate validation splits the data into three chunks, two of which are used for iterative learning and testing. The remaining one is used rarely to evaluate the model.

Listing 10.6 shows the training of the random forest classifier. You'll notice that instead of using the classifier directly to fit the data, we pass the `RandomForestClassifier` to the `CrossValidator` object and use the `CrossValidator`'s `.fit` method. From there, though, the evaluation process is similar. We can find the area under the operating receiver characteristic curve using the `BinaryClassificationEvaluator`. Lastly, we can print the best model from our cross-validation attempts and see what rules we ended up with.

Listing 10.6 A robust random forest model using PySpark

```
from pyspark.ml.classification import RandomForestClassifier
forest = RandomForestClassifier()
grid = ParamGridBuilder().\
            addGrid(forest.maxDepth, [0, 2]).\
            build()
cv = CrossValidator(estimator=forest, estimatorParamMaps=grid,
                    evaluator=bce,numFolds=10,
                    parallelism=4)
cv_model = cv.fit(df)
area_under_curve = bce.evaluate(cv_model.transform(df))
print("Random Forest AUC: {:0.4f}".format(area_under_curve))
#
print(cv_model.bestModel.toDebugString)
#
```

Creates an instance of our desired classifier

Creates a parameter grid search over some parameters

Initializes the cross-validator to train several models

Fits the models

Prints the best model

In these rules, we can see the different trees that make up the decision forest. In your own output, you'll notice that some trees have the same rules—this must be a good way to make judgments about mushrooms!

```
Tree 0 (weight 1.0):
   If (feature 7 in {0.0})
    Predict: 0.0
   Else (feature 7 not in {0.0})
    Predict: 1.0
 Tree 1 (weight 1.0):
   If (feature 4 in {0.0,4.0,5.0,8.0})
    Predict: 0.0
   Else (feature 4 not in {0.0,4.0,5.0,8.0})
    Predict: 1.0
 Tree 2 (weight 1.0):
   If (feature 11 in {0.0,2.0,3.0})
    Predict: 0.0
   Else (feature 11 not in {0.0,2.0,3.0})
    Predict: 1.0
 Tree 3 (weight 1.0):
   If (feature 20 in {1.0,2.0,3.0,4.0,5.0})
    Predict: 0.0
   Else (feature 20 not in {1.0,2.0,3.0,4.0,5.0})
    Predict: 1.0
```

Summary

- PySpark's SQL module has a tabular `DataFrame` structure that provides table-like features, such as column names, on top of `RDD`-powered parallelization.
- PySpark has a machine learning library that includes tools for every step of the machine learning pipeline, including data ingestion, data preparing, machine learning, cross-validation, and model evaluation.
- Machine learners in PySpark are represented as classes that learn using the `.fit` method. They return a model object, which can judge data using the `.transform` method.
- We can use PySpark's feature creation classes—such as `StringIndexer` and `VectorAssembler`—to format `DataFrames` for machine learning.
- The feature creation classes are `Transformer`-class objects, and their methods return new `DataFrames`, rather than transforming them in place.

Part 3

Part 3 explains how to bring the tools and techniques we've covered throughout this book into the cloud. We'll cover the fundamentals of cloud computing, object storage in the cloud, and how to set up your own computing clusters in the cloud. Through hands-on examples, we'll run the distributed computing frameworks covered in Part 2—Hadoop and Spark—in the cloud. This part focuses on large data category 3: data that is too big for either storing or processing locally. Once you've mastered the content in this chapter, you'll be able to tackle data of any size.

11 Large datasets in the cloud with Amazon Web Services and S3

This chapter covers

- Understanding distributed object storage in the cloud
- Using the AWS web interface to set up buckets and upload objects
- Working with the boto3 library to upload data to an S3 bucket

In chapters 7–10, we saw the power of the distributed frameworks in Hadoop and Spark. These frameworks can take advantage of clusters of computers to parallelize massive data processing tasks and complete them in short order. Most of us, however, don't have access to physical compute clusters.

In contrast, we can all get access to compute clusters from cloud service providers such as Amazon, Microsoft, and Google. These cloud providers have platforms that we can use for storing and processing data, along with a variety of services that automate common tasks we may want to do. In this chapter, we'll take the first step of analyzing big data in the cloud by uploading data to Amazon's Simple Storage Service (S3). First, we'll review the basics of S3; then we'll create a bucket and upload an object using the browser-based AWS console; and finally we'll upload several objects to a bucket with the boto3 software development kit.

11.1 AWS Simple Storage Service—A solution for large datasets

Amazon Web Service's Simple Storage Service, better known as S3, is a data storage service used to hold some of the largest datasets, such as the datasets of General Electric, NASA, Netflix, the UK Data Service, Yelp, and—of course—Amazon itself. S3 is the go-to service for large datasets for the following five reasons:

1. *S3 has effectively unlimited storage capacity.* We never have to worry about our dataset becoming too large.
2. *S3 is cloud-based.* We can scale up and down quickly as necessary.
3. *S3 offers object storage.* We can focus on organizing our data with metadata and store many different types of data.
4. *S3 is a managed service.* Amazon Web Services takes care of a lot of the details for us, such as ensuring data availability and durability. They also take care of security patches and software updates.
5. *S3 supports versioning and life cycle policies.* We can use them to update or archive our data as it ages.

CLOUD OPTIONS: AWS, AZURE, AND GOOGLE CLOUD The three prominent cloud providers—Amazon (AWS), Microsoft (Azure), and Google (Google Cloud)—all offer a standard suite of core services. The core services include virtual machines for computing and object-based storage. In this chapter, I'll go into detail on Amazon's S3 service because AWS is the most popular of the cloud platforms. That said, the principles in this chapter apply to all the object storage systems of the three cloud providers. Indeed, we can use everything in this chapter and chapter 12 on Microsoft Azure and Google Cloud.

In this section, I'll go over the five advantages to using S3 and, in the process, explain what S3 is and how it works.

11.1.1 Limitless storage with S3

When a dataset becomes so big that we start to worry about where and how to store it, we know we're dealing with a large dataset. For these situations, S3 is always an option because it allows for effectively limitless (but potentially costly) storage (figure 11.1). In fact, S3 is such a good option for large datasets, AWS even has a service designed to help organizations migrate local petabyte-scale datasets into S3.

What makes S3 effectively limitless? Large data centers with lots of disk space. There's no secret when it comes to cloud-based storage. AWS stores the data on disk volumes much like you would if you were to store it locally. What makes it so appealing for us is that instead of us buying the disk space and managing it ourselves, AWS is willing to rent it to us. And when we need more, AWS is willing to rent us more.

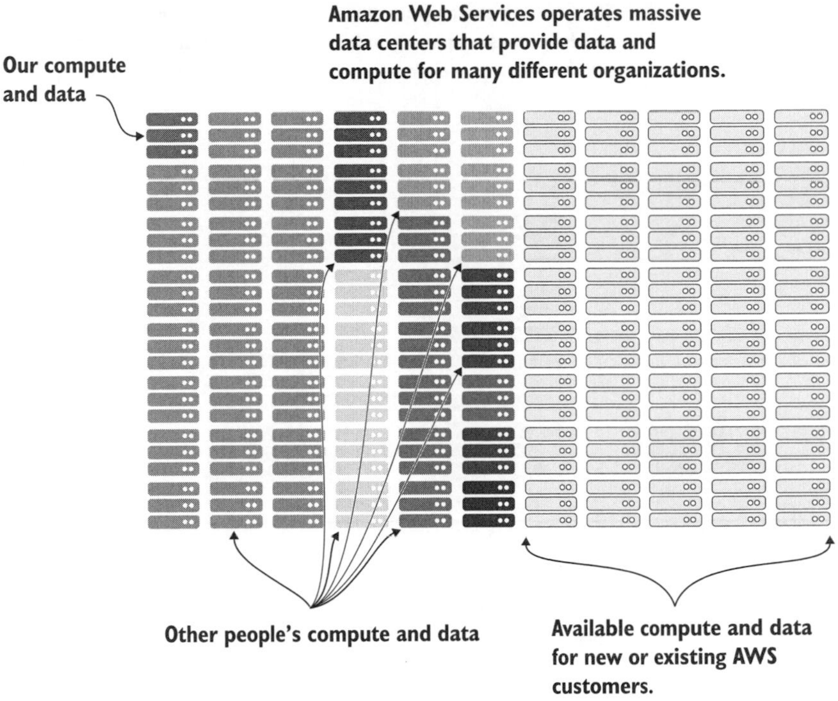
Amazon Web Services operates massive data centers that provide data and compute for many different organizations.
Our compute and data
Other people's compute and data
Available compute and data for new or existing AWS customers.

Figure 11.1 Because AWS data centers are so large in proportion to the size of our data, S3 offers effectively limitless storage.

11.1.2 Cloud-based storage for scalability

Because S3 is a cloud-based storage service, we get scalability benefits that we wouldn't get if we were storing the data ourselves. In the cloud, we never need to buy more physical storage devices, we only need to pay for more of the storage service. And we can purchase more of that service anytime we want and give it up anytime we want (figure 11.2). AWS refers to this as *elasticity*, and others refer to it as *scalability*.

Consider the following scenario: you're running a small survey company, and you've bought some storage to hold the survey data for your first few customers. This has a few drawbacks:

- You need to find a good way to estimate how much space the surveys will require.
- You need to pay for the storage space all at once.

Because S3 is in the cloud, we can avoid both these problems. With S3, we pay for the storage we use for our data when we store it, and we can be confident that there will always be storage available when we're ready to purchase it.

Now imagine that your first round of surveys went so well that a hospital has asked you to run a massive nationwide survey for them. You need to prepare to hold their

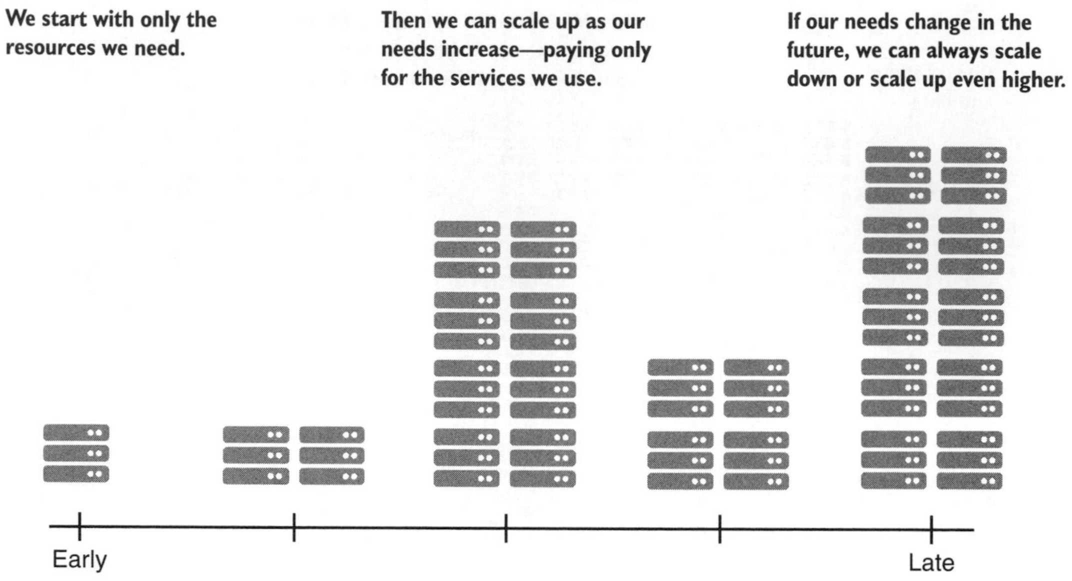
We start with only the resources we need.
Then we can scale up as our needs increase—paying only for the services we use.
If our needs change in the future, we can always scale down or scale up even higher.
Early
Late

Figure 11.2 Cloud-based storage is useful when we need to be flexible, because the storage space is available to us on-demand as we have more and more data to store.

data—and fast. You have a new challenge: you need to quickly find and set up a large data storage solution.

If you were storing your data in S3, the large data storage solution could be the same as your smaller data storage solution: it could all go in S3. Because the service is limitless and available on demand, when there's more data for us to store, we can pay more to store it.

11.1.3 Objects for convenient heterogenous storage

Another advantage of S3 is that it follows the object storage paradigm. Object storage—as opposed to traditional file storage—is a storage pattern that focuses on the what of the data instead of the where. With traditional file storage, a file is referred to by its name and which directory it's in. With object storage, we recognize objects by a unique identifier (figure 11.3).

Because unique identifiers themselves are not usually enough to help humans keep track of their data, object storage supports arbitrary metadata. This means that we can tag our objects flexibly based on our needs. Do we need to tag data by day? By user or customer? By product or marketing campaign? By the tides or the moon? We can apply any tags we want. Additionally—though we won't cover them in this book—querying tools are available for S3 that allow SQL-like querying of these metadata tags for metadata analysis.

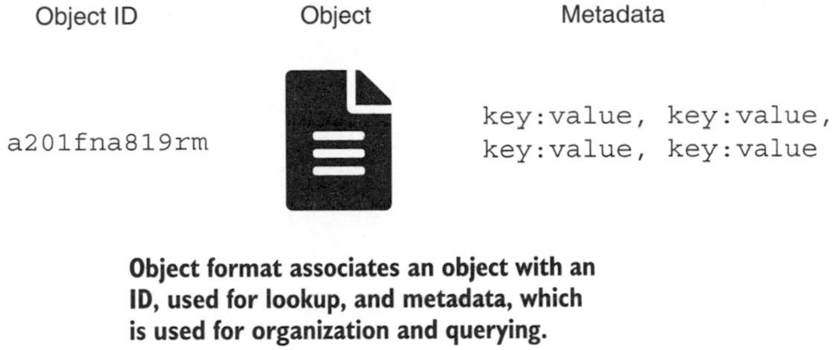
Object ID
Object
Metadata
a201fna819rm
key:value, key:value,
key:value, key:value
Object format associates an object with an ID, used for lookup, and metadata, which is used for organization and querying.

Figure 11.3 Object storage associates data with a unique identifier, which we can call to perform file operations on the object.

Having unique identifiers as the approach to calling all our objects means that we can store heterogenous data in the same way. Say we're running a social media platform, and our users are uploading pictures and videos to our website. We can store both of those file types in S3 and tag them with the same metadata even though they're different types.

11.1.4 Managed service for conveniently managing large datasets

One problem that we'd run into if we were managing a large dataset ourselves is the day-to-day maintenance of the dataset. If we want our data to be highly available, we have to take steps to replicate the data in multiple storage environments while also setting up failovers, so that when our data is unavailable in one location, we can find it quickly in another. For large datasets, this is no trivial matter.

Because S3 is a managed service, Amazon Web Services handles all of the low-level implementation of our data and ensures high durability and availability. That means that we can expect our data to be available when we need it without having to think about it too much. This will free us up to do other things, like actually working on the large dataset we now have stored in S3.

11.1.5 Life cycle policies for managing large datasets over time

One of the issues we'll have with large datasets—which we've already alluded to in this section—is that large datasets are growing datasets. Over time, our dataset grows larger and larger. That said, not all of the data in that large dataset stays relevant.

Image we're a running subscription-based online video service. We want to store records of all the videos our users have watched so we can make recommendations to them about which other videos they may enjoy. That said, we may want to limit the recommendations we generate so that we're only generating recommendations for currently subscribing users and only using data from the last year.

One way to go about doing this would be to filter the data. We've used filter operations throughout the book—starting in chapter 4—and we've seen that they're natural to implement with the Hadoop and Spark frameworks. Filtering still requires us to pay for the data to be available to us and pay to process it. Another option would be to archive data we know we don't need, such as old log files that we wouldn't regularly analyze.

For this, S3 has a life cycle policy feature that we can use to make data that we're unlikely to need less available and store it more cheaply. A standard approach (figure 11.4) is to

- start the data we have in S3 Standard
- then when we need it less, relegate it to S3 Infrequent Access
- then when we're ready to archive the data, move it to S3 Glacier

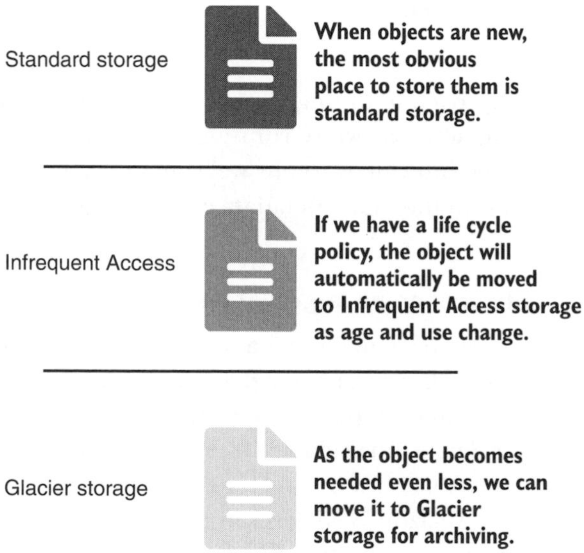
Standard storage
When objects are new, the most obvious place to store them is standard storage.
Infrequent Access
If we have a life cycle policy, the object will automatically be moved to Infrequent Access storage as age and use change.
Glacier storage
As the object becomes needed even less, we can move it to Glacier storage for archiving.

Figure 11.4 We can use the life cycle policy to ensure that old data we're less likely to want to analyze costs us less, while still maintaining the same storage strategy.

The different storage formats all have different cost structures. Table 11.1 summarizes the differences between the storage classes.

Table 11.1 Three major S3 storage classes are available, depending on how often you need to access your data.

S3 storage class	Cost to store	Cost to use	Availability
S3 Standard	Low	Very low	Very high
S3 Infrequent Access	Very Low	Low	Very high
S3 Glacier	Lowest	*Medium	Low

*Includes the cost of moving an object from S3 Glacier to another S3 format before use

S3 Standard has the greatest storage cost but the lowest per-transaction cost, which is great when we have data we'll be using a lot. S3 Infrequent Access has lower storage costs than S3 but greater transaction costs—storing data in this format is cost-effective when we'll be accessing the data less, but we want it available for when we do need it. S3 Glacier has the lowest storage cost but must be elevated to another S3 type for us to use it. The time it takes to do this can be adjusted in the range of several minutes to several hours.

In general, using S3 Standard is fine. I recommend using S3 Infrequent Access and S3 Glacier only if you have specific needs. For example, if you know you'll only need to analyze the data once each month, you could consider storing it in S3 Infrequent Access. If you need the data only for quarterly or annual analysis and can plan ahead, you may want to use S3 Glacier for cost savings.

11.2 Storing data in the cloud with S3

S3 is a place we can store large datasets. In this section, we'll go over two ways we can store that data by using

- a browser-based graphical interface
- the boto Amazon Web Services/Python Software Development Kit (SDK)

The browser-based interface is a convenient and user-friendly way to upload data and manage metadata. We can use the Python SDK library, boto, to harness the full power of Python and embed S3 actions in our scripts and software.

11.2.1 Storing data with S3 through the browser

We'll start with learning how to store data in S3 through the browser. The browser-based interface to S3 *buckets* offers some advantages over the programmatic SDK access we'll look at later. In particular, the browser

- provides visuals queues that aid in understanding the concepts of S3 storage
- has wizards that enumerate the available options

These advantages make the browser-based interface a good option for getting used to S3 storage.

Loading data into S3 is a two-step process:

1. Set up a bucket—a place to store the data.
2. Upload an object—a piece of data to be stored.

We'll tackle these steps in order. First, we'll set up a bucket and talk about the options available to us there; then we'll upload an object and talk about object-level options.

Setting up buckets in S3

Buckets are areas in S3 where we can store data. When we upload data to S3, we upload that data to a specific bucket. When the object is uploaded, it becomes accessible to only those who have access to the bucket. This makes buckets a great way to separate our data and control access to it.

WORKING ON AWS In this section through the rest of the book, the exercises involve using live Amazon Web Services resources. These services are a business for Amazon. To follow along, you'll need to set up an AWS account with a credit card, debit card, or prepaid cash card. The resources needed for the examples in chapters 11 and 12 cost less than $5 as I'm writing this. To conserve cost, make sure you shut down all your compute resources when you no longer need them. Idle compute clusters can quickly raise the cost of using AWS.

For example, imagine we're an airline and we have an application that allows users to see where all our planes are flying at any given time. We might want to store full flight location logs in S3 so that we can access this data for future analysis. At the same time, we want to keep curious third parties—potentially our competitors—from downloading our data. Buckets and their privacy controls allow us to limit access to such data.

To start setting up a bucket, we'll need to navigate to the S3 page in AWS. We can find Amazon Web Services at https://aws.amazon.com. From there, you can click the Services drop-down menu in the upper left corner of the screen and select S3, which you can find under Storage. Additionally, we could search for S3 in the Services search (figure 11.5).

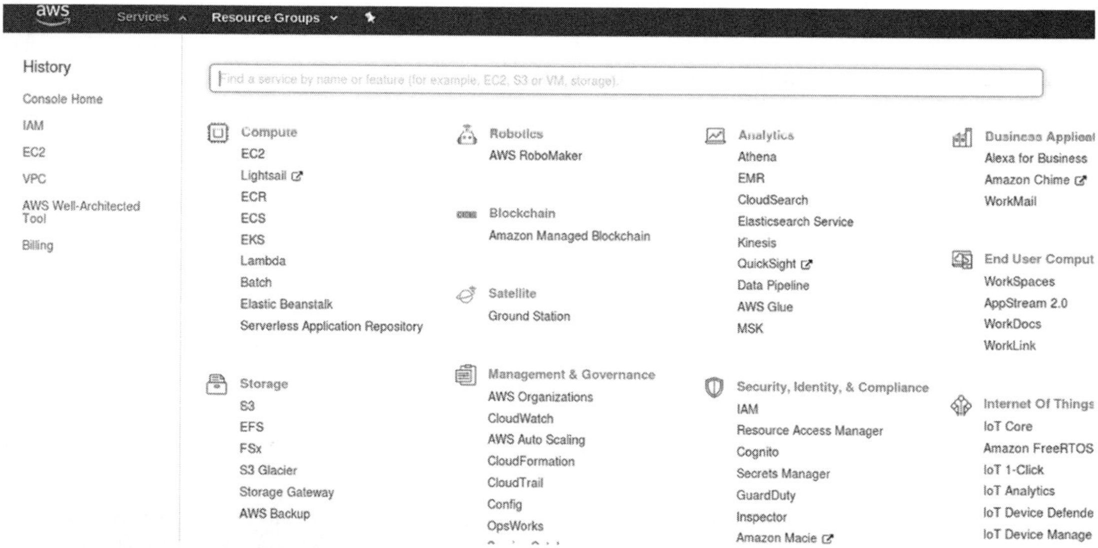
aws
Services
Resource Groups
History
Console Home
IAM
EC2
VPC
AWS Well-Architected Tool
Billing
Find a service by name or feature (for example, EC2, S3 or VM, storage).
Compute
EC2
Lightsail
ECR
ECS
EKS
Lambda
Batch
Elastic Beanstalk
Serverless Application Repository
Storage
S3
EFS
FSx
S3 Glacier
Storage Gateway
AWS Backup
Robotics
AWS RoboMaker
Blockchain
Amazon Managed Blockchain
Satellite
Ground Station
Management & Governance
AWS Organizations
CloudWatch
AWS Auto Scaling
CloudFormation
CloudTrail
Config
OpsWorks
Analytics
Athena
EMR
CloudSearch
Elasticsearch Service
Kinesis
QuickSight
Data Pipeline
AWS Glue
MSK
Security, Identity, & Compliance
IAM
Resource Access Manager
Cognito
Secrets Manager
GuardDuty
Inspector
Amazon Macie
Alexa for Business
Amazon Chime
WorkMail
End User Comput
WorkSpaces
AppStream 2.0
WorkDocs
WorkLink
Internet Of Things
IoT Core
Amazon FreeRTOS
IoT 1-Click
IoT Analytics
IoT Device Defende
IoT Device Manage

Figure 11.5 To navigate to the S3 landing page, we can always use the Services navigation drop-down menu and either do a search or find S3 under Storage.

This will take us off of the main AWS landing page and onto the S3 landing page. This page will list the buckets we have once we have one or more buckets set up. For now, though, it offers us a search bar and a button that we can click to launch the S3 Create Bucket wizard (figure 11.6). Click that button.

S3 buckets
Search for buckets
Create bucket
Edit public access settings
Empty
Delete

Figure 11.6 The S3 Create Bucket wizard and bucket search are available from the S3 landing page.

Once we enter the Create Bucket wizard, it will walk us through the options for setting up an S3 bucket. The first two options we'll face are deciding on a bucket name and selecting a region for our bucket. The name of our S3 bucket has several restrictions. The three major restrictions for S3 bucket names are that they

- must be unique among all S3 bucket names (see figure 11.7)
- can't use capital letters or underscores
- must be between 3 and 63 characters

A common way to name S3 buckets is to break bucket names into a series of labels. For example, wolohan.mastering.largedata could be a bucket for this book. That name consists of three labels—wolohan, mastering, and largedata—each of which is separated by a period. If I wanted to create a second bucket for a similar purpose, I could create wolohan.mastering.largedata2. If I wanted to create a bucket for a book on small data, I could call it wolohan.mastering.smalldata. Another common approach is to use hyphens instead of periods.

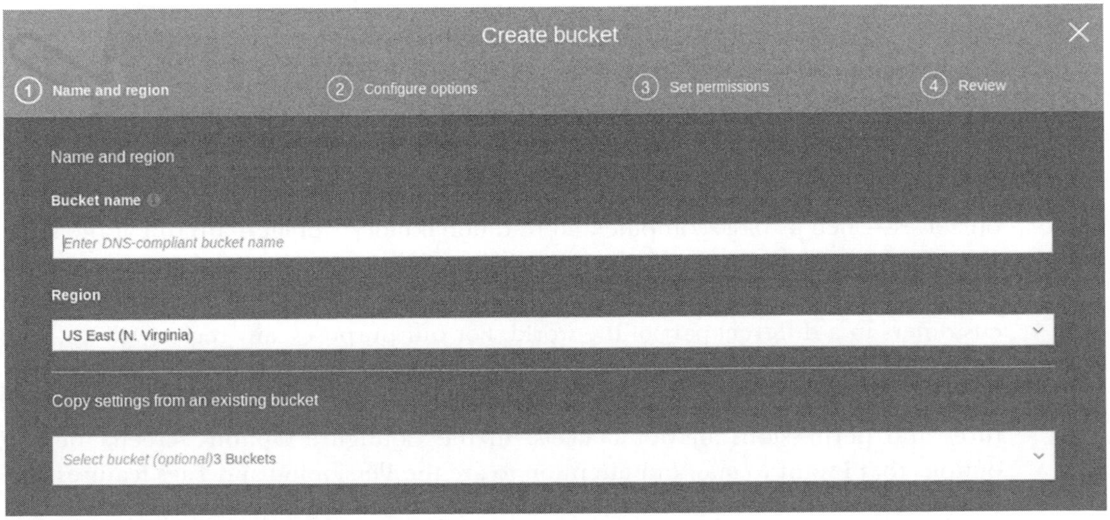
Create bucket
1 Name and region
2 Configure options
3 Set permissions
4 Review
Name and region
Bucket name
Enter DNS-compliant bucket name
Region
US East (N. Virginia)
Copy settings from an existing bucket
Select bucket (optional)3 Buckets

Figure 11.7 The bucket wizard is helpful in selecting a bucket name, which must be unique across all S3 buckets, and a region.

Additionally, on the first Create Bucket page, we need to select a region for our bucket. The region refers to the group of data centers where AWS will store the bucket's data. In AWS parlance, a region is a group of availability zones, which are themselves data centers or groupings of data centers (figure 11.8). The availability zone level offers the lowest redundancy and fault tolerance (which is still quite good), with a region-level service offering more fault tolerance (which is great), and a multi-region setup offering the most fault tolerance (excellent).

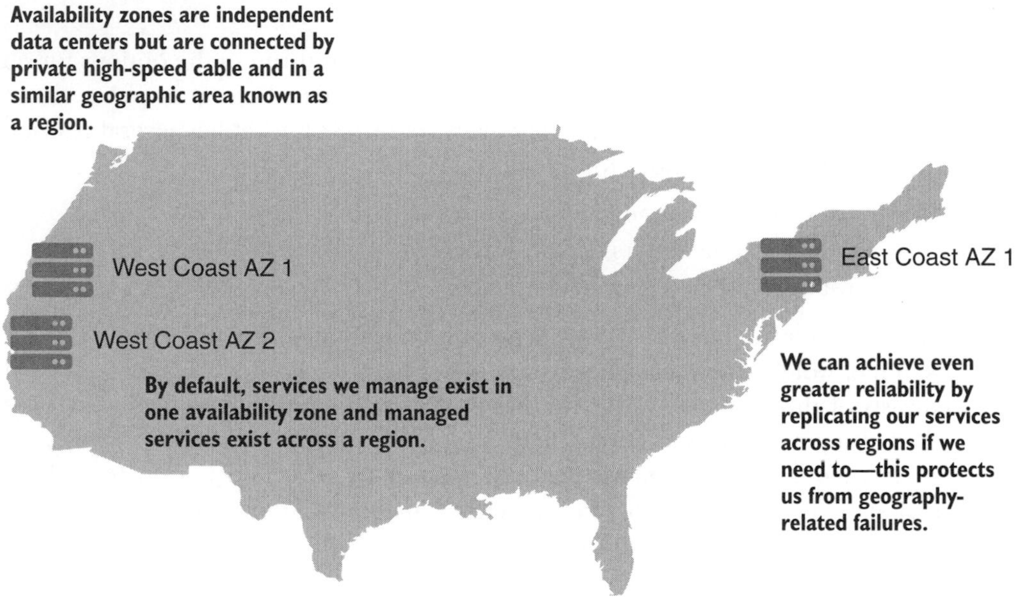
Availability zones are independent data centers but are connected by private high-speed cable and in a similar geographic area known as a region.
West Coast AZ 1
West Coast AZ 2
East Coast AZ 1
By default, services we manage exist in one availability zone and managed services exist across a region.
We can achieve even greater reliability by replicating our services across regions if we need to—this protects us from geography-related failures.

Figure 11.8 Regions and availability zones in AWS refer to the data centers that are used to run compute operations or store data. Moving from small scale (availability zone) up to large scale (multiple regions) improves fault tolerance.

Managed services in AWS typically run at the region level. Services that we manage ourselves—such as basic compute and traditional block storage—are run at the availability zone level. We can replicate managed services and self-managed services across regions if we need the extra redundancy or need to make our application available to customers in a different part of the world. For our purposes, any region will do. Pick the one closest to you and click Next.

The next two screens in the S3 Create Bucket wizard allow us to select optional features and permissions for our buckets. In the Configure Options screen, the two options that I want to draw our attention to are the Versioning and Tags features (figure 11.9).

S3 versioning is a very useful feature because it allows us to keep track of objects through time. For example, we can use S3 to store snapshots of a database all in a

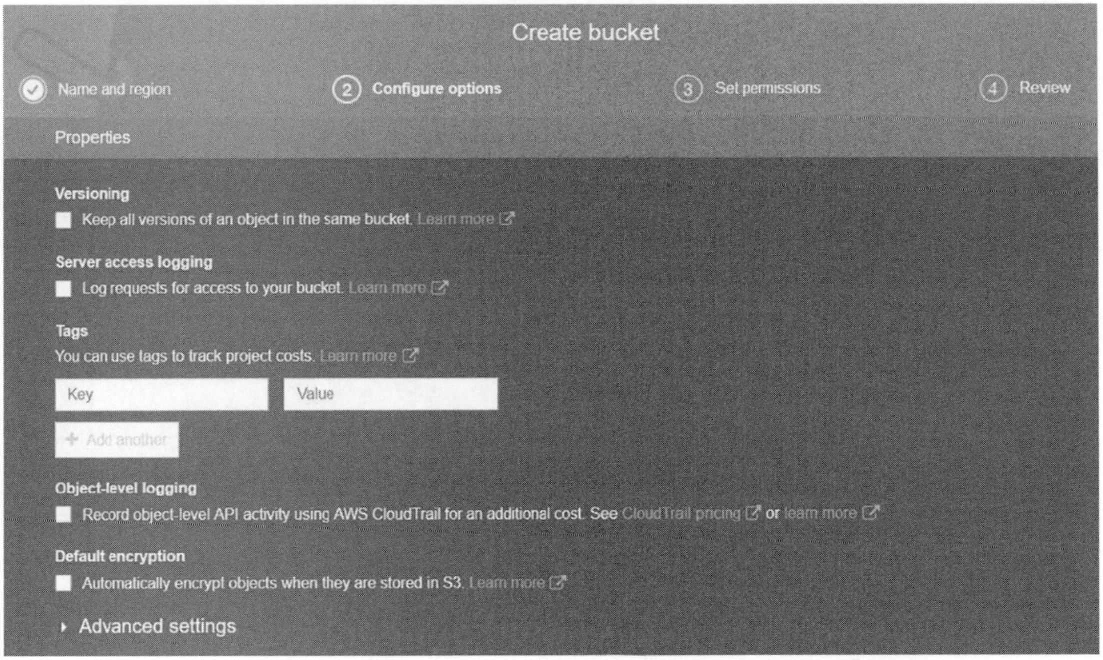
Create bucket
Name and region
2 Configure options
3 Set permissions
4 Review
Properties
Versioning
Keep all versions of an object in the same bucket. Learn more
Server access logging
Log requests for access to your bucket. Learn more
Tags
You can use tags to track project costs. Learn more
Key
Value
+ Add another
Object-level logging
Record object-level API activity using AWS CloudTrail for an additional cost. See CloudTrail pricing or learn more
Default encryption
Automatically encrypt objects when they are stored in S3. Learn more
Advanced settings

Figure 11.9 Configure Options offers options for generating S3 buckets in the AWS browser wizard.

single object. That being said, with S3, we do pay to store every version of the object uploaded. If we upload four versions of an object at 10 MB, we're paying for 40 MB or storage. If we store 100 versions of an object at 100 GB each, we're paying for 10 TB of storage. Versioning is an important feature, but don't get caught off-guard if you're versioning large objects.

The Tags option for S3 buckets allows us to use arbitrary metadata to keep track of projects. For example, it may make sense for you to enter a tag for your S3 bucket with a key of "project" and a value of "chapter-11." You can add as many of these tags as you need for your project. For example, if you have a bucket for movies, you may want to add a key of "content" and a value of "movies." Once you're done adding tags, click through to the next screen.

From the Set Permissions screen, we can set restrictions on the public access of our bucket. Public access refers to access that comes in directly from the public internet. For data analysis, assuming we want to do our analysis on AWS as I demonstrate next chapter, we won't need this (figure 11.10). For other use cases, public access can be helpful. Amazon recommends limiting public access to S3 buckets as much as possible. Go ahead and block all public access for this bucket, click through the next two pages, and create the bucket.

At this point, we've created an S3 bucket. You should see a bucket show up on the main S3 landing page. Click on the bucket's link, and you'll be brought to a landing

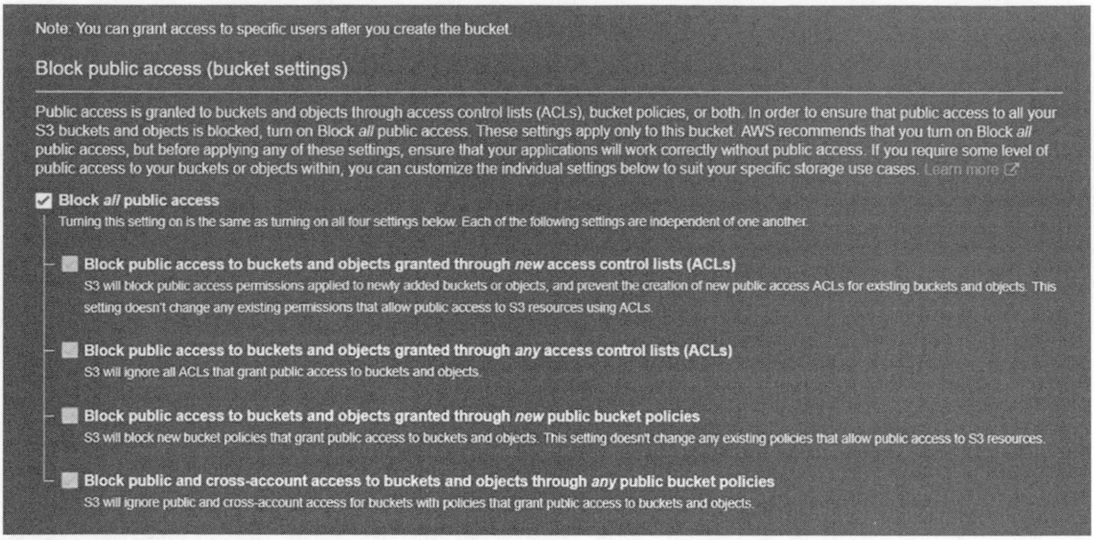
Note: You can grant access to specific users after you create the bucket.
Block public access (bucket settings)
Public access is granted to buckets and objects through access control lists (ACLs), bucket policies, or both. In order to ensure that public access to all your S3 buckets and objects is blocked, turn on Block all public access. These settings apply only to this bucket. AWS recommends that you turn on Block all public access, but before applying any of these settings, ensure that your applications will work correctly without public access. If you require some level of public access to your buckets or objects within, you can customize the individual settings below to suit your specific storage use cases. Learn more
Block all public access
Turning this setting on is the same as turning on all four settings below. Each of the following settings are independent of one another.
Block public access to buckets and objects granted through new access control lists (ACLs)
S3 will block public access permissions applied to newly added buckets or objects, and prevent the creation of new public access ACLs for existing buckets and objects. This setting doesn't change any existing permissions that allow public access to S3 resources using ACLs.
Block public access to buckets and objects granted through any access control lists (ACLs)
S3 will ignore all ACLs that grant public access to buckets and objects.
Block public access to buckets and objects granted through new public bucket policies
S3 will block new bucket policies that grant public access to buckets and objects. This setting doesn't change any existing policies that allow public access to S3 resources.
Block public and cross-account access to buckets and objects through any public bucket policies
S3 will ignore public and cross-account access for buckets with policies that grant public access to buckets and objects.

Figure 11.10 Public access to S3 buckets is not generally necessary for analytics workflows.

page specific to that bucket. As long as that bucket is empty, it will show you a landing page giving you three options (figure 11.11):

- Upload an object
- Set object properties
- Set object permissions

Of these three, we'll want to upload an object. If we click the blue Upload button in the top left corner, we'll be brought to another wizard like the one we just went through. This wizard is for adding data to an S3 bucket.

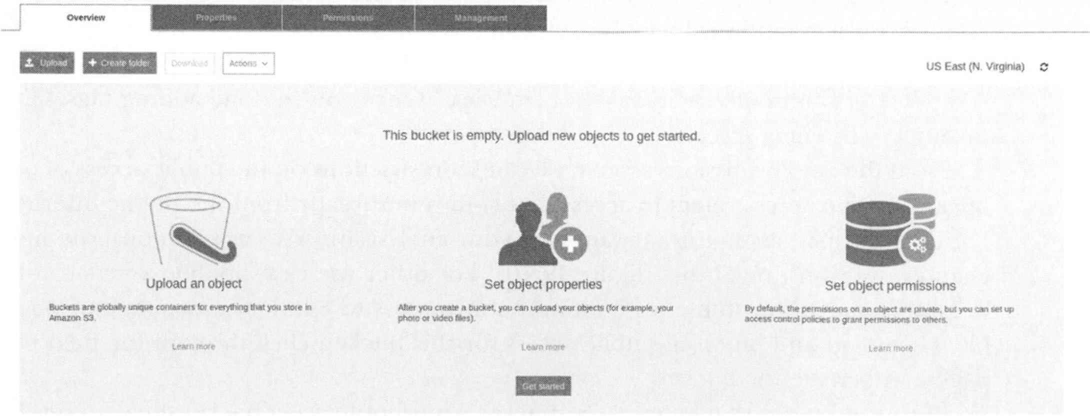
Overview
Properties
Permissions
Management
Upload
Create folder
Download
Actions
US East (N. Virginia)
This bucket is empty. Upload new objects to get started.
Upload an object
Buckets are globally unique containers for everything that you store in Amazon S3.
Learn more
Set object properties
After you create a bucket, you can upload your objects (for example, your photo or video files).
Learn more
Set object permissions
By default, the permissions on an object are private, but you can set up access control policies to grant permissions to others.
Learn more
Get started

Figure 11.11 The main thing we'll do with S3 buckets is upload objects to them.

The bucket Upload wizard (figure 11.12) allows us to upload a single file or multiple files. Go ahead and click Add Files and choose a file from your file system. The chapter 11 repository (you can find it at this link: https://www.manning.com/downloads/1961) for this book includes several files for the programmatic example later in this chapter that you can use for this part.

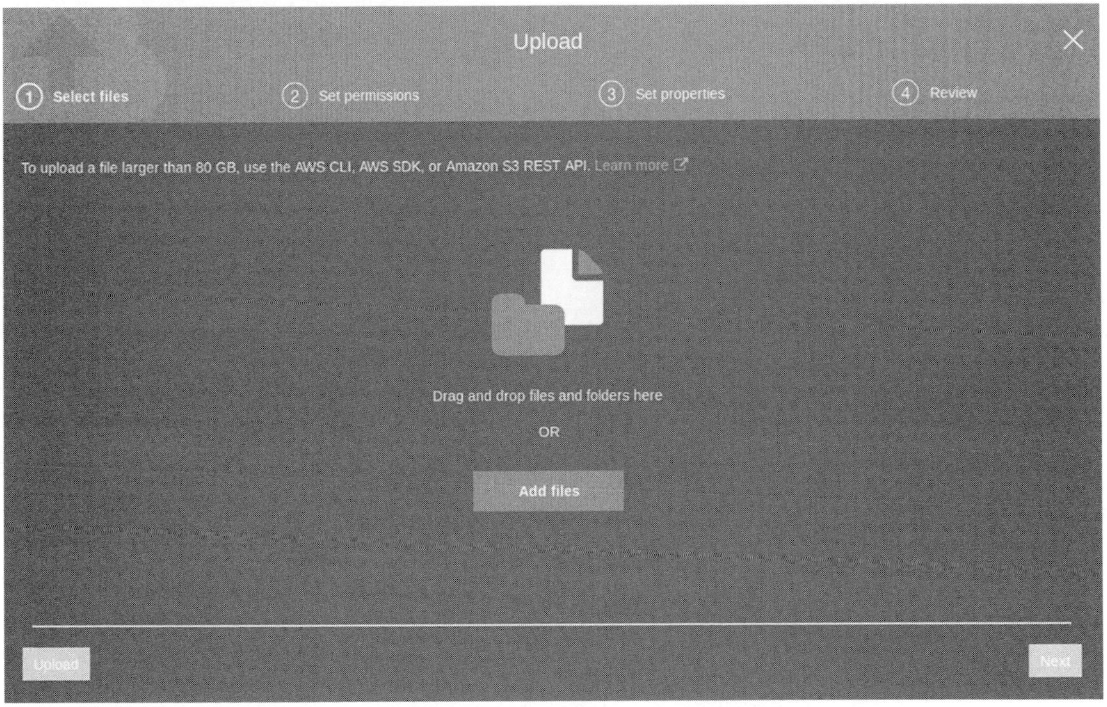
Upload
1 Select files
2 Set permissions
3 Set properties
4 Review
To upload a file larger than 80 GB, use the AWS CLI, AWS SDK, or Amazon S3 REST API. Learn more
Drag and drop files and folders here
OR
Add files
Upload
Next

Figure 11.12 The bucket Upload wizard allows us to upload files to an S3 bucket.

Click through the next screen, selecting to use the bucket-level permissions, and you'll be brought to a Set Properties screen (figure 11.13). On this screen, we can select the storage class of the object we're uploading.

We covered three of these storage classes in section 11.1.5:

1. Standard storage is appropriate for most use cases.
2. Infrequent Access storage is for data we want to have available but won't need often.
3. Glacier storage is for data we want to keep but will need infrequently and about which we'll have plenty of notice before we need it.

On this screen, we can see those three classes, plus several more. You'll notice that AWS provides its own descriptions of when the different storage classes are useful. At the top of the page in the wizard, the link to the current S3 pricing will let us compare

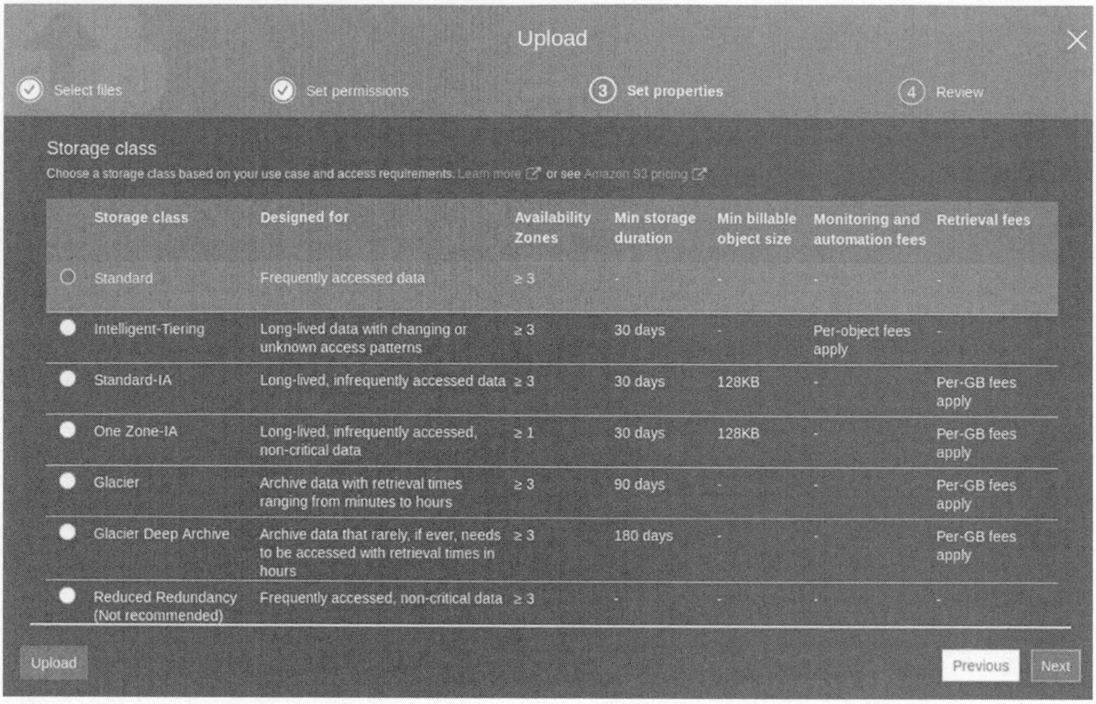
Upload
Select files
Set permissions
3 Set properties
4 Review
Storage class
Choose a storage class based on your use case and access requirements. Learn more or see Amazon S3 pricing
Storage class
Designed for
Availability Zones
Min storage duration
Min billable object size
Monitoring and automation fees
Retrieval fees
Standard
Frequently accessed data
≥ 3
Intelligent-Tiering
Long-lived data with changing or unknown access patterns
≥ 3
30 days
Per-object fees apply
Standard-IA
Long-lived, infrequently accessed data
≥ 3
30 days
128KB
Per-GB fees apply
One Zone-IA
Long-lived, infrequently accessed, non-critical data
≥ 1
30 days
128KB
Per-GB fees apply
Glacier
Archive data with retrieval times ranging from minutes to hours
≥ 3
90 days
Per-GB fees apply
Glacier Deep Archive
Archive data that rarely, if ever, needs to be accessed with retrieval times in hours
≥ 3
180 days
Per-GB fees apply
Reduced Redundancy (Not recommended)
Frequently accessed, non-critical data
≥ 3
Upload
Previous
Next

Figure 11.13 The storage classes in S3 are all tailored to a different use case. The standard S3 storage class is appropriate for most use cases.

the costs of the different storage options. I recommend using S3 Standard for this upload and other uploads where the case for another class is not obvious.

Additionally, via this screen, we have the option of adding metadata tags to our object (figure 11.14). These tags are key-value pairs that can be anything we want. They can be helpful for storing our data. For me, I'm uploading the data file named 2014-01.json—which I know is a JSON file with data from January 2014 in it. For that reason, I'll give it three tags:

- A header declaring the content type of the object
- A custom tag indicating the month of the object
- A custom tag indicating the year of the object

I can use these tags in the future to find the object among all of the objects that I upload to this bucket.

Once you've added the metadata you want, click through this screen, review your choices, and upload the object to your bucket. Now, when you're on the landing page of your S3 bucket, you should see a listing of all the objects in that bucket. There should only be one object: the one you just uploaded. Click on that object, and you'll be brought to an object page (figure 11.15).

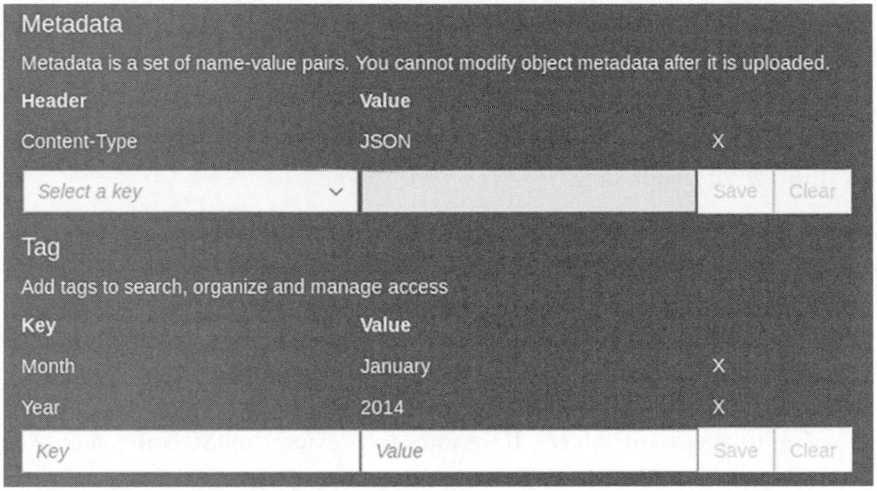
Metadata
Metadata is a set of name-value pairs. You cannot modify object metadata after it is uploaded.
Header
Value
Content-Type
JSON
X
Select a key
Save
Clear
Tag
Add tags to search, organize and manage access
Key
Value
Month
January
X
Year
2014
X
Key
Value
Save
Clear

Figure 11.14 Adding metadata to S3 objects helps us find those objects later when we need to use them.

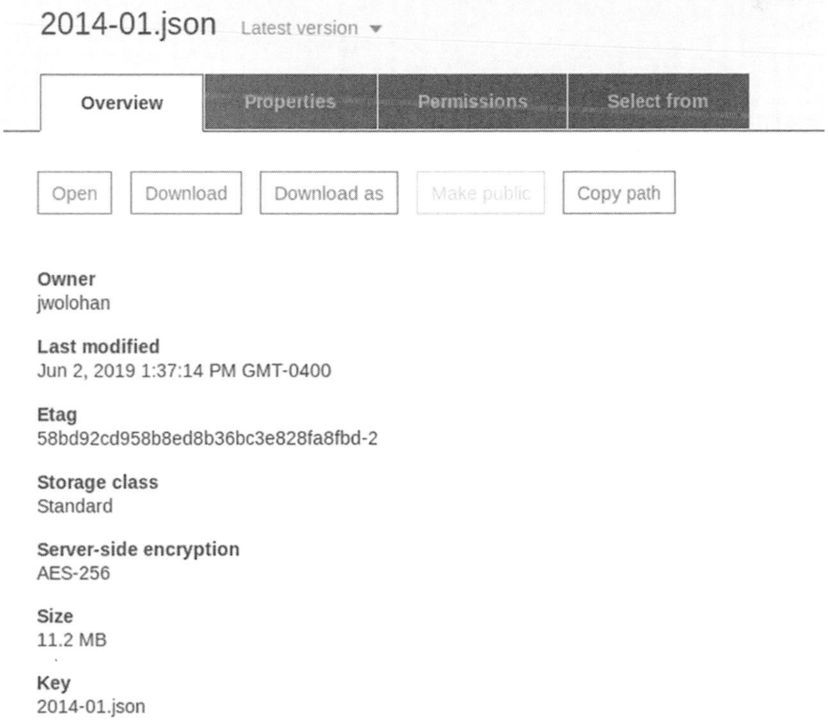
2014-01.json
Latest version
Overview
Properties
Permissions
Select from
Open
Download
Download as
Make public
Copy path
Owner
jwolohan
Last modified
Jun 2, 2019 1:37:14 PM GMT-0400
Etag
58bd92cd958b8ed8b36bc3e828fa8fbd-2
Storage class
Standard
Server-side encryption
AES-256
Size
11.2 MB
Key
2014-01.json

Figure 11.15 The S3 object page shows metadata about the object and lists actions—such as downloading the object or opening the object—that we can take.

The object page shows you properties of the object you just uploaded, including

- the owner of the object
- the date the object was last modified
- the storage class of the object
- the size of the object

Additionally, options at the top of the page indicate actions we can take. Try to open the object using the open option, and you'll be brought to an error page. Why is this happening?

We're getting the error page because we're attempting to access the object from our browser over the public internet, and we blocked public internet access to all the objects in our bucket. This is the same response that anyone else would see if they were trying to access our object. If we want to preview the JSON file, a convenient way to do that is on the Select From tab.

The Select From tab gives us options for querying our data (figure 11.16). If we select the JSON file format and JSON lines type, AWS will give us a preview of the document. We can also click through and use SQL-like expressions to query our document. For large files, this may be an effective way of preprocessing our data, although we also can use the map and filter techniques we have learned through this book.

Parquet: A concise tabular data store

In figure 11.16, you'll notice three file format options: CSV, JSON, and Parquet. The first two we've already used in this book. CSV is a simple, tabular data store, and JSON is a human-readable document store. Both are common in data interchange and are often used in the storage of distributed large datasets. Parquet is a Hadoop-native tabular data format.

Parquet uses clever metadata to improve the performance of map and reduce operations. Running a job on Parquet can take as little as 1/100th the time a comparable job on a CSV or JSON file would take. Additionally, Parquet supports efficient compression. As a result, it can be stored at a fraction of the cost of CSV or JSON.

These benefits make Parquet an excellent option for data that primarily needs to be read by a machine, such as for batch analytics operations. JSON and CSV remain good options for smaller data or data that's likely to need some human inspection. For more on Parquet, see chapter 7 of *Spark in Action*, Second Edition, by Jean-Georges Perrin: http://mng.bz/eD7P.

Uploading objects manually is useful because it can be a good introduction or a reminder of all the options that are available to us. It does, however, require a lot of clicking. In the next section, we'll look at how we can upload an object programmatically.

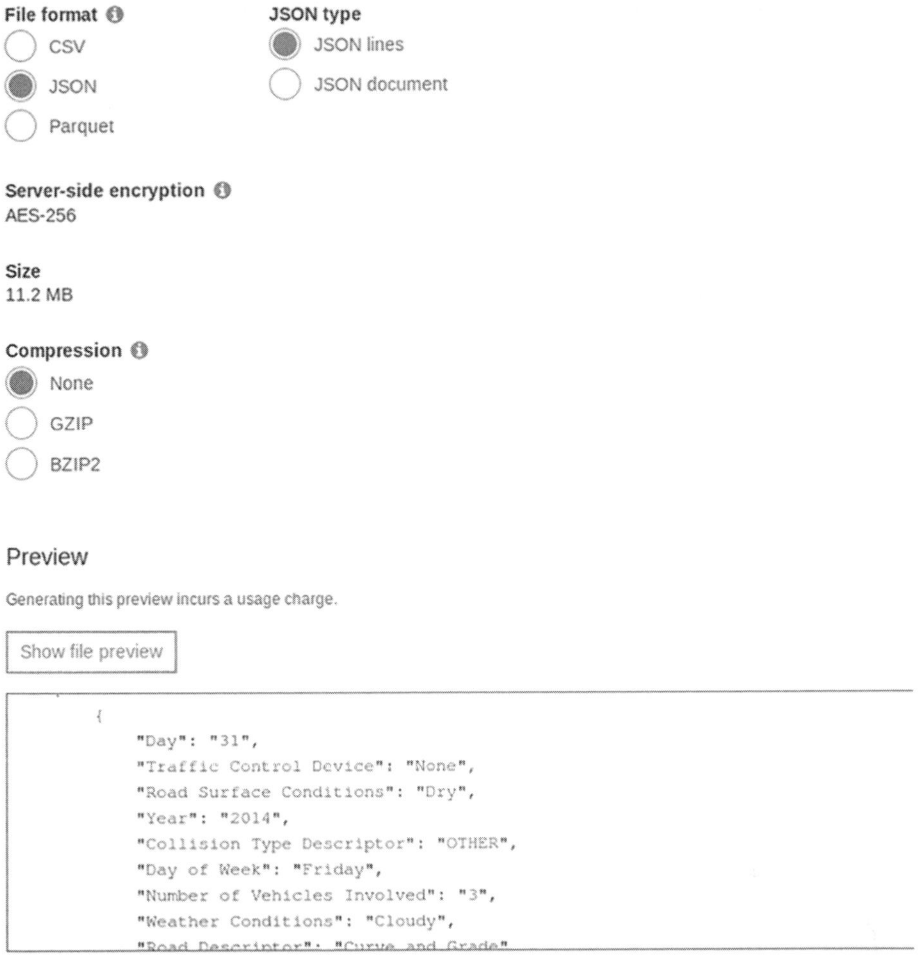
File format
CSV
JSON
Parquet
JSON type
JSON lines
JSON document
Server-side encryption
AES-256
Size
11.2 MB
Compression
None
GZIP
BZIP2
Preview
Generating this preview incurs a usage charge.
Show file preview
{
"Day": "31",
"Traffic Control Device": "None",
"Road Surface Conditions": "Dry",
"Year": "2014",
"Collision Type Descriptor": "OTHER",
"Day of Week": "Friday",
"Number of Vehicles Involved": "3",
"Weather Conditions": "Cloudy",

Figure 11.16 We can use S3 Select to preview JSON, CSV, or Apache Parquet files that we've uploaded to S3. S3 Select provides SQL-like access to data in all three formats.

11.2.2 Programmatic access to S3 with Python and boto

Although the browser-based interface to S3 is nice, at times we want to upload objects to S3 without as much human involvement. For these situations, we can use one of the AWS SDKs. For Python, that would be the boto library.

Boto is a library that provides Pythonic access to many of the AWS APIs, including the S3 API. We can use boto to write Python code—including all of the map and reduce perks we've used so far in this book—to upload objects to S3. The current version of boto is boto3, and we can install it using `pip`:

```
pip install boto3
```

We'll be able to use boto to interact with AWS on our behalf. To do so, we need to give it authorization. This authorization comes in the form of an access key and an access key secret. To create these keys, we'll have to go back to AWS in our browser. Specifically, we'll want to go to our Identity Access and Management (IAM) console.

A SECURE CLOUD WITH IAM

Through the Amazon Web Services IAM interface, we can create accounts with different access permissions. For example, we may want to give our developers access to our compute resources but restrict the finance team to only the billing. This is a powerful tool—similar to user accounts on an operating system.

By default in AWS, we operate as root. As you may know from working on a Unix system, root access gives us a lot of power, but it also can allow a malicious or ignorant actor to cause a lot of damage. For that reason, we want to limit the amount of time we spend at root. To do so, we'll create separate IAM accounts to work from.

Navigate to the Users tab of the IAM console by doing one of the following:

- Clicking your name in the top right corner, then Security Credentials, then Users in the sidebar
- Going to https://console.aws.amazon.com/iam/home?#/users

From here, you'll see a blank list of users. It's blank because we haven't created any IAM users yet. Up top, there will be a big blue Add User button. Click that button, and you'll be brought to yet another AWS wizard (figure 11.17). This wizard will walk us through setting up an IAM user.

In the first screen, give the user a User Name and check the box for Programmatic Access. This will provide that user credentials to use the Python SDK for AWS: boto. Don't click the checkbox for AWS Management Console Access. Leaving it unchecked will prevent that user from accessing AWS over the web.

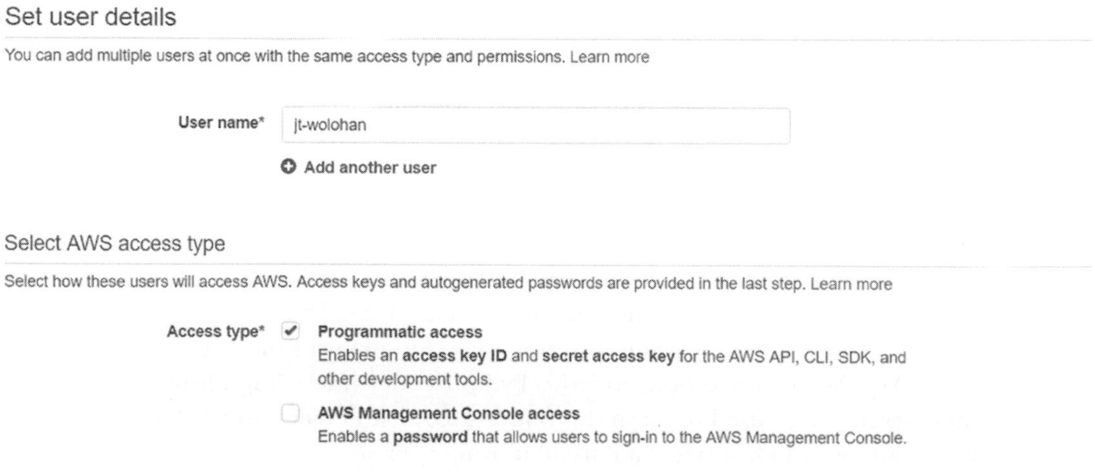
Set user details
You can add multiple users at once with the same access type and permissions. Learn more
User name*
jt-wolohan
Add another user
Select AWS access type
Select how these users will access AWS. Access keys and autogenerated passwords are provided in the last step. Learn more
Access type*
Programmatic access
Enables an access key ID and secret access key for the AWS API, CLI, SDK, and other development tools.
AWS Management Console access
Enables a password that allows users to sign-in to the AWS Management Console.

Figure 11.17 The AWS Create User wizard will help us create a user that will have programmatic-only access to our AWS resources.

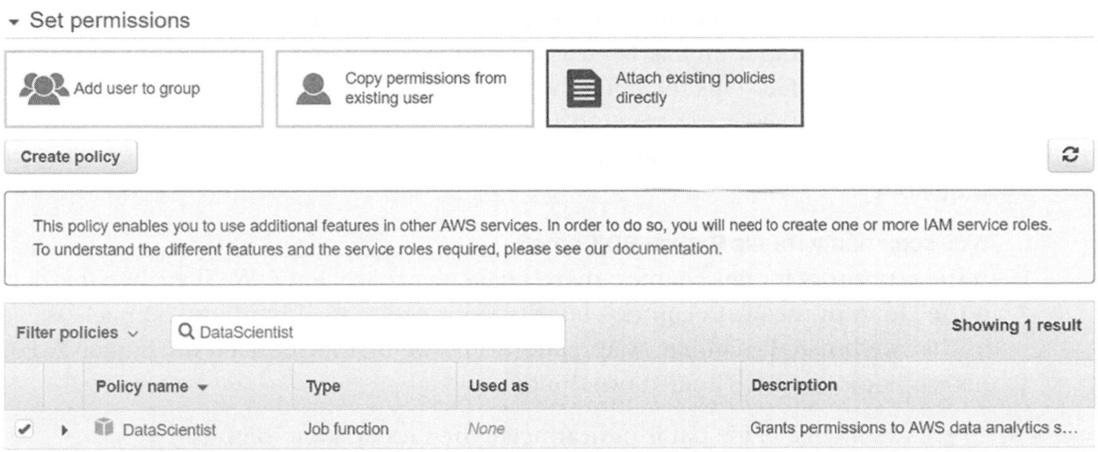
Set permissions
Add user to group
Copy permissions from existing user
Attach existing policies directly
Create policy
This policy enables you to use additional features in other AWS services. In order to do so, you will need to create one or more IAM service roles. To understand the different features and the service roles required, please see our documentation.
Filter policies
DataScientist
Showing 1 result
Policy name
Type
Used as
Description
DataScientist
Job function
None
Grants permissions to AWS data analytics s...

Figure 11.18 Adding a data scientist policy to our new IAM user will allow the user to access the resources necessary for working with large datasets in the cloud, but nothing else.

Click through to the second page, and you'll be asked to set the user permissions (figure 11.18). This is where we decide what the user can and can't do. We'll want our user to be able to access and modify AWS resources necessary for working on large datasets. AWS refers to this type of user as a data scientist. To give the user we're creating the permissions of a data scientist, do the following:

- Click Attach Existing so we can see the AWS suggested permissions policies.
- Type DataScientist in the search bar and select the result that appears.

Note that AWS has a variety of other permissions sets for other roles—such as system administrators, billing only, read only, and database administration only—that we can use to ensure folks only have access to what they need. See table 11.2 for more information.

Table 11.2 Useful AWS Security Policies and common situations in which you would assign them

AWS Security Policy	Use case
AdministratorAccess	Individuals who need to be able to manage other users; start up and shut down all services
DataScientist	Users who are performing general data analytics tasks, requiring a mix of S3, EC2, and Elastic MapReduce services
AmazonElasticMapReduceRole	Users who need to use the Elastic MapReduce cluster-computing abilities of AWS
AmazonS3FullAccess	Programs/scripts that need to both read and write data to AWS S3
AmazonS3ReadOnlyAccess	Programs/scripts that only need to read data from AWS S3
PowerUserAccess	Users who need to access all features of all services but don't need to manage other users

Once you're ready—click through the next two screens until you see a success message indicating the user has been created. On this page, you'll see an option to download a .csv file. This file contains the user credentials for the user you just created, including the access key and the secret key we'll need to programmatically access S3 through boto. Download this file and get it ready—we're about to write some code.

AWS SCRIPTING WITH THE PYTHON SDK BOTO3

In the repository for this chapter, there's data on car accidents. We'll analyze this data in the cloud in the next chapter—but first, we need to load it up into S3 buckets. To do this, we'll use the familiar map pattern that we first introduced in chapter 2. For this map operation, we'll need two things:

- A sequence of file paths indicating all the files we want to upload
- A helper function that does the work of uploading those files

Let's start with the helper function to get working with boto3. Our map helper functions typically have taken one parameter, but for this map helper function, let's design it to take two parameters. The first will be the path to the file we're trying to upload, and the second will be the bucket to which we want to upload. This will let us reuse the function for other buckets if we'd like.

We'll start by focusing on the first parameter of the function: the file path. Let's take this file path and use the `os.path.split` function to extract the filename from the path. We'll assign the file this name—the same name that it has on our local system—when we upload it to S3.

From here, we're ready to create an AWS client instance. The client instance is a class that has methods representing actions we can take on AWS, such as uploading files to a bucket. This is available in boto as `.client`, and we'll initialize it with three parameters:

- The name of the service we want to use—in this case `"s3"`
- The access key id for the DataScientist account we created
- The secret access key for the DataScientist account we created

Importantly, we don't want to pass these keys in as plain text. Doing so could potentially expose our account credentials if we upload our code to a code repository. Instead, we want to read them from environment variables. You can assign the access key and access secret to environment variables with the `export` command on a Unix machine or from the environment variables wizard on a PC.

```
export AWS_ACCESS_KEY=YOUR-ACCESS-KEY-HERE
export AWS_SECRET_KEY=YOUR-ACCESS-SECRET-HERE
```

Credentials, AWS, and boto3

You have several ways to establish your identity when using boto3. The method I've chosen here balances ease and security. Two other popular options are to specify your access key and secret key in a credentials or configuration file, located at either `~/.aws/credentials` or `~/.aws/config`. Amazon provides information on how to set up those files in their AWS Command Line Interface documentation: http://mng.bz/O9oo.

An advantage of the credentials file is that you can specify multiple profiles—for example, for development and environments—and easily alternate between them when setting up a boto3 session. That's beyond the scope of this chapter, but I encourage you to take a look at the boto3 configuration documentation for more information: http://mng.bz/G4ER.

Providing those three parameters returns a client that can take S3 actions on our behalf. This client has a method `.upload_file` that we can use to upload our files. We'll also pass three parameters to the `.upload_file` method:

1. The file path of the file we want to upload
2. The name of the bucket to which we want to upload
3. The name of the file as we want it to show up on S3

This method performs the upload to AWS and may return an HTTP response. Let's take this response and return it, along with the file name, as the value of our function upon completion. We can see this helper function in full in the following listing.

Listing 11.1 A helper function to upload files to S3

```
import boto3 as aws #A
import os

def upload_file(file_path, bucket):
    _, file_name = os.path.split(file_path)
    s3 = aws.client("s3",
        aws_access_key_id = os.environ["AWS_ACCESS_KEY"],
        aws_secret_access_key = os.environ["AWS_SECRET"]
    )
    response = s3.upload_file(file_path, bucket, file_name)
    return file_name, response
```

To use this function, we need to map it across a sequence of files. Use the `iglob` function, which we covered in chapter 4, to assign a sequence of the files we're interested in to a variable for that purpose. Once we have that sequence, we need to apply our `upload_file` function to each of the files, as shown in the following listing.

Listing 11.2 Uploading files from the filesystem to S3

```
from glob import iglob

if __name__ == "__main__":
    files = iglob("/path/to/data/files/*")
    [upload_file(f, bucket="your-bucket-name") for f in files]
```

Running this code will take some time, but it shouldn't provide you with any clues of its completion in the terminal. Instead, navigate in the browser to the S3 bucket you created. Once there, you should see a bucket full of data files ready to analyze (figure 11.19).

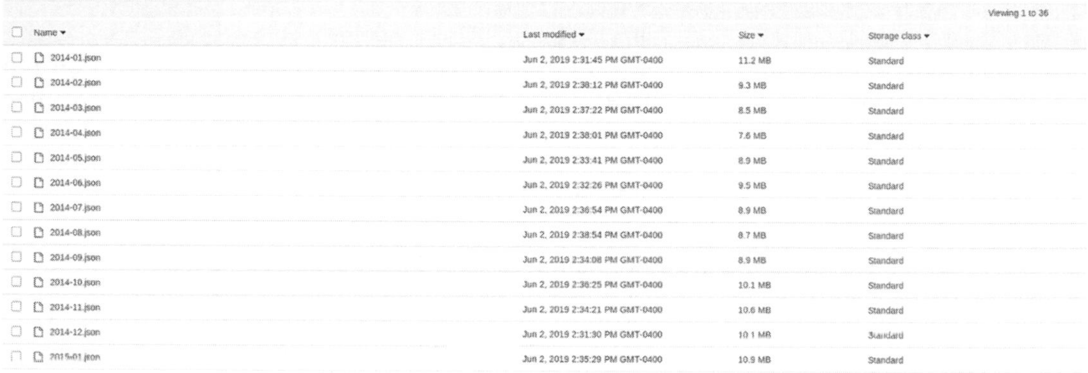
Viewing 1 to 36
Name
Last modified
Size
Storage class
2014-01.json Jun 2, 2019 2:31:45 PM GMT-0400 11.2 MB Standard
2014-02.json Jun 2, 2019 2:38:12 PM GMT-0400 9.3 MB Standard
2014-03.json Jun 2, 2019 2:37:22 PM GMT-0400 8.5 MB Standard
2014-04.json Jun 2, 2019 2:38:01 PM GMT-0400 7.6 MB Standard
2014-05.json Jun 2, 2019 2:33:41 PM GMT-0400 8.9 MB Standard
2014-06.json Jun 2, 2019 2:32:26 PM GMT-0400 9.5 MB Standard
2014-07.json Jun 2, 2019 2:36:54 PM GMT-0400 8.9 MB Standard
2014-08.json Jun 2, 2019 2:38:54 PM GMT-0400 8.7 MB Standard
2014-09.json Jun 2, 2019 2:34:08 PM GMT-0400 8.9 MB Standard
2014-10.json Jun 2, 2019 2:36:25 PM GMT-0400 10.1 MB Standard
2014-11.json Jun 2, 2019 2:34:21 PM GMT-0400 10.6 MB Standard
2014-12.json Jun 2, 2019 2:31:30 PM GMT-0400 10.1 MB Standard
2015-01.json Jun 2, 2019 2:35:29 PM GMT-0400 10.9 MB Standard

Figure 11.19 Your browser shows the traffic data files that have been uploaded to an AWS Simple Storage Service bucket.

In the next chapter, we'll use those files and this bucket to learn how to analyze large datasets in the cloud.

11.3 Exercises

11.3.1 S3 Storage classes

Which S3 storage class is best for each of the following three situations?

1. Data we know we'll only need rarely and with plenty of warning
2. Data we know we'll only need a few times each month
3. Data we'll need access to regularly

11.3.2 S3 storage region

AWS resources exist inside either availability zones or regions. Does highly durable S3 storage exist in an availability zone or across a region?

11.3.3 Object storage

Which three elements are the integral components of object storage?

- Object, object name, object location
- Object, object path, object color
- Object, object size, metadata
- Object, object ID, metadata

Summary

- Amazon Web Services Simple Storage Solution—known as S3—is a great option for large datasets we'll want to operate on in the cloud because it's effectively limitless in size.
- S3 is also a managed service—AWS acts as a custodian for our data, and we can focus on getting value from it.
- In S3, objects, which can be any data file we upload, are stored in buckets. We can assign metadata tags to both buckets and objects for organization.
- We can store S3 objects in the Standard storage class, if we'll access them frequently; an Infrequent Access storage class, if we'll access them infrequently; and Glacier storage class for archiving.
- We can create buckets and upload objects through the browser using AWS's graphical interface. The interface shows us lots of options for every action we take.
- We also can upload objects through the Python software development kit for AWS: boto3.

12 MapReduce in the cloud with Amazon's Elastic MapReduce

This chapter covers

- Launching and configuring cloud compute clusters with Elastic MapReduce
- Running Hadoop jobs in the cloud with mrjob
- Distributed cloud machine learning with Spark

Throughout this book, we've been talking about the ability to scale code up. We started by looking at how to parallelize code locally; then we moved on to distributed computing frameworks; and finally, in chapter 11, we introduced cloud computing technologies. In this chapter, we'll look at techniques we can use to work with data of any scale. We'll see how to take the Hadoop and Spark frameworks we covered in the middle of the book (chapters 7 and 8 for Hadoop; chapters 7, 9, and 10 for Spark) and bring them into the cloud with Amazon Elastic MapReduce. We'll start by looking at how to bring Hadoop into the cloud with mrjob—a framework for Hadoop and Python that we introduced in chapter 8. Then, we'll look at bringing Spark and its machine learning capabilities into the cloud.

12.1 Running Hadoop on EMR with mrjob

In chapter 8, we reviewed two methods of working with Hadoop:

1. *Hadoop Streaming*—Which uses Python scripts for its mappers and reducers
2. *mrjob*—Which we can use to do Hadoop jobs using only Python code

When we used both of these approaches, we focused on implementing the map and reduce style in Hadoop. With the techniques in chapter 8, you could take advantage of a Hadoop cluster if you already had one available, but most people don't. In this section, we'll review running Hadoop jobs on Amazon Web Services' Elastic MapReduce (EMR), a service we can use to create compute clusters whenever we need them.

12.1.1 Convenient cloud clusters with EMR

Hadoop clusters used to be reserved for only those who needed them often or could afford to have a large amount of computing resources laying around idle much of the time. This meant that 10 years ago, for the most part, only corporations and academic institutions had cluster computing. Now, with the cloud increasing in popularity, everyone can have access. One convenient way to get access to a compute cluster is Amazon's Elastic MapReduce service.

Other cloud compute services

Amazon is not the only provider of cloud-based clustering computing services. Their two major competitors, Microsoft Azure and Google Cloud, both offer services you'll find similar to Amazon Web Services. Microsoft's Azure HDInsight service and Google's Cloud Dataproc service both support Hadoop and Spark. That means you can use the knowledge from chapters 7–10 with both of those services. mrjob, which we covered in chapter 8 and go into more depth on in this section, also supports Google Cloud Dataproc. mrjob doesn't support Azure HDInsight.

In this chapter, we'll use AWS because we'll want to work with the resources we used in the previous chapter.

Amazon Web Services' EMR is a managed data cluster service. We specify general properties of the cluster, and AWS runs software that creates the cluster for us. When we're done using the cluster, Amazon absorbs the compute resources back into its network. You can think of this like the S3 cloud storage. Because Amazon has so much compute power, we can ask for some whenever we want, and they'll rent it to us. Then, when we don't need it anymore, Amazon is happy to take it back.

With this setup, if we need to run a large data processing task once a month or even once a year, we don't need to pay to maintain the cluster all month or all year. We can ask AWS to provide us the compute resources when we need to do the processing, then we can return the compute resources to Amazon when we're done. If we need to do this work more often, or at irregular intervals, we can maintain a small cluster that can grow based on usage.

For example, say we run text analytics on all the comments posted about our products on Facebook, Twitter, and Instagram every six hours. We may maintain a small cluster all the time to reduce startup time and then have the cluster expand based on how much new data there is to analyze. If there are only a few thousand comments about our products, we might get by without expanding our small cluster. If something surprising happens—say an A-list celebrity is caught using a product of ours—and we have hundreds of thousands of comments to parse through, our cluster can automatically expand to accommodate the increased volume.

Importantly, too, the pricing model for Amazon's EMR service is a per-compute-unit per-second charge. If we run 100 machines and our job finishes in 2 minutes, we'll pay the same amount as if we processed it on one machine and it took us 200 minutes. That means there are no cost savings to doing things slowly. Amazon encourages us to parallelize our problems away. All three cloud providers—Microsoft, Google, and Amazon—price their managed compute services in this way, though prices vary by provider.

12.1.2 Starting EMR clusters with mrjob

The easiest way to start an EMR cluster is by using a Python library we're already familiar with: mrjob. Although we can—and did, in chapter 8—use mrjob locally, mrjob was designed to automate the procurement of EMR clusters. By writing a Hadoop job with EMR and specifying the right settings, we can quickly set up a Hadoop cluster in the cloud.

Because we'll do machine learning with Spark later in this chapter (section 12.2), let's do a bit of data analysis that will help us understand the files we uploaded to S3 in chapter 11. Back in chapter 11, we uploaded data about car accidents, including features such as the time of day and the number of vehicles involved. For our first Hadoop job on EMR, let's write a MapReduce job that counts up the number of times crashes occurred with different numbers of vehicles (figure 12.1).

To do this, we'll create a custom class that inherits from the main mrjob class. Then we'll write two methods for that class:

1. A `.mapper` that takes in the line and returns the number of vehicles involved
2. A `.reducer` that groups the vehicles and sums the counts

Because our data is stored in the JSON lines format, when we process each line with our `.mapper`, we'll read it into a Python object using `json.loads`, as shown in listing 12.1. From there, we can use dictionary notation to retrieve the number of vehicles involved in the crash. Yielding this value and a 1 in a `tuple` will put us in good shape to count the values up in our `.reducer`.

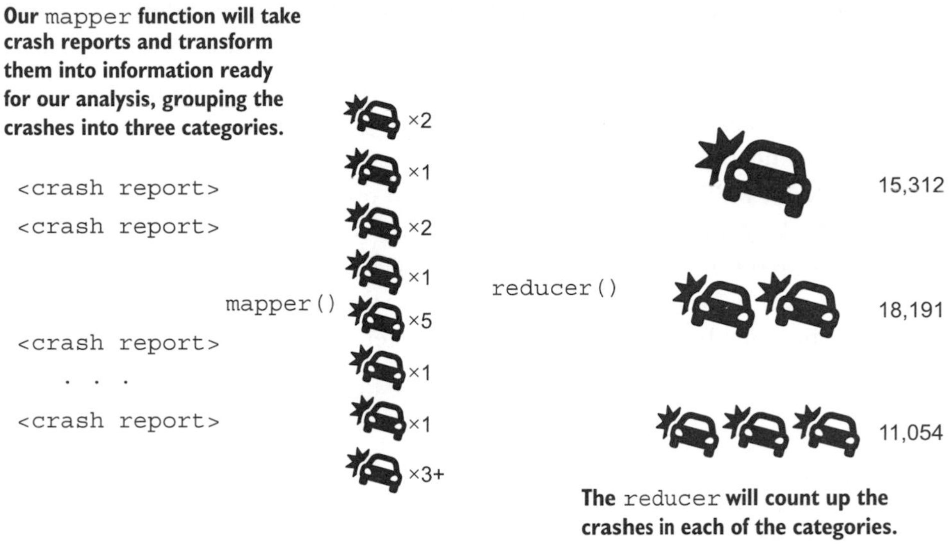
Our mapper function will take crash reports and transform them into information ready for our analysis, grouping the crashes into three categories.
<crash report>
<crash report>
<crash report>
. . .
<crash report>
mapper()
×2
×1
×2
×1
×5
×1
×1
×3+
reducer()
15,312
18,191
11,054
The reducer will count up the crashes in each of the categories.

Figure 12.1 We can use EMR to scale our MapReduce jobs up to any size. In this case, we'll use EMR to analyze the number of car crashes with different numbers of vehicles involved.

Listing 12.1 Counting crashes by number of vehicles with mrjob

```
from mrjob.job import MRJob
import json

class CrashCounts(MRJob):

    def mapper(self, _, line):
        crash_report = json.loads(line)
        vehicles = crash_report['Number of Vehicles Involved']
        yield vehicles, 1

    def reducer(self, key, values):
        yield key, sum(values)


if __name__ == '__main__':
    CrashCounts.run()
```

In our `.reducer`, we use the standard counting reduction. The key stays the key, but the value becomes the sum of all the values. If we ran this locally, the result would be a sequence of keys and values printed to the terminal. The first value indicates the number of vehicles involved, and the second value indicates how many crashes involved that number of vehicles. If you have the data files locally, you can run the mrjob script and validate this for yourself.

To run this in the cloud on EMR, we need to pass three additional parameters to our mrjob script on the command line, as shown in listing 12.2:

1. The first parameter we need to specify is called the runner. This tells mrjob how to process our command. By default, it processes locally. To process on EMR, we will need to specify `-r emr`.
2. Next, we'll need to provide a path to our input files. So far, we've been using blob syntax and pointing to where those files reside locally. Here, though, we have our data in S3. That path will need to be our bucket.
3. Lastly, let's specify a folder to which we'll write our output. We can place it in the same bucket or in a separate bucket.

Listing 12.2 Running Hadoop on EMR with mrjob

```
python mrjob_crash_counts.py \
      -r emr \
      s3://your-bucket-name-here/ \
      --output-dir=s3://your-other-bucket-name/crash-counts
```

In addition to these variables, which define where the script will go, we need to provide our credentials. mrjob uses them to create a compute cluster on our behalf. To keep these credentials secret, mrjob insists that you have these variables exported to your local environment. This prevents you from exposing your credentials in plaintext in your source code. If you didn't provide your credentials in chapter 11 when using boto3 to upload data to S3, the following listing shows how to do that for Mac and Linux. For Windows, search for "environment variables" and follow the wizard.

Listing 12.3 Setting AWS credentials for mrjob

```
export AWS_ACCESS_KEY_ID=<your AWS access key>
export AWS_SECRET_ACCESS_KEY =<your secret AWS access key>
```

Once you have your environment variables set, you'll be able to run mrjob on EMR with the command from listing 12.2. By default, this command will spin up a small test cluster for you. For learning the tool, this small cluster is plenty. For bigger jobs, you'll want to use more resources. A common way to use more resources is to use an mrjob config file. This file allows us to use YAML notation to specify the type of cluster we'd like.

For example, if we wanted to

- run our Hadoop job with 20 instances
- have all those instances be m1.large
- have those resources be in the us-west-1 region (Northern California)
- tag those resources with a "project" tag that had a value of "Mastering Large Datasets"

we could specify all of that in the config file. We can see an example of a config file for just that in the following listing.

Listing 12.4 An example configuration file for mrjob

```
runners:
  emr:
    num_core_instances: 20
    image_version: 5.24.0
    instance_type: m1.large
    region: us-west-1
    tags:
      project: Mastering Large Datasets
```

Specifying settings in a configuration file makes it possible for us to use and reuse multiple settings. For example, it may be enough to use 20 instances to run a nightly extract-transform-load process. For the monthly executive report, though, we may need to use 100 instances. We can use two configuration files to allow us to save our parameters.

We can pass those parameters to mrjob on the command line when we invoke it with Python using the `conf-path` parameter. The following listing shows an example of this action.

Listing 12.5 Adding a config file to an mrjob call

```
python mrjob_crash_counts.py \
       -r emr \
       s3://your-bucket-name-here/ \
         output-dir-s3://your-other-bucket-name/crash-counts
       --conf-path=</path/to/your/config/file.conf>
```

Once you've successfully run your Hadoop job on EMR with mrjob, we can open up the AWS console to see what happened.

12.1.3 The AWS EMR browser interface

In section 12.1.2, we looked at how we can use AWS EMR with the mrjob tool. In this section, we'll look at how we can use the browser interface to run Spark jobs. Just as AWS provides a browser-based interface to S3, the object storage system that we looked at in chapter 11, AWS also provides a browser-based interface to EMR. You can access that interface by going to https://console.aws.amazon.com/elasticmapreduce/home.

If you ran the job from section 12.1.2 and that job completed successfully, you should see a task with the status "Terminated—All steps completed" (figure 12.2). If you see another message, the job may still be running, or there may have been an error.

mrjob_crash_counts.jt-w.20190615.221956.445583
j-1AMC8NN8JT9TF
Terminated
All steps completed
2019-06-15 18:20 (UTC-4)
13 minutes

Figure 12.2 The Amazon browser-based console provides a convenient overview of the status of our clusters, including their names, IDs, status, time started, and total uptime.

VIEWING CLUSTER STATUS FROM THE AWS CLUSTER CONSOLE

Whatever you see after you run the job, click on the name of the cluster, and you'll arrive at the cluster-specific console page. On this page, you'll see the name and status of the instance along with other information about your cluster (figure 12.3).

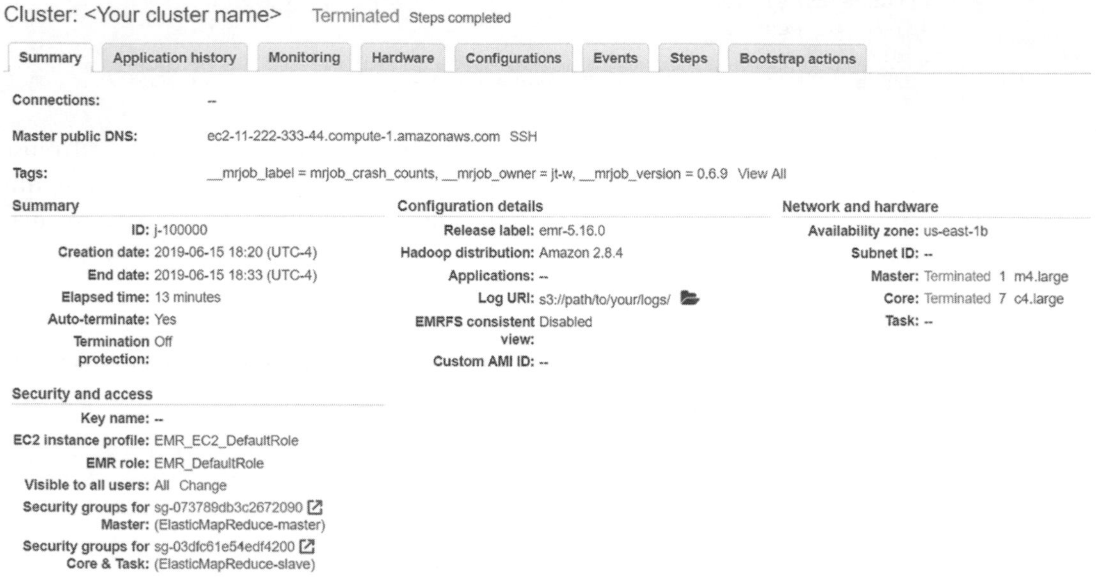
Cluster: <Your cluster name> Terminated Steps completed
Summary
Application history
Monitoring
Hardware
Configurations
Events
Steps
Bootstrap actions
Connections: --
Master public DNS: ec2-11-222-333-44.compute-1.amazonaws.com SSH
Tags: __mrjob_label = mrjob_crash_counts, __mrjob_owner = jt-w, __mrjob_version = 0.6.9 View All
Summary
ID: j-100000
Creation date: 2019-06-15 18:20 (UTC-4)
End date: 2019-06-15 18:33 (UTC-4)
Elapsed time: 13 minutes
Auto-terminate: Yes
Termination protection: Off
Configuration details
Release label: emr-5.16.0
Hadoop distribution: Amazon 2.8.4
Applications: --
Log URI: s3://path/to/your/logs/
EMRFS consistent view: Disabled
Custom AMI ID: --
Network and hardware
Availability zone: us-east-1b
Subnet ID: --
Master: Terminated 1 m4.large
Core: Terminated 7 c4.large
Task: --
Security and access
Key name: --
EC2 instance profile: EMR_EC2_DefaultRole
EMR role: EMR_DefaultRole
Visible to all users: All Change
Security groups for Master: sg-073789db3c2672090 (ElasticMapReduce-master)
Security groups for Core & Task: sg-03dfc61e54edf4200 (ElasticMapReduce-slave)

Figure 12.3 The cluster console shows information specific to that AWS cluster, such as the ID of the cluster and the number of machines in it. You can also use this console to modify the settings of running clusters.

Click the Steps tab, and you'll find a list of all the steps submitted to your cluster. In EMR, steps are tasks that we send to the cluster through the EMR API—either using the console, through an SDK like boto3, or through the command-line AWS tools. In our case, there should be only a single step (figure 12.4). AWS created this step when we ran mrjob with the EMR runner.

It's possible to submit multiple steps to the same cluster. If we do that, the steps will run one after another. Each step will wait until all steps in front of it have finished before it begins. If we want to run multiple steps simultaneously, we can request multiple clusters at the same time from EMR.

This tab is useful because it provides convenient access to the logs for each step. If your EMR steps fail—which they inevitably will if you use the service enough—this page can be helpful in your debugging process. Additionally, when jobs fail, mrjob will parse through the logs created by the Hadoop job and attempt to provide you with a user-friendly diagnosis of what went wrong. Hadoop's logs are Java logs, and Java error messages can require some getting used to. If you're more familiar with Python than with Java, the mrjob diagnosis can be quite a benefit.

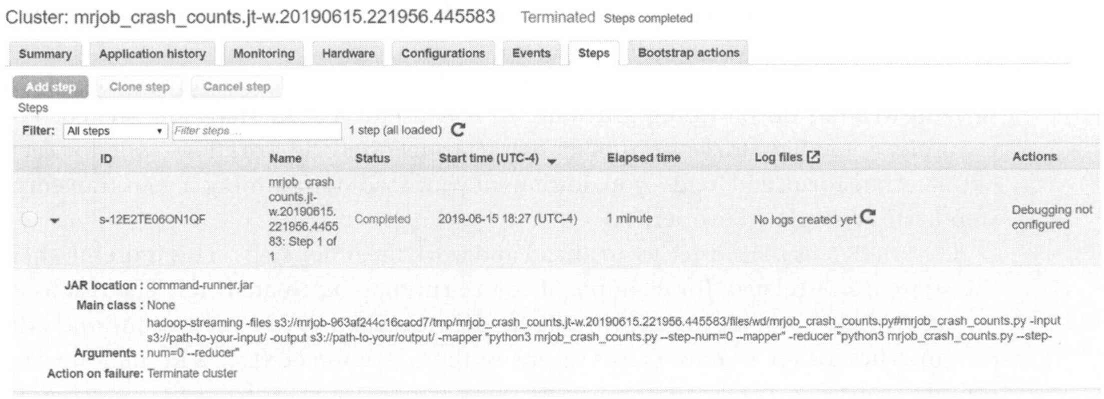
Cluster: mrjob_crash_counts.jt-w.20190615.221956.445583 Terminated Steps completed
Summary
Application history
Monitoring
Hardware
Configurations
Events
Steps
Bootstrap actions
Add step
Clone step
Cancel step
Steps
Filter: All steps
1 step (all loaded)
ID
Name
Status
Start time (UTC-4)
Elapsed time
Log files
Actions
s-12E2TE06ON1QF
mrjob crash counts.jt-w.20190615.221956.445583: Step 1 of 1
Completed
2019-06-15 18:27 (UTC-4)
1 minute
No logs created yet
Debugging not configured
JAR location : command-runner.jar
Main class : None
Arguments : hadoop-streaming -files s3://mrjob-963af244c16cacd7/tmp/mrjob_crash_counts.jt-w.20190615.221956.445583/files/wd/mrjob_crash_counts.py#mrjob_crash_counts.py -input s3://path-to-your-input/ -output s3://path-to-your/output/ -mapper "python3 mrjob_crash_counts.py --step-num=0 --mapper" -reducer "python3 mrjob_crash_counts.py --step-num=0 --reducer"
Action on failure: Terminate cluster

Figure 12.4 The step-specific detail screen of the EMR console shows information about tasks we've asked our cluster to work on.

Running lots of small EMR jobs

On this tab, you will also note the amount of time that was spent working each particular step. For example, in figure 12.4 you can see that my crash counts script only spent 1 minute running. Compare that to figure 12.3, where the cluster as a whole ran for 13 minutes. The remaining time was spent in setup and teardown. In the setup phase, the machines are procured and connected, and the necessary software is installed on them (such as Python, Java, and Hadoop). In the teardown phase, AWS returns the resources and produces logs.

If you'll be running lots of small tasks, that's a use case where you may want to submit multiple steps to a single cluster. mrjob makes it easy for us to set up clusters with the `create-cluster` command. We can pass this command to our configuration file so the cluster behaves just like it would if we created it with a single job. Additionally, the cluster will keep running after our job has finished. When we do run a persistent cluster like this, we'll usually want to specify a maximum number of hours it can be idle before it shuts down entirely:

```
mrjob create-cluster --max-hours-idle 1 --conf-path=path/to/conf/file.conf
```

This prevents us from paying for resources we don't need.

To submit jobs to an existing cluster, we'll need to specify the cluster ID to which we want to submit our code. On the command line, the parameter is `--cluster-id`, and it should be followed by the ID of the cluster on which we want to run.

Another parameter to note is `emr_action_on_failure` (in the config file) or `--emr-action-on-failure` (on the command line). These parameters specify what should happen to the cluster if our jobs fail. When we run a single step, this defaults to `TERMINATE_CLUSTER`. Having terminate on fail as the default means that if our job has any errors, our cluster will shut down. The two other options for `emr_action_on_failure` are `CANCEL_AND_WAIT` and `CONTINUE`.

`CANCEL_AND_WAIT` tells the cluster to cancel the other steps that have been queued up and to hold off on doing anything. This is useful if your steps are related. For example, if you have three steps in an extract-transform-load workflow—one for each extract, transform, and load—you don't want your load step running if your transform step hasn't completed properly.

`CONTINUE` tells the cluster to go ahead and work the other steps. This is useful when the steps aren't related; for example, if you're running batch analytics. The results of one analytics step won't necessarily impact the next step, so it's fine to continue with our analytics jobs if we have errors in one of them. We use `CONTINUE` in the following listing.

Listing 12.6 Specifying cluster ID and failure behavior in an mrjob config file

```
runners:
  emr:
    num_core_instances: 6
    image_version: 5.24.0
    instance_type: m1.large
    region: us-west-1
    cluster_id: j-000000000
    emr_action_on_failure: CONTINUE
    tags:
      project: Mastering Large Datasets
```

Specifying a cluster ID and an action on failure from the command line allows us to save time repeatedly setting up clusters to run fast jobs.

VIEWING OUR OUTPUT IN S3

Let's take a look at the output of our Hadoop job. When we called our mrjob script, we specified an output directory. This was a folder in an S3 bucket. Our output was written as objects to that bucket. If you navigate to that bucket in the browser, you should see a list of objects (figure 12.5).

Each of these objects was created as a result of our crash counts Hadoop process and contains a part of the results. Each line of these files will have the same pattern as the output from our mrjob class's `.reducer`. The first element on each line will be the

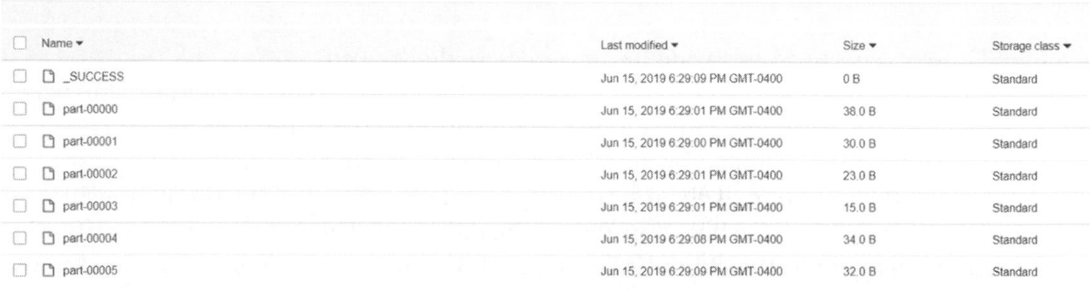
Name
Last modified
Size
Storage class
_SUCCESS
Jun 15, 2019 6:29:09 PM GMT-0400
0 B
Standard
part-00000
Jun 15, 2019 6:29:01 PM GMT-0400
38.0 B
Standard
part-00001
Jun 15, 2019 6:29:00 PM GMT-0400
30.0 B
Standard
part-00002
Jun 15, 2019 6:29:01 PM GMT-0400
23.0 B
Standard
part-00003
Jun 15, 2019 6:29:01 PM GMT-0400
15.0 B
Standard
part-00004
Jun 15, 2019 6:29:08 PM GMT-0400
34.0 B
Standard
part-00005
Jun 15, 2019 6:29:09 PM GMT-0400
32.0 B
Standard

Figure 12.5 In your browser, the bucket lists the objects created as a result of our Hadoop process.

number of vehicles involved in the crash, and the second element will be the number of times we saw a crash involving that number of vehicles.

If we don't want to have our results stored to an S3 bucket, omitting the `--output-dir` parameter will instead print those values to our screen. Outputting the values to our screen can be useful in situations where we know we won't need to use those results in future workflows through EMR. One example might be when we're testing our job. We can run it with a few small instances and print the results locally for testing, then use many instances and save the results when we've validated that the job works.

In this section, we've reviewed how to submit a Hadoop job to a cloud-compute cluster using mrjob and Amazon Web Services' EMR. Hadoop on EMR is excellent for large data processing workloads, such as batch analytics or extract-transform-load. In the next section, we'll review using Spark on EMR.

12.2 Machine learning in the cloud with Spark on EMR

When I introduced Hadoop and Spark in chapter 7, I introduced both of them as frameworks for distributed computing. Hadoop is great for low-memory workloads and massive data. Spark is great for jobs that are harder to break down into map and reduce steps, and situations where we can afford higher memory machines. In this section, we'll focus on how we can use Spark to train a machine learning model on large data in the cloud on EMR.

12.2.1 Writing our machine learning model

Before we can run our machine learner in the cloud, let's start by building a model locally on some testing data. This will mirror a process we might perform if we were running machine learning algorithms on a truly large dataset:

1. Get a sample of the full dataset.
2. Train and evaluate a few models on that dataset.
3. Select some models to evaluate on the full dataset.
4. Train several models on the full dataset in the cloud.

This process has the virtue of making it possible for you to test lots of models quickly and cheaply on your local machine. And later, because we're using scalable frameworks and a scalable computing style, we can bring the models we like into the cloud and test them on the full dataset (figure 12.6).

For this scenario, we'll continue to work with the car crash data we uploaded in chapter 11 and explored in the first section of this chapter.

> **SCENARIO: CAR CRASH ANALYSIS** Root-cause analysis of car crashes is a key way governments and safety organizations make driving safer. We've been asked by one such organization to develop a machine learning model that can predict which conditions lead to crashes that involve several vehicles (three or more) and which conditions lead to crashes that involve only one vehicle.

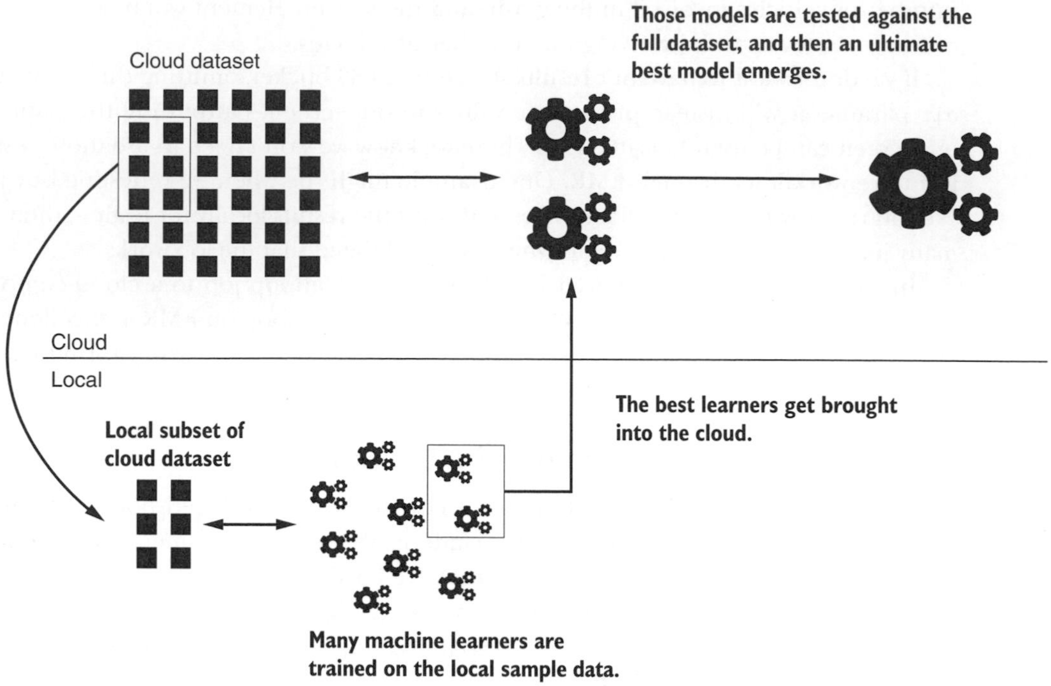
Those models are tested against the full dataset, and then an ultimate best model emerges.
Cloud dataset
Cloud
Local
The best learners get brought into the cloud.
Local subset of cloud dataset
Many machine learners are trained on the local sample data.

Figure 12.6 A common machine learning process for large datasets is to sample many models locally and then evaluate the best models in the cloud.

If you worked through chapter 10, where we learned about machine learning in Spark, you may want to try this part yourself as a challenge. We'll use a naïve Bayes classifier as the machine learning model for this scenario. The naïve Bayes algorithm is a simple, probabilistic classifier that is often used for baseline assessments of the difficulty of machine learning problems, especially in text analytics. Problems where naïve Bayes algorithms perform poorly can be considered difficult, whereas problems where naïve Bayes algorithms perform well are easy.

The first thing we need to do to run a naïve Bayes algorithm is the same as the first thing we did for decision trees in chapter 10: we need to read in data. Our data is in the JSON lines format, so the best way to read in our data is to use the `.textFile` method of a `SparkContext` and then chain `.map` methods together to transform the data into a version ready for transformation into a Spark `DataFrame`. Spark `DataFrames` are the required data format for Spark's built-in machine learning libraries.

To transform the data from JSON lines into a sequence of Python objects, we first need to split the data into lines. We can do this with a `.flatMap` and a `.split` on all newline characters. We use `.flatMap` here instead of normal `.map` because our original sequence is a sequence of files. If we used a standard `.map`, we'd have a sequence of sequences resulting from each file being transformed into a sequence of lines. What we want is a single sequence of lines. The `.flatMap` method flattens our sequence of sequences into a single sequence. From here, we can map the `loads` function from the `JSON` module across all the lines. This method, which we've used a few times already, converts a JSON-formatted string into a Python object.

Additionally, we'll want to improve the way the times are recorded. In the data, the times are recorded as raw times. That's not useful because our machine learning model likely won't have enough data to learn that 11:45 a.m. and 1:03 p.m. are closely related, but 3:45 p.m. and 5:03 p.m. likely have very different driving conditions (because of the beginning of evening commute traffic). Listing 12.7 includes a small function that makes some sense of the times.

Once we have the data in a sequence of Python objects, we also want to make two more cleanup transformations. First, we'll want to group the crashes into three categories:

1. Single-vehicle crashes
2. Two-vehicle crashes
3. Three-or-more-vehicle crashes

The number of crashes will be the target variable for our analysis. To do this grouping, we'll need to write a helper function that transforms the `'Number of Vehicles Involved'` field, as shown in the following listing.

Listing 12.7 Reading and cleaning crash data from JSON lines

```
def group_crashes(x):
    if int(x['Number of Vehicles Involved']) > 3:
        x['Number of Vehicles Involved'] = "3"
    return x

def improve_times(x):
    time = x['Time']
    if time < "5:00":
        x['Time'] = "Early morning"
    elif time < "7:00":
        x['Time'] = "Morning"
    elif time < "9:00":
        x['Time'] = "Morning commute"
    elif time < "12:00":
        x['Time'] = "Late morning"
    elif time < "16:00":
        x['Time'] = "Afternoon"
    elif time < "18:30":
        x['Time'] = "Evening commute"
    elif time < "22:00":
        x['Time'] = "Evening"
    else:
        x['Time'] = "Late night"
    return x

  sc = SparkContext(appName="Crash model")
  spark = SparkSession.builder \
                     .master("local") \
                     .getOrCreate()
```

```
texts = sc.textFile("/path/to/your/files/")
xs = texts.flatMap(lambda x:x.split("\n")) \
          .map(json.loads) \
          .map(group_crashes) \
          .map(improve_times)
```

From this point, we're ready to convert our `RDD` into a `DataFrame` and prepare our `DataFrame` for Spark's machine learners. To transform the `RDD` into a `DataFrame`, we use the `.createDataFrame` method of our `SparkSession` (figure 12.7). `SparkSession` objects are central to Spark's SQL, `DataFrame`, and machine learning capabilities and serve as a mirror to `SparkContext` objects for `RDDs`.

When we set up our machine learning job, we can import both the `SparkContext` and `SparkSession` utilities to use both the `RDD` and `DataFrame` methods.

```
from pyspark import SparkContext
from pyspark.sql import SparkSession
sc = SparkContext(appName="Crash model")
spark = SparkSession.builder \
                    .master("local") \
                    .getOrCreate()
```

We can use the `RDD` methods to read in JSON files and do some preprocessing with the map and reduce methods provided by `RDDs`.

```
texts = sc.textFile("/path/to/your/files/")
xs = texts.flatMap(lambda x:x.split("\n")) \
          .map(json.loads) \
          .map(group_crashes) \
          .map(improve_times)
```

When we're ready, we can explicitly convert our `RDD` to a `DataFrame`.

```
df = spark.createDataFrame(xs)
```

Figure 12.7 We can use both the `SparkContext` and the `SparkSession` to take advantage of `RDDs` and `DataFrames`. We'll need to explicitly convert our `RDD` to a `DataFrame` when we want to use the `DataFrame` methods for machine learning.

Once we have our data in a `DataFrame`, we need to use the `StringIndexer` to transform our variables into the indexed format that Spark expects (listing 12.8). We won't go into the details of the indexer code here, because our focus for this section is on Spark and EMR. If you'd like a refresher, we originally discussed these concepts in chapter 10, specifically section 10.2.2 with listings 10.2, 10.3, and 10.4.

Listing 12.8 Preparing the crashes RDD for machine learning

```
df = spark.createDataFrame(xs)

feature_labels = df.columns
feature_labels.pop(feature_labels.index('Number of Vehicles Involved'))
df = reduce(string_to_index, feature_labels, df)
indexes = ["i-"+f for f in feature_labels]

df = VectorAssembler(inputCols=indexes,
                     outputCol="features").transform(df)

df = StringIndexer(inputCol='Number of Vehicles Involved',
                   outputCol='label').fit(df).transform(df)
```

With our DataFrame ready for machine learning, the last step is to set up the actual machine learning algorithm. As noted earlier, for this example we want to use a naïve Bayes algorithm. Like in our final example from chapter 10, we'll use cross-validation to assess model performance. As you might guess from the algorithm's name (*naïve*), the naïve Bayes model has relatively few parameters compared to more sophisticated models, so we'll only optimize a single parameter of the model: smoothing. The smoothing parameter refers to how much additive smoothing is used in the model. The additive smoothing process prevents zeros from dominating the model, instead treating zeros as *very small* numbers. Typical values are 1/1000, 1/100, 1/10, and 1. You can see the machine learning code in the following listing. You'll notice a lot of similarities between this code and the code we wrote for our random forest classifier in section 10.3.2.

Listing 12.9 A naïve Bayes classifier for vehicles in crashes

```
mce = MulticlassClassificationEvaluator()
nb = NaiveBayes()

grid = ParamGridBuilder().addGrid(nb.smoothing, [.0001, .001, .01, 1]) \
                        .build()
cv = CrossValidator(estimator=nb, estimatorParamMaps=grid,
                    evaluator=mce,numFolds=5,
                    parallelism=4)
cv_model = cv.fit(df)
transformed = cv_model.transform(df)
f1 = mce.evaluate(transformed)
print("NB F1: {:0.4f}".format(f1))
cv_model.bestModel.save("/path/to/your/model")
```

One thing you may notice about this code that's different from the code in chapter 10 is that we refer to our evaluation metric as F1 instead of AUC. F1, like AUC, is a metric that assesses trade-offs between false positives and false negatives. It's most prominently used in information retrieval and document classification. For our purposes, it's enough to know that F1 scores can range between 0 and 1, with higher numbers being better.

You can run this code locally, pointing the `.textFiles` method and the `.bestModel.save` method to locations on your local machine. For the inputs to `.textFiles`, I recommend using a subset of the full crashes dataset. This will speed up the test process—the entire dataset will take several minutes to process on a single machine. For the output, you're specifying a location where Spark will try to create a directory and store a description of the model. This should be a directory that doesn't exist yet.

> **REMINDER: SPARK-SUBMIT** Remember to run your Spark code with the `spark-submit` utility instead of Python. The `spark-submit` utility queues up a Spark job, which will run in parallel locally and simulate what would happen if you ran the program on an active cluster.

12.2.2 Setting up an EMR cluster for Spark

To run this machine learning job in the cloud, we'll need a cluster on which to run our Spark job. Earlier in this section, we saw two ways to set up an EMR cluster programmatically using mrjob:

1. We can set up single-step clusters by submitting a Hadoop job with the `-r emr` flag set.
2. We can set up persistent clusters by running the `mrjob create-cluster` utility.

In this subsection, I'll show you how to set up a Spark cluster with mrjob and introduce you to the EMR cluster wizard.

SETTING UP A SPARK CLUSTER WITH MRJOB

Back in section 12.1, we set up EMR clusters using mrjob so that we could run our Hadoop jobs in the cloud. As part of this, we wrote an mrjob config file (listing 12.4). The mrjob config file was a declaration of what we wanted our cluster to look like, as shown in listing 12.10. We can use that same approach to set up a Spark cluster. All we'll need to do is specify a few extra options.

Listing 12.10 Refresher: mrjob config for EMR

```
runners:
  emr:
    num_core_instances: 20
    image_version: 5.24.0
    instance_type: m1.large
    region: us-west-1
    tags:
      project: Mastering Large Datasets
```

Note that this configuration defines a cluster of 21 machines—20 workers and 1 master. Those machines are of type m1.large and are using AMI version 5.24.0. Additionally, we'll be setting the cluster up in the us-west-1 region and tagging it with "project: Mastering Large Datasets."

For our Spark cluster, the first thing we'll need to do is change the instances we're using to one that has more memory. Hadoop, as I've mentioned before, was designed to take advantage of low computing power environments. Spark has greater resource requirements. For Spark, the smallest instance type we can us is m1.xlarge. When running Spark jobs in production, we can achieve better performance by using the AWS C-series instances, which are compute optimized.

> **EC2 instance types and clusters**
> We'll want to know about three types of EC2 instances for cluster computing: M-series, C-series, and R-series. M-series instances are the default for cluster computing. These instances are solid, general-purpose instances. I recommend using them for Hadoop jobs, and for testing Spark jobs. AWS provides C-series instances for compute-heavy workloads, which includes Spark analytics. Batch Spark jobs are best run in production on C-series instances. Lastly, the R-series of instances is a high-memory series. We'll want to use this series of instances if we're dealing with streaming analytics.

Next, we'll need to tell mrjob that we want to use Spark. For this, mrjob provides an option called `bootstrap_spark`. This takes a boolean variable, so we'll set that to `true`.

Lastly, we'll want to be able to access our instance over the command line through SSH. SSH is a utility we can use to log in to and run commands on remote servers. To set up the cluster so we can log in through SSH, we'll need to specify an AWS .pem key pair.

If you haven't set up an AWS EC2 key pair, you can create one using the AWS command line tool, which you installed along with boto3. The command for that is `aws ec2 create-key-pair`. You'll also want to set the mandatory `--key-name` option so that you can refer to your key.

```
aws ec2 create-key-pair --key-name my-emr-key > /path/to/my/key.pem
```

AWS EC2 keys are region specific, and this command will create the key in your default region. If you're not sure what your default region is, you can go to https://console.aws.amazon.com. The region will display as a parameter in the URL; for example, http://mng.bz/ZeA5.

With that, we'll have a configuration file ready to set up a Spark cluster. Our Spark mrjob configuration file looks like the following listing.

Listing 12.11 mrjob configuration file for a Spark EMR cluster

```
runners:
  emr:
    num_core_instances: 4
    image_version: 5.24.0
```

```
max_hours_idle: 1
instance_type: m1.xlarge
region: us-west-1
bootstrap_spark: true        <- Tells EMR to install Spark on the cluster
ec2_key_pair: my-emr-key     <- Provides EMR the name of the key we'll use for SSHing into the cluster
tags:
  software: Spark
  project: Mastering Large Datasets
```

You can run this cluster with the `create-cluster` command. When you do, you should receive a JSON string as a response. You'll also be able to go to the AWS EMR Console and see your cluster setting up. Once you're satisfied that the cluster is running, feel free to shut it down. To do that, merely select the checkbox next the cluster and click the Terminate button at the top of the screen.

THE AWS EMR CLUSTER WIZARD

In addition to setting up EMR clusters using mrjob, we can also do so using the AWS console. Like we saw in chapter 11 with S3, the AWS console is a good way to see all of the options that we have when we use AWS. To get started, navigate to the EMR console main page: https://console.aws.amazon.com/elasticmapreduce/.

On this page, you should see a list of clusters, including the ones you may have created while running the Hadoop jobs and the one you created from the previous subsection on Spark and mrjob. At the top of this page, you should see a button inviting you to create a cluster. That button launches the AWS EMR cluster wizard.

When you click it, you'll immediately be brought to a quick setup page. On this page, there are four sets of options:

1. General options that describe our cluster
2. Software options that tell AWS what we'll be doing on the cluster
3. Hardware options that tell AWS which instances to reserve for us
4. Security options that tell AWS how we'll be accessing the cluster

In the general options (General Configuration) section (figure 12.8), you'll want to give your cluster a name you'll recognize. There are two other options there defining the Logging behavior and Launch Mode—these are both fine by default. Next, in the software options (Software Configuration) (also figure 12.8), you'll want to use the latest EMR release and select the software configuration that contains Spark. This tells AWS to install Spark when it's setting up our cluster.

Scroll down and you'll see hardware and security configuration options (figure 12.9). For the hardware options (Hardware Configuration), set Instance Type to m1.xlarge and the Number of Instances to 3. If you change the number of instances, you'll notice that the number of core nodes—the nodes that will run work on your cluster—is always one less than the total number of instances you've selected. This is because one instance always needs to serve as the master instance. Lastly, select your EC2 Key Pair from the drop-down menu. If you don't see your key pair listed here, try changing availability zones using the drop-down menu in the top right corner of the screen.

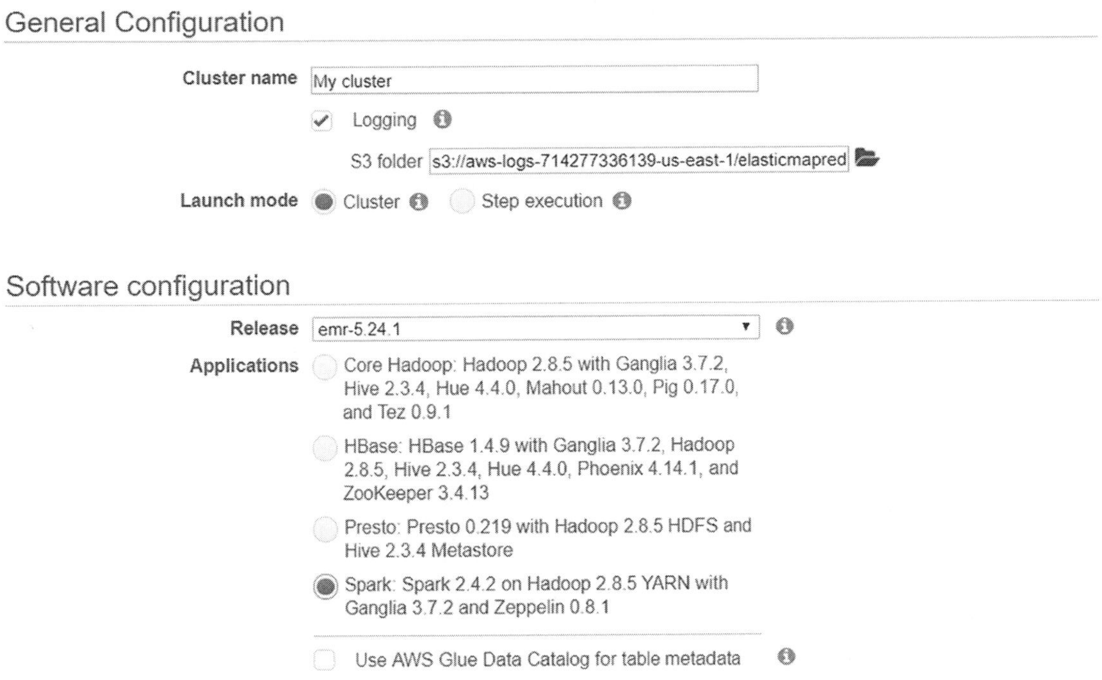
General Configuration
Cluster name
My cluster
Logging
S3 folder
s3://aws-logs-714277336139-us-east-1/elasticmapred
Launch mode
Cluster
Step execution
Software configuration
Release
emr-5.24.1
Applications
Core Hadoop: Hadoop 2.8.5 with Ganglia 3.7.2, Hive 2.3.4, Hue 4.4.0, Mahout 0.13.0, Pig 0.17.0, and Tez 0.9.1
HBase: HBase 1.4.9 with Ganglia 3.7.2, Hadoop 2.8.5, Hive 2.3.4, Hue 4.4.0, Phoenix 4.14.1, and ZooKeeper 3.4.13
Presto: Presto 0.219 with Hadoop 2.8.5 HDFS and Hive 2.3.4 Metastore
Spark: Spark 2.4.2 on Hadoop 2.8.5 YARN with Ganglia 3.7.2 and Zeppelin 0.8.1
Use AWS Glue Data Catalog for table metadata

Figure 12.8 The General Configuration section of the AWS EMR wizard lets you specify the Cluster Name and other configuration options.

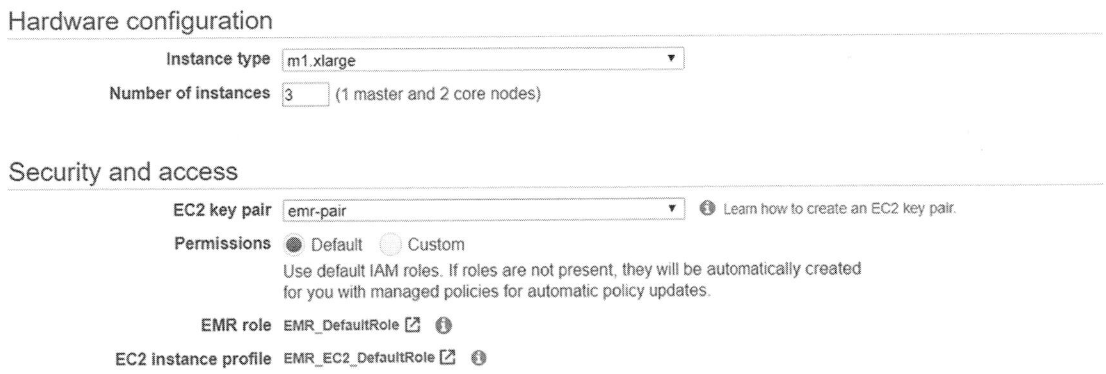
Hardware configuration
Instance type
m1.xlarge
Number of instances
3
(1 master and 2 core nodes)
Security and access
EC2 key pair
emr-pair
Learn how to create an EC2 key pair.
Permissions
Default
Custom
Use default IAM roles. If roles are not present, they will be automatically created for you with managed policies for automatic policy updates.
EMR role
EMR_DefaultRole
EC2 instance profile
EMR_EC2_DefaultRole

Figure 12.9 The hardware and security configuration options in the EMR setup wizard offer a simple GUI for launching a right-sized cluster.

If you proceeded from here to launch your cluster, you'd launch a cluster that is more or less the same as the cluster you launched using mrjob. Instead, though, go to the top of the page and select Go to Advanced Options. This will take you to a four-step wizard that shows you all of the options for an EMR cluster.

First, you'll see a long list of software that is available to you, including

1. Hadoop
2. Spark
3. JupyterHub
4. Hive
5. Pig
6. TensorFlow

We've covered the first two pieces of software—Hadoop and Spark—in this book: Hadoop in chapters 7 and 8, and Spark in chapters 7, 9, and 10. Additionally, we've looked at both Hadoop and Spark in this chapter. Depending on your background, you may be familiar with the remaining four tools.

JupyterHub is a cluster-ready version of the popular Jupyter Notebook software. Installing that software means you can run interactive Spark and Hadoop jobs from a notebook environment. This is a great tool for data analysts and data scientists.

Hive and Pig are similar tools that provide SQL or SQL-like interfaces to large datasets. Analysts can use Hive to compile SQL code to Hadoop MapReduce jobs. Likewise, we can use Pig to compile *Pig-latin* commands to run Hadoop MapReduce jobs. Both pieces of software are aimed at making large datasets accessible to traditional business analysts.

The last of the four, TensorFlow, is a popular deep learning library. The library is used for many state-of-the-art implementations of deep learning. The ability to run TensorFlow on AWS can reduce training time dramatically, because it enables us to run jobs on GPU (Graphic Processing Unit—processors designed for fast arithmetic) clusters or TPUs (Tensor Processing Units—processors designed for deep learning) that would be cost-prohibitive if not in the cloud.

If you click through to the next page in the wizard, you'll see detailed options for defining the hardware available to your cluster (figure 12.10). In particular on this page, pay attention to the instance groups at the bottom. You'll notice that here you not only

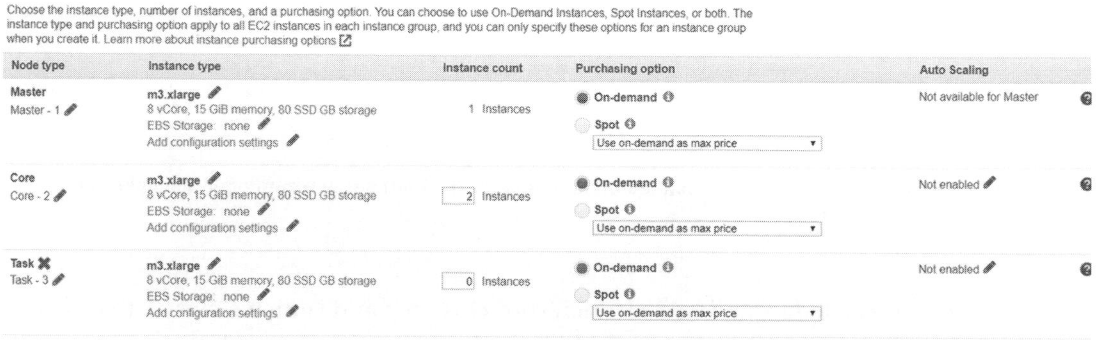
Choose the instance type, number of instances, and a purchasing option. You can choose to use On-Demand Instances, Spot Instances, or both. The instance type and purchasing option apply to all EC2 instances in each instance group, and you can only specify these options for an instance group when you create it. Learn more about instance purchasing options
Node type
Instance type
Instance count
Purchasing option
Auto Scaling
Master
Master - 1
m3.xlarge
8 vCore, 15 GiB memory, 80 SSD GB storage
EBS Storage: none
Add configuration settings
1 Instances
On-demand
Spot
Use on-demand as max price
Not available for Master
Core
Core - 2
m3.xlarge
8 vCore, 15 GiB memory, 80 SSD GB storage
EBS Storage: none
Add configuration settings
2 Instances
On-demand
Spot
Use on-demand as max price
Not enabled
Task
Task - 3
m3.xlarge
8 vCore, 15 GiB memory, 80 SSD GB storage
EBS Storage: none
Add configuration settings
0 Instances
On-demand
Spot
Use on-demand as max price
Not enabled

Figure 12.10 The advanced hardware configuration options allow us to bid for spot instances and set up auto-scaling for our cluster.

have the ability to define which type of instance you want, you also can see and set resource and pricing information for those instances. For example, we can see that the m3.xlarge instance that AWS suggests for us has 8 virtual cores and 15 GB of memory.

Additionally, we can select either On-Demand or Spot pricing for our instances. Spot pricing is a short-term market rate price that we can use to save money on our compute jobs. When we enable spot pricing, Amazon gives us access to unused instances at a low rate. This low rate comes with some risk, though. If the spot price ever exceeds what we bid—such as when demand for AWS resources is high—Amazon may shut down our instances and lease them to another buyer. That said, if we're running batch analytics jobs over night, this is often an excellent way to save money.

Lastly, in the Create Cluster—Advanced Options view, we can see the Auto Scaling option. When we turn Auto Scaling on, AWS will watch our resource usage and scale our cluster up or down as necessary. For example, if we're running a big Spark job, the cluster may scale up to the maximum number of instances we've set. When that job finishes, the cluster will eventually scale down to the minimum until we're ready to run another job.

Clicking through to the next two pages, you'll be able to

- define logging settings
- add free-form key-value tags to your cluster
- add an EC2 key pair for SSH access

Once you've had a chance to look at all the options available to you on these pages, you can create a cluster using either the Quick or Advanced settings. If you preferred using mrjob, you also can relaunch your cluster with the `mrjob create-cluster` command from the previous subsection. You'll need a running cluster, with Spark, with an attached EC2 key pair for the next subsection when we will SSH into our cluster.

NOTE You can run the examples in this chapter for less than $5 at the time of this writing.

12.2.3 Running PySpark jobs from our cluster

Once we have our cluster up and running, we're almost ready to run our machine learning job. There are only five steps left:

1. Modifying our script for the cloud
2. Adding our script to S3
3. SSHing into the master node
4. Installing the required software
5. Configuring our Spark cluster to run Python3
6. Running our Spark job

These steps will take us from having a local-only machine learning script to having run our machine learning job on the cloud. But first, we need to make two small modifications to our machine learning script.

In the naïve Bayes script from earlier in this section, we used local file paths as inputs and outputs. That was important because we wanted to test the script locally. When we're running the script in the cloud, we won't have access to our local resources—only resources that are in the cloud. We'll need to change those paths to point to cloud locations. Specifically, we'll point both of them to S3 locations.

To reference an S3 bucket, prepend S3:// to the name of your bucket. For example, if you had a bucket named my-favorite-S3-bucket, the path to that bucket would be S3://my-favorite-S3-bucket/. For S3 folders, you can add any word after the bucket name. Point the input path to target the bucket that contains your car crash data files and point the output path to target a folder in another bucket, as shown in the following listing. Once you've done that, save this as a new file.

Listing 12.12 Cloud-ready paths for input and output

```
texts = sc.textFile("S3://your-crash-data-bucket/")
. . .
cv_model.bestModel.save("S3://your-output-bucket/nb-model")
```

With these paths defined, we have a cloud-ready script. Unfortunately, we can't access this script from the cloud if it's on our local machine. We also need to move the script into the cloud. Again, we'll use S3. If you're up for a challenge, you can try on your own to create a new bucket and upload the script there using either the AWS console or boto3. Otherwise, you can follow the instructions from section 11.2.1 to create a new bucket and upload your new script.

Once the script is uploaded, we're ready to log in to our cluster. If you're on a Mac or Linux machine, you'll be able to use the built-in SSH utility. On Windows, you'll need to download a terminal emulator that supports SSH: PuTTY is the conventional choice for this. You can download it here: http://mng.bz/RP4D.

Once you know you'll be able to use SSH, head to the EMR console in your browser and find your running EMR cluster. At the top of the page you'll see a path to the cluster (figure 12.11). This is the path you'll SSH into.

To enter the cluster, open up your terminal or PuTTY and enter the address of the cluster. (AWS provides documentation for connecting using PuTTY at http://mng.bz/2Jn9.) Additionally, you'll need to identify yourself by pointing SSH to your key:

```
ssh -i /path/to/your/key.pem ec2-00-000-000-00.compute-1.amazonaws.com
```

Summary
Application history
Monitoring
Hardware
Configurations
Events
Steps
Bootstrap actions
Connections:
Enable Web Connection – Zeppelin, Spark History Server, Ganglia, Resource Manager ... (View All)
Master public DNS:
ec2-00-000-000-00.compute-1.amazonaws.com SSH
Tags:
-- View All / Edit

Figure 12.11 You can find the address of the master node of your cluster at the top of the console page for your cluster.

If this goes through successfully, you should see EMR in ASCII art on your terminal screen (figure 12.12). This is how you'll know you're logged into the master node. From this screen, the entire cluster is in your control. You can install software and run scripts just like you would if you were at the command line of your local machine. For our machine learning script, we'll need NumPy—a Python library for numerical processing. Let's make sure it's installed, and we'll install the toolz package for good measure.

```
       __|  __|_  )
       _|  (     /   Amazon Linux AMI
      ___|\___|___|

https://aws.amazon.com/amazon-linux-ami/2018.03-release-notes/
3 package(s) needed for security, out of 5 available
Run "sudo yum update" to apply all updates.

EEEEEEEEEEEEEEEEEEEE MMMMMMMM           MMMMMMMM RRRRRRRRRRRRRRR
E::::::::::::::::::E M:::::::M         M:::::::M R::::::::::::::R
EE:::::EEEEEEEEE:::E M::::::::M       M::::::::M R:::::RRRRRR:::::R
  E::::E       EEEEE M:::::::::M     M:::::::::M RR::::R      R::::R
  E::::E             M::::::M:::M   M:::M::::::M   R:::R      R::::R
  E:::::EEEEEEEEEE   M:::::M M:::M M:::M M:::::M   R:::RRRRRR:::::R
  E::::::::::::::E   M:::::M  M:::M:::M  M:::::M   R:::::::::::RR
  E:::::EEEEEEEEEE   M:::::M   M:::::M   M:::::M   R:::RRRRRR::::R
  E::::E             M:::::M    M:::M    M:::::M   R:::R      R::::R
  E::::E       EEEEE M:::::M     MMM     M:::::M   R:::R      R::::R
EE:::::EEEEEEEE::::E M:::::M             M:::::M   R:::R      R::::R
E::::::::::::::::::E M:::::M             M:::::M RR::::R      R::::R
EEEEEEEEEEEEEEEEEEEE MMMMMMM             MMMMMMM RRRRRRR      RRRRRR
```

Figure 12.12 Some nice EMR ASCII art will greet you when you log in to an EMR cluster.

The way we install Python libraries doesn't change whether we're on our local machine or on a remote server; we use `pip`. Because we want to use Python3, however, we'll need to install `pip3`, which doesn't come installed by default. You can install `pip3` with the command `sudo yum install -y pip3`. You can then use `pip3` to install NumPy and toolz with the command `sudo pip3 install -y numpy toolz`. Additionally, you can install any other software you may wish to use. Installing software on the master node will replicate this install across all of the other nodes.

At this point, if you want to test NumPy, toolz, or any other library, you can

- call Python with the `python3` command
- import the library you want to test
- run any Python code you'd like from the console

Now our Python3 environment is set up to run our machine learning script. Unfortunately, Spark is still configured to run with legacy Python. Let's configure our Spark environment so it runs Python3. To do this, we'll need to modify a shell file on the server. On the server, we can only use terminal-based text editors. The easiest of these editors to use is *nano*.

To open a file in nano, we type `nano` and then the file's name. To open the file where the Spark environment variables are stored, we'll type

```
nano $SPARK_HOME/conf/spark-env.sh
```

When you open this up, you'll see a shell script. At the bottom of the script, modify the line that says `PYSPARK_PYTHON` so it reads `PYSPARK_PYTHON=python3`. When you're done, you can save and exit the file by pressing the following keys (these will be the same on Mac, PC, and Linux):

1. *Control-O*—Begins to save the file
2. *Enter*—Writes the file to the disk
3. *Control-X*—Begins to exit nano
4. *Y*—Tells nano that yes, you want to exit

Finally, to put these changes into action, activate the Spark environment you just modified:

```
source $SPARK_HOME/conf/spark-env.sh
```

Now we're ready to run our Spark machine learning script! You can run your PySpark script just like you did on your local machine. Remember that your script lives in an S3 bucket, and you'll need to point PySpark to the file there.

```
spark-submit S3://bucket-holding-my-script/my-script.py
```

When you run your script, you'll see the standard output from Spark. It will tell you what it's doing and give you progress on the task. Depending on how many instances you allocated to this cluster, this job may take a little or some time. When it's finished, you'll be able to go into the S3 bucket you targeted for your output and see a folder named nb-model. This folder contains the compressed description of the naïve Bayes model you trained.

12.3 Exercises

12.3.1 R-series cluster

Write an mrjob config file that you could use to start a cluster of five R-series instances.

12.3.2 Back-to-back Hadoop jobs

Configure an EMR cluster to be persistent and then execute two Hadoop MapReduce jobs on that cluster. For example, select only a few fields from JSON-line data with the first job, then transform that data into CSV format with another job.

12.3.3 Instance types

We use three major instance types in cluster compute workflows: M, C, and R. Which of these types is good for each of the following?

- Streaming workflows
- Hadoop workflows
- Test workflows
- Spark workflows

Summary

- Elastic MapReduce, known by the acronym EMR, is an AWS managed service we can use to quickly and conveniently obtain cluster computing capability.
- We can run Hadoop jobs on EMR with the mrjob library, which allows us to write distributed MapReduce and procure cluster computing in Python.
- We can use mrjob's configuration files to describe what we want our clusters to look like, including which instances we'd like to use, where we'd like those instances to be located, and any tags we may want to add.
- When running Hadoop on EMR, we can operate directly on data in S3, which facilitates petabyte-scale analytics and extract-transform-load operations.
- When we need to run advanced analytics and machine learning on large datasets, AWS EMR also supports Spark.
- Running Spark jobs on EMR requires more powerful instances than Hadoop jobs, which can increase cost. But for some workflows, Spark jobs will be faster than Hadoop jobs.

index

N

O

P

R

S

T